The End of Loyalty

THE END *of*
LOYALTY

. . . . .

*The Rise and Fall
of Good Jobs in America*

. . . . .

RICK WARTZMAN

PUBLICAFFAIRS
NEW YORK

Book Design by Jack Lenzo

Library of Congress Cataloging-in-Publication Data
Names: Wartzman, Rick, author.
Title: The end of loyalty : the rise and fall of good jobs in America / Rick
    Wartzman.
Description: First edition. | New York : PublicAffairs, [2017] | Includes
    bibliographical references and index. | Description based on print version
    record and CIP data provided by publisher; resource not viewed.
Identifiers: LCCN 2017006668 (print) | LCCN 2017011940 (ebook) | ISBN
    9781586489151 (ebook) | ISBN 9781586489144 (hardcover)
Subjects: LCSH: Labor—United States—History. | Industrial relations—
    United States—History. | Corporations—United States—History. |
    Industrial policy—United States—History. | Labor policy—United
    States—History. | United States—Economic conditions—1945–
Classification: LCC HD8072.5 (ebook) | LCC HD8072.5 .W37 2017 (print) |
    DDC 331.700973—dc23
LC record available at https://lccn.loc.gov/2017006668

For my dad, Paul Wartzman,
who showed me what it means to be a mensch

For Randye, forever

CONTENTS

PREFACE

As I waited for an Uber to pick me up at Google, my mind was racing.

It was late February 2015, and a light breeze blew through the Mountain View, California, night sky. I'd spent the past couple of hours at a meeting of a group called i4j, which stands for Innovation for Jobs. The buffet had been resoundingly mediocre—a surprise considering that we were at the Googleplex, the technology giant's corporate headquarters, famous for its great perks. The cognitive power in the room was sure dazzling, though.

There was Vint Cerf, a Google vice president and one of the fathers of the Internet; Byron Auguste, a former Obama administration economic-policy official who was now running an organization called Opportunity@Work, which was aiming to "rewire the US labor market"; Robin Chase, the cofounder of Zipcar; Marjory Blumenthal, executive director of the President's Council of Advisors on Science and Technology; and a couple dozen other entrepreneurs of both the business and social variety.

This being Silicon Valley, we'd been kicking around how to "disrupt unemployment," which officially stood at 5.5 percent in the United States at that moment, a substantial drop from the double-digit jobless rate that had wracked the nation four and a half years earlier, following the Great Recession. Yet for many folks across the country, the recovery was less than full-bodied. "Right now, as many as 30 million Americans are either out of work or severely underemployed," Jim Clifton, the president of Gallup, the research and consulting firm, noted just a few weeks before my visit to Mountain View. "Trust me, the vast majority of them aren't throwing parties to toast 'falling' unemployment.

"The great American dream," he added, "is to have a good job, and in recent years, America has failed to deliver that dream more than it has at any time in recent memory."

High-tech tends to be full of optimists, and i4j didn't disappoint in this regard. Many on hand could see a day coming soon when algorithms would connect job seekers of all stripes with just the right options for employment—a development that would be terrific for everyone, including business. "There are trillions of dollars to be made in raising the value of people, which are, perhaps, our world's most underutilized resource," asserted David Nordfors, the cochair of i4j.

I, too, am an optimist at heart, and I truly hoped that Nordfors was correct. But as someone who'd spent more than five years examining how the social contract between employer and employee in America had changed since the end of World War II, I was skeptical of any remedies that seemed too quick or easy.

As my Uber driver, Jorge, pulled onto Plymouth Street to take me to San Francisco, it was hard not to think about what kind of job he had. On one level, far too much has been made of Uber, Task-Rabbit, and the rest of the online "gig economy," which accounts for less than 1 percent of the US workforce. But on another level, Uber is a perfectly appropriate symbol for positions that are now found all across America: ones that don't pay well, have terrible or nonexistent medical and retirement benefits, and command not the slightest bit of long-term loyalty from one's employer.

Labor economist Guy Standing has a term for those with such jobs: "the precariat," a group of people who invariably live lives defined by economic insecurity and are all too aware that they're stuck in the mud, if not falling ever further behind. Their ranks extend well beyond those in gig jobs or other forms of "contingent work," and their disenchantment with how poorly they're faring is hardly new. Indeed, members of the working class have been feeling aggrieved since political pundits in the early seventies referred to them as the "Archie Bunker vote," a nod to the star character of the hit sitcom *All in the Family*.

Since then, not much has improved for most workers; a lot has gotten tougher. Compensation for some 80 percent of the American labor force, in fact, has barely gone up since Archie ruled the airwaves—a 10 percent raise over forty years, after adjusting for inflation. During the prior twenty-five years, by contrast, pay and benefits for this huge demographic climbed by 90 percent.

Today, nearly half the nation's workforce earns less than fifteen dollars an hour. About a third of men in their prime don't make enough to keep a family of four out of poverty or are altogether unemployed—double what it was thirty years ago. More than 10 percent of jobless men ages twenty-five to fifty-four have stopped looking for work—a trend particularly prevalent among those without a college degree. In the mid-1950s, only 2 percent of this group of men was on the sidelines.

Meanwhile, few Americans have sufficient savings to retire on, in no small part because employers have cut their pension benefits. And businesses continue to push more health-care costs onto their employees.

Some unequivocally good news came when the US Census Bureau reported that median household income rose more than 5 percent in 2015. But this surge didn't come close to offsetting decades of stagnation. For those on the middle rungs of the economic ladder, their income was still more than 4 percent below where it was at the start of the financial crisis in 2007, and more than 5 percent below where it was at the end of the nineties. Even after the latest jump, earnings for male workers were less than they were in the 1970s. Median pay for women has essentially been flat since 2000.

Why is this happening? It's certainly not because American companies have been struggling overall and therefore haven't had the means to do better for those in their employ. Corporate profits have reached historic highs in recent years. A big part of the trouble is that this wealth has not been distributed like it was previously. Workers have been largely left out. Instead, the winners have been the fortunate few: investors (who've reaped dividend increases and stock buybacks) as well as top corporate executives and others at the very high end of the pay scale. Most Americans, even those who work their tails off, can't count on the job market to give them the lift it once did.

"Some say that our current income inequality is no longer like the Roaring Twenties or even the Gilded Age," labor lawyer Thomas Geoghegan has written. "We're reaching inequality that we haven't known since feudalism. Charlemagne, not J. P. Morgan, is the relevant comparison."

Within weeks of my evening at the Googleplex, a slate of candidates would officially announce that they were entering the 2016 race for the White House. The resentment voiced by Geoghegan—and so many others—would now find its expression through the campaigns of Bernie Sanders on the left and, especially, Donald Trump on the right. "The forgotten men and women of our country will be forgotten no longer," Trump vowed in his victory speech on election night. The working class (really, the white working class) had helped to catapult Trump to the presidency, taken in by his promises to restore the kind of blue-collar employment that had once guaranteed a good life. "I want him to bring America back," said Youngstown, Ohio, resident Kerri Smith, a caregiver for disabled children and a former Democrat who voted for Trump. "Bring back the jobs, bring our country back."

But while the electorate's anger was understandable, it was tough to see how shaking up Washington would have the intended effect. There is "the pretense in American elections that choosing the right president will magically fix the nation's wide economic problems," observed journalist Hedrick Smith, the author of, among other books, *Who Stole the American Dream?* But what "plagues the middle class is much less the product of presidential policies and much more the result of the private-sector trickle-down business model. In the economy, the power to divvy up the nation's pie lies in the hands of corporate CEOs."

This reality—that most Americans' fortunes depend directly on whether they have work and how their company treats them, not on the maneuverings of government—is what compelled me to explore the shifting relationship between employer and employee. It is a narrative that I've been watching play out for a long time from a variety of angles.

For fifteen years I was a reporter at the *Wall Street Journal*, where I tracked the coal, steel, and aerospace industries, getting to know frontline laborers along with those in the C-suite. I covered economic policy from the Treasury, Federal Reserve, and White House—and was also there when a minimum-wage worker in Louisiana came home after a ten-hour day to discover that her gas had been shut off because she couldn't afford to pay her bill. More recently, I've done management consulting for major corporations at the Drucker Institute and have sat side by side with union leaders on the board of a progressive publication called *Capital & Main*. From all of these different vantages, I have noticed the growing worship of Wall Street; the increasingly one-sided chess match between employers and their workers; the mounting hoopla around "corporate social responsibility" that, in most cases, has very little to do with companies looking out for their own people.

I bring to these issues a strong belief that by better understanding where we've been, we can be smarter about where we're going. To that end, since 2009 I have been delving into the histories of four companies: General Electric, General Motors, Kodak, and Coca-Cola. By tracing their ups and downs over a seventy-year span—through the Golden Age of the fifties and sixties, the tumultuous years of the seventies and eighties, and the past two and a half decades, when the corporate compact has been completely undone—I tell the bigger story of how America has transformed.

I have tried not to romanticize what was or wash out the complexities and contradictions. Most workers, for instance, did do quite well during the aforementioned Golden Age—but only if they were white and male. For women and people of color, corporate America was a hostile environment. (In many cases, it still is.) The hatred between organized labor and management was often savage. Many look back at that older era and fondly remember it as a time of rock-solid stability, marked by "lifetime employment." I even use that felicitous phrase in a few spots. But it's actually not so cut-and-dried. Even in the 1950s and '60s, it wasn't uncommon for someone to have ten or twelve different jobs over his career. The ability of workers to move around has always been a positive feature of the American economy.

That said, workers in more recent years have found themselves moving less because they've wanted to and more because they've had to. Job security in the private sector is much weaker than it once was, a big reason that many people's incomes have become tremendously volatile, swinging up and down a lot more than they did before. For workers, the American corporation used to act as a shock absorber. Now, it's a roller coaster.

As seen through the lens of GE, GM, Kodak, and Coke, a combination of forces has led us here: globalization and heightened competition from low-wage countries; the fading influence of unions; the introduction of labor-saving technology; a newfound willingness—and at times eagerness—to lay off enormous numbers of people even when there's no crisis at hand; the outsourcing of all manner of work; the decline of manufacturing; and the rise of knowledge jobs for those with the skills and education to grab them and, simultaneously, the rise of third-rate service jobs for those without.

Yet from my reading of these four iconic companies—and the larger universe of businesses that they reflect and represent—I'd single out one other factor as more important than all the others: a reconstituting of corporate culture that has explicitly elevated shareholders above employees. American workers won't be able to overcome these other challenges unless this perversion ceases.

What the future holds is a mystery, of course. Some maintain that we are destined for a prolonged period of slow economic growth, which would be bad for workers. Others see the spread of artificial intelligence setting off the next boom. Some warn that robots will take away so many jobs that masses of people will be left with nothing to do. Others suggest that all sorts of new avenues of employment are about to open up because of cloud computing, Big Data, and the Internet of Things.

Whatever comes, what's clear is that we as a country have to find a way to share our prosperity more broadly again. At stake is nothing less than the well-being of our democracy.

A good place to begin is simply to ensure that more people are working. A tight labor market causes employers to bid up compensation—something that finally started to be realized toward the end of 2016—and split profits more equitably. "With just a few exceptions, our economy has failed to generate the necessary quantity and quality of jobs," Jared Bernstein, who served as director of the White House Task Force on the Middle Class under President Obama, has written. He has calculated that when wages were expanding at a healthy clip for most everyone, from the late 1940s through the late 1970s, the country was at "full employment" more than 70 percent of the time. That's the point at which all eligible people who want a job can find one. Since 1980, we've been at full employment less than 30 percent of the time.

Given his perch, Bernstein has offered numerous policy prescriptions (some of them also supported, to varying degrees, by the Trump administration): putting people to work repairing roads, bridges, railways, airports, and the like through a government infrastructure program; more aggressively overseeing Wall Street so as to protect Main Street jobs from being wiped out in another speculative bubble; more seamlessly reintegrating into the workforce those with criminal records; giving special attention to residents of "job deserts"—depressed urban and rural areas with stubbornly high unemployment rates. All of these recommendations are vital.

But Washington's prod can't alone turn things around. Corporate executives must step up. It is their companies that must do the bulk of the hiring. It is their companies that must reinstitute a sturdier social contract with their workers.

If that sounds Pollyannaish, this is where history is a useful reminder. In the 1940s, those heading some of our biggest companies took it upon themselves to help create tens of millions of decent jobs. And they did so not only to make a buck but also to strengthen society.

PART I
THE GOLDEN AGE

While General Electric touted its contribution to the war effort in this 1943 advertisement, it was also starting to plan for peace, including the creation of good jobs for returning US troops.

1

THE SCRAMBLE FOR
58 MILLION JOBS

In March 1943, as they had for three and a half grim years, men across much of the world fought and killed each other on fields of battle, while others brutalized innocents beyond the normal pale of war. Early in the month, US and Australian aircraft bombed a crucial Japanese supply convoy in the Bismarck Sea, prevailing in what Gen. Douglas MacArthur would single out as "the decisive aerial engagement" in the southwest Pacific theater. A few weeks later, the British Eighth Army overran German and Italian forces along the Mareth Line in southern Tunisia, a bloody struggle punctuated by torrential shelling and heavy machine-gun fire. Hitler's SS rounded up the remaining Jews in Poland's Krakow ghetto, sending 8,000 men, women, and children to the Plaszow concentration camp and murdering 2,000 more on the streets. Aboard the Japanese destroyer *Akikaze*, the crew matter-of-factly gunned down some sixty Germans—Protestant missionaries and Catholic priests and nuns—accused, speciously, of being spies. Then they flung the dead over the side of the ship into the waters off New Guinea.

Meanwhile, at month's end, thousands of miles from the combat and the mayhem, nineteen American businessmen gathered at the Harvard Club in New York to plan for peace. This mission didn't sit well with everyone. Some people found it unseemly to be talking about postwar America while husbands and brothers and sons were still dying halfway around the globe. They fretted that corporate interests were jumping the gun—literally.

The group went by the bureaucratic-sounding name of the Industrial Advisory Board of the Committee for Economic Development, yet their assignment was anything but humdrum: Once the war was over and America's factories were no longer churning out tens of billions of dollars in armaments, how could they prevent the country from falling back into the crippled economic state it had experienced in the 1930s? How could they make sure that legions of servicemen wouldn't find themselves jobless, impoverished, and forced to queue up in bread lines upon their return home? How could they render misguided all of the forecasters who were predicting that as many as 30 million people would soon find themselves unemployed while, in the words of one observer, "the worst depression in history would sweep the land"?

The Committee for Economic Development was far from the only organization trying to grapple with these thorny questions. Over the next two years, the federal War Production Board, the National Resources Planning Board, the Senate's Special Committee on Postwar Economic Policy and Planning, and dozens of other public bodies would all wrestle with these same difficult issues. The United Auto Workers union and various business lobbies, including the US Chamber of Commerce and the National Association of Manufacturers, would take them on as well. But the CED, more than any other entity, gained a reputation for the thoroughness of its analysis, the boldness of its action, and the progressive nature of its thinking—progressive, at least, for a bunch of businessmen.

Some dubbed their worldview "enlightened capitalism." Others called it "liberal conservatism." Still others affixed harsher labels: one Detroit industrialist went so far as to brand the CED's leaders "the most dangerous men in America." What prompted such contempt was that the CED was far more accepting of organized labor than either the Chamber or the Manufacturers, asserting that unions can, in fact, "serve the common good." The CED also endorsed the idea that federal debt could be added in service of "promoting and maintaining high levels of productive employment"—a perspective at odds with the deficit hawks more commonly found in the corporate community. Taken aback by the CED's position, the *Nation* ran an article headlined "Heresy in High Places," in which it declared: "Some of the basic concepts of Keynesian economics have at last penetrated into the upper stratum of American business society."

Despite taking such unconventional stances, those shepherding the CED didn't fit the profile of rebels. Many of the executives instrumental in the organization's early days were big bosses at some of the nation's largest corporations. Among them were Eastman Kodak's treasurer, Marion Folsom, a technocrat of the first order; the inventor of the all-electrical car ignition (and holder of 139 other patents) and General Motors vice president, Charles Kettering; and Coca-Cola chairman Harrison Jones, a man so silver-tongued he once boasted that he "could sell bottled horse piss." Charles Wilson, General Electric's president, would join the CED board by the war's end.

For each of these men, generating more jobs was a top priority. To Kettering, or "Boss Ket" as he was known within the corridors of GM, employment and innovation were inextricably linked. "In the future," he said, a major corporation "must accept as a moral obligation the task of propagating new industries. It must pay more and more attention not alone to the improvement of old things but to the development of new things." To Folsom, "well-organized statistical and planning departments" were the vehicles through which companies could project sales fluctuations, regulate inventories, and thus keep employee turnover to a minimum. "If management applies brains and effort to this problem of stabilizing employment," he said, "real progress can be made." To Jones, the trick was to get enough companies to start hiring so that the nation's economic flywheel would begin to turn—workers becoming consumers, leading to demand for more products made by more workers. "The furnishing of jobs starts the cycle, which builds and gathers momentum, and the more men employed, the greater the prosperity," he said. And to Wilson, the idea was similar: companies must consciously keep prices low and paychecks high so that "the common man" would trigger a virtuous circle of economic growth. This was the "dynamic logic of mass production" that Henry Ford had famously dramatized in 1914, when he had instantly doubled his workers' income by decreeing the five-dollar day.

"How am I going to sell my refrigerators if we don't give 'em wages to buy with?" Wilson asked.

The CED was the ideal megaphone to amplify these viewpoints. The US Commerce Department had launched the CED as an independent, self-financed organization in September 1942 in a bid to combine the best in economic scholarship with the real-world input of those in industry. The mix proved powerful. "When I started this job, I thought we were going to hatch a hen egg," Paul Hoffman, the president of the automobile company Studebaker and the CED's chairman, confided to the executive committee of the organization six months after its founding. "It has turned out to be an eagle." With the CED's momentum building, its agenda quickly formed. "We are being pressed to go off on a dozen tangents," Hoffman said. "We shall have to hold enthusiasm in check a bit in order to stick to our main purpose—jobs."

On this day, March 29, the man in charge of winning the peace was David Prince, a vice president of General Electric, who called to order the meeting at the Harvard Club at 9:45 a.m. Bespectacled and mostly bald, with stray wisps of gray hair, Prince looked every bit like the engineer he was. His specialty was switchgears. But GE had directed him to concentrate on a switchover of a different sort: the eventual transition to a peacetime economy. Indeed, GE was widely seen as the most advanced company in the nation when it came to postwar planning, having meticulously estimated the output of its products under a host of possible circumstances, and the CED had tapped Prince to spread this know-how.

Much of GE's blueprint involved straightforward, if exhausting, legwork—methodically surveying producers and consumers to gauge supply and demand market by market. "There is nothing mystic or magic or revolutionary about advance planning," said GE's Charlie Wilson. The process was, however, inherently controversial. Some businesspeople worried that the CED's approach was synonymous with centralized control. "To many Americans economic planning denotes totalitarianism," Prince admitted. "They visualize an economic system in which individuals and corporations would follow the dictates of a super economic bureau, and they therefore quite properly suspect it because it is opposed to their ideas of personal liberty."

Yet to Prince and his CED colleagues, this logic was totally backward. Minus sound planning, Prince cautioned, "we will certainly develop overproduction" in a raft of industries, "and I doubt whether we can weather another case of that sort without the government taking over." To the CED, the very best way to keep Washington from exerting too heavy a hand was for companies to plan assiduously and thereby prevent a relapse of the 30 percent jobless rate that had bedeviled the country in the preceding decade. "In the absence of such activity on our part," Prince said, "I fear government will take over by default." Later, he added: "This expectation of mass unemployment gives a perfect charter for all of the crackpots to promote government regulation . . . make-work projects, etc." By getting out in front of the problem, "this should be an opportunity for the business community to be the champions of courage and optimism," rather than getting dragged down by "the counsel of despair."

Much of the Harvard Club meeting—attended by officials from Kodak; Firestone Tire & Rubber; Sears, Roebuck; the Automobile Manufacturers Association; and other companies and trade groups—focused on selling this vision through a variety of industry handbooks and other publications. One report they discussed at length, "Markets After the War," turned out to be so popular that more than 1,000 requests a day poured in for it. The study, which relied on extensive data crunching by the Commerce Department, revealed a huge gulf between prospective employment one year after the end of the war and the anticipated size of the peacetime labor force. The only way to close the gap, remarked Gardiner Means, the eminent economist who joined the CED staff in 1943, was to spur "a radical change in business attitudes."

Casting itself as "a merchant of ideas," the CED urged managers to jot down the new goods they were hoping to sell after the war, while it also gave advice on how to leverage knowledge gained from military production. In the future, both consumer and industrial offerings "will contain many 'hidden values' resulting from the use of new materials and better methods," the CED suggested in a treatise called "Planning the Future of Your Business." "They will reflect wartime experience, which companies will put to good use to provide the public with products having greater value in performance, in lasting qualities, in appearance and, most important, in price."

In time, the CED set up a massive field operation, with a presence in nearly 3,000 communities all over the United States, through which some 250,000 local trade-association members regularly received information. A relentless push for 58 million private-sector jobs propelled the entire effort. This, said Hoffman, was the target that America would need to hit to avoid catastrophe. His math went like this: in 1940, the year before Pearl Harbor, some 49 million people were employed in the United States, turning out $98 billion dollars worth of goods and services. Thanks to the war, 62 million people now had jobs, and US economic output had soared more than 50 percent. If the country were merely to fall back to where it had been in 1940, the ranks of the unemployed could reach 15 million—an "intolerable" situation in Hoffman's mind. He thought 58 million jobs was the total required to keep the nation humming.

Unpretentious and self-deprecating, Hoffman liked to portray himself as a "simple-minded man with simple objectives." But an explicit goal of 58 million employed—with private industry on the hook for 50 million of those jobs—was, in many eyes, downright audacious. "I don't believe that you made this statement. I hope you didn't," George Sloan, a prominent New York businessman, told Hoffman. "I am strongly of the opinion that we, as representatives of industry, must be very careful that we do not make statements or implied promises that will be thrown back at us when the war is over by enemies of a free economy . . . that while they were fighting in Tunisia or Guadalcanal, industry, through its spokesman Paul Hoffman, had assumed the responsibility of supplying 58 million full-time jobs when they returned—and that industry had failed completely in living up to this responsibility."

What Hoffman and the others at the CED knew, however, was that anything less would deprive Americans of the thing they craved most in the wake of the Great Depression—perhaps even more than peace: a strong sense of security. "We believe in the American system of free enterprise," the CED proclaimed. "By that we do not mean that the government should let business alone, nor that economic opportunity should take precedence over political liberty, nor that the 'good old days' of the twenties should return.

"By free enterprise," it continued, "we mean freedom of opportunity, opportunity to work, to live decently, to educate children in the arts of citizenship and human happiness and in the skills of a trade or profession to provide against sickness and old age. We stress opportunity, not contrasted with security, but identified with security."

In the years to follow, members of the CED would work earnestly toward achieving these principles. They pursued them, in large measure, by analyzing and opining upon the proper federal role in shaping and steering the nation's economy. Specifically, they encouraged the government to manipulate the levers of fiscal and monetary policy so as to put an end to the boom-bust cycles that had long roiled American businesses and their workers.

The CED would also support select pieces of social legislation. Most contentious was the Employment Act of 1946. When the bill was first introduced in the Senate, it was titled the Full Employment Act, and it held that "every American able to work and willing to work has the right to a useful and remunerative job in the industries, or shops, or offices, or farms, or mines of the nation." This language, which echoed President Roosevelt's 1944 Economic Bill of Rights, set off alarm bells among many business groups. The US Chamber of Commerce derided the legislation's "Utopian objective," while the National Association of Manufacturers said it would lead to "state socialism." The ultraconservative Committee for Constitutional Government, which had substantial corporate backing, attacked the bill as "Russian spawn" whose other "ancestors" included Adolf Hitler and Benito Mussolini.

When the bill finally crossed President Truman's desk, ready to be signed into law, it was vastly watered down, going only so far as to say that the government should "draw on all of its resources and functions to promote maximum employment." Any hint that the government guaranteed full employment, or that individuals had an absolute right to work, had been erased. Still, the fact that the legislation didn't die outright in the face of such virulent opposition was itself remarkable. And its survival was due, in no small way, to the CED's general approval of its aims.

Regarding full employment, "I like the phrase as an expression of a goal for national policy," Beardsley Ruml, the treasurer of the retailer R.H. Macy, told Congress on behalf of the CED. "Why not leave the term 'full employment,' like 'liberty' and 'justice,' to stand as a goal of democratic government, and to derive its specific content from the will of the people as expressed from time to time by their free institutions."

Paul Hoffman likewise slammed the notion that the bill would somehow transform the government into an employer for masses of Americans. "The crucial role, the most vital function of government in
fostering employment," he said, "is to establish conditions under which
the free enterprise system can operate most effectively and to counteract the tendencies in the system toward booms and depressions."

Yet even with all this, those in the CED saw clear limits as to
what Uncle Sam could and should do. Ultimately, they believed, it was
up to corporate America to offer pensions, health insurance, and an
array of other benefits to its workers. It was up to corporate America
to create jobs. "We speak of 'full employment.' But, under any name,
it doesn't happen automatically or in response to government fiat," said
Ralph Hayes, a Coca-Cola executive. The CED wasn't suggesting that
government was an insignificant player. Beyond nurturing an environment in which business could flourish, with regulations and rates of
taxation that were sensible, the government had an obligation to erect
a safety net for all citizens. But this was meant to be only "the basic
floor of protection," said Kodak's Marion Folsom, who was influential
in the passage of the Social Security Act in 1935. At the end of the
day, most working people would find the security they were looking for
as participants in the private sector, not as wards of the public sector.
Companies practicing modern forms of "welfare capitalism"—and not
the welfare state—would meet the bulk of their needs. It was industry
that should "lend a helping hand to its workers," said General Motors
chairman Alfred Sloan, shielding them "against the vicissitudes of life."

This wasn't a matter of business being altruistic. Many executives were concerned that unless they made sure there were enough
jobs to go around, and unless the benefits that came with them were
sufficiently abundant, communism or socialism might well take root
on America's shores. "Any nation with a great unemployment wave
becomes a seedbed for -isms," said Harrison Jones of Coca-Cola.

Nor did companies look at this as a one-way deal. They would
give a lot to their employees as well as insist on much in return: dili-
gence, productivity, good morale, and above all, devotion to the corporation—or, as Kodak president Frank Lovejoy characterized it,
"the whole-hearted interest and cooperation of the worker." General
Electric codified the expectations on both sides, listing the following

among its primary corporate objectives: "to provide good jobs, wages, working conditions, work satisfactions, and opportunities for advancement conducive of most productive performance and also the stablest possible employment, all in exchange for loyalty, initiative, skill, care, effort, attendance, and teamwork on the part of employees."

For most of American history, there had been no such give-and-take. Through much of the nineteenth century, companies kept a distant relationship with their workers. Many used skilled contractors rather than hiring too many full-timers. Clothiers and shoemakers favored a "putting-out" system in which they would give people the materials they needed and then have them produce the finished goods at home. By the early twentieth century, businesses were bringing more and more workers in-house as they sought to gain new efficiencies and to better control quality. Mass production supplanted artisan labor. But just because companies now wanted their own employees didn't mean they were going to coddle them; management led by intimidation, not accommodation. "Bill, has anyone been fired from this shop today?" the assistant superintendent of one factory asked his foreman. Told no, he shot back: "Well, then fire a couple of 'em. It'll put the fear of God in their hearts." Members of the working class were typically unemployed for long stretches of the year, and decisions about whom to hire and fire were often capricious and cruel. The best way to ensure job security was to bribe your boss—and many did.

The new social contract emerging between employer and employee in the United States represented a drastic departure from this punishing past. It was forged between men and women—some of them unionized, some of them not; some of them blue collar, some of them white collar—and corporations such as Kodak, GM, Coca-Cola, and GE. These four giants, as well as thousands of other large businesses, would affect job security, pay, benefits, and worker engagement through this compact. In other words, not only would they make cameras and cars, refreshments and refrigerators; over the next seventy years, they would also make, and sometimes break, millions of lives.

In March 1932, George Eastman smoked a Lucky Strike cigarette, lay down in his bed, pointed a Luger automatic to his heart, and squeezed the trigger. The great man—who in 1885 had given America and the world the first transparent photographic film and later birthed amateur snapshot picture-taking by introducing the Kodak camera to the market—had been in ill health for more than a year. A condition affecting the nerves in his spinal cord had made walking difficult and painful. At age seventy-seven, Eastman had had enough. His suicide note, written on a piece of yellow-lined paper, read:

To my friends
My work is done—
Why wait?
GE

Notably, Eastman's body of work included not just stupendous technological feats but equally impressive accomplishments in the realm of human relations. The instinct to do well by his workers stemmed from an incident that occurred when he was a young employee at a bank and was passed over for a promotion that unquestionably should have been his; the job went instead to a relative of one of the bank's directors. "It wasn't right. It wasn't fair," Eastman recalled. "It was against every principle of justice." Insulted, he struck out on his own, resolving that everybody who worked for him "should feel, under every condition relative to employment, that the fair thing, the just thing is being done by him or her. . . . There is no panacea that can cover all the wounds that must necessarily come in a relationship of employer to employee. But there is such a thing as making a worker feel that his contribution to the success of the organization is important and deserving of recognition."

In 1911, Eastman established the Kodak Welfare Fund with an initial infusion of $500,000 to assist those employees who couldn't work because of illness or accident or might have to retire because of their age. "We have got to be prepared to do something for men who have grown old in our service," Eastman stated, adding that "now while we are making so much money is the time to provide such a fund."

The following year, Eastman introduced what was to become Kodak's signature benefit: a profit-sharing plan known as a "wage dividend." The payout was based on the common stock dividends disbursed to the company's shareholders, with the total pot then proportioned to reflect each employee's individual earnings over the previous five years. For someone with at least five years of service, it was a sizable bonanza—worth about a month's pay. Receiving that inaugural wage dividend was "like a godsend to me," especially given "how much ground it covered," one Kodak veteran would recount decades later of his $57 bonus—a sum equal to more than $1,300 today. Eastman wouldn't have been surprised by such delight. "You can talk about cooperation and good feeling and friendliness from morn to midnight," he said, "but the thing the worker appreciates is the same thing the man at the helm appreciates—dollars and cents."

In 1919, Eastman offered employees $10 million in Kodak stock—one-third of his personal holdings—at far below the market rate, directing that all resulting proceeds be added to a supplemental welfare fund. "For fifteen or twenty years back," Eastman said, "I have had a provision in my will to distribute this stock among the employees who have helped make the company a success, but I am so discouraged about the prospect of dying soon that I am afraid many of the possible beneficiaries will get to Heaven ahead of me, so have concluded to expedite the distribution." The basic intent of this bounty was plain: "Our employees are well satisfied and loyal," Eastman said, "and this can only act to make them more so."

Year after year, Eastman's largesse grew. Kodak added a sickness allowance in 1920, and in 1928 the company unveiled an employee benefit plan that it touted as "the most advanced yet by a corporation." The comprehensive program featured life insurance, disability coverage, and a retirement annuity. Kodak's reach also extended far beyond the pocketbook. The company developed two suburban housing developments right outside its home base of Rochester, New York—one for rising executives and another, with more modest housing, for rank-and-file workers. They could buy a lot from the Kodak Employees Realty Corporation and secure their mortgage from the Eastman Savings and Loan Association.

Employees' children were educated at the Kodak Union Free School, while workers themselves could receive tuition subsidies when they took classes at the University of Rochester or other local colleges. They competed in company-sponsored sports leagues—basketball, softball, bowling, and more—and were entertained at lunch by string quartets that Eastman hired. And when they were feeling under the weather, they could depend upon the Kodak Medical Department, complete with dentist and nutrition adviser. If a worker was house-bound, one of the company's ten visiting nurses came calling, adminis-tering "hope and joy and . . . advice." In all of these things, the "Kodak King," as Eastman was known, had turned his company—alongside Procter & Gamble, DuPont, Standard Oil of New Jersey, American Telephone and Telegraph, International Business Machines, and a slew of others—into a paragon of welfare capitalism.

For many of these corporations, the Depression changed every-thing. As the downturn worsened, they slashed costs and curtailed the activities that had been designed to win their employees' fealty. Some killed the personnel departments that had been in charge of dispensing goodies to their workers—and keeping them in line. Kodak was jolted too. It tried to save jobs by reducing people's hours and putting them on part-time status. "We hoped that this would be sufficient," Kodak president William Stuber told employees in April 1932, a month after Eastman had killed himself. But it wasn't, and layoffs followed. That summer, the company trimmed executives' pay by 10 percent, while those with lower salaries and wages were hit with a 5 percent cut. In 1934, Kodak failed to issue a wage dividend for the first time in the plan's history.

Still, Kodak—and its workers—fared far better than most. The company kept its benefits largely intact through the Depression, and even added paid vacations for factory hands in 1938. With the econ-omy in shambles, Kodak also spearheaded a private, community-wide hospital insurance program in Rochester (later integrated into the Blue Cross system), and it led an alliance of area businesses in forming a vol-untary unemployment insurance plan. Fortunately for them, Kodak's workers didn't need to withdraw from the reserve all that often. From 1935 to 1939, the separation rate—the total of quits, retirements, layoffs, and firings—at the company's Rochester factories averaged a mere 11 percent annually, far below the 45 percent for US manufacturing.

Much of this stability was due to the deft planning of Marion Folsom, who first exhibited his gift for statistical analysis long before he showcased these skills for the CED. The McRae, Georgia, native had stepped in and improved his father's bookkeeping techniques at the family's general store shortly after going to work there at the age of twelve. Folsom went on to graduate from the University of Georgia when he was just eighteen, and then enrolled at Harvard Business School. In 1914, on the recommendation of the Harvard dean, Eastman personally wooed Folsom to join Kodak. For the next forty years, before President Eisenhower picked him to be his secretary of health, education, and welfare, Folsom was central to seeing that, as he framed it, "all employees receive a 'square deal'" at Kodak.

But as much as Eastman was genuinely humane, and as much as Folsom was sincerely interested in trying to help "the poor guy who's always up against it," something else compelled them to be so munificent with their employees: a desperate desire to thwart the unions.

Many companies were engaged in similar efforts, yet Kodak was particularly dogged. In 1919, Eastman appealed directly to his workers when labor organizers came to Rochester. "Right now there are those who are trying to poison the minds of the people of this community and of this company with a line of so-called argument that reeks of incendiarism—are circulating propaganda that, if followed to its full conclusion, can bring us only to the pitiable condition of prostrate, starving Russia," he told them. "Such propaganda and propagandists can not easily be reached by the management. But you men at the bench, you know! And you have the remedy in your own hands. . . . Your comfort and prosperity and the growth and prosperity of the company are interdependent." Unionization went nowhere.

Nine years later, organizers were still trying to make inroads at Kodak Park, the company's main factory complex. "As individuals we are helpless," *The Kodak Worker*, an openly Communist publication, opined in May 1928. "We must learn the lesson of class solidarity. We must learn to appreciate the value of organization. We must resolve . . . to take the offense against our bosses, demand higher wages, shorten work days, and put an end to the oppressive conditions within the plant." But for all the paper's swagger about ensuring that "the master class trembles in its boots," Kodak employees still weren't buying it.

By the 1930s, many companies could no longer hold back unions, be it with carrot or with stick, as the Depression exposed fundamental weaknesses of American business and New Deal era laws greatly strengthened labor's standing. But Kodak kept on as it had, buying the loyalty of its 22,000 workers with fat paychecks, regular wage dividends, ample benefits, and a complaint system known as "the Open Door"—all of it trumpeted on the pages of *Kodakery*, the employee newspaper started during World War II. At the same time, Kodak managers kept tabs on what unionized companies in Rochester were about to offer their workers and made sure they at least matched it. "As long as there's somebody else has got it a little bit better," Folsom explained, "the industrial relations people say we have to go along."

In the late 1940s, Kodak faced perhaps its toughest test yet on the labor front: a drive by the United Electrical, Radio, and Machine Workers to organize the company's Camera Works. But, again, management triumphed, as Kodak president Thomas Hargrave pressed his employees on whether "these outsiders" from the union "had anything to do with bringing . . . into existence" the many benefit programs they were receiving from the company. "I know, and I am sure you know, that they did not," he said. The UE campaign ended soon thereafter.

Unionists may have thought "industrial paternalism" was a more accurate choice of words than "welfare capitalism," but Kodak's employees didn't seem to care. And the brass was bent on keeping it that way. "When Eastman died in 1932, he left behind two generations of inbred managers, men who . . . shared his commitment to welfare capitalism as well his views that unions were anathema and an affront to private property," the historian Sanford Jacoby has written. "It was well understood by Kodak managers . . . that a sacred tradition would be broken if a union came into the company on their watch." When all was said and done, none ever would.

Through the 1920s and '30s, Coca-Cola's recipe for capturing its employees' allegiance consisted of three main ingredients: charisma, culture, and cash.

Two figures, in particular, possessed the charisma: Robert Woodruff and Harrison Jones, who had grown up just blocks apart in Atlanta and then found themselves leading the company—Woodruff as Mr. Inside, Jones as Mr. Outside. "Since we were knee-pants boys together in grammar school," Woodruff said, "our paths and our lives have been interlocked, and during our mature years the common bond and cement has been the dedication of both our lives and careers to Coca-Cola." For all that joined them, though, Woodruff and Jones were a study in contrasts.

Jones, a lawyer by training, had the dynamism of a Chautauqua tent preacher: the booming voice emanating from his 6-foot, 220-pound frame; the gesticulating hands; the flowing river of words. Perhaps the only thing separating him from a man of the pulpit was that nearly all of his sentences were pockmarked by "goddamn this" and "goddamn that"—as well as vernacular far more vulgar. "Every observation by Harrison," Coca-Cola's Ralph Hayes once commented, "begins with a spate of profanity, followed by an explosive negative in heated denial of whatever has just previously been said." Ralph McGill, the editor of the *Atlanta Constitution*, called Jones "a steam engine in pants."

Jones's prime responsibility was dealing with Coca-Cola's bottlers, a web of mostly independent businesses that converted the parent company's syrup into soda and then packaged and sold the final product—all backed by the marketing, advertising, and branding juggernaut that has always been Coca-Cola. Interactions between the mother ship and its franchisees were often fractious, and Jones took it upon himself to smooth things over, while pushing the troops to sell, sell, sell. "Did it ever occur to you that Coca-Cola, the finished beverage, is a child of a marriage between the Coca-Cola Company and the bottler?" Jones thundered to a group of executives from throughout the Coca-Cola system. "It comes from the womb of one and the loins of another. Oh, there is mutuality in this deal. But the only thing that counts to any worthwhile parents, and the only thing that counts here, is offspring, and Coca-Cola is the child, the offspring, of that marriage. . . . The millions of people in the world don't give a hoot who the parents of this child are. They know the child. They believe in the offspring. That is our life; that's our blood, and it's that we must perpetuate. And we must adopt the motto that the one spring that springs eternal is offspring. So, we must have unity. We must have cooperation."

Back at headquarters in Atlanta, Jones would assume the same role, sitting in the company cafeteria and listening to employees' gripes—all while expounding on the need for unity and cooperation. "People would try to talk, but before it was over they'd be spellbound," said his grandson, Harrison Jones II. "He'd sit there, and people would just be amazed that he would spend so much time with them. He'd spend forty-five minutes with an employee with a problem." Evidently mollified, the workers of Coca-Cola proper never unionized, though plenty of the bottling plants were organized, mostly under the auspices of the Teamsters.

Woodruff, known as "The Boss," had a much different personality. For starters, he wouldn't have been caught dead in the employee cafeteria. An adroit behind-the-scenes operator, Woodruff preferred to eat with a few handpicked executives and friends in his private dining room, just off his office, which he reached by private elevator. He was a natural tycoon, right down to the ever-present cigar in his mouth—usually a Cuesta-Rey, though on occasion a Havana encircled by a special Coca-Cola band. But Woodruff was a tycoon with a southern twist. His pride and joy was Ichauway Plantation, a 30,000-acre paradise in rural Georgia, where politicians, athletes, and entertainers joined him to ride horses, fish, hunt quail, and drink bourbon. "One of the high points," one visitor related, "is when the colored chorus comes up to the 'big house' . . . to sing Negro spirituals."

Woodruff could be gruff at certain times and aloof at others—something never true of Jones—but he radiated his own commanding presence. Just six feet tall, he still dominated a room. "You knew when The Boss had arrived, even if you were facing the other way," said one associate. "You could feel it."

The blend—Jones, rousing and riotous; Woodruff, refined and respected—worked beautifully. Each in his own way made sure a common message was conveyed constantly to everyone in the Coca-Cola universe, from top manager to floor sweeper, from bottler to advertiser: being part of this company was truly something special. In a certain respect, it was a funny refrain. Other products, arguably, had far more import than did a bottle of soda. General Electric, for one, could claim that it was at the very center of what Henry Ford called "the Age of Edison"—the early twentieth-century period of electrification that sparked America's new industrial future. General Motors played a key part in making Americans mobile, forever changing the basic structure of community and society. But Coca-Cola had a singular grip on the American imagination, giving the nearly 7,000 people that the company employed in the mid-1940s an unusual sense of pride in their work.

As legend has it, it was 1886 when Atlanta pharmacist John Stith Pemberton hunched over a three-legged brass pot in his backyard and cooked up the first batch of the syrup that would build an empire. He poured his concoction into a jug and carried it down the street to Jacobs' Pharmacy, where it was sold at the soda fountain for five cents a glass. Soon, whether by design or by accident, it was mixed with carbonated water. People loved it.

During World War II, the company shipped its billionth gallon of syrup, and through the 1940s it outsold its rival Pepsi by roughly five to one. But even more striking than the company's market share was its mind share. Coca-Cola, wrote newspaperman William Allen White, "is a sublimated essence of all that America stands for—a decent thing, honestly made, universally distributed, conscientiously improved with the years." During the war, American factories clamored for Coke to keep their workers contented, leaving Woodruff's men feeling immensely gratified. Such demand, Ralph Hayes told The Boss, spoke to "the unique position of this beverage as a part and symbol of a way of life for which a war is being waged." It was heady stuff for a soft drink.

Aware perhaps of the psychic value that the company offered, Coca-Cola paid its factory workers relatively well but stinted somewhat on executive salaries. When manager Harold Sharp joined the legal department in the early 1920s, "I was making about three times as much money" elsewhere, he recalled. Yet he signed on anyway, "interested in becoming connected with a clean, commercial enterprise, regardless of the compensation." And, sure enough, Sharp found real purpose in his work. "We have the product, and we are aiming at a definite objective of bringing refreshment, pure and wholesome, to the millions of people who inhabit the earth," he said.

Despite the occasional grumbling about tight pay, Woodruff was able to get a lot out of his employees. One way he did this was by always giving executives a second chance. "I hate to see a fellow fail when, with just a little more thinking and a little more work, he could succeed," Woodruff said. Among The Boss's best traits, Hayes averred, was his fierce "loyalty to his enterprise, fidelity to his associates, constancy toward his friends." Along with the constancy came cash—well-timed cash bonuses, to be exact.

These payments were very different from Kodak's wage dividend, which was strictly objective and egalitarian. A windfall from Woodruff, by contrast, was highly subjective and personal—the type of benevolent gesture, one imagined, to which the help at Ichauway Plantation had also grown accustomed. "This company has sure been good to a lot of us country boys," Sharp said in 1939, having just been handed his bonus for the year. Holland Judkins, another recipient of Woodruff's good graces, told The Boss: "Thank God for you and Santa Claus in the order named." Some offered a quid quo pro upon the receipt of their bonus. "To show my appreciation," said W. J. Brogunier, who worked in Coca-Cola's Baltimore office, "I will do all that I can to help make next year better."

At times, Woodruff would adjust people's base salaries—a move that also engendered warm expressions of loyalty. Upon learning that "my rate had been hijacked, my feeling of utter surprise was followed by other feelings of quiet, confusion, gratitude, and determination," said Hayes. By "determination," he added, he meant that he didn't want to let Woodruff down by not doing everything he could to help the company. It's the determination "to avoid giving anyone cause to say that your judgment or confidence was too badly misplaced," Hayes wrote. "I don't mind you losing bets on horses, cards or dice, but I don't want to be a party to your losing one on a person, particularly if I'm the person." He closed his letter this way: "Bob, what I started to say was, 'Thank you,' and that I do—proudly and humbly and faithfully."

Gerard Swope earned a degree in electrical engineering from the Massachusetts Institute of Technology, but his real education—the one that would turn his tenure as the president of General Electric into something strange and extraordinary—came from a very different place: Hull House, the settlement agency that provided a range of services for immigrants (mostly Italians, Czechs, and Russian Jews) and sought to close the divide between rich and poor.

Swope, the son of a St. Louis manufacturer of watchcases, had made his way to Chicago after graduating from MIT in 1895 and landing a machine-shop job with the Western Electric Company. Soon thereafter, he began teaching algebra and electricity classes at night at Hull House, which Jane Addams and Ellen Gates Starr had opened on the city's Near West Side in 1889. Their converted mansion would expand over the years into a thirteen-building complex, stretching for nearly a block, with a gymnasium, theater, art gallery, music school, boys' club, auditorium, cafeteria, cooperative residence for working women, kindergarten, nursery, libraries, post office, and meeting rooms—often used by labor organizers.

But Addams's real contribution had less to do with bricks and mortar and more to do with flesh and blood—the way she attracted wealthy women and men to Hull House to serve those who were less fortunate. They came as volunteers "to help out with the house's many activities in art, drama, music, recreation, education, and charity," Jane Addams's biographer, Louise Knight, has written. "While they often arrived with a sense of moral superiority, if they stayed long enough and their minds were open, their class condescension evaporated and was replaced by democratic beliefs: outrage at the unjust conditions working people strove to overcome and eagerness to be their political allies in those struggles."

For Swope, such ideals were a potent magnet, and always had been. While at MIT, he had studied business law with Louis Brandeis, who would go on to join the US Supreme Court and memorably sum up his own philosophy on income distribution this way: "We can have democracy in this country, or we can have great wealth concentrated in the hands of a few, but we can't have both." Swope was wicked smart, intense, and exacting—"a spring under tension always, never spent and never relaxed," as one friend painted him. But he was no stuffed shirt. While in college, he took a job at the 1893 Chicago World's Fair, working at the General Electric exhibition for a dollar a day. Tearing down transformers and other gear in need of repair, he immersed himself in oil, grease, and dirt. Swope would eventually become a full-time resident of Hull House. There he met his wife, Mary Hill, who was a social worker. Addams herself officiated at their wedding. Moving back to St. Louis at one point for Western Electric, the Swopes even opened their own settlement house, right next door to their home, where Mary taught immigrant women to sew.

By the time, then, that he was named president of General Electric in 1922, having spent the previous couple of years organizing the company's foreign operations, Gerard Swope had a head full of well-thought-out ideas about how the laboring class should be treated. "There are three factors in our economic system today that must be taken into consideration in our work: the shareholders, the employees, the community," Swope told GE's foremen on his first cross-country tour of the company's factories. As for the shareholders, he said, "happily, there is little to worry over in regard to the financial end of our business.

"My greatest concern," he went on, "is in the other two phases of our responsibility, that towards the employee and to the community at large. As to the employees, I infer every man here realizes that he is dealing with men and not with material or machinery. In our human relations between employees and employers there must be justice and sympathy. We spend so much of our time, so much of our life, in industry that we can get a very much greater satisfaction out of life if we have the conditions which surround our work pleasant and congenial."

Much like Kodak, GE was already a pioneer in this arena. Under Charles Coffin, who became GE's first president after merging his Thomson-Houston Company with Thomas Edison's businesses in 1892, a number of steps were taken to cushion the workforce. The company instituted a pension plan in 1912 and in 1913 formed a mutual benefit association to succor employees and their families in case of sickness, hospitalization, or death. A profit-sharing system kicked in in 1916, a life-insurance plan in 1920 (partly a response to the flu pandemic two years earlier), and a savings plan in 1922.

Swope then improved these benefits and added a bevy of new ones: hospital coverage, loan funds, housing assistance, and recreational activities for employees. Along the way, Swope had the consummate partner: Owen Young, who had shown himself to be an exemplary problem solver as GE's general counsel before rising to be chairman. Like Swope, Young, who'd grown up as a poor farm boy in upstate New York, knew what it was like to get his hands dirty. Like Swope, Young had been exposed to the thinking of those who questioned the excesses of capitalism and put the worker first—in Young's case, the muckraking journalists Lincoln Steffens and Ida Tarbell, who lauded Young for "a labor policy . . . in harmony with liberal notions." And like Swope, Young believed that it was possible to bind together the interests of employer and employee.

In the past, "capital was the employer, buying labor as a commodity in the cheapest market and entitled to all the profits of the undertaking," Young told an audience at the Harvard School of Business in

1927. "Managers were considered the paid attorneys of capital to devise ways and means to squeeze out of labor its last ounce of effort and last penny of compensation. Is it any wonder that in this land of political freedom men resented the notion of being servant to a master? . . . Fortunately, we are making great progress in America in these difficult relationships. We are trying to think in terms of human beings—one group of human beings who put their capital in, and another group who put their lives and labor in a common enterprise for mutual advantage."

To promote that spirit, Swope and Young kept GE's pay rates as high as possible—an essential element, they were convinced, to help those on the line feel valued and, in turn, inspired to help management meet its objectives. "Slowly we are learning that low wages for labor do not necessarily mean high profits for capital," Young said.

Beyond their own brand of welfare capitalism, Swope and Young utilized two other methods to try to motivate their employees. The first was "scientific management," the principles that Frederick Taylor had popularized a few years before World War I (and a cousin of Fordism, which standardized mass production). Under Taylorism, the time required for each element of a job was to be measured so as to ascertain the best way for tackling every task. The aim was to boost productivity. Although many would come to regard time-and-motion studies as instruments of management repression—an image that Charlie Chaplin helped to make indelible in his 1936 film *Modern Times*—Taylor himself had a completely different goal. "The principal object of scientific management," he wrote, "should be to secure the maximum prosperity for the employer coupled with the maximum prosperity for the employee."

Lillian Gilbreth, a Taylor protégé, taught GE how to apply this methodology in the mid-1920s, and by and large, the workforce seemed to like it—or at least they learned to like it, bending the system so as to raise their incentive pay while reducing the most tyrannical aspects of being monitored by a stopwatch. Often, groups of employees would work together, calibrating things so that they cranked out neither too much product (an offense known as "rate-busting") nor too little ("chiseling").

The other tactic that GE used to win over its workers was to cultivate "company unions"—an appellation every bit as oxymoronic as "Jews for Jesus." Real unions despised these management-sanctioned groups, which could be found not only at GE but also at Goodyear, Dennison Manufacturing, AT&T, and more than 1,000 other companies across America. Samuel Gompers, the labor leader, called them a "pretense admirably calculated to deceive." But many workers weren't so condemning, at least not at GE. The bosses treated the leaders of GE's company unions as junior partners, not as opponents, and they were even given access to corporate financial data. The upshot: management was able to "educate and secure sympathy and support from a large body of employees," the manager of GE's plant in Lynn, Massachusetts, reported. Esprit de corps ran high; turnover was low.

Then the Depression hit. Swope responded by thinking big—really big. In 1931, he put forth a proposal to shore up all of industry and cure the nation's unemployment crisis. "A job for every man!" became his watchword. After President Hoover rejected "the Swope Plan"—an intricate scheme involving the adoption of a large-scale social insurance system, funded by employer and employee, and the formation of corporate cartels—GE moved on its own, extending unemployment benefits to those who'd been laid off from the company.

Over time, however, GE was forced to cut back on many benefits, while reducing average pay by nearly 30 percent. Its payroll shrank by more than half, from 88,000 employees in 1929 to fewer than 42,000 in 1933. The company restored wages and benefits as rapidly as it could, but in the meantime, the lean years had given an unprecedented opening to a faction that had never really made much headway at GE before: outside labor organizers. Among this band was James Carey, who in 1936 became president of the new United Electrical and Radio Workers of America.

Swope and Young's reaction to the UE stood in stark contrast to that of their peers at a company like Kodak. Rather than stiff-arm organized labor, as Eastman had done and his successors would continue to do with a kind of religious fervor, the two GE executives openly embraced the national union movement. Their impulse wasn't new. As early as 1926, Swope and Young had met secretly with William Green, the head of the American Federation of Labor, to invite him to organize their company's factories. They even suggested that the AFL could parlay the dues it collected at GE into a war chest that would help the union infiltrate other electric companies. Their main demand was that GE's workers be organized into a single, broad industrial union, which they believed would be easier to negotiate with than a series of competing craft unions. The overture to Green fizzled, but it signaled that Swope and Young were, even among the "industrial statesmen" of the 1920s, well ahead of their time.

In 1935, President Roosevelt signed into law the National Labor Relations Act, the landmark measure that established the rights of workers to organize unions and bargain collectively. The law, known as the Wagner Act (for its chief sponsor, Sen. Robert Wagner, a Democrat from New York), also created the National Labor Relations Board and the legal infrastructure through which union-related disputes would be settled. Many companies fought the law bitterly—so much so that *Business Week* magazine was undoubtedly speaking for the mainstream of its readership when it called the Wagner Act "a piece of despotism" that corporate America would "unitedly resist." But not Young and Swope, who had been among a handful of corporate executives to make constructive suggestions on the drafting of the bill. To them, it was inescapable that labor was going to organize itself, and so it made good business sense to get out in front. But more than pragmatism was at play. Working with unions, instead of wrangling with them, was an extension of Young and Swope's credo that employees should sit atop the corporate pecking order, ahead even of shareholders. "In the long run," Swope said, "the people who should be management's chief concern are those who give their lives to the business, the workers, and not primarily those who buy in and out because a company pays good dividends."

Not every GE executive felt so comfortable about the UE's ascent. When Carey, newly elected to head the union, asked Swope for a meeting in February 1937, Swope's lieutenants advised him to spurn the request. After all, it wasn't a normal part of the corporate president's job to sit down with a labor representative, and they feared that a face-to-face session with GE's top man would give Carey too much cachet. What's more, GE's managers liked the plant-by-plant bargaining that took place under the company-union system—an arrangement endangered by the UE's pursuit of a single, national contract. But Swope ignored his men, and he and Carey had "a fine intimate talk," as Swope would remember it—the sixty-four-year-old corporate lion peppering the twenty-five-year-old "boy wonder" of labor with questions about his background and beliefs. It was the only time that the two met directly, but Swope came away persuaded that Carey could be trusted, and vice versa. "If you can't get along with these fellows and settle matters," Swope told the vice president handling labor relations, "there's something wrong with you." By the spring of 1938, GE's old company unions had been swept aside and the UE had won its first national contract without any real resistance from management.

The amity would be short-lived, however. Swope and Young retired in 1944, and the executives who followed them—including Charlie Wilson—had a decidedly different view of unions. The new guard were still moderates in some ways, as evidenced by their active involvement in the CED. But in dealing with organized labor, they took a sharp turn to the right, a turn that was all the more pronounced because for so long GE had stood so far to the left.

I n the spring of 1938, *Sales Management* magazine sent a squad of researchers to Muncie, Indiana—the prototypical American "Middletown"—where at every twentieth home they asked questions about ninety big corporations. One of them was, "Which companies, in your opinion, treat their employees fairly?" The three that topped the list were General Motors, Coca-Cola, and General Electric. For those actually working at these behemoths, however, reality was more cloudy and complicated. This was especially so at GM.

Like GE, GM was an early adopter of an assortment of employee benefits. A bonus system for salaried personnel was started in 1918, a savings and investment plan for all workers in 1919, a training institute providing continuing technical education in 1926, disability and life insurance that same year, and sickness and accident insurance in 1928. In 1932, as the Depression deepened, GM tried to keep as many people as possible employed through the use of job sharing. In 1939, the company would begin offering no-interest loans in the event a worker with five or more years of seniority faced a sudden reduction in hours or was laid off. And in 1940, it would implement a retirement plan. Wages were good.

Most of these pluses for employees came while Alfred Sloan ran GM. Born into an upper-middle-class Connecticut family, Sloan was a classmate of Gerard Swope's at MIT. Following graduation, he joined the fledgling Hyatt Roller Bearing Company, which after several years—and with the help of his father—he bought from the original owner. Over the next two decades, Sloan greatly expanded the business by supplying two companies at the fore of the fast-growing auto industry: Ford and General Motors, which had been founded in 1908 by William Crapo Durant. Sloan was well on his way to being a rich man.

Billy Durant would make him even richer. In 1916, he approached Sloan and offered to acquire Hyatt, part of a strategy in which the ever-scheming Durant would buy up and put under one roof various components manufacturers. Although Sloan and his father each walked away from the deal with $5 million—an amount equal to more than $100 million today—Sloan wasn't the type to retire and be idle, especially at age forty-one. So, Sloan went to work for Durant, where he learned all he needed to know about how *not* to manage a company. By 1920, the freewheeling Durant had pushed General Motors to the financial brink. He "was a great man with a great weakness—he could create but not administer," Sloan would say. The chemical company DuPont, which had become a major investor in GM, forced Durant out in November of that year. Beginning in 1921, Sloan worked closely with a coterie of DuPont executives to get GM back on track. They did, and in May 1923, Sloan was made president of GM.

He was an organizational genius. The management writer Peter Drucker, who knew Sloan well, would credit him with being "the first to work out systematic organization in a big company, planning and strategy, measurements, the principle of decentralization," and more. Sloan's role "as the designer and architect of management," Drucker added, "surely was a foundation for America's economic leadership in the forty years following World War II." Sloan's no-nonsense manner could make him seem impersonal and cold. But Drucker insisted that this was an unfair portrait. He had "tremendous personal warmth and was unbelievably generous—with his time as well as with his money," Drucker wrote. "Wherever I went in GM . . . I was told, often by fairly junior people, how Sloan had come to their rescue, usually unasked—how, for instance, he had given up an entire Christmas vacation to find the hospital where the badly burnt child of a plant manager could get the best medical care, and he had never even met the plant manager. I always asked, 'To whom would you go if you were in a serious jam?' Most people immediately answered, 'Alfred Sloan, of course.'"

Rather than make a fuss about his own openhandedness, Sloan preferred to crow about GM's open-mindedness. "The ability to get people to work together is of the greatest importance," he said. "General Motors, by its method, gets the fullest possible benefit of every ounce of brainpower in the whole organization. It also, in this way, gets the fullest possible contribution of every man, because everybody has been won over by open, aboveboard discussion to every policy adopted."

Well, almost every one. Even Sloan couldn't possibly have said with a straight face that GM was open and aboveboard in its policy toward organized labor. Fearful of the ascendant United Auto Workers, GM hired Pinkerton and other detective services to spy on its employees from early 1934 through mid-1936. In all, the automaker spent nearly $1 million—about $17 million in today's terms—on its espionage activities, though their full extent will never be known. That's because executives purged their files when they caught wind that a special US Senate committee, under the direction of Wisconsin Progressive Robert La Follette Jr., was about to investigate the matter as part of a sweeping probe into how some of America's largest companies were routinely violating the civil liberties of workers attempting to organize. The timing of the purge was impeccable, with GM's records cleaned out just before La Follette's staff could serve subpoenas. "I was astonished at the amount I could get rid of," Louis Seaton, a GM manager in charge of labor relations, acknowledged to La Follette.

The picture that did come together, while incomplete, was damning enough. In order to feed a steady stream of reports to GM about the UAW and its plans, Pinkerton had placed informants inside a number of union locals, and the agency had even lured an organizer from the UAW's international office into its pocket. It set up a dummy office inside the Hoffman Building in downtown Detroit, where the union had its headquarters, to keep a close eye on who came and went. According to one of its former agents, Pinkerton tapped the phone of the UAW's president, Homer Martin. Operatives also maintained surveillance of union leaders, including Martin and the man who would succeed him as head of the UAW, Walter Reuther. GM wasn't as apt to turn to violence as was Ford Motor—with its infamous service department, populated by gun-wielding thugs—but its behavior was just as creepy.

During the summer of 1936, with congressional investigators beginning to piece things together, GM dismantled its spying apparatus.

Six months later, in February 1937, the company's executives were called to appear before La Follette's committee. In between, without any more Pinkertons snooping around and making things difficult, the UAW made significant strides in organizing the workers at GM.

It all began on December 30, 1936, when union activists sprang into action at the Fisher No. 1 factory in Flint, Michigan, which supplied car bodies to Chevrolet and Buick. Rather than picket outside the plant, which would give the company an opportunity to send in scabs, workers loyal to the union camped inside, effectively seizing control of the facility and shutting down production. In the coming days and weeks, the sit-down strike spread across the area—to a Cadillac assembly plant, and then to a Fleetwood factory, and then to Fisher No. 2. There, on January 11, 1937, the police tried to take back the facility by firing rounds of tear gas at the strikers, only to be rebuffed by a barrage of stones, bottles, and steel door hinges. The cops turned and bolted—a retreat that led laborites to call the confrontation the Battle of the Running Bulls. But the bulls didn't stay away long. The police returned and opened fire with pistols and riot guns, wounding thirteen people. The clash strengthened the resolve of the strikers, who pressed on. On February 1, under the leadership of Walter Reuther, the union occupied Chevy Engine Plant No. 4—a linchpin of the GM factory system.

From the outset, GM contended that the strikers were breaking the law, having commandeered private property. The company also did its best to make the case that it was a fair employer. "Wages are higher today, by far, than the corporation ever paid before," Sloan told his workers. "No one can honestly say otherwise." Yet, while that was true, employees did have their frustrations—mostly about the ever-increasing speedup of the assembly line. The old "drive system," which had governed much of the American workplace from about 1880 to 1915, was still in full throttle at GM. "Everywhere workers indicated that they were being forced to work harder and harder," read a 1934 National Recovery Administration report on the auto industry. "They are vigorous in denouncing management as slave drivers, and worse." It was said that William Knudsen, a GM executive who would become corporate president in May 1937, could yell, "Hurry up!" in fifteen languages. As a rejoinder, the strikers in Flint sang:

When the speedup comes, just
twiddle your thumbs.
Sit down! Sit down!
When you want them to know
They'd better go slow,
Sit down! Sit down!

On February 11—with pressure mounting from US labor secretary Frances Perkins; Michigan governor Frank Murphy; and John L. Lewis, the president of the Committee for Industrial Organization, the umbrella group to which the UAW belonged—GM finally gave in. It didn't have much choice. The company had pumped out 50,000 automobiles in the month before the start of the strike. Now, output was at a virtual standstill, with just 125 cars rolling off the line in a week.

The four-page agreement that GM signed with the UAW was groundbreaking, for it recognized the union as the exclusive bargaining agent for the company's workers. The pact was also monumental for the labor movement as a whole, marking the beginning of a thirty-year period in which industrial unionism would serve as a countervailing force against corporate power in America.

As a clutch of GM labor officials made their way to room 357 of the Senate office building in Washington, just four days after the Flint sit-down strike had been settled, it was clearly too soon for anyone to grasp the historic weight of the accord. The executives were simply trying to explain how they'd ended up overseeing "the most colossal supersystem of spies yet devised in any American corporation," as La Follette's committee termed it.

They did their best, reminding the panel that unions could play rough, too, like the time in 1933 when organizers dynamited a power station at one of the plants in Flint, causing several hundred thousand dollars in damage. They also took care to make a distinction between their own laborers and labor unions—"outside organizations" that promoted "a great deal of radicalism," as Alfred Marshall, director of personnel at GM's Chevy operation, put it.

"I have hired upward of 250,000 men in my day," Marshall said. "I personally hired every man that went into the Chevrolet division for five years at Flint. I personally headed up the welfare." He went on to tell the committee that three principles guided him: "Hire a man; keep him busy." "Pay him well for what he does." "And treat the man as you would be treated yourself."

Sen. Elbert Thomas, a Democrat from Utah, was skeptical. "Just carry that logic through with regard to spying and see where you are," he told Marshall.

"We try to be very fair with regard to spying," Marshall replied.

As mockable as Marshall's rationalization may have been, he wasn't being insincere: many GM executives really did feel as if their domain had been invaded by a group of outsiders, threatening the company's independence to the point that they could justify spying (at least to themselves). "Will a labor organization run the plants of General Motors Corporation or will management continue to do so?" asked Sloan, who was so opposed to the New Deal and its support-ive posture toward unions that he helped fund the American Liberty League, a fanatical group that stooped to racism and anti-Semitism in its frenzy to bring down President Roosevelt.

Some inside GM's executive suite weren't so dogmatic, how-ever. At least a few of Sloan's top men thought the use of spies a bad practice. The chief heretic was Charles Wilson—"Engine Charlie," as he would come to be known, to distinguish him from GE's "Electric Charlie" Wilson. He had joined GM from Westinghouse in 1919 as an engineer and nine years later was made a corporate vice president. In 1941, he would replace Knudsen as president of GM, having taken an especially close interest in labor relations.

Given Wilsons's roots, this focus wasn't surprising. His father had organized a toolmakers' local in Pittsburgh, and Wilson himself had been business agent for a Pattern Makers union as a young man. He liked to tell people that when Socialist labor leader Eugene Debs ran for the White House in 1912, he'd voted for him. Wilson even kept a framed copy of his union card on his desk at GM.

To be sure, Wilson was no pushover, and he and his underlings—some of the same men who had orchestrated the spying in the 1930s—would fight the UAW hammer and tongs over all sorts of contract provisions and corporate policies throughout the forties. But as less of a hard-liner than Sloan, Wilson was open to collaborating with the union, making lasting peace where possible. "The test of labor relations isn't rhetoric," he once said. "The test is results."

It was striking that GM had room for both men—a staunch conservative like Sloan, who would remain GM's chairman until 1956, and a more free-thinking executive such as Wilson—and it highlights an often-overlooked facet of the way that corporations have always dealt with their workers and, more generally, defined the social contract: with terrible inconsistency. And so Charles Kettering could sit on the founding board of the CED, while GM vice chairman Donaldson Brown lent considerable intellect and energy to the National Association of Manufacturers and its assault on the Full Employment Act. The very concept of "full employment," Brown told Sloan, was the kind of "abstract economic theory" that could result in government planners "laying down a dictum" as to how much industry must produce. Some scholars like to put a thick line between the two groups: the CED has become shorthand for those companies at the center-left of American big business in the 1940s; the NAM has become code for those much further to the right. What often gets missed, however, is that many corporations—not only GM, but also GE, Kodak, and Coca-Cola—had at the very same time executives who were involved with both organizations, a display of corporate schizophrenia that would make it difficult to shove any of these enterprises into a single political box.

The Germans surrendered, just as the CED knew they would, in May 1945, and the Japanese followed suit in August. More than 400,000 American soldiers, sailors, airmen, and marines had died in what would be called the Good War.

As millions more veterans made their way home, the bread lines that many had foreseen never materialized. In January 1946, *Time* magazine reported that the nation's economy was going full tilt, leaving it to the CED's Paul Hoffman to tote up "the cheery figures": some 52 million workers were already employed in civilian jobs, household earnings were rising steadily, and private production was also surging.

Whether this excellent fortune was due to the advance planning of the CED and all the corporations it had enlisted in its cause, or whether it was the result of other factors—pent-up demand, government policy, demographic change—who could say for sure? And who really cared? "The problem," said *Time*, "is no longer how to achieve full employment. The question now is: how can it be maintained?" For America's workers, their long-elusive quest for security finally seemed within reach.

In 1947, General Motors officials launched the MJC—the "My Job Contest"—in which employees were invited to write on the topic, "My Job, and Why I Like It." About 175,000 GM workers entered, an extraordinary showing.

2

TAKE THIS JOB AND LOVE IT

Not long after V-J Day, General Motors president "Engine Charlie" Wilson addressed a group of his executives in Detroit, laying out half a dozen fundamentals to ensure the company's "continuing success" and "to maintain our competitive position" as the automaker embarked on the transition from a military to a peacetime economy. Most of these guidelines hinged on giving workers what they needed to thrive on and off the job—tangibles and intangibles alike. "Put the right people in the right places," Wilson advised. "Train everyone for the job to be done; make the organization a coordinated team; supply the right tools and the right conditions; give security with opportunity, incentive, recognition; look ahead, plan ahead for more and better things."

As platitudinous as these principles may have seemed to some, they were sufficiently inspiring to be invoked two years later, in the fall of 1947, by William Kitts, a junior engineer in the company's Fisher Body Division, as he sought to shed light on why he appreciated working for GM. Citing Wilson's words was a nice touch—nice enough, at least, to help Kitts's composition stand out from the nearly 175,000 others submitted as part of a company-sponsored letter-writing contest. Everyone who'd entered had been directed to explore the same topic: "My Job, and Why I Like It." Bill Kitts's prize: a brand new black Pontiac Streamliner four-door sedan. At the grand awards banquet, Wilson himself would hand Kitts and thirty-nine other winners keys made of gold.

In all, about 59 percent of GM's hourly and salaried workforce participated in the contest—a deluge of entries so large that, had they been stacked one on top of another, the pile of paper would have extended six stories high. The frenzied response was prompted by a crush of promotional activities, which began in September with a two-week teaser campaign in which the initials "MJC" were tossed out unexplained, adding an air of mystery to the proceedings: it was then revealed that they stood for "My Job Contest." Spurred on by more than one hundred contest chairmen spread across GM's factories and offices, foremen and supervisors urged their underlings to write letters. Buildings were festooned with streamers and posters, letting everyone know that their views were welcome. "You Don't Have To Be A Highbrow . . . Know How To Spell . . . Be A Skilled Writer . . . Fine Penmanship . . . Use English . . . Or Even Own a Pen," read one placard. Plants held open houses, exhibits, and parades to gin up interest. Six full-color postcards were mailed to employees, reminding them to get their letters in. And they did—in every form and fashion imaginable.

The average letter ran about 250 words, though one wag put down but a single sentence. Others ballooned to 20 typewritten pages. About 700 were in foreign languages—Polish, Spanish, German, Hungarian, French, Lithuanian, Hebrew, and Arabic—and required translation. One was written in Latin, another in braille. Some employees took the "or even own a pen" line literally, sending in phonographic recordings. One worker put together a six-minute silent film, showing him talking about the contest with his family, writing his letter, and then placing it in the corner mailbox. Poems, acrostics, and renderings were also part of the mix.

Without a doubt, many of the missives were barefaced attempts by GM employees to snare one of the forty cars (one Cadillac, three Buicks, six Oldsmobiles, ten Pontiacs, and twenty Chevrolets) or the more than 5,000 other items offered to those deemed best: refrigerators, freezers, ranges, washing machines, radios, and more. To this end, some engaged in pure sycophancy—nothing but "apple-polishing," as *Time* bluntly put it in a write-up of the company contest. But many others, the magazine added, penned pieces that "had a ring as authentic as the clang of the drop-forge hammer" used to stamp out engine parts or axles at one of GM's giant factories. Kitts, whose job was to make improvements to the assembly line at Fisher Body's St. Louis plant, was among those who weren't blowing smoke. "The better the tools, facilities, and working conditions," Wilson had stated back in 1945, "the more that can be produced with the same human effort and the lower the cost of the product. When this results, higher wages can be paid and more good jobs provided." Wrote Kitts in his essay: "I feel that in some small way I am helping to put into effect one of the basic points that Mr. Wilson set up. . . . The reason I like my job is because I'm doing a job that is important and at the same time is exactly what I wanted to do to make a living. What more could any man desire?"

Kitts, who was twenty-three, had been fascinated by cars since he was a little kid. After high school, he took a job as a stock clerk at the Fisher Body plant in his hometown of Memphis, Tennessee. One day, shortly after Kitts started, the head of industrial relations at the site asked him if he would consider applying to the General Motors Institute—the company's technical training center in Flint, Michigan. He did, and was accepted. "This was one of the biggest moments of my life," Kitts recounted in his winning letter. "It was about this time that I first began to feel a great like for the corporation, for I realized that it not only had an interest in production, but also had an interest in the individual employee as well." By taking advantage of this break, Kitts was put on a pathway that big businesses such as GM loved to tell the world they afforded. "Think of the corporation as a pyramid of opportunities toward the top with thousands of chances for advancement," Alfred Sloan had written in his 1940 book, *Adventures of a White-Collar Man*. "Only capacity limited any worker's chance to grow, to develop his ability to make a greater contribution to the whole and to improve his own position as well."

In Kitts's case, he wasn't going to let anything limit him. "I learned early on that I wasn't as smart as some people," he said, "but I could outwork them." For four years, Kitts traveled every eight weeks by rail between the General Motors Institute—where he took courses in metallurgy, math, and physics—and Fisher Body operations in Memphis and, after the war, St. Louis. In Flint, he cleaned blackboards and swept out classrooms to earn a little extra money. "That's how you learned responsibility," he said. Once he'd completed his studies, having displayed particular talent on the lathe, his assignment was to recommend the best portable hand tools to heighten efficiency at Fisher Body. "I had immense pride working at General Motors," Kitts said. "You'd be surprised how much pride you had. I'd compare it to Annapolis or to West Point."

There was more to liking a job than deriving from it personal honor and satisfaction, of course. Kitts noted in his MJC submission that he was "receiving good wages," and many others also highlighted the company's pay policy. Overall, 52 percent of those writing contest letters applauded how much they earned at GM, making income the most frequently mentioned of eighteen broad themes identified by the company. Mary Linabury, who held a job in the Electro-Motive Division's engineering department, wrote that she "never yet had to ask for a raise" because "they have come through steadily with my increasing abilities." Vernon Halliday, a grinding-machine operator for Buick, whose letter was playfully written in the style of a bumpkin, said: "I gets paid every Friday," and "the pay is good, too"—though there were other ways that GM took care of him. Halliday, who had joined the company in 1922, lived with his family in one of about 1,000 houses that GM had constructed in a Flint neighborhood called Civic Park, offering workers sweetheart financial incentives to buy.

Other MJC winners also touted the company's fringe benefits. Betty Kraft, of the GM patent office, pointed to the retirement program as an essential reason for her "happiness and peace of mind." Delphia Baugh, who'd joined Fisher Body's Fleetwood Plant in 1929, wrote that her "neat little white cottage" in Detroit was, in a sense, "a gift to me" from the company because it had awarded her a $1,000 bond for an idea that she'd had to increase production during the war—part of the GM Suggestion Plan. "With this bond," she said, "I made the down payment on my home." Wrote C. Wales Goodwin, who worked in the engineering department at Pontiac: "In my twenty-seven years with General Motors, I have not only seen marvelous mechanical progress, but I have also seen great humanitarian progress" with "old-age benefits established, pension and retirement funds set up, group and hospital insurance set up, shorter working hours, higher wages, and vacations with pay for all employees."

GM did pay well—an average of more than $3,000 per employee across the company in 1947 (equal to about $32,000 today). That compared with about $2,700 for all US workers. But in this regard, GM was merely at the fore of a much larger trend. Nationally, full-time workers had seen their wages and salaries rise markedly since the end of the war, up more than 18 percent in two years. A good chunk of this gain reflected the need for Americans to keep up with the cost of consumer goods, which was now surging after the lifting of wartime price controls. And there had been some serious bumps along the way, especially in certain industries like autos, which experienced massive layoffs right after the war's end. Yet the US unemployment rate remained below 4 percent through 1946 and 1947, and it wasn't long before a real and lasting prosperity began to sweep across the country, elevating millions of families "from poverty or near poverty to a status where they can enjoy what has been traditionally considered a middle-class way of life," Frederick Lewis Allen, the editor of *Harper's Magazine*, observed in his book *The Big Change*. In concrete terms, this meant "decent clothes for all, an opportunity to buy a better automobile, install an electric refrigerator, provide the housewife with a decently attractive kitchen, go to the dentist, pay insurance premiums, and so on indefinitely." Benefits were expanding widely as well. The National Industrial Conference Board discovered that group accident and health insurance was in place at 64 percent of the 3,500 companies it surveyed in 1946, a sharp increase from the 31 percent with such protections in 1939. Pension plans were now being offered by 42 percent of the companies, up from a scant 13 percent seven years earlier.

Yet, in the end, many GM workers reached past such practicalities and, like Kitts, found tremendous pride in the company and its products. Indeed, nearly half of all the MJC letters captured such feelings—almost as many as those referring to the magnitude of GM's remuneration. "I've got a job I'm really proud of!" Linabury wrote. "It is from this engineering department that come all of the changes in design that produce stronger, lighter cars with smoother, more efficient engines and motors." Taylor Phillips, a color-spray man, said he wore his GM "badge as proudly as the proudest G.I. wears his honorable-discharge button because I know that my job is an important and necessary one in this gigantic organization."

Eliciting comments like these was just what Charlie Wilson and his senior colleagues wanted. Workers were always going to beef about something, they figured, but just getting them to articulate some of the pluses at GM was bound to help keep them more content. "In the words of the popular song, it caused these men and women to 'accentuate the positive,'" Wilson said. "As one letter writer indicated, he had never before stopped to think about the good things connected with his job, but when he did stop to think, he was surprised with the number of 'positives' there really were." Harry Coen, GM's vice president for employee relations, added: "A bit of homespun philosophy has run like a thread through all of the material issued during the contest, and that is—'Let's look at the doughnut instead of the hole.' It's just as simple as that."

The contest had a second purpose, too: to allow management to peer inside the minds of GM's workers. To help them determine the best way to interpret the letters, Coen's staff met with experts in the fields of education, social psychology, psychiatry, and political science. Readers, specially trained by the Statistical Analytics Company, coded every entry, carefully tabulating on IBM "mark-sense" cards which prevailing subject or subjects the writer had brought up. Peter Drucker, who served as an employee-relations consultant to Wilson and was also one of the MJC final judges, called the contest "the richest source of information ever about workers, their needs, desires, and capabilities."

This claim, even if half-true, was impressive, given the widespread use of employee-attitude testing at the time. From the mid-1940s through the mid-1950s, two in five large companies in America would conduct at least one such survey. Sometimes, the aim was to generate results that could be used to propagandize: "Ninety-seven percent of employees think this is an above-average plant!" Other times, the intent was to give workers a place to vent their complaints—a safe avenue for a calming catharsis. Kodak, for instance, set up a program in which department heads would meet regularly with small groups of hourly workers for an open-ended conversation. One of its primary aims was "to serve as a psychological 'safety valve' for individual employees." In either case, such efforts were often used to blunt union organizing, helping management unearth and assuage workers' concerns before they could fuel official demands by an outside labor representative.

Despite these manipulative moves, real insights were gleaned from attitude testing. From the time that the technique had been pioneered in the 1920s, researchers found that managers hoping to foster good morale tended to overestimate the value of paying their workers well and underestimate how crucial it was to treat them fairly, provide jobs that have real meaning, and communicate clearly the way in which each individual's role fit into the larger mission of the organization. "Apparently it is not enough to have an enlightened company policy, a carefully devised (and blueprinted) plan of manufacture," wrote Elton Mayo, the famous Harvard professor, who in the late 1920s guided the interviewing of some 21,000 employees (half the total) at the Western Electric Company's Hawthorne Works in Cicero, Illinois. "To stop at this point, and merely administer such plan, however logical, to workers with a take-it-or-leave-it attitude has much the same effect as administering medicine to a recalcitrant patient. . . . This is the essential nature of the human; with all the will in the world to cooperate, he finds it difficult to persist in action for an end he cannot dimly see." Other scholars—Abraham Maslow, Douglas McGregor, and Frederick Herzberg, among the most highly esteemed—would also stress how critical it was for people to find a loftier purpose in their jobs. "Unless there are opportunities at work to satisfy these higher-level needs," McGregor wrote, "people will be deprived; and their behavior will reflect this deprivation."

The MJC reinforced these notions. As Drucker summarized it, "the contest fully proved" that extrinsic rewards such as pay and promotion—what Herzberg termed "hygiene" factors—could cause dissatisfaction among workers if handled poorly. "But satisfaction with them," Drucker continued, "is not particularly important and an incentive to few. Achievement, contribution, responsibility, these are the powerful motivators and incentives." Taken by this core finding, Wilson floated an idea: he wanted to test a new organizational structure in which management and blue-collar employees would work closely together to find ways to improve GM's operations. For the first time, frontline laborers would have real input into the corporation's decision making.

The concept was immediately shot down from both directions. Sloan, who as chairman of GM remained by far the most influential person at the company, "had little use" for Wilson's progressive views, Drucker remembered. "For the great majority of GM executives—and for executives in American industry altogether at that time—anything like" what Wilson was advocating "represented the abdication of management's responsibility," Drucker added. "'*We* are the experts, after all,' they argued. '*We* are being paid for knowing how to organize work and job, or at least for knowing it better than people with much less experience, much less education, and much lower income. We are accountable,' they argued, 'and not only to the company, its shareholders, and its customers, but above all to the workers themselves, to make them as productive as they possibly can be—or how else can we pay them a decent wage?'"

Although Wilson invited the union to be a part of his program—and although Walter Reuther privately characterized the GM president as "a very decent, genuine human being"—the opposition from the leadership of the United Auto Workers was every bit as violent as that from the company's executive suite. "To the UAW," Drucker said, "anything that would establish cooperation between company and workers was a direct attack on the union." Without an ally in sight, Wilson's vision died swiftly—or at least it would remain in a deep coma for the next thirty years.

In the meantime, Reuther and the UAW did all they could to discredit the MJC. "The General Motors contest is an attempt to conduct a one-sided opinion poll of the workers," Reuther contended. "The corporation hopes, by offering a number of valuable prizes, to buy employee statements to the effect that General Motors is a kindly, fatherly, and understanding employer, sympathetic to the workers' problems and needs, which will later be used in so-called goodwill advertising. If GM is sincerely interested in a true opinion poll of its workers, the corporation should be willing to offer equal prizes for letters stating what is wrong with GM employer-employee relations with constructive suggestions for improving such relationships."

At least a few union men ripped down MJC posters from plant walls. Others, like R. E. McDonald, writing in *The Searchlight*, the newspaper of UAW Local 659 in Flint, resorted to verse instead of vandalism:

> *They ask me why I like my job*
> *And offer several prizes.*
> *Some household things, some odds and ends*

And cars of different sizes.
They all look good from where I sit
Say! Maybe I could lie
And tell 'em how I love my job
And give 'em reasons why.
For instance, I like my job
Because the boss is kind.
(He reprimands me from in front
And kicks me from behind).
Or else I like my job because
My wages here are greater,
(I have bologna once a week
And with it, boiled potater).
I like my job because they keep
The plant so clean and purty.
(The flies don't come in anymore,
The dining room's too dirty.)
They look out for my comfort, too.
At least that's how I feel,
(In summertime I slowly melt,
In winter I congeal). . . .
Your mail will surely bulge with notes
That praise you to the skies,
Delude yourself how much you may
You'll know it's simply lies.
And guys like that should stop and think,
They'd see the whole thing's funny,
For Judas did the same damn thing
For a hell of a lot less money!

UAW supporter Phil Singer, writing under the pseudonym Paul Romano in a widely distributed tract called *The American Worker*, also reported that attitudes about the MJC were sour. The rank-and-file's "remarks vary from: 'The biggest liar will win' to 'The winners are already picked out,'" he wrote. "Others say: 'I like my job because I can feed my family,' 'I like my job because I want to win a new Cadillac,' 'I like my job because I want to keep my job,' etc. . . . The company is pressuring the workers to enter the contest. The foreman and plant superintendents have been going around trying to coerce workers into entering. One long-employed worker was in the office about it. He noticed that the boss had a mark next to his name. He became furious and had an argument with him. He said that he would write a letter only if he himself decided. So far he had decided not to, and no one was going to compel him."

For all of this tough talk, though, there was no escaping it: by the fall of 1947, it was organized labor—and not companies like GM—that had been knocked back on its heels.

On June 23, 1947, Congress voted into law a piece of labor legislation that would turn out to have as much impact on the relationship between employer and employee as any other in American history: the Taft-Hartley Act. As is often the case, the measure's full wallop would not be felt for quite a while; despite a number of restrictions that Taft-Hartley placed on union organizers, the ranks of labor continued to grow in the immediate wake of its passage, and the share of the nation's nonagricultural workers who were unionized would not fall below 30 percent for fifteen years. Still, whether because they were prescient or just trying to be provocative, labor advocates were apoplectic about Taft-Hartley from the outset. Less than a week after the law's approval, pickets surrounded the Cincinnati church where Lloyd Taft, the son of the bill's Senate cosponsor, Republican Robert Taft, was getting married. "CONGRATULATIONS TO YOU. ____ TO YOUR OLD MAN," read one of the protestor's signs, leaving it up to onlookers' imaginations to fill in the blank with all manner of invective.

President Truman, whose veto of Taft-Hartley had been overridden by overwhelming majorities in both the House and Senate, called it "a slave-labor bill." Walter Reuther excoriated the law, known formally as the Labor-Management Relations Act, as "a vicious piece of Fascist legislation." Said Thomas Johnstone, assistant director of the UAW's General Motors Department: "If allowed to stand, the clock may be turned all the way back . . . to the days of the open shop and industrial war." Actually, Taft-Hartley came about through industrial war, in a fracas that pitted, among others, GM against the UAW.

The union had followed its electrifying triumph in the 1937 Flint sit-down strike with another huge victory, winning a contract at GM in 1940—this time, without needing to implement any work stoppage. The wage increase in the accord was small, just one and a half cents an hour. But it forced GM to give up paying different amounts to workers who did the same jobs. No longer would the whim of the boss hold sway. No longer were laborers subject to the sort of individual bias they had encountered in the past. No longer could a particular plant supervisor pay his employees based on his own proclivity for stinginess. "GM's shift toward a uniform, nationwide wage pattern represented one of the industrial union movement's most significant steps toward the New Deal era's transformation of the American class structure," the historian Nelson Lichtenstein has written. "Factories within the same firm, and companies within the same industry, would cease to compete for lower wages, and within those factories and occupations wage differentials would decline" for millions of blue-collar workers.

The 1940 agreement was also pathbreaking in its establishment of a grievance arbitration system. Under it, the stickiest shop-floor disputes were decided by an "umpire" who considered written briefs and oral arguments from UAW officials on one side and members of GM's industrial-relations staff on the other. Many of Sloan's top men were uncomfortable with this arrangement, fearing that it gave the union an invitation to interfere with the prerogatives of management and would further drive a wedge between the company and its workers. "Often, through union activity directed at gaining the exclusive allegiance of the union membership, there is lost the essential element of loyalty and recognition of dependency upon effectiveness of management," groused Donaldson Brown, the GM vice chairman. "An understanding of the mutuality of interests of management and labor is dissipated. Efficiency is reduced, and the interests of all concerned suffer as a consequence." But Wilson realized that having the union's explicit involvement in a corporate disciplinary system was paramount to promoting peace—or at least to preserving what many would regard over time as an "armed truce."

The arrival of World War II introduced its own complications into the dynamics between union and company. Reuther talked up the ideal of "victory through equality of sacrifice." And in a show of patriotism, the UAW and other leading trade unions offered an unconditional no-strike pledge. But many workers resented having their wages held in check by the War Labor Board, which was trying to tame inflation by keeping a lid on pay, while corporate coffers grew fat on military contracts. Union membership in America swelled during the war, increasing from about 9 million to 15 million from 1940 to 1945. Grievances piled up, and wildcat strikes—actions unauthorized by the union brass—proliferated across heavy industry: autos, coal, rubber, steel, and shipbuilding. During 1944, more than 2 million laborers across the United States walked off the job, an all-time high. More than half of all autoworkers took part in some kind of work stoppage that year, including 7,000 employees at GM's Chevrolet Gear and Axle, who were enraged over the firing of five workers who'd failed to meet stepped-up production schedules. "When we found that there was no other solution except a wildcat strike," said one GM worker, "we found ourselves striking not only against the corporation but against practically the government, at least public opinion, and our own union and its pledge." Many of these were quickie strikes, of limited economic consequence. But they were a potent symbol of working-class solidarity—and a harbinger of more unrest to come.

Leaders of labor and management tried to head off additional trouble. In March 1945, the presidents of the US Chamber of Commerce, the American Federation of Labor, and the Congress of Industrial Organizations signed a seven-point charter that acknowledged "the inherent right and responsibility of management to direct the operations of an enterprise," as well as "the fundamental rights of labor to organize and engage in collective bargaining." The idea was to "substitute cooperation and understanding for bitterness and strife," as the AFL's William Green described it. That turned out to be wishful thinking. By the fall, with Germany and Japan having now surrendered, 200,000 coal miners, 44,000 lumbermen, 43,000 oil workers, 35,000 longshoremen, and thousands more in the glass, textile, and trucking industries had struck their respective employers. In the final four and a half months of 1945, 28 million "man days" of work were lost to walkouts—more than double the high reached over a full year during the war. The key issue was wages: wartime bonuses and overtime had been cut and the cost of living was climbing rapidly.

On November 5, with the public growing increasingly dismayed over the seemingly endless strike wave, President Truman convened seventy-two delegates from the AFL, CIO, Chamber of Commerce, National Association of Manufacturers, and other groups at a labor-management conference in Washington. He implored them to figure out a way past their differences. "There are many considerations involved," the president said in opening the colloquy. "At the base of them all is not only the right but the duty to bargain collectively. I do not mean giving mere lip service to that abstract principle. I mean the willingness on both sides, yes, the determination, to approach the bargaining table with an open mind, with an appreciation of what is on the other side of the table—and with a firm resolve to reach an agreement fairly. If that fails, if bargaining produces no results, then there must be a willingness to use some impartial machinery for reaching decisions on the basis of proved facts and realities, instead of rumor or propaganda or partisan statements. That is the way to eliminate unnecessary friction. That is the way to prevent lockouts and strikes. That is the way to keep production going."

Not everyone was thrilled with the message. GE's president, "Electric Charlie" Wilson, thought that Truman's oratory had tilted unfairly against the corporate community. "It was too one-sided to do other than egg labor on to get all they can," he said. Whether Truman's speech served as the impetus or not, packinghouse, steel, coal, and railroad workers would lead protracted strikes in the coming months. During the year after V-J Day, the scope and intensity of labor-management conflict would go down as unmatched in US history. About 5 million men and women were involved in more than 4,500 work stoppages. At GE alone, 100,000 members of the United Electrical, Radio, and Machine Workers walked out in January 1946, seeking higher pay. "The problems of the United States can be captiously summed up in two words: Russia abroad, labor at home," Wilson said, as the nation's unions remained restive and the Cold War dawned.

But by far the longest impasse—lasting 113 days—would play out at GM. The strike's principal architect was Walter Reuther, who at the time was running the UAW's GM Department and was still four months away from assuming the union presidency. The son of a German immigrant union activist, Reuther was born in Wheeling, West Virginia, on September 1, 1907—Labor Day eve. As an eleven-year-old, he went with his father to visit the old man's hero, then in prison: the Socialist leader Eugene Debs. Reuther moved to Detroit in 1927, where over the next few years he'd show great skill as a die maker at Ford Motor, stump for Socialist presidential candidate Norman Thomas, and take economics and sociology classes at Detroit City College. In January 1933, Reuther and his younger brother Victor set off for Europe and then Russia, hoping to learn more about the Soviet system. Taking jobs at the fledgling Gorky Auto Works, they were impressed. "In all the countries we have thus far been in," Victor Reuther told a friend, "we have never found such genuine proletarian democracy. It is unpolished and crude, rough and rude, but proletarian workers' democracy in every respect."

In late 1935, the Reuthers returned to Detroit, where Walter rejoined the Socialist Party and began to make his mark as a UAW organizer, most dramatically during the Flint sit-down strike at GM and, several months later, at the Battle of the Overpass at Ford. In that brawl, several company union-busters had kicked and slugged Reuther and another UAW organizer near the Miller Road overpass outside Ford's sprawling Rouge plant. For good measure, Reuther was thrown down a flight of stairs. He came away bloodied and battered—but proud and able to claim the moral high ground in the union's tussle against corporate America. As deft as Reuther was at fighting the large companies, he demonstrated equal aptitude for dispatching his foes inside the union, adroitly navigating the internecine rivalries that plagued the UAW in the 1930s and '40s. At first, Reuther allied himself with the union's more radical faction, which included a group of Communists, in part because it allowed him to differentiate himself from those leaders who favored a policy of accommodation with GM. Later on, when it suited his ambitions, he turned against the Communists and resigned from the Socialist Party as well. By 1940, according to Lichtenstein, Reuther had emerged as "a national spokesman for the pro-defense, pro-Roosevelt 'right wing' within the American labor movement"— a standing he cemented with a bold plan, known as "500 Planes a Day," to speed the auto industry's conversion to military output.

Now, with GM focused on how it would reconvert its lines for postwar production, Reuther again thrust himself into the spotlight— leading 180,000 workers to walk out of the company. The strike began on November 21, 1945, just two weeks after President Truman had tried to smooth things over at his labor-management conference. "It is time to debunk the notion that labor can meet in parleys with government and management and by some miracle fashion a compromise that will keep all parties happy and contented," Victor Reuther said, speaking for his brother. GM initially proposed to raise average pay by 10 percent, from a $1.10 an hour to $1.21. In early December, in response to newly issued wage and price regulations from Washington, the company upped its offer by two and a half cents, an overall boost in pay of 12 percent. But the union was pressing GM to increase average hourly income all the way to $1.43—a 30 percent jump—so as to make up for the mountain of overtime that workers no longer would receive because of the end of the war. "Never in the history of this industry has there been so perfect a chance to correct the inequalities . . . and to obtain a real increase in wages," the UAW asserted, "for the major auto companies are swollen with war profits and are hungrily reaching for the greatest potential market for automobiles that has ever been seen, or ever will be seen again in our lifetime, in all probability."

Reuther didn't stop there. The company was so flush, he insisted, it could meet the UAW's 30 percent demand without charging any more for its cars. "Wage increases without price increases" became Reuther's rallying cry—a strategy that widened the circle of support for the strike. "In this struggle," he later explained, "we were defending the interests not only of autoworkers alone, but of labor as a whole and of all the millions of small farmers, white-collar workers, intellectuals, pensioners, etc. who stood to be damaged just as much as we if living costs were permitted to spiral upward."

The company countered that it was in no position to pay anything close to the amount that Reuther was trying to exact. GM's sales may have doubled during the war, it said, but profits had actually fallen 12 percent over that time. And even though the company's income could conceivably surge going forward amid a blossoming consumer economy, there were many uncertainties and no guarantees. "We had the gun put to us awfully quick," Wilson said. "When we were still hearing echoes of the atomic bomb, we got 30 percent" as the UAW's ultimatum. What's more, said Wilson, to think that wages could be raised without affecting prices was sheer folly. Should the union get what it wanted, "prices to customers would have to be raised 30 percent," he warned. "If wage raises in automobile plants forced such increases in car prices, the market for automobiles would be restricted. Fewer cars would be sold; fewer people would be able to afford and enjoy them, and fewer workers would be employed in making them."

Reuther didn't back down. If GM's financial condition was really as precarious as the company claimed, he said, prove it—open the books. For GM, this was the ultimate indignity: a challenge far outside the normal framework of union negotiations. Federal labor law covers "such areas as rates of pay, hours of work, working conditions," the company said in a full-page newspaper advertisement it took out across the country. "No mention is made of earnings, prices, sales volume, taxes, and the like. These are recognized as the problems of management." The ad, which bore the headline "A 'Look at the Books' or 'A Finger in the Pie?,'" went on to add that Reuther's gambit would "surely lead to the day when union bosses, under threat of strike, will demand the right to tell *what* we can make, *when* we can make it, *where* we can make it, and how much we must charge *you*—all with an eye on what labor can *take out* of the business, rather than on the *value that goes into the product.*"

In January 1946, a federally appointed fact-finding board recommended that GM hike average pay by nineteen and a half cents an hour, or 17.5 percent. Although this was far less than the UAW had been pushing for—a terrific letdown for Reuther—the panel embraced the union's basic reasoning: a fast-growing marketplace for autos, it suggested, would stimulate a buildup in production and profits that could easily absorb higher wages without higher prices. Reuther hailed the board's report as "a complete endorsement of the union's position" and a "historic step." GM's Donaldson Brown fretted that the Truman administration had bestowed upon Reuther "a moral victory." But as time dragged on, it became apparent that the company had the much stronger hand to play. Early in the strike, the government had sent GM more than $34 million as part of a refund of "excess profits" taxes paid during the war, giving it a sizable cash cushion. Those in the union, conversely, were running out of dough. By March, Detroit's Public Welfare Department said the city's relief funds had been nearly exhausted by GM workers on strike. Meanwhile, a string of other companies were able to sign contracts for far less than the thirty-three cents an hour that constituted Reuther's line in the sand. Ford, Chrysler, Radio Corporation of America, and most notably, the nation's big steelmakers had all settled for gains of eighteen or eighteen and a half cents an hour. Precedent had been set. The United Electrical Workers, which bargained on behalf of about 30,000 GM employees who were not part of the UAW, similarly settled with the company for eighteen and a half cents, with no concession on prices—a move denounced by Reuther as a Communist-inspired double-cross.

Despite the setbacks, Reuther's bluster continued. "The president's offer of nineteen and a half cents was a compromise of our demand," he said. "I will be God damned if I will compromise a compromise. . . . This is all horseshit about going back to work." Yet within a few weeks, Reuther was out of tricks. The final agreement with GM, reached with the help of a federal mediator, called for a base wage increase of eighteen cents an hour, plus an extra penny to correct certain inequities—a 19 percent increase overall. In addition, the union won some new language regarding seniority, along with a mechanism to facilitate the collection of dues from workers. All in all, however, it wasn't much to show for a strike that had lasted nearly four months. If there was any real winner, it was Reuther, who was narrowly elected president of the UAW on March 27, 1946, a couple of weeks after the contract's ratification. His nerve in taking on GM, the leviathan of American industry, unquestionably had helped his cause.

But there would also be a heavy price to pay—for the UAW and for all of American labor. Having unleashed strike after strike after strike, the union movement had gone too far in many people's estimation. "The public will not tolerate a continuance of the civil war which prevailed in 1946," the Committee for Economic Development said in its appraisal of the situation. Even President Truman, who usually could be counted on as a friend of labor, had become so irritated that a handful of men could cripple the economy, he threatened to conscript striking railroad workers in May 1946. "No longer the underdog in the public's mind," historian James Gross has written, "'too powerful' became the most-used adjective for labor unions." Editorial cartoonist Thomas Little, who'd later win a Pulitzer Prize for the *Nashville Tennessean*, neatly encapsulated the country's mood by depicting swirls of factory smoke that curled into the air and spelled out the word STRIKES. The caption read, "Better Get It Under Control." To do that, the nation turned to the GOP, which campaigned under the slogan "Had enough?" "We know that in the year after V-J Day we had lost $6 billion in the standard of living in America due to industrial strife," said Richard Nixon, who came to Washington as a congressman from California in 1947, part of a Republican rout in the midterm elections that saw the party wrest control of both the House and Senate from the Democrats. "We had seen unprecedented force and violence in labor disputes throughout the country. We had seen abuses by labor leaders. . . . We had seen, as well, in the labor-management field how a few persons, irresponsible leaders of labor, could paralyze the entire country by ordering a strike by the stroke of a pen."

Although America's antiunion sentiment had come to a fast boil—"The public was happy with labor on V-J Day, but in the years since we have seen a shift in public opinion," Nixon said—the reaction on Capitol Hill was more of a slow burn. Ever since the Wagner Act had been passed a dozen years earlier, giving workers the right to organize and bargain collectively under the vigilant eye of the National Labor Relations Board, the law had been under constant assault. Business interests, including the Alfred Sloan–backed Liberty League, at first challenged the act's constitutionality. When the Supreme Court upheld the act in April 1937, the battleground relocated to Congress. Over the previous decade, lawmakers had put forward 169 amendments to national labor policy, most of them repeating "the same chant of hate: 'Regulate labor, curb labor, destroy labor,'" said Philip Murray, who served as president of the CIO as well as president of the United Steelworkers. In general, these proposals had sought to ramp up the regulation of internal union affairs, limit the ease with which strikes could be called, restrain picketing and boycotting, and make illegal the "closed shop" (a business in which membership in a union is a condition for being hired and continuing to work there). The Taft-Hartley Act, just one of 200 labor-related bills introduced at the start of the 1947 congressional session, was more of the same—and then some. Opponents called it a "death warrant" for unions. But others had a gentler interpretation. Reform, said GE's "Electric Charlie" Wilson, was needed "to save labor from its own excesses—excesses which, if unrestrained, will in the long run be injurious to labor itself."

It is tempting to dismiss Wilson's comment as a total charade—an attempt to make himself seem fair and reasonable when what he really wanted was to see America's industrial unions obliterated. But issues like this are rarely so black and white. By 1945, even the hard-nosed National Association of Manufacturers had given up trying to have the Wagner Act repealed outright. In part, this was a calculated bid by the NAM to seem less reactionary and burnish its image. Beyond that, many executives of larger companies had learned to like collective bargaining because it provided a measure of predictability and stability on the shop floor. What was needed, the CED said, were some "orderly ground rules" moving forward. For others, putting up with a union man like Walter Reuther was simply superior to the alternative. These executives "believe that pension plans, good lighting, and personnel counseling are better than socialism," C. Wright Mills wrote in his 1948 classic *The New Men of Power: America's Labor Leaders.*

Given this stance of most of big business—it wanted to rein in, not do away with, unions—there couldn't have been a more fitting person recruited to write the Taft-Hartley Act: a one-time New Deal Democrat who would remain lifelong friends with FDR's labor secretary, Frances Perkins, but who'd drifted more and more to the right over the years and would soon become a high-priced lawyer and lobbyist for GE and GM. His name was Gerard Reilly.

Reilly grew up in Boston, the oldest of three children, in a working-class household that was long on discipline. His father, an accountant, "would beat the boys—not because they did anything wrong, just to keep them straight," Reilly's daughter, Margaret Heffern, said. Reilly earned a scholarship to Harvard, where he graduated with honors in 1927. Gangly in appearance and possessing a slight stutter, "he was socially awkward and very cerebral," said his son, Jack. To help pay his expenses through school, Reilly worked as a gas-station attendant and as a substitute mail carrier. After earning his diploma, he became a newspaper reporter in Rhode Island, where one coworker recalled him as "a very idealistic young man with a liberal social philosophy." Reilly eventually went to Harvard Law School, where he studied with Felix Frankfurter, and then joined the Roosevelt administration. He wound up in the Labor Department and quickly worked his way up to be the top lawyer there. The Senate confirmed him as solicitor in 1937, and he became a close and trusted adviser to Secretary Perkins.

Reilly's views were not as far to the left as those held by some New Dealers, and he worried that certain individuals in the Labor Department were ignoring administration policy "because of mistaken zeal." Still, official Washington was a tight community, and with his easy laugh Gerry Reilly befriended many who were part of it, including White House aide James Rowe Jr. and the Hiss brothers, Alger and Donald. (Alger Hiss would become one of the most controversial figures of the Cold War after being accused of spying for the Soviets and convicted of perjury in 1950.) Even with his relatively moderate leanings, Reilly had little doubt that many aspects of the capitalist system had crumbled amid the Great Depression and might never be rebuilt. "The days of 'laissez faire' economy are past" in Reilly's judgment, the *Washington Star* wrote. "He is an unqualified advocate of federal regulation in the field of . . . social insurance as 'safeguards to workers.'" In particular, he urged Perkins to fight for tough labor standards. "Millions of employees are being paid wages insufficient to maintain themselves and their families in decency and comfort, and are being forced to work unconscionably long hours," he told Perkins in August 1937. "The need for correcting these evils has long since been recognized by commentators, legislators, administrators, and the public at large."

In 1939, House conservatives went after Perkins and Reilly, accusing them of conspiring to avoid the deportation of Harry Bridges, the Australian-born leader of the International Longshoremen's and Warehousemen's Union and a suspected Communist. The secretary and solicitor maintained that they were just following the law in not moving precipitously against Bridges, but a resolution was introduced in Congress demanding their resignations. "Do you remember the priest that walked beside Joan of Arc when she went to the stake?" Perkins asked Reilly as the two entered a House Judiciary Committee hearing. It isn't known whether Reilly indulged any of his vices that day, pouring himself an extra glass of bourbon or puffing on a few extra Chesterfields, but he couldn't be blamed if he had. Settling in before the hostile panel, "you could see them all sharpening their knives and their pencils," Reilly later said. In spite of the pressure, he comported himself very well. Emanuel Celler, a Democrat on the committee, told Perkins afterward that Reilly's "sincerity and guilelessness were most disarming." The two survived the ordeal, and in September 1941, President Roosevelt picked Reilly to join the National Labor Relations Board. Upon Reilly's departure from the Labor Department, Perkins thanked him not only for his service—"You have had an extremely important part in . . . lifting the standard of living of the people of this country in compliance with our new conception of what makes a healthy economy in a mass-production system"—but also for his "warm personal friendship."

By this point, the NLRB had accumulated "a fine roster of enemies," *Time* pointed out. This included, not surprisingly, antiunion businesses that were upset over the board's vigorous enforcement of the Wagner Act. What outraged them, apart from any substance of the board's actions, was its tone. In those days, the NLRB had a habit of "not only telling the employers they were wrong . . . but telling the employers they were immoral," said Paul Herzog, who would later chair the board. The AFL also pilloried the NLRB, accusing it of "brazen favoritism" toward the CIO in a series of jurisdictional disputes in which the rival labor coalitions were vying for members. "I have never seen a more united or extensive protest against a federal board," said Rep. Howard Smith, a Virginia Democrat, who was the NLRB's chief antagonist through the late 1930s. Even worse, the NLRB had garnered a reputation as a hotbed of communism.

Much of the condemnation of the NLRB was exaggerated, with little real evidence to indicate that the board was exercising partiality in its decisions. Still, hoping to quiet the critics, President Roosevelt shook up the three-member NLRB after the election of 1940 by nominating two men who didn't have the baggage that their predecessors did. One of them was Reilly. "It may be said of Solicitor Reilly . . . that he has at least kept himself above the great ideological controversies in his field to remain comparatively unknown to the general public," the *Baltimore Sun* wrote. What no one had yet detected was that Reilly had become deeply disillusioned. He was aghast that staffers at the NLRB and in other parts of the federal government were, as he said later, "waist deep in the Communist Party." And he was offended by the "skullduggery" that some at the board had perpetrated to tip official rulings in labor's favor. Workers may well have needed a guardian angel more than businesses did during the 1920s and early '30s, Reilly reasoned, "but certainly by the time of the war, the pendulum had swung too far the other way." As he saw things, it was unions—not companies—that had begun to exploit workers for their own aggrandizement, with an unabashed assist from the NLRB. "It's a very paternalistic attitude . . . these union leaders take toward the rank-and-file," he said. Many inside the NLRB were infuriated by Reilly's politics. He had started his career "as a kind of sneaker-wearing Georgetown type, very bright and very liberal" but "ended up a kind of legalistic spokesman for industry"—a switcheroo that led to "more cussing" at the NLRB than almost anything else at the time, said Herbert Fuchs, who worked there.

But what appalled some appealed to others. After leaving the NLRB in 1946, Reilly was invited to draft legislation that would vitiate the Wagner Act and the NLRB, first by Republican senator Joseph Ball of Minnesota and then by Robert Taft. Reilly would help, as well, with the bill being advanced in the House by Republican Fred Hartley of New Jersey. And when differences in the Taft and Hartley measures needed to be reconciled by a conference committee, Reilly was on hand there, too. At times, his old world and his new one collided. "I'd go and play with Alger Hiss's son, and that evening Representative Nixon would come by and meet with my father at our house," Jack Reilly recalled. Through it all, somehow, Reilly and Frances Perkins remained devoted to each other: he, now a Republican insider; she, the epitome of New Deal liberalism—"Saint Frances of the Labor Department, Our Lady of Working Americans," as one of her Democratic successors called her. Even though Reilly's and Perkins's politics had totally diverged, "he adored her," his daughter said. He even became the executor of her estate and would always cherish the cufflinks that President Roosevelt had given to her and she had passed on to him.

The act that finally became law—despite President Truman's objections that it contained "new barriers to mutual understanding" between employer and employee—put a hard bridle on union organization and operations. Taft-Hartley created a Federal Mediation Board to decrease strikes and reorganized the NLRB, shunting much of its policy-making authority to the courts. It gave the president the power to limit a union's right to strike in peacetime by requiring a sixty-day cooling-off period on national security grounds. It prohibited jurisdictional strikes between the AFL and CIO, which were still feuding over turf, and designated sympathy strikes and secondary boycotts as "unfair labor practices." A "free speech" provision made it easier for employers to try to dissuade their workers from even joining a union. It barred the unionization of "managerial and supervisory" employees. And it put an end to the "closed shop" while expressly sanctioning state "right-to-work" laws under which no person could be obligated, as a condition of employment, to join or pay dues to a labor union. In sum, Taft-Hartley didn't outlaw collective bargaining, but it emphasized the rights of individual workers—just the way Gerard

Reilly wanted it. "He morphed into a very thoughtful conservative," said Frank Nebeker, who sat with Reilly on the federal bench in the 1970s before being appointed by Ronald Reagan to direct the Office of Government Ethics. "He even out-conservatived me."

If the full effect of Taft-Hartley would come slowly for most of America's rank-and-file, one group found itself pinched right away: factory foremen, who as part of the "managerial and supervisory" class no longer had any right to organize and bargain collectively. Companies like GM had been hankering to clamp down on them for years, ever since the Foreman's Association of America had evolved into a disruptive force during the war—amassing a membership of as many as 50,000, staging walkouts at Chrysler and other manufacturers, winning contracts at Ford Motor and United Stove Company, and cutting a deal with the Congress of Industrial Organizations by which the CIO agreed that its members wouldn't replace any foremen should they go out on strike.

They had a lot to strike for. Once paid as much as 60 percent more than the hourly workers they oversaw, foremen at some companies were now earning less than their subordinates because, unlike those in the United Auto Workers and other industrial unions, they couldn't plump their salaries with overtime. Their fringe benefits often trailed as well. Hoping to turn that around, the foremen's demands were not much different than those of the workers they supervised. They wanted, among other things, a seniority system, sick leave, and a premium for covering the night shift. They were also angling to recover some lost respect. Through the 1920s, foremen played God inside many of America's factories—hiring, firing, driving, and rewarding those on the line. But as industry became more technologically advanced and was managed with greater sophistication from above, their clout diminished and in some cases disappeared.

As warranted as the foremen's frustrations may have been, GM and most other companies viewed their unionizing as an utterly preposterous proposition. In their eyes, foremen were the first-line officers of management; they spoke for the enterprise and, therefore, had no choice but to take sides. The laborers under them could simultaneously feel loyal to both company and union—a phenomenon that management theorists called "dual allegiance"—but this division of sympathies was untenable for foremen, a nonstarter. What, for instance, would happen if a group of foremen was to affiliate with the CIO, the same labor organization that the UAW was part of? How could they possibly represent the company when ironing out grievances submitted by their union brethren? "The dual allegiance which will arise when foremen are unionized will imperil their ability to fulfill their responsibilities to maintain efficiency and discipline of the men under their direction," GM's Charlie Wilson said. "In such circumstances, management cannot continue to give them such authority any more than the Army can risk granting a commission to a man who holds partial allegiance to another country."

Taft-Hartley removed, once and for all, the chance that America's foremen would feel any such pangs of dual allegiance. But the law left them feeling something else: stuck in the middle. If the foreman "don't get it from the people below him, he gets it from those above," said Joseph Kundla, who ran a crew of thirty-six men in the car conditioning department at GM's Framingham, Massachusetts, factory. One of Kundla's peers from the chassis department, William Keinath, also had the sensation of being squeezed. Whenever something goes wrong, he said, "no matter who the fault actually lies with, the foreman gets blamed." Added James Frederickson, a foreman in the plant's paint department: "When it comes down to it . . . management pulls the strings on us like we were puppets. They call us members of management, but they don't treat us like we are." Too far down in the hierarchy to have any real voice in company decisions, but high up enough to incur the antipathy of the guys on the line, foremen like Kundla, Keinath, and Frederickson were caught in a corporate netherworld—their vulnerability foreshadowing that of the cubicle-dwelling middle manager of the 1980s and '90s.

Still, not everyone despised the job, not all the time anyway. Kundla thought the pay was fine, and he was pleased with the varied nature of his work. "It's not monotonous," he said. Keinath looked forward to moving up the ladder at GM. "I hope to go a long way," he said, "and I think I have the potential." For Frederickson, there was dignity in his work: "I do have a strong drive to want to do a good job and be trusted to do it."

For most employees—salaried or hourly, unionized or not—this was (and would remain) their day-to-day reality: they found lots of things about their jobs to be exasperating, but they found others to be exhilarating, with most falling somewhere in between. After all, these are "human beings," Peter Drucker wrote, and not "the statistical abstractions that most management men and many sociologists and industrial relations people see in their mind's eye when they say 'worker.'" They "do not 'like' everything, nor do they completely 'dislike' everything," he added. "They discriminate. They are never 'satisfied' but also seldom totally 'dissatisfied.' They judge." In this light, GM's My Job Contest wasn't meaningless; employees' letters were valid expressions of what they liked about their work. But, as Drucker noted, this was only half the equation. A more rounded, more nuanced, more illuminating picture would come from hundreds of interviews conducted by a team of Yale University researchers several years after the MJC. Roaming two GM factories (Framingham and Linden, New Jersey), they talked to foremen (including Kundla, Keinath, and Frederickson) and production workers of every occupation. From this, they heard it all: the positives and the negatives, compliments and brickbats, professions of gratitude and outbursts of anger.

Steve Domotor, a forty-five-year-old Hungarian immigrant, had bounced around several industries—shipping, autos, textiles—before he found his way to the Linden plant in 1937. He was seduced instantly. Working with metal "was in my blood," Domotor said, and the money that GM offered was above the national average. He started off at seventy-five cents an hour, pounding out imperfections in car bodies before they were painted. A week later, he was making eighty-five cents, "and in no time," Domotor recalled, "I was up to a dollar." By the early 1940s, he'd become a "ding man," a painstaking job that required him to remove dents and fix damage without marring the paint or polish that already had been applied. This took so much dexterity that only 8 of 2,000 people in the whole plant rose to be "ding men." It was one of the highest paying jobs at Linden—not bad for someone with a sixth-grade education and, in that way, a telling example of how workers with minimal schooling could pull down solidly middle-class wages in the postwar era. Yet it was the size of the challenge, and not just the size of his check, that really excited Domotor. Each banged-up piece of metal that came his way had to be puzzled out. "Every day there's something new," he said. "You see those wrecks on the highway? There's no two alike, is there?"

But Domotor also learned that people could be as twisted as fenders. "If the foreman treats you like a man, everything is alright," Domotor said. "An experienced foreman will listen to you. You talk to him, and you can compromise with him." But others, he found, use language "that's not fit for pigs." One supervisor was "authority crazy," Domotor complained. "He wants you to bow down to him." Many others said the same thing: whether they liked a job depended, to a large extent, on whether or not they reported to a jerk.

Some were naturally suspicious of all foremen, carrying a level of animus so intense it seemed almost tribal. "The company trains them guys," said John Sillup, who during his fifteen years at GM had mounted cushions, seats, and side-arm panels on Buicks, Oldsmobiles, and Pontiacs. "They teach them how to pat your back and feel for a soft spot to put the knife in." Others were more generous. "The pressure is on the foreman just as on the worker," said Bradford DeGroat, a welder. "It's the higher-ups who brew all the trouble."

Amid this welter of opinion, there was one well-defined area of agreement: everybody, virtually without exception, abhorred the unremitting pace under which they worked. "The line keeps moving, moving, moving—and there's no avoiding it," said John Donohue, who assembled heaters to be installed inside Oldsmobiles. In many sections of the factory, the din was continuous, and the air befouled by oil, smoke, or other contaminants. "Here, look at my cap," said Stanley Tomsky, a metal finisher, holding up a hat full of steel dust. "Imagine what my lungs are like." Production workers were supposed to take breaks, with "relief men" swinging into position to keep the line moving in their absence. But many times, "you can't get relief until they see the piss running out of your eyeballs," said Robert Scales, a glass installer.

Overtime delivered extra pay. But it also intruded into the normal rhythms of workers' households. "You never know when you're going to eat lunch, and my wife doesn't know when to have supper for me," said DeGroat. "They not only hire you; they run your life." Men went home irritable, exhausted, beaten down. "I can't go bowling or shoot pool anymore," said John Hajducsek, a thirty-eight-year-old seat-installation man, who was hired by GM in 1940. "I have no energy to go out. As far as I'm concerned, I'm finished."

"Here they know a man is being overworked, and they try to get that last ounce of blood out of him," said Glace Bright, a welder. "The whole thing is that you're constantly working under pressure. Your mind is never at ease.

"It isn't a question of liking the job," Bright said. "You just do what you're told, whether you like it or not."

GM feted the forty top winners of the "My Job, and Why I Like It" contest at the Statler Hotel in Detroit a couple of weeks before Christmas 1947. The six MJC judges made brief remarks. Charlie Wilson gave a speech. "The results of the . . . contest have exceeded all our expectations," he said, "not only because of the number of General Motors employees who participated, but more particularly because of the tone and quality of the letters themselves. . . . They are the most sincere and most moving human documents it has ever been my privilege to read. They give one a feeling that so long as people such as the men and women who wrote those letters live and work as Americans, our country and our institutions are safe." The evening wasn't all so earnest. Del Delbridge and his orchestra played, while guests feasted on shrimp cocktail Neptune, essence of chicken royal, and filet mignon. The high point was when Wilson handed over the golden keys to the winners' new cars. Thomas Anslow, a forging machine operator, got the top prize: a Cadillac. Bill Kitts drove off in his Pontiac Streamliner. Mary Linabury, Betty Kraft, and C. Wales Goodwin each received Chevy Fleetline Sportmasters. Both Taylor Phillips and Delphia Baugh went home in a Buick Model 51 sedan.

There was just one snag. Vernon Halliday, the grinding-machine operator from Flint, didn't go to the banquet because his son Douglas, a GM engineer, had been mistakenly told he should attend instead. It wasn't until the end of the festivities, when Wilson read excerpts of the winning entries, that Douglas realized something was wrong. "The names of the authors of these excerpts were not given," Vernon later told his own parents, "but Douglas instantly recognized mine and at the end of the banquet announced to Mr. Wilson the error. The head of the personnel division here at the Buick, who sat at the same table with Douglas, told me privately that he knew something of the mental anguish which Douglas suffered during the reading of my entry when the truth dawned upon him. . . . No one but our son knew of the error, of the whole four hundred assembled." Vernon sold his new car, an Oldsmobile Series 76 Dynamic Cruiser, and tried to split the money with Douglas. "But he won't hear to taking a cent," Vernon said. "What would have been such joyful news, had there been no error, just left us feeling sort of numb. . . . Not that he wasn't proud to have his dad win—only that it was such a letdown to discover that his expected and planned-for prize belonged to another, especially after we had talked together of his selling it and using the proceeds as an investment fund against a time of need."

Some days you like your job. Some days you don't.

After years of high tension, General Motors and the United Auto Workers negotiated the "Treaty of Detroit" in 1950, ushering in an era of labor peace. Walter
Reuther, the UAW president, stands third from right.

3

THE MAKING OF
INDUSTRIAL PEACE

In the aftermath of Taft-Hartley, the Congress of Industrial Organizations and the American Federation of Labor reacted like any wounded animals would: they bared their teeth and became aggressive. Strikes were leveled at an unusually broad range of industries in 1948—"from the stock market to the stockyards," one report on the situation noted. Coal miners stopped working in March, West Coast dockworkers went out in September, and longshoremen at East Coast ports hit the picket lines in November. Meanwhile, the United Auto Workers kicked off what it described as "an intensive organizational and educational drive" to cope with the passage of the "infamous" and "insidious" law, a campaign modeled on none other than General Motors' own "My Job Contest." The fliers promoting the union's efforts weren't nearly as slick as the ones that the company had produced for the MJC, but whatever they lacked in polish they made up for with the mordancy of the message: "GM Workers—Win a Prize Without Telling Any Lies."

The aim, in this case, was to help Walter Reuther and his men meet the new realities of Taft-Hartley, which demanded that all union members now sign a card allowing their UAW dues to be pulled automatically from their paychecks. "Failure to promptly obtain these signed check-off cards seriously jeopardizes the welfare of our union," the UAW warned. At the same time, the UAW was eager to attract as many new members as possible, concerned that Taft-Hartley had made it easier for rival unions to infiltrate GM and the other automakers. "A lot of the fellows we are after just haven't been around long enough to feel the union in their bones—or in their hearts," the UAW asserted. "They don't remember what it was like in the not-so-good-old days. We have the answers for them. Take them back over the years. Corner them at lunch, or at the gate, or over a beer, and give it to them straight. . . . Let's finish the job in GM. Let's build the union. The UAW makes us strong—so let's make the UAW stronger. A strong union is much more than an answer to Taft-Hartley. It's a beachhead on the future we all want."

The union's prize drawing—open to anyone who joined the UAW, recruited a new member, or signed a dues check-off or union security card—was paltry compared with the MJC. In fact, the union could afford only a handful of inducements to dangle in front of workers: two automobiles (a Packard and a Ford), three Kelvinator refrigerators, and two Co-Op Home Freezers. Still, at least Reuther's boys could add a little levity to the loot they had, displaying the Ford and the Packard in front of union headquarters in Detroit, in plain view of the General Motors Building across the street. "There's a Ford in a GM Union Member's Future," a giant banner hanging outside the UAW offices proclaimed. It was all a poke at GM, which had refused to sell the UAW one of its own cars at a discount. The union even convinced one of the MJC winners, Delphia Baugh, to write an open letter supporting the UAW initiative. "I won a Buick in the 'My Job Contest,'" said Baugh. "But just because I like my job does not mean that I think it cannot be improved. . . . I am going to try to sign up as many members as I possibly can in the UAW-CIO contest."

In all, the campaign was a success, motivating more than 25,000 workers from GM plants to join the UAW—a bump in membership, said one union official, that "greatly strengthened the hand" of labor as it prepared for 1948 contract talks. The union played its cards determinedly, making an unprecedented 132 separate demands of GM and vowing to wage "the damnedest struggle ever." Union negotiators pushed for a pay increase of twenty-five cents an hour, a guarantee of at least 40 hours a week of income, a pension plan for factory work-ers, and a new "social security" program that would provide a full 52 weeks of disability coverage, double the current level. "What to do about doctor bills and grocery bills when sickness or accident stop pay-checks," the UAW said, "is the top worry among autoworkers."

The company, unmoved, anticipated another epic showdown. "We regarded these demands as extravagant beyond reason and feared that if the UAW persisted in them we would have another disastrous strike similar to the 1945–1946 one," Alfred Sloan later recalled. There was, however, a saving grace: despite the caustic tenor of the UAW's mem-bership drive, the union agreed with GM to negotiate the new contract out of the public eye. "In previous years," Sloan said, "our collective bargaining had come to resemble a public political forum in which the union fed a stream of provocative statements to the press, and we felt obliged to answer publicly. The privacy of the 1948 negotiations made their tone more realistic from the start." Another factor may also have helped tamp down the rhetoric: some of the sharpest tongues in the room had been removed. On the company side, Harry Coen—who had accused Reuther of revealing "Socialistic desires" during the 1945 bargaining—had been replaced as GM's labor-relations chief by Harry Anderson, an attorney with a more sophisticated style, and Louis Sea-ton, who was as blunt as a wrecking bar but known for keeping his composure. Then, on April 20, about five weeks into negotiations, Reuther was quieted as well. That's when an assassin nearly killed him.

It was about ten at night, and Reuther had just returned to his home in Northwest Detroit from a UAW executive board meeting. When he went to fetch a bowl of peaches out of the refrigerator, a blast from a twelve-gauge shotgun tore through the kitchen window. The buckshot caught Reuther in the right arm and in the chest. Somehow, he stayed conscious and crawled onto the back porch. "Those dirty bastards!" he yelled. "They have to shoot a fellow in the back. They won't come out in the open and fight." The doctors pumped four pints of blood into him, as Reuther survived two and a half hours of surgery. No one would ever be arrested in the case, though Reuther himself al-ways suspected that his Communist rivals in the UAW must have had a role in the attempted murder.

At the negotiating table in room 5–202 of the General Mo-tors Building, the big breakthrough came in late May, following

thirty-seven previous bargaining sessions. With UAW members having walked off the job at Chrysler just a week and a half earlier and
the union's strike deadline at GM looming, the strain was growing
fast. But progress toward a settlement had stalled. And the talks had
become so mind-numbing that Seaton switched to smoking cigars
during the bargaining after noticing one day that three different cigarettes were burning in the ashtray in front of him. Now, he sought to
stir things up, offering a new wage formula whose main goal was to
make sure that workers' wages didn't keep falling behind rising prices.

In tangible terms, it meant that GM would give an hourly pay increase of eleven cents to 225,000 production employees—far less than
the UAW had been seeking. Yet what was momentous was that eight
cents of the total would be tied to the government's Consumer Price
Index and adjusted going forward so as to track the general cost of
living. The other three cents, labeled an "annual improvement factor,"
were supposed to reflect productivity gains at the company—an explicit linking of higher wages to higher output and stronger corporate
performance. "I prefer to think of it as a group merit raise of sorts,"
Sloan said.

The concept of a cost-of-living adjustment, or COLA, was not
new. In 1916, Kodak had increased pay for its workers based partly
on a cost-of-living index that Marion Folsom had put together. In
1936, General Electric adopted a similar scheme, which in the face of
mounting consumer prices soon helped to push the company's wage
rates to record levels. "The cost-of-living adjustment is automatic and
will be paid without any necessity of complaint or collective bargaining on the part of employees," GE announced. GM itself had flirted
with a COLA in the mid-1930s, and Charlie Wilson then refined the
plan in 1941. During the 1945 negotiations, GM offered a COLA—but
the UAW rejected it, focusing instead on its call for "wage increases
without price increases."

Despite the UAW's resistance, the COLA wasn't just a corporate
tool. Leon Trotsky, the Marxist leader, had popularized the notion
among laborites in the late 1930s. And before the latest round of negotiations, a number of UAW locals were also insisting on a "sliding
scale of wages" that would move in concert with consumer prices. But
Reuther was incredulous—anxious, in particular, about what would
happen if a postwar depression set in and prices began to flow in only

one direction: downward. What's more, observed Sloan, it seemed that union leaders "would prefer to play an active role in setting wages." A COLA took away part of the UAW's raison d'être.

Nevertheless, Reuther came around. Consulting with top aides from his bedside, where he was recuperating from his gunshot wounds, he blessed the 1948 agreement, persuaded by two things: First, the union negotiated a floor for the COLA, so that this portion of the formula could not fall below three cents. And second, the UAW could continue to press for a raise in the annual improvement factor in subsequent contracts. "Thus," said Reuther, "the General Motors' workers are not chained to the same standard of living. They are protected against increased living costs and at the same time make progress with respect to living standards. From now on our fight will be to increase and accelerate the extent of that progress." As was his nature—and the nature of his position—Reuther pledged to keep battling "against the greedy industrialists."

Yet the truth was, having a built-in COLA addressed a huge problem that had vexed GM's workers—and the entire country, for that matter—since the end of the war: nonstop inflation. By late 1946, exploding prices had all but erased the wage increases won by the UAW and other unions the previous winter. Inflation continued to soar at a rate of nearly 20 percent through the first half of 1947, generating so much angst and anger among working Americans that they started to sing about it:

> *My mother gave me a penny*
> *To buy some candy;*
> *I didn't buy no candy;*
> *It cost a nickel.*
> *A piece of penny candy,*
> *It cost a nickel;*
> *Oh, everything is higher;*
> *It's sure outrageous;*
> *Yes, everything is higher;*
> *Except my daddy's wages.*
> *My mother gave me a nickel*
> *To buy a pickle;*
> *I didn't buy no pickle;*

It cost a quarter.
A qua-qua-qua-qua quarter,
It cost a quarter;
A little nickel pickle,
It cost a quarter.
My mother gave me a quarter
For seltzer water;
I didn't buy no water;
It cost a dollar.
A da-da-da-da dollar;
It cost a dollar;
For bubbles in the water,
It cost a dollar.
My mother gave me a dollar
So I wouldn't holler;
But you should hear me holler,
'Cause what can you buy with a dollar?

Ultimately, Reuther defended the COLA as "a tremendous victory"—a stance made all the easier by Charlie Wilson's inclination to stick up for the union on this one. Wilson remained, all in all, plenty hard-bitten. Heading into the 1948 talks, for example, he had lashed out at organized labor, condemning the nation's industrial unions as "the most powerful monopolies that have ever existed in our country . . . operating with little or no regard for the public interest." But on the issue of inflation, Wilson showed the progressive streak that set him apart from so many of his colleagues at GM and throughout much of corporate America. Most executives castigated big labor's insatiable hunger for higher pay and blamed inflation on the "wage-price spiral." Wilson, though, would hear none of it. "The working people did not make that inflation," he said. "They only want to catch up with it in order to pay their grocery bills. I contend that present high wages are more the result of fundamental inflationary money pressures than of unreasonable wage pressures by the union." He added: "Arrangements like ours, for lifting and lowering wages in step with the cost of living are commonly called 'escalator clauses.' They are attacked by people who insist upon talking about the 'wage-price spiral.' We should say the 'price-wage spiral.' For it is not primarily wages that push up prices, it is primarily prices that pull up wages."

With the COLA, then, Reuther and Wilson found themselves side by side, absorbing flak from both the left and the right. A representative of the American Federation of Labor called the COLA "a violation of the whole philosophy of progress," and the United Mine Workers criticized the GM-UAW settlement as "a definite backward move." In 1912, the miners had eliminated COLAs from their contracts after finding that companies had manipulated the price of coal—to which wages were pegged—and "the workers were gypped by the sliding scale." For its part, the National Association of Manufacturers also raised questions about the logic of a COLA, and *Barron's* considered it "a vicious mechanism." One survey of executives found that four in five believed that such a formula would not work in their industry, half thought it would have unfavorable competitive effects, and three out of four felt that it would be inflationary. Wilson professed to take comfort in being hammered from all directions. "Frankly, I am personally encouraged by criticism from such extreme points of view," he said, "and I feel that perhaps we have found a safe middle ground." Besides, as much as any company in America, GM was a pacesetter in the area of human relations, having "initiated labor trends in the past," *Business Week* pointed out. Although the COLA "is still so new that it may not have immediate acceptance in many other managements," the magazine said, "GM is betting blue chips that eventually it will be." And it was. By the early 1960s, COLAs would be incorporated into about half of all union contracts nationwide and spread as well into the pay packages of various white-collar workers, including government employees and retirees and Social Security beneficiaries.

Yet the significance of the 1948 GM-UAW contract lay not only in its substance but also in its symbolism. It signaled the beginning of the end of the incessant warring in which American labor and management had engaged through most of the 1930s and '40s. The political scientist Samuel Lubell could sense the change when he dropped in on a UAW local in Detroit in 1940 and then again in 1948. By the time of his second visit, he said, "the strike photographs had come down from the bulletin boards and had been replaced by idyllic snapshots of the union's annual outings and sporting events. . . . The 'class-conscious' educational director was gone—ousted in the UAW-wide fight against Communists which Walter Reuther led. On their desks, the new officers had propped the slogan, 'UAW Americanism for Us.' They were wearing green jackets and green silk legion caps. In 1940 the flavor of the local was one of street barricades and sit-down strikes; eight years later, it was almost like a lodge hall."

In May 1950, still riding these amicable feelings, GM and the UAW reached a new contract that would extend for half a decade—an unparalleled time span that promised to "have a stabilizing influence not only on our business but on the economy of the whole country," Wilson said. "We believe that removing the fear or possibility of a strike for five years is a tremendously constructive achievement for our employees and their families, our business, our dealers, our suppliers, and the general public. The settlement should mean that all concerned can face the future with added confidence."

All told, the contract guaranteed GM's autoworkers a 20 percent increase in their standard of living by 1955. The "Treaty of Detroit," as *Fortune* magazine famously called it, would accomplish this, first, by continuing the COLA—a crucial reaffirmation of the basic formula set in 1948, even though the way that the US Bureau of Labor Statistics calculated the Consumer Price Index led to a fair bit of consternation for both GM and the UAW. The agreement also added an annual improvement factor of four cents for every year it was in force. In addition, it gave GM's blue-collar employees enhanced life, sickness, and accident insurance, new hospitalization and surgical coverage, and, in an enormous triumph for the UAW, pensions to which the company would contribute at least $1.50 per month for each year of service up to thirty years. Reuther and the leaders of other unions, especially the Mine Workers and the Steelworkers, had been persistently pursuing the creation and expansion of health, welfare, and retirement funds since the end of the war—a cause bolstered by a 1949 Supreme Court decision, involving Inland Steel, which held that such benefits were subject to collective bargaining.

In addition to these economic gains, the UAW also obtained a version of the "union security" clause that it had been coveting since its membership drive in early 1948. In return, Reuther and his men agreed that "a continuing improvement in the standard of living depends upon technological progress . . . and a cooperative attitude on the part of all parties"—an open acknowledgment of what lay at the core of the social contract: that the union and its members had to help keep the corporate machine purring if they themselves were to thrive.

On a day-to-day level, the Treaty of Detroit augured something else: a newfound equanimity in how labor and management would interact. "This kind of collective bargaining calls for intelligent trading rather than table-pounding, for diplomacy rather than belligerency, and for internal union discipline rather than grassroots rank-and-file activity," the labor economist Frederick Harbison commented, adding that the GM-UAW agreement should help bring a welcome calm "throughout the mass-production industries." One union leader went so far as to complain that, when asked in 1950 to help draft a platform for a state CIO meeting, he had nothing much to reach for. "Ten or fifteen years ago," he said, "I would have welcomed the assignment. There were so many things I was mad about. But what can I agitate for now? We don't have any really big issues left."

For Charlie Wilson, such contentment was very much the intention. "It is our hope," he said, "that this agreement will set a pattern for bargaining based on principles that will ensure industrial peace and prosperity and minimize strife and industrial warfare." And indeed it would—sort of.

In the grandest sense, the GM-UAW contract helped to usher in the era of industrial peace that Wilson had envisioned, and many would come to see the 1950s as a Golden Age of American business, in no small part because of the accommodation that labor and management had reached. The United Mine Workers also signed multi-year pacts with coal operators in 1950, setting the stage for thirteen years of tranquility in company towns across Kentucky, Pennsylvania, West Virginia, and elsewhere. "Coal can offer more value and better service if it has an opportunity to settle down and really work," Ivan Given, the editor of the trade journal *Coal Age*, wrote. "With the 1950 contracts appreciably broadening that opportunity, the situation can be truly described as a new start." The rubber industry likewise experienced a stretch of harmonious relations through the 1950s, and even the steel industry—where work stoppages had occurred every three years since the early forties—had by the end of the decade hit upon a no-strike posture that would last for the next quarter of a century. "I never went on strike in my life, I never ordered anyone else to run a strike in my life, I never had anything to do with a picket line," said George Meany, who served as president of the AFL and then as president of the AFL-CIO when the two labor federations merged in 1955. "In the final analysis, there is not a great deal of difference between the things I stand for and the things that the National Association of Manufacturers stands for."

Still, for all of these indications of reconciliation, "peace" between employer and employee remained a relative concept. Even at GM, the volume of grievances increased more than fivefold in the ten years after the 1950 contract was signed. Across American industry, the intensity of work stoppages did drop in the 1950s, so that about 4 percent of those employed participated in some kind of walkout during the decade, down from more than 10 percent during the strike wave of 1946. But that still meant millions of workers were involved in strikes in any given year.

"The problem is not one of whether or not there will be labor peace," the industrial psychologist Robert McMurry wrote in *Harvard Business Review*. "Fundamentally, there can never be true peace in the sense of a total integration of goals and objectives; the underlying interests of the parties are too greatly at variance. . . . The real question is not how to avoid or prevent labor warfare, but how to confine it within manageable bounds."

For decades, this tug-of-war "within manageable bounds" would go on. Different companies dealt with unions in different ways, whether by trying to outfox them during negotiations or by casting doubts in the minds of the rank-and-file about whether they even needed representation. Some employers played nice; others were nasty. But because of their ability to act collectively—even after Taft-Hartley—workers across the economy were able to counterbalance the inherent strength of corporate America. This would translate into higher wages, better benefits, and improved working conditions not only for those who carried a union card but for millions more blue-collar workers whose employers followed the patterns set by organized labor. Benefit packages for millions of nonunion white-collar workers would also be based on what unfolded at the bargaining table. In short, the nation never would have had so many good jobs without unions.

Winning these good jobs never came easily, however. The constant push and pull between labor and management often drained both sides. At a Coca-Cola bottling plant in Cumberland, Maryland, for example, tensions had been brewing since the summer of 1951, when the Teamsters began trying to organize the factory.

The prospect of unionization so spooked the southern clan that owned the place that the patriarch made a special trip to Western Maryland to address the rank-and-file—a rare personal appearance by Walter Sams. He appealed to the same logic of loyalty that Kodak's George Eastman and GM's Donaldson Brown had before him: the company and its workers had a commonality of interests, Sams suggested, and nobody from the outside needed to get in the middle of the deal.

"I have been married thirty-six years and sometimes my wife and I become confused," Sams said. "Now, when we do, we don't call in a neighbor. . . . We are in a business partnership, so we discuss the matter and get things straightened out. . . . We are a big family. Certainly if I eat, you are going to eat. If I stay warm, you will stay warm too."

Sams went on, beseeching his salesmen to get out there and peddle hard, pushing far beyond the 400,000 cases of soft drinks that they currently sold each year to area grocery stores, restaurants, hotels, filling stations, and other businesses. "There is no reason why this plant cannot go to 600,000 cases," he said, "and I know every man here is going to benefit by it." With that, Sams requested that everyone pause for a moment for—what else?—a thirst-quenching drink of Coca-Cola; it was a sweltering day outside, with temperatures topping ninety. Then he agreed to take questions "about money or anything else."

The dialogue that followed was not exactly hostile. But slowly, the complaints seeped out, like fizz from a shaken bottle of soda. One salesman asked Sams why the men had to work holidays. Another questioned whether he was working too many routes at once. "We don't have time to turn around," he told the boss. Another said he'd had only one raise in five years. Another said the work he was getting wasn't steady enough. At each turn, Sams responded with a mix of firmness, spelling out what he saw as economic reality, and benevolence. "Nothing pertaining to you and your happiness is unimportant to me," he said.

The outreach by Sams made little difference. The Teamsters succeeded in calling for an election, which the National Labor Relations

Board slated for late September. The company mailed letters to the nineteen salesmen and laborers eligible to vote—a no-holds-barred effort to remind them how good they had it. "Certainly you have security in your job," the letter said. "You have, in addition to a normal weekly wage, other benefits which do not cost you one penny. These are group insurance, hospitalization insurance, and an opportunity to join a pension plan to take care of you at age sixty-five or before. . . . You are given your full pay when out for sickness. Uniforms and uniform laundry are provided without charge. You have never been forgotten at Christmas. . . . Are you very sure that you do not desire to retain your capacity to act as an individual in all matters pertaining to your welfare in so far as your employment with this company is concerned? How can your situation be improved by turning over your leadership to those who are unfamiliar with your local and personal problems, as well as the problems which beset the management of this company?"

Coca-Cola's plea fell flat. By a count of fourteen to five, the workers in Cumberland made Teamsters Local 453 their bargaining agent. And by October, the union was making demands—first and foremost, a call for a 15 percent rise in wages. The company said there was no way to afford such an increase, especially given its unwillingness to charge its customers more. "The greatest single factor in Coca-Cola's success today," it told the Teamsters, "is that we are able to maintain a retail price of five cents." Animosity deepened. The union alleged that the company was refusing to bargain in good faith. "The employees had been notified that as long as they belonged to the union, the company will not grant any increases but will grant them increases when they discontinue their membership," the Teamsters reported to the NLRB. Negotiations picked up again in early 1952, but by spring, things had fallen apart. The Teamsters struck on May 10.

The complexion of the fight—a stalemate over local wages involving fewer than two dozen workers—was revealing: although mass strikes by the Auto Workers, Electrical Workers, and so on grabbed the headlines, the majority of the work stoppages in America have always been small, involving fewer than a hundred employees. And yet the small conflicts can get every bit as ugly as the big ones. In Cumberland, Sams and his managers tried to keep their customers stocked with Coca-Cola by having nearby plants serve them. But the Teamsters weren't about to make things easy. Union goons assaulted two salesmen from Chambersburg, Pennsylvania, on May 21, as they stopped to get gasoline. "Unload the damn truck!" one of the union men shouted, as his five associates smashed three cases of empty Coca-Cola bottles. "Beat their damn brains out!" another of the attackers yelled. The cab door flew open, and a barrage of fists rained down on the salesman behind the wheel before he managed to drive away.

By August, the strike was turning into a war of attrition. The company had made several counter-offers to the Teamsters, but the most it put on the table was a 6 percent boost in wages—less than half the amount that the union had initially sought. The Teamsters dug in. Each day, eight or so pickets lined up in front of the factory. "They are bound to wear out eventually," Roy Lottig, the manager of the Cumberland plant, told Sams.

September turned to October, October to November, and November to December. Finally, a few weeks before Christmas, a deal was reached, with wage gains of 6 percent to 8 percent, depending on the job classification. The union seemed relieved. Coca-Cola was miffed. On paper, the contract was set to remain in force for a year, but the company was already plotting how to toss the Teamsters—and its strongest backers from among the rank-and-file—before the plant could even get up and running again. "I wake up at night worrying about how I am going to handle those S.O.B.s when we do open," Lottig told Sams. "They know I will never let up until I nail each and every one of them."

By late in the year, Sams and Lottig were right where they wanted to be: on the verge of dislodging the Teamsters from the plant. The company cancelled its labor contract in December 1953, a month after petitioning the NLRB for a new election, confident that a majority of workers no longer supported the union. In March 1954, the vote was held, and this time the company came out on top. Labor peace had arrived in Cumberland, but by way of a far different kind of strategy than GM's: the Teamsters had been snuffed out.

The outcome, while affecting few people and isolated in scope, laid bare two essential truths about labor relations in America in the 1950s: First, lots of workers didn't want to be organized. From the mid-1930s through the mid-1940s, unions won 83 percent of the representation elections held in America. But their "win rate" was now approaching 70 percent—and falling fast. During a later walkout, at a Coca-Cola plant in Boston, one worker expressed his distaste for the Teamsters in a poem he called "The Wail of the Picket: The Coke Man's Psalm." It began by referring to the union shop steward, a fellow named Gildea:

> *Gildea is my shepherd; I am in want.*
>
> *He maketh me to sit in parked autos; he picketeth me before still Coke plants. He emptyeth my bank account; he leadeth me in the path of unemployment, for his union's sake.*
>
> *Yea, though I march at the end of the picket line, I will fear no evil Coke company; for Gildea art with me. Thou mouth and thy pipe comfort me.*
>
> *Thou preparest a contract before me in the presence of mine union brothers: thou filleth my head with nonsense; now my cup runneth empty.*
>
> *Surely misery and poverty shall follow me all the days of his strike: and I will dwell in a leaky tent forever.*

Second, despite the giddy reaction in the press to the Treaty of Detroit and pronouncements by corporate leaders that organized labor was now a welcome part of the business landscape, many executives continued to loathe unions (even if they wouldn't always say so in polite company). "If American management, upon retiring for the night, were assured that by the next morning the unions with which they dealt would have disappeared," two experts from MIT told the Industrial Relations Research Association, "more management people than not would experience the happiest sleep of their lives."

Sams, for sure, was poised to have a wonderful rest in light of the Teamsters' ouster. "With our troubles out of the way," he said, "we should certainly be able to begin showing better results" as a business. Lottig was pleased, too, and hopeful that the union wouldn't return anytime soon. "I feel that I have so many loyal men now," he said, "that all of us would sense any inkling of trouble in the future."

If it seemed presumptuous that workers would be as loyal to their place of employment as Roy Lottig indicated, he wasn't the only one thinking this way. In late 1953, as Coca-Cola Bottling scuffled with the Teamsters, the US Supreme Court had made it clear: companies were to be governed by a spirit of "cooperation, continuity of service, and cordial contractual relation between employer and employee that is born of loyalty to their common enterprise."

This conception of loyalty, with workers and their bosses coming together in the quest for something larger than themselves, had deep roots in the American tradition. "What we want . . . from some of the managers of great corporate interests is more loyalty, and less of the individualism of those who seek power," the philosopher Josiah Royce wrote in 1908. "And I myself should say that precisely the same sort of loyalty is what we want from both the leaders and from the followers of organized labor." Now, with the Supreme Court's ruling, the heart of the social contract—an allegiance between worker and employer based on what was supposed to be their mutual aspiration to see the business succeed—was no longer just the emergent ethos of corporate life; it was the law of the land.

The case that came before the high court grew out of an incident that began in the summer of 1949, when contract negotiations broke down between the International Brotherhood of Electrical Workers and WBT, the radio and television station in Charlotte, North Carolina, owned by the Jefferson Standard Broadcasting Company. The lone sticking point between them was whether the IBEW would have the right to bring in an outside arbitrator in the event that the station fired one of the fourteen broadcast technicians represented by the union. The IBEW said this was a question of job security, since there was no way to protect its members from being dismissed capriciously—"for any reason, whether just or unjust." Company officials framed the issue completely differently: "If we are going to be able to run our business, we certainly think that we should have the right to decide who shall be our employees and whether we shall keep a person in our employment or not."

The technicians didn't strike. But they began picketing outside the station in July and sent taunting telegrams to management: "Every day you lose measurable amount of dollars and immeasurable amounts of prestige. What does it cost us? Just a little beneficial exercise by being exposed to fresh air and sunshine." Then, on August 24, the IBEW turned up the heat. It openly questioned whether Jefferson Standard's brand new TV service—the first in the Carolinas—was delivering high enough quality.

"Is Charlotte a Second-Class City?" the union's handbill read. "You might think so from the kind of television programs being presented by the Jefferson Standard Broadcasting Company over WBTV. Have you seen one of their television programs lately? Did you know that all the programs presented over WBTV are on film and may be from one day to five years old? There are no local programs presented by WBTV. You cannot receive the local baseball games, football games, or other local events because WBTV does not have the proper equipment to make these pickups. Cities like New York, Boston, Philadelphia, Washington receive such programs nightly. Why doesn't the Jefferson Standard Broadcasting Company purchase the needed equipment to bring you the same type of programs enjoyed by other leading American cities? Could it be that they consider Charlotte a second-class community and only entitled to the pictures now being presented to them?" The handbill—some 5,000 of which were distributed around town—was signed, "WBT Technicians."

For Jefferson Standard, which only a month earlier had unveiled this "new thing called television" before thousands of locals packed into the Charlotte Armory, the technicians' charges were more than embarrassing. The whole uproar was starting to cost money. "We are losing some business here in Charlotte because of the mix-up between the engineers and WBT," a salesman for the company's life-insurance division told Bryan. "These boys are walking the streets in front of the building passing out leaflets, and some people are getting a little bitter taste toward Jefferson Standard."

On September 3, WBT fired the ten technicians it believed responsible for distributing the handbills. "Ever since early July, while you have been walking up and down the street with placards and literature attacking us," Charles Crutchfield, the station's general manager, wrote to each of those who were dismissed, "you have continued to hold your job and receive your pay. . . . Even when you began to put out propaganda which contained many untruths about our company and a great deal of personal abuse and slander, we still continued to treat you exactly as before. For it has been our understanding that under our labor laws, you have a very great latitude in trying to make the public believe that your employer is unfair to you. Now, however, you have turned from trying to persuade the public that we are unfair to you and are trying to persuade the public that we give inferior service to them. While we are struggling to expand into and develop a new field . . . you are busy trying to turn customers and the public against us in every possible way, even handing out leaflets on the public streets advertising that our operations are 'second-class,' and endeavoring in various ways to hamper and totally destroy our business. Certainly we are not required by law or common sense to keep you in our employment and pay you a substantial salary while you thus do your best to tear down and bankrupt our business."

Over the next couple of months, both sides pressed their case. The union started a postcard campaign, urging people to tell Southern Dairies, Interstate Milling, Shell Oil, Brown & Williamson Tobacco, and other businesses large and small to stop advertising on WBT because of the station's "inexcusable" action of having "unjustly discharged ten engineers for union activity." The company countered with its own mailer, telling all who would listen: "If any employer was ever justified in discharging employees, we were." Through the fall of 1949—while WBT broadcast a test pattern with news and weather announcements during the day, and *Kukla, Fran, and Ollie; The Perry Como Show; Hopalong Cassidy;* and other fare aired at night—the war of words between the company and the union ground on.

Then in early 1950, it nearly became a war on a whole different scale: police arrested Sterling Hicks, the local IBEW business manager, and charged him with conspiring to dynamite WBT's 435-foot-tall AM transmission tower. Acting on a tip, the cops first arrested another man as he was in the act of hurling five sticks of dynamite, their fuses lit, at the intended target. (The authorities had earlier discovered the cache of explosives, hidden under a pile of leaves, and removed the percussion caps, rendering them harmless.) The man, a part-time housepainter, told police that Hicks had hired him to bring down the steel structure for $250. Hicks, who was well-known in the community not only for his union duties but also as a deacon of his church and a member of Charlotte's parks and recreation commission, denied involvement. But he was eventually convicted and ordered to serve two years in state prison.

As Hicks's conspiracy case wound its way through the legal system, so did the union's case against Jefferson Standard. In August

1950, an NLRB trial examiner ruled that the company had engaged in certain unfair labor practices and recommended that the technicians who were fired be reinstated in their old jobs. The company objected, and in June 1951 the full NLRB went against its own trial examiner's findings and, by a four-to-one vote, ruled in Jefferson Standard's favor. The board reasoned that the technicians' broadside—"Is Charlotte a Second-Class City?"—fell outside the scope of the IBEW's labor dispute with WBT, and therefore, the workers weren't entitled to protection under federal law. "In our judgment," the NLRB wrote in its decision, "these tactics . . . were hardly less 'indefensible' than acts of physical sabotage." The crux of the technicians' argument, the board added, was that "the employer ought to be boycotted because he offered a shoddy product to the consuming public—not because he was 'unfair' to the employees who worked on that product."

Next it was the union's turn to try to have things reversed, and in November 1952 it won. The federal Court of Appeals in Washington, on narrow technical grounds, sent the entire matter back to the NLRB for reconsideration. The NLRB and the company then took up the game of judicial ping-pong, appealing the DC Circuit's ruling. The Supreme Court agreed to take it on, and arguments were heard in October 1953. Two months later, Justice Harold Burton issued his opinion for the six-to-three majority. Jefferson Standard was totally vindicated.

"There is no more elemental cause for discharge of an employee," wrote Burton, a Truman nominee, "than disloyalty to his employer." That line, more than any other, reverberated through the media: "Test in Firing: Loyalty to Firm," read the headline in *US News & World Report*. "Loyalty to the Boss," said *Newsweek*. North Carolina's *Greensboro Free Press* cheered the high court's decision in an editorial: "If the time ever comes that an employer cannot dismiss an employee for open disloyalty, particularly when that disloyalty strikes at the existence of the employer, we might as well call off the dogs and let the Reds take over."

Although Burton's opinion also referred to the fact that loyalty was supposed to be a two-way street, in the furtherance of the employer and employee's "common enterprise," that aspect of the decision didn't receive much attention. Instead, people seemed to put the onus squarely on the employee. A few weeks after the Supreme Court made its ruling, one of the technicians who'd picketed WBT, Robert Hilker, wrote to Crutchfield. "I was a little young when I worked for WBT to understand both sides of the picture," Hilker said. "Even after leaving there it took several weeks to see anything but a one-sided view. However, in about six months' time, things gradually changed and looked different to me. And, frankly, after a year's time I was at a point where I began to think you were a pretty intelligent fellow for getting rid of the whole bunch. Now, after three years, I wonder why you didn't fire the bunch of us sooner. . . . If you ever need any help holding down any other problem 'children,' I'll be glad to explain to them publicly or privately why 'not to bite the hand that feeds you.'" Another of the fired technicians, A. O. "Buster" Richardson, wrote a similar letter to Crutchfield—and asked to return to WBT. "I'm truly sorry for acting like a headstrong 'child' and being such a fool," he said. "If you do see fit to rehire me I will do my level best to make you and the company a good man, and cause nobody no trouble and give the company my full loyalty." Richardson, alas, never got his job back.

Somewhere between GM's embrace of the UAW and Coca-Cola Bottling's thrashing of the Teamsters, General Electric carved out a third course for dealing with its unions: it tried to end-run them. The playbook for this move was commissioned by "Electric Charlie" Wilson, the company's president, and drawn up by his chief spinmeister, Lemuel Ricketts Boulware, whose name more than any other—save, perhaps, for Taft and Hartley—would come to be reviled among the nation's union leaders. The *New York Times* called him "the author of the most controversial labor-relations program in a major industry." Boulware described himself, only half-jokingly, as "the tough guy of General Electric who went around frightening little children and grown men." Yet for a moment in time, in 1955, even Lem Boulware could look like a peacemaker.

Born in Springfield, Kentucky, in 1895, Boulware had learned at a young age what hard work was like, thanks to his father's uncompromising sense of discipline. "When I was caught loitering in front of the drugstore or pool room with no paying job immediately in sight," Boulware recounted, "I was dispatched promptly to a farm he had handy. This interfered greatly with baseball, fishing, and quail shooting." Through high school, he held all manner of jobs—at a bank, grocery, harness shop, butcher, tobacco market, and water and light plant. Boulware graduated in 1916 from the University of Wisconsin, where he captained the baseball team, and then briefly taught accounting and commercial law. He served as an infantry officer during World War I and later became sales manager at the Easy Washing Machine Company. He went on to be vice president and general manager of two other manufacturers, Carrier Corporation and Celotex, and also had a stint as a vice chairman of the War Production Board, where he worked with Wilson. In January 1945, Boulware joined GE as a consultant to Wilson on marketing and merchandising. He was also put in charge of the company's affiliated manufacturing operations, which sold products under their own brands. Then came the big strike of 1946 by the United Electrical, Radio, and Machine Workers, which changed everything—for Lem Boulware and for GE and its employees.

The raw power shown by the UE stunned Wilson and his fellow executives. Hundreds of pickets encircled GE factories around the country, keeping just about everyone, including white-collar workers, from entering. Wilson seemed to take it personally. "To me," he said, "it is the height of stupidity that we, as a corporation, should not be allowed to get into our plants, people who are not members of the union." Even worse, the strikers—not the company—captured the public's sympathy and support. Restaurants delivered hot lunches to the picket lines. College students walked alongside the strikers. Politicians championed the union cause. In Bloomfield, New Jersey, seven local policemen helped lead a union rally, while a band from the American Legion post played in the strikers' parade. The town's mayor opened with this invocation: "Help us so that when we pray each day, 'Give us this day our daily bread,' the 'us' will include all people." In the end, GE followed the national pattern and settled with the UE for a wage increase of eighteen and a half cents—all while having been made out to be the bad guy. Yet one part of the company had altogether sidestepped the ignominy: Boulware's affiliated operations. There, conspicuously, no workers had struck.

As Boulware would later tell it, with no small amount of dramatic flair, he was caught totally off guard when Wilson called him into his office one day in May 1947 and informed him that as of Monday he was to drop everything he was doing and take on a new job: "finding a more rewarding approach to General Electric's employee-relations problem." "All this was quite a shock to me," Boulware said, adding that he "weakly reminded" Wilson that "I had no experience in the field." In truth, Boulware had been contemplating how to neutralize the unions' message machine since shortly after his arrival at GE.

According to Boulware, GE was in "the ridiculous situation where—despite the best of intentions and the best practices known—the company" has become "distrusted and disapproved of by employees and neighbors in some very important matters," as the 1946 strike "so clearly demonstrated." To turn things around, Boulware adopted the role he knew best: that of a salesman. He devised a method of "job marketing" for "job customers," in which GE would first research what its employees "wanted in their jobs and how they felt their present jobs fell short of their desires." Said Boulware: "We tried to diagnose what they consciously liked and disliked about their jobs; what they understood, misunderstood, or just didn't know or ignored about their jobs. We inquired into what they did not understand about the economic, social, and political influences which surrounded their jobs with opportunities, obligations, and limitations. We looked for the motives and beliefs which determined whether they gave their full interest, skill, care, and effort while working, and the events and impressions that determined whether they went home reasonably satisfied with their accomplishments and associations at the end of the day."

From these extensive worker interviews, Boulware fashioned a 9-point checklist that, as he put it, "General Electric employees wanted their job package . . . to contain":

1. Compensation, including "pay that is right—all things considered—for the skill, care, and full day's effort as measured by reasonable modern standards," as well as pensions, insurance, and other "extra financial benefits."
2. Working conditions that are "as good as they can be made at the moment" and "regularly improved."
3. Supervision that is "technically competent" and able to elucidate the reasons behind any management decision, as well as give good advice.
4. Job security "to the greatest degree possible."
5. Respect "for basic human dignity."

6. Promotion "as fast as opportunities arise or can be created and on a strictly fair basis."

7. Information "on management's objectives, plans, problems, successes, and failures."

8. Belief in "the individual job's importance, significance, and challenge, and in the employee's contributions to the great good accomplished by the final GE product."

9. Satisfaction derived "from going home to the family after a hard day's work with the feeling that something important has been accomplished."

To help sell his 9-point plan, Boulware developed a 120-page guide for GE's 12,000 foremen and 3,000 other members of the company's managerial staff. The bulk of the manual, he noted, was "devoted to overcoming employee objections to giving full skill, care, and effort" on the job: that is, to the workers' half of the social contract. Buttressing management's pitch was one of the most elaborate propaganda campaigns ever undertaken by a corporation, replete with films, posters, handbills, and letters home. Week in and week out, Boulware also flooded GE's employee newspapers with cartoons and stories that both conveyed the company's point of view and ripped the unions': "General Electric Keeps Trying to Make Jobs Better," "Steady Jobs Through Steady Friends," "We Will Keep Trying to Do Right—About Your Pensions, Insurance, and Pay," "Who Is Telling the Truth—and Who Isn't?" GE's executives were ecstatic about the corporate agit-prop. "It is the kind of straightforward, hard-hitting, factual material that I think we should have been directing to our employees for a long time," Robert S. Peare, a GE vice president, told Boulware in December 1947.

Like any good salesman, Boulware knew he wouldn't get very far if he didn't actually have a decent product to sell; it couldn't all be bombast. And so he made sure that GE followed through on at least some of its promises, overhauling the salary structure for the company's 15,000 managers to bring it more in sync with the overall market. The effect was to raise the pay of many employees whose compensation had long been neglected. For GE's 120,000 unionized workers, however, the story was far more complicated. Boulware maintained: "We are not antiunion or prounion. We are proemployee." In reality,

GE was fervently antiunion—a disposition stemming from Boulware's deep suspicion of anything he felt inhibited unfettered capitalism. This bottomless faith in laissez-faire doctrine fueled Boulware's other sales effort: flogging the "creativeness, efficiency . . . and essential humanity of the 'private sector'" while tearing down the "inevitable stultification, wastefulness, and dictatorial regimentation of the 'public sector.'"

For Boulware, these two crusades—one ballyhooing GE's treatment of its employees, the other "a ceaseless education campaign in the ideology of the free market," as the historian Kim Phillips-Fein has written—were inseparable. If workers would only understand the basic tenets of America's economic system, Boulware figured, they would better appreciate that the company was doing all it could for them. To help make his case, Boulware regularly distributed pie charts and statistical tables showing where every dollar of GE revenue went. During one typical quarter, for example, 42.6 cents was passed to outside suppliers, 36.4 cents to employees (in the form of wages and benefits), 15.1 cents to the government in taxes, 3.1 cents for reinvestment back into the company, and 2.8 cents to shareholders. The lesson, in Boulware's words, was unmistakable: "General Electric was not a toe-to-toe struggle between an employee 'class' and an owner 'class.' It was a sort of clearinghouse where people came together to do things for each other" by contributing their respective resources, whether capital or labor.

In turn, it was up to GE to look out for "the balanced best interests of all": its customers, shareowners, employees, and the communities in which it operated. This way of thinking—which would be upended in the coming decades, as maximizing shareholder wealth was put ahead of all other considerations—was far from exclusive to GE. Gen. Robert E. Wood, the chief executive of Sears, said "the four parties to any business" were, "in order of importance": customers, employees, community, and stockholders. Johnson & Johnson said its "first responsibility" was to "the doctors, nurses, and patients, to mothers and fathers and all others who use our products and services." It next listed its employees, communities, and stockholders as those to whom it also had a responsibility. General Motors said it was "in business to make a profit," so that "over the long term" it could "pay for research and improved tools and methods" in order to make better products for its customers; "provide jobs and opportunities for employees"; "earn a satisfactory return for investors"; "help others progress, including dealers and suppliers"; and "pay our share of the heavy cost of government." And Kodak said it was guided by SPICE: an attempt to serve Shareowners, the Public Interest, Customers, and Employees.

Not all of Boulware's teachings were so benign, however. Much of economics, unlike physics or astronomy, isn't value-free science. And Boulware infused GE's take on the subject with the specter of "socialist enemies," a group into which he lumped "Roosevelt, Truman, Reuther, and their ilk." His ultimate ambition was to turn GE's workforce, some 200,000 strong, into an activist army that would help disseminate his conservative gospel and, over time, elect into public office like-minded politicians who would help foster a better business climate. The way to get there, said Boulware, whose deep voice retained a trace of his Kentucky twang, was to help GE's workers and others whom the company touched "learn more thoroughly the arithmetic of our way of life . . . to realize the wonders of both the mechanics and results of our free system."

Assisting Boulware with his antitax, antigovernment proselytizing was a beloved Hollywood star who had started out as a proud Democrat and union leader but would, under Boulware's tutelage, become a passionate conservative. For eight years, beginning in 1954, Ronald Reagan hosted the Sunday-night TV show *General Electric Theater* and also served as a roving corporate ambassador, speaking to employees (and sometimes their neighbors) at GE's 139 plants across the nation. "For almost two centuries," Reagan told those at GE, "we have proved man's capacity for self-government, but today we are told that we must choose between a left and right or, as others suggest, a third alternative, a kind of safe middle ground. I suggest to you there is no left or right, only an up or down—up to the maximum of individual freedom consistent with law and order, or down to the ant heap of totalitarianism."

Reagan, who as the country's fortieth president would have a profound impact on the social contract between employer and employee, called his time at GE his "postgraduate course in political science." Others must have felt as if they were in school as well. GE employees—white- and blue-collar alike—received as part of Boulware's program a specially commissioned economics textbook written by Lewis Haney, a harsh critic of the New Deal. Boulware encouraged the company's managers to read the *Wall Street Journal* editorial page, William Buckley's columns in the *National Review*, and *The Freeman*, a journal published by the libertarian Foundation for Economic Education. A number of tracts from conservative standard-bearers, such as Henry Hazlitt's *Economics in One Lesson*, were put on recommended reading lists. All managers received a copy of John T. Flynn's *The Road Ahead*, which cautioned that "our American system is being destroyed not merely by Communist conspirators" but by those who had set the country on a track toward Socialism. "The Communist would like to ruin the American system by clubbing it over the head," Flynn wrote. "The Socialist planner would like to do it by slow poison."

GE borrowed and put its workers through a DuPont course called "How Our Business System Operates," while Boulware also had thousands of GE supervisors attend an additional series of classes on "the basic facts about our industrial system." Leading them was Neil Carothers, the head of the business school at Lehigh University and a darling of the far-right American Liberty League. At GE, he lectured on "The Nature of Production," "What Sets Wages?" "The Distribution of Wealth," and "Popular Economic Errors." But he saved some of his most strident opinions for the course on "Labor and Management." A hundred years earlier, during the Second Industrial Revolution, employers did abuse their workers, Carothers posited. But now, he said, "it is the workers who hate and attack management," especially when goaded by unions. As he related it, "Thousands of workers whose livings depend entirely on the men who supply the capital and take the risks of enterprise have been led by propaganda to picture these owners and hired managers as Shylocks and exploiters." The unions' enmity, Carothers added, stemmed from memories of those dark days of the nineteenth century, "even though the majority of American employers have long since learned that fair treatment of labor is good policy not only for decency's sake but good policy from the standpoint of profits."

All of this must have been quite dizzying for James Carey, the union chief who had found common ground with Gerard Swope in the late 1930s. As the young president of the United Electrical and Radio Workers of America, he hadn't taken a direct part in too many bargaining sessions with the company. But he became much more involved after the Communist-led UE splintered and he founded the

International Union of Electrical, Radio, and Machine Workers, or IUE, in 1949. Like Walter Reuther, Carey had gone from being in league with Communists and Communist sympathizers earlier in his career to ardently opposing them, as the IUE and UE battled it out at one manufacturing plant after another for the right to represent GE (as well as Westinghouse) employees. "American Workers Want No Part of UE's Reds!" a standard piece of literature from the IUE exclaimed. "American workers want a real union. They want a union that works for them; not the Communist Party." In short order, the IUE had become the much larger organization, representing five times as many workers as the UE.

On the surface, it might have seemed as though Carey's anti-UE agenda would endear him to Boulware. After all, the two had a common enemy in the nation's Communists. Any such buddying up was not to be, however. Carey "marched triumphantly back in to the General Electric Company bargaining conference room in 1950 expecting to be treated as a conquering hero who had delivered the employees and the company from communism," said Herbert Northrup, an employee-relations consultant to Boulware. "Instead of accolades, Carey found that the congeniality at the top corporate level, which had characterized the early collective bargaining days under Swope, had vanished."

What greeted Carey was what would soon become widely known—and pejoratively so in labor circles—as "Boulwarism." The idea was to move away from the usual negotiating process in which the union would ask for way more than it thought it would get, and the company would offer far less than it thought it would have to give, only to meet somewhere in the middle. "There is no sense in having to go through a lot of rigmarole as though we were a bunch of thieves haggling over some stolen trinket in a flea-bitten Eastern bazaar," GE said in one of its newsletters. Rather, under Boulwarism, GE put forward an offer that it deemed "feasible and fair" given its level of profit and its commitment to balancing the interests of all of its stakeholders. In GE's eyes, no dickering was required; this was truly the best the company could do after considerable study of the relevant details—all part of what Boulware said was "trying to do right voluntarily."

The company would then do two things: First, it would put the terms of the offer into effect for all of its nonunion workers and give the IUE a deadline to accept the package. If the union missed the date, any monetary increase would not be retroactive for its members. Next, GE would take its case directly to the rank-and-file, as Boulware's unceasing salesmanship continued. "It must now be obvious to our employees," the company said, "that membership in a union will not get them anything they would not be able to get without a union." Admitted one CIO official: "Mr. Boulware has created excellent employee relations and very bad union relations."

Boulware put on quite a show. On the day that union and corporate negotiators sat down to face each other in New York, "local company managements would gather workers together . . . as captive audiences," one union man who was part of the bargaining recalled. "Supervisors distributed literature containing the company terms and the promotion therefor. Similar material would be found in full-page ads in community newspapers. Instead of one grand opening in Manhattan, there were a hundred or so, all timed, scheduled, and run off like clockwork as if by pushbutton signal from GE headquarters." As for the man with his finger on the button, he insisted that there was "nothing new or unorthodox or even experimental" about what GE was doing. "It is simply aimed at pleasing people with jobs in exactly the same way our company's product marketing program has been pleasing people with products for seventy-five years," Boulware said.

To Carey, all this talk of "job marketing" was bunk, and the company's claims of truth and fairness rang even more hollow. In his view, Boulware's take-it-or-leave-it tactics had but one purpose: to undermine the basic integrity of collective bargaining. And Carey wasn't about to roll over. As a ten-year-old boy, he liked to brag, he had led his Philadelphia schoolmates in a classroom strike against excessive homework. Carey was a bantam, small in physical stature but profane and truculent, once telling a company negotiator in the middle of contract talks: "I'll break every bone in your body. Damn it, I'll come over there and bust you right in the mouth." One union man remembered that they had to change the ashtrays in the bargaining room to aluminum because Carey would smash the glass ones.

But for all his brashness, Carey was now limited in his effectiveness. This was in part because of the IUE's constant fighting with the UE—an "orgy of interunion conflict," as the historian Ronald Schatz has written—and in part because of frequent jockeying for control within the IUE itself. In 1950, for example, Carey called for a chain of "rolling strikes" against GE, only to have the big IUE local in Pittsfield, Massachusetts, vote against the plan, effectively killing it. Carey came out of the meeting at Pittsfield High School, in which he had unsuccessfully sought strike authorization, burning mad. "Why those S.O.B.s would have treated Charlie Wilson better than they treated me," Carey said. In 1952, Carey threatened a nationwide strike against GE, but several locals again shut him down.

IUE members at GE did win wage gains through the early 1950s—3 percent in 1950, 2.5 percent in 1951 and 1952, a shade over 3 percent in 1953, and a shade under 3 percent in 1954—plus cost-of-living increases and other benefits: pension coverage, insurance, and holidays. But each round of contract talks was difficult, and IUE members didn't receive the full pay increases they would have enjoyed had the union settled sooner and met GE's deadline for retroactivity to kick in. Boulwarism was taking a real bite. All along, the epithets flew between Boulware and Carey. "Even after Mr. Boulware goes," the union leader said, "he will leave scars it will take years and years to heal." Boulware belittled Carey as an "unsound, unwise, untruthful, and ineffective representative of our employees."

As the two sides prepared for negotiations in 1955, the acrimony showed no signs of letting up. In January, Carey told a group of IUE locals that they weren't just fighting for themselves anymore. "Make no mistake about it," he said. "Boulwarism will spread to other sections of our industry and to other industries also if we permit it to succeed in General Electric. . . . In a strict sense, therefore, our fight against Boulwarism is the fight of all organized labor." This wasn't just a theory. Westinghouse, Sylvania Electric Products, North American Aviation, Goodyear Tire, and some of the steelmakers had in the past year started trying out versions of GE's labor policies.

By spring, Boulware was bracing for a full-blown work stoppage. "Carey very much wants a companywide strike this year regardless of what the offer is," he said. But while the rancor remained the same, one thing had changed: the nation's economic outlook. A ten-month recession in 1953 and '54 had dictated that the previous package GE offered to its workers "was thin," Northrup said. "This required the hard sell and tough stance for Boulware's 'job marketers.'" But now, things were looking up—way up. As bargaining began in July, GE reported record earnings for the first half of 1955. One of the company's goals "is a staggering 10 percent profit after taxes on sales," David Lasser, the IUE's research director, told Carey. "GE is approaching this." With such rosy financial results, there was no way for GE to escape making a generous offer. The question was what it would get in return. "In 1955," Northrup said, "the aim was long-term peace to prepare for the projected long-term boom."

The union had gone into the talks with a bold demand: "a guaranteed annual wage" for its members, which would ensure a worker received 85 percent or more of his pay for up to an entire year of unemployment. In response, the company tried to lower expectations. "Naturally, no one ever gets all he wants in every respect," GE said in its employee-relations newsletter. Carey was the sort to dig in on an issue like the guaranteed annual wage. But, as luck would have it, just as Walter Reuther was sidelined for most of the UAW's talks with GM in 1948 while he recovered from his gunshot wound, Carey fell ill during the GE negotiations. When he did show up, Boulware occupied him—the stocky, six-foot-three executive towering over Carey—so the actual thrust and parry at the bargaining table was left to others. Prenegotiation conferences had also helped to allay certain problem areas in advance.

Not that the atmosphere was suddenly amiable. As in the past, the exchange between GE's chief negotiator, Virgil Day, and the IUE bargainers—Lasser, John Callahan, and Leo Jandreau—became very heated at times, with each side accusing the other of "scurrilous attacks":

> CALLAHAN. Isn't it true that the company made deals with the
> UE . . . and Communists in Louisville to beat us
> there?
> DAY. That's a libelous statement, and we could sue.
> LASSER. You had captive audience meetings to have work-
> ers bring pressure on their stewards, stewards on
> their officers, etc.
> DAY. We express our views. We think it's in the best
> interest of the union.

JANDREAU. Suppose it worked in reverse—if our stewards
were allowed to call a meeting in the plant to
bring pressure on the foremen?

DAY. The union in Schenectady and other locations
has been spreading the theory of work stoppages,
which is in violation of the law and the contract,
and we are going to look down the barrel of a gun
to correct the situation.

Despite the sniping, GE and the IUE worked briskly through the meat of the contract. The union didn't get its guaranteed annual wage, but the company agreed to the richest accord in its history, including a sizable wage increase, cost-of-living protection, and substantial improvements in health, life insurance, and pension coverage. For the IUE negotiators, the rub was that GE wanted the pact to extend for five years—and that made them nervous. "A lot can happen in five years," Callahan said. "You would have an opportunity . . . to close down operations and move them to lower-paid areas. Furthermore, we would have no job security and might be at the mercy of the company. We're not happy about this." But Day wouldn't budge. "We're serious about the structure of confidence and stability" that such a lengthy agreement would bring.

The IUE's protests didn't go on for long. On August 12—more than a month before the expiration of the existing contract—the union accepted the GE package. The wage jump, nearly 20 percent over the five years, and the other provisions were too much to pass up. Boulware was gleeful. "You may as well take this," he said, handing Callahan his necktie. "You've taken everything else I have." Carey called it "a splendid settlement." So did Boulware. "We are maturing into a kind of relationship that people ought to have," Boulware said. "After all, we are dealing with a $1.2 billion payroll that affects 500,000 people. This is serious and it ought to be handled in a businesslike way." Said Carey: "I believe that this new contract can provide new and better foundations for labor relations in General Electric."

Such optimism would soon fade. But for now, at least, Lem Boulware and Jim Carey had shown that, with all the money sloshing around in 1950s America, it was possible to buy labor peace even at GE.

In the 1950s, companies such as Kodak provided lavish benefits and sponsored lots of recreational activities, helping to make it a Golden Age for workers and their families. Here, youngsters play softball through the Kodak Park Athletic Association.

4

SMUG NATION

At the Rochester Trust branch at Lake and Ridgeway Avenues, in the shadow of the mammoth industrial center known as Kodak Park, small crowds lined up all day and into the night, taking advantage of the extra hours that the bank, like many others around the city, had extended. Yet even with the bottleneck, most of those patrons forced to stand around and wait wore smiles. And why not? A slug of money is a powerful intoxicant, and Kodak had just handed out the largest wage dividend in its history: more than $28 million to 51,000 workers. That amounted to about $500 per person, the equivalent today of more than $4,000 each. Twenty million of the total went to 35,000 employees right in the company's hometown—a place so rolling in it that Rochester would soon become branded "Smugtown, USA."

It was March 14, 1955, and while Jim Carey's International Union of Electrical Workers was gearing up to see how much it could pry out of GE, the men and women of Kodak were already cashing in. The profit-sharing program that George Eastman had introduced in 1912 had grown so substantially that for Rochester's merchants it was practically like having a second Christmas a week before the official start of spring. "Kodak's annual wage dividend payment," said *Life* magazine, "is the big financial event of the year in Rochester." For days preceding the payout, local newspapers were thick with advertising:

Garson & Wood marketed luxurious bedroom suites, in limed oak or cherry cordovan; the Peerless appliance shop pushed the new Philco electric range with its "Miracle Roastmeter"; and the National haberdashery showed off its selection of imported Italian worsted suits. Now, employees were snapping up these goods and much, much more. "At many stores," the Rochester *Democrat and Chronicle* reported, "major items put aside long ago on 'Will Call' orders were delivered against cash on the barrelhead." The banks—Monroe County Savings, First Federal Savings and Loan, Rochester Savings, Security Trust, and others—also competed for customers. (Were he looking down upon his old city, George Eastman surely would have been pleased, for he had originally conceived of the wage dividend as a reserve for workers' retirement years.) "Congratulations to all you Kodak folks on your good fortune," Community Savings declared in its ad. "And when you come in to cash your check, why not stash away a good share of it to earn Community's generous dividends? You've worked for it . . . now let it work for you."

But the temptation to spend, rather than to save, was strong, with Rochester's car dealers supplying some of the sweetest cajolery. "Get a bonus for your bonus," was the come-on from Ralph Pontiac, while over at Heinrich Motors, "Kodakers" were encouraged to choose from ninety different "Bonus Buys": everything from a 1947 Chevy for $125 to a '54 Buick Riviera for a shade over $2,000. Piehler Pontiac, Huff Pontiac, Ken Ralph Ford, and Corey Nash all held wage-dividend sales as well. Even the most frugal Kodak employees must have found it difficult not to treat themselves to something special when, just six weeks after the disbursement, the company filled their wallets even more: on the heels of record earnings, it raised workers' base pay by 5 percent. The increase, President Albert Chapman said, "recognizes that the interest, loyalty, and effective work of Kodak people are among the most important reasons for the company's progress."

Kodak gave its workers far more than just money, however. Continuing the practices that Marion Folsom had begun decades earlier, it also strove to maintain as much job security as possible. "For more than fifty years," Geneva Seybold of the National Industrial Conference Board observed, "the company has planned its production schedule as best it could to avoid seasonal layoffs. And usually any technological changes are delayed until plans have been made for the retraining and transfer of those affected." Craig Cochrane, Kodak's director of industrial relations, put it like this: "The paramount consideration here will always be the opportunity to work full-time. . . . And that, I believe, is the one answer that appeals to the conscientious worker."

Kodak, which had perpetually lavished benefits on its employees, was by 1955 spending about $1,000 per person on life insurance; retirement annuities; sick pay; disability, unemployment and old-age insurance; holiday and vacation pay; and hospital, surgical, and major-medical coverage. Recognizing that health costs were bound to escalate as people got older, Kodak in the mid-1950s began to offer its health insurance plans—at company expense for life—to those who'd retired with at least fifteen years of service, as well as to their dependents. "I can hardly convey to you the nature of the response that came from our retired people when this was announced," Donald McConville, Kodak's director of industrial relations, told a meeting of the American Management Association. "To say they were grateful is my understatement for the day. Nothing else the company has ever done, I am certain, helped so much in relieving worry and giving the retired person assurance of a secured future."

Kodak's promotion of extracurricular activities was also outstanding, as illustrated by the company's 18-hole golf course and its 300,000-square-foot recreation center. It sponsored movies, picnics, bridge, dancing, baseball, and badminton. But the most popular pastime among Kodak employees was bowling. In fact, when the American Bowling Congress came to Rochester in the midfifties, 324 different company teams entered the tournament. Kodak justified its considerable spending on these pursuits as good for employer and employee alike. "In this highly complex age," said Louis Eilers, a senior executive who would go on to become Kodak president, "industry has a great need of people who are healthy, vigorous, and competitively keen." Evidently, knocking down pins at one of the recreation center's twenty automatic lanes was viewed as a good way to heighten a worker's animal spirits.

Like Gold Rush California, with its proliferation of brothels, bars, and pick and shovel salesmen, Rochester became fertile ground for those with the shrewdness to exploit a lucrative situation. One of these go-getters was H. Dean Quinby Jr., a local native who came up with a mechanism for people to buy stock on a regular basis, regardless of what each share cost at any given moment. Participants in the Quinby Plan would simply specify how much they wanted to spend—twenty five dollars a month, say—and Quinby would then acquire on their behalf as many shares as he could from a select menu of blue-chip companies; it was like buying equities on installment. "Buy stocks the same way you buy gasoline for your car—by the dollar's worth" became his motto. As for dividends, they would go not to the investor but, rather, were plowed back into the plan for further purchases. "The laws of compound interest apply with equal force to dollars, rabbits, and shares of stock," Quinby said. "One hundred shares with an average dividend yield of 6 percent will double in twelve years."

Born in 1898, the scion of a prominent Rochester family, Quinby was a gentleman and a charmer. Standing six foot two and strongly built, he was part of the local country-club scene, played squash, and had a taste for Manhattans and good wine. He worked on Wall Street as a bond broker until the crash of 1929 and then started an air-conditioning business—but his first love was always the markets. He dreamed up the Quinby Plan while lounging on a yacht on Lake Ontario in 1938, and for many years those who signed on could buy into only one company: Kodak.

It took some time for Quinby's innovation—the democratization of investing—to gain traction, and so he lived off his wife's trust fund for a while. But he stuck with it, and as Rochester found itself awash in more and more cash, so did Quinby. "He was a salesman by nature," said his son, Congreve. In 1945, as World War II ended, 241 people invested about $250,000 in the Quinby Plan. A decade later, some 4,400 Quinby Plan contributors had committed more than $3.3 million to buy stocks for the year.

By this point, the Quinby portfolio included other corporations: General Motors, General Electric, DuPont, Standard Oil of New Jersey, and AT&T. But Kodak remained the focus, especially after the company in 1953 set up a voluntary payroll-deduction system through Quinby so that its employees could buy its common stock. By 1955, the Quinby Plan held 96,000 shares of Kodak—as a block, one of the ten largest holdings in the company. And Quinby could always count on more, particularly with Kodak's wage dividend getting bigger. "As my father used to say, it was like somebody would stand at the top of the

Kodak building with bales of money and then just throw it out to the winds," his son recalled.

A Quinby & Company ad in the *Democrat and Chronicle* challenged workers to invest: "Wage dividend time should be thinking time." It urged employees to fortify their nest eggs with Kodak shares—a terrific way to augment "your financial strength" and "bring you enduring satisfaction." "Faith in the future of Eastman Kodak Company," the ad promised, "has been well received."

Rochester was a boomtown, and the way to partake in its riches was obvious to many.

"It is a comparatively simple matter to . . . amass a modest fortune, a $25,000 home, and a circle of friends with the same determination," wrote Curt Gerling, a local newspaperman who gave the city its Smugtown moniker. "Some believe the formula as unburdensome as getting a job at Kodak and learning to pat the proper posteriors. This perhaps is an oversimplification but not enough to detract from the basic premise."

It would similarly be an oversimplification to say that to get ahead in America in the 1950s you would take a job at a big employer, not screw up, and watch your standard of living rise—but not enough to detract from the basic premise. In this way, Rochester and Kodak were both mirrors and magnifiers of national life. "US capitalism is *popular* capitalism," the editors of *Fortune* magazine wrote, "not only in the sense that it has popular support, but in the deeper sense that the people as a whole participate in it and use it." General Electric also marveled at this new "People's Capitalism," pointing to workers' high wages and high purchasing power.

Much of this rah-rah rhetoric was overblown. Tens of millions across the country—about a quarter of the population—lived in poverty, causing John Kenneth Galbraith, in his 1958 book *The Affluent Society*, to express grave concern about those suffering from "inequality and deprivation." A few years later, in his 1962 landmark *The Other America*, Michael Harrington would shine a light on those relegated to the margins of the economy. "Here are the unskilled workers, the migrant farmworkers, the aged, the minorities, and all the others who live in the economic underworld of American life," Harrington wrote. But even this reality was not enough to alter three fundamental truths: American business flourished during the fifties, an extraordinarily wide swath of the populace enjoyed the fruits of its prosperity, and the social contract between employer and employee was the primary instrument through which this wealth was shared.

Fewer than 500 companies employed more than a fifth of all American nonfarm workers in the fifties—an incredible concentration of smarts and sweat responsible for about half of the nation's industrial output and a quarter of that of the entire free world. All told, America was manufacturing roughly half of all items produced around the globe by 1955, even though it had only 6 percent of its population. Many of these goods were destined for export. If Rochester was Smugtown, the United States was Smug Nation.

Some of America's competitive edge was the result of the industrial infrastructure in Germany and Japan having been so badly damaged during World War II. And much was dependent on a burst of government spending aimed at countering the Soviets—during the Korean War, the Cold War, and the Space Race. The military-industrial complex, as President Eisenhower would soon label it, accounted for as much as 20 percent of total economic output in the 1950s. In 1957, government-supported research and development performed by federal contractors outstripped the funding put up by the companies themselves. By 1960, the nation's electronics industry had come to rely on Uncle Sam for 70 percent of its R&D dollars.

Still, much of America's upper hand was due to public investment not in science or technology, but in workers themselves. The G.I. Bill of Rights, which President Roosevelt had signed into law in 1944, had disbursed college and training funds to nearly half of the nation's 16 million World War II veterans by the time the program expired in 1956. "The expansion of higher education and the subsidization of students have led to marked gains in the educational background of workers," Charles Hession and Hyman Sardy wrote in *Ascent to Affluence*, their history of American economic advancement. "Better education for workers has improved the quality of the nation's labor force and this has manifested itself in increased productivity."

As workers' productivity soared, corporations spread the returns. Hourly employees in some industries—steel, autos, manufacturing equipment—saw especially large boosts in pay. But wages and salaries climbed sharply during the course of the fifties for most everyone: up 54 percent overall for full-time blue- and white-collar workers. Jumps in income outpaced inflation. Besides issuing bigger paychecks, companies also provided what *Business Week* termed "big fringes." By the middle of the decade, almost half of all large- and medium-sized employers in the United States were giving their workers pensions, and more than two-thirds were kicking in insurance of some kind, up from a negligible number just ten years prior. "The status of the American worker, broadly speaking, attained a new peak in 1955," said Joseph Goldberg, a US Labor Department official. There was no shortage of small fringes, too—the everyday perks that helped to sustain employee loyalty. When someone retired from Coca-Cola, for example, he was reminded that he could always grab a meal at no cost in the company dining room in Atlanta: "We would like for you to avail yourself of this opportunity often." In 1950s America, there really was such a thing as a free lunch.

With their financial station upgraded, people spent as never before—on cars, on Levittown-style suburban houses, on TVs, and on jet travel, which began to take off at the end of the decade. It's as if someone had set the economy on fire, a conflagration fueled by easy credit and fanned by Madison Avenue. "The reason we have such a high standard of living," said Robert Sarnoff, president of the National Broadcasting Company, "is because advertising has created an American frame of mind that makes people want more things, better things, and newer things."

The 1950s were part of a thirty-year, postwar period that saw America take its final steps toward being truly modernized. In 1940, a good-sized portion of households around the country still had no flush toilets, electric lights, or even running water. By 1970, hardly any homes were without these things. Less than half of all residences had refrigerators and washing machines in 1940, but thirty years later more than 90 percent did. Vice President Richard Nixon was so enchanted by America's consumer economy—and what its brisk development said about the merits of capitalism—that he'd show off a newfangled dishwasher to Soviet premier Nikita Khrushchev in 1959 as the two toured an exhibit of a typical American kitchen at the US Embassy in Moscow. "Any steelworker could buy this house," Nixon told him proudly.

Not everyone was so enamored of the nation's sudden preoccupation with accumulating more things. Galbraith, for one, warned in *The Affluent Society* that it was dangerous to go from "a world where more production meant more food for the hungry, more clothing for the cold, and more houses for the homeless to a world where increased output satisfies the craving for more elegant automobiles, more exotic food, more erotic clothing, more elaborate entertainment—indeed, for the entire modern range of sensuous, edifying, and lethal desires."

Yet as repulsive as this acquisitive culture was to some commentators, America's buying binge had a definite virtue: it was no longer just the well-heeled who got to join in. "Certainly evidence is plentiful that some of the old barricades of class warfare are toppling," A. H. Raskin, the renowned labor writer for the *New York Times*, wrote in August 1955. Top executives were still living large, but not quite as large as, say, their counterparts of the 1920s. Their ostentatiousness restrained, they seemed more like everyone else—and everyone else seemed more like them. "Among other things that have changed in the executive's life has been the ritual connected with city club life," a 1955 *Fortune* article asserted. "Ceremony has all but vanished with the migration to the suburbs. Executives now use town clubs merely for lunching or having a fast drink at the end of the day before catching their commuting trains. The old, annual club dinner with its solemnities and reports, its printed menus, elaborate dishes, and long cigars, has deteriorated into a gobbling of commonplace steak by members numbed by martinis." Changes in tax policy—the top rate went from 38 percent in 1949 to 52 percent through most of the fifties—also helped level the playing field. "The large yacht," said *Fortune*, "has . . . foundered in the sea of progressive taxation." Moreover, the magazine added, "as executives' homes have dwindled in size, so have their parties. Frederick J. Thibold, catering manager at Sherry's in New York, can remember dances for 2,000 with a 'sumptuous supper' 25 years ago. A big dance today is one for 400, and at some of these, Thibold confides in a whisper, Sherry's has served hot dogs and hamburgers." Fittingly, Harvard business professor Richard Tedlow has written, it was a bottle of Coca-Cola that in the mid-1950s became "the international symbol of the American consumer culture, the quintessential democratic luxury."

Actually, class divides in the United States had started to come down in the 1940s, when the gap in wages between rich and poor shrank significantly. The wage differential between the middle class and poor also tightened during this time, and the same narrowing was found irrespective of education, job experience, or occupation. Economists would come to call this era "the Great Compression." The trend could be chalked up, at least in part, to government intervention during World War II—specifically, the actions of the War Labor Board, which regulated pay and generally approved higher earnings for only the lowest-paid workers. As a result, this dramatic flattening wouldn't continue for very long. But neither would the wage structure widen for the next twenty-five years or so, making this an unrivaled age of American egalitarianism. "Incomes stopped converging around 1952," the journalist Timothy Noah has explained. "But what happened next is even more remarkable. Although incomes ceased becoming more equal, they didn't start becoming less equal (as they had during the 1920s after World War I). The income ratios stayed more or less the same. For instance, in 1952 the share of national income going to the top 10 percent was 33 percent. In 1962 it was 34 percent. In 1972 it was . . . 34 percent. The rich were getting richer, but not disproportionately to everyone else."

Wealth came to workers in various forms. The Employee Stock Ownership Plan would make its debut in 1956. Hundreds of other businesses, including corporate goliaths such as Sears and Procter & Gamble, had long had their own profit-sharing schemes. In all, about half of US workers in the mid-1950s were paid by some type of group-based incentive program, the most talked about of which was developed by Joseph Scanlon, a lecturer in industrial relations at the Massachusetts Institute of Technology. His was, in many ways, the purest demonstration of the mutuality of interests that was supposed to underpin the social contract between employer and employee.

Although *Time* magazine in 1955 pronounced him "the most sought-after labor-relations adviser in the U.S," the fifty-six-year-old Scanlon didn't fit anyone's image of an MIT management expert. The son of Irish immigrants, Joe Scanlon joined Empire Steel, a small company in Mansfield, Ohio, as a cost accountant in 1924. He also boxed on the side, earning as much as $1,000 a bout as a featherweight prizefighter. When his boss told him that he didn't stand much of a chance of getting promoted if he kept coming to work with black eyes, Scanlon promptly shed his white collar for a blue one, becoming an open-hearth tender—a hazardous job, dirty and blazing hot. He then served as a union local president for the Steelworkers.

During the Depression, Empire nearly went under. It let go half its workforce, and everyone who stayed with the company had to swallow a 25 percent pay cut. Searching for answers, Scanlon consulted with Clinton Golden, a top Steelworkers official. "Develop some method for reaching down into the mind of each employee," Golden told him, "and see what he has got to propose that may possibly result in a reduction of cost or improvement of the quality of the product. See if you can come out in a spirit of teamwork, of working together to save your company." Scanlon went back and put Golden's advice into action. A special joint research committee of management and workers was established, kinks in the production process were identified, and fixes were found—most based on the suggestions of those on the front lines. Profits rose, workers' pay was restored, and Empire began to hire again.

Scanlon continued to refine various cooperative constructs through the mid-1940s, first as a part of the Steelworkers' industrial-engineering department and then as member of the staff at MIT. What emerged was different than straight "profit sharing"; the Scanlon Plan was a groundbreaking example of what would come to be designated "gainsharing"—a system involving not only paying out bonuses based on corporate performance but also ensuring that all employees participate in the key decisions intended to spur higher productivity and lower costs. The Scanlon Plan was, in this regard, as much a philosophy as a formula. "What Joe Scanlon was driving for was broad decentralization and genuine delegation, clear to the bottom of the organization," said Douglas McGregor, Scanlon's MIT colleague. His vision, McGregor added, was completely antithetical to "the typical industrial-engineering approach . . . of the last half century, which takes all the human elements out of work and turns man essentially into a glorified machine tool."

The Scanlon Plan contained three crucial elements: First, the workers (or their union representatives) would collaborate with management to figure out the total cost of compensating people in the organization and compare that to the total market value of what the organization produced. Monthly bonuses would be paid whenever the company beat this baseline ratio. Second, everyone was to be compensated under the same rules, so as to not pit individuals or groups of workers against each other. "We like to see everybody from the president of the company to the floor sweeper all in the same plan," said Fred Lesieur, who assisted Scanlon. Third, a network of production councils was set up, each charged not only with brainstorming ideas but with putting the good ones into practice. Scanlon had "a deeply rooted faith in democracy and democratic processes," Golden, the Steelworkers official, remarked. "He believed that every worker, no matter how humble and seemingly unimportant his task, is capable of making a contribution not only to the success of the enterprise but to the happiness and well-being of his fellows."

Bringing these concepts to life was not easy. To begin with, it demanded an unqualified commitment from those at the top of the corporation. Gathering meaningful input from each and every part of the organization, as Scanlon said, required much more than "the boss greeting the worker with a 'cheerio.'" Foremen and superintendents, who were accustomed to having complete authority over technical production decisions, had to give up that control. And workers had to get beyond feeling ripped off if their bonuses were lower than expected.

Yet when things clicked, the results were stunning. At the Cornelius Company, a Minnesota producer of aircraft parts, productivity shot up 100 percent in the four months after adoption of Scanlon's system. Herman Miller, the Michigan furniture company, smashed all production records in the first month it had a Scanlon Plan. And at the Adamson Company, a maker of steel tanks in Ohio, profits skyrocketed 500 percent and employees earned bonuses as high as 98 percent—all because of Scanlon, executives said.

At Lapointe Machine Tool, of Hudson, Massachusetts, a Scanlon Plan was put in after the Steelworkers had gone out on strike for eleven weeks. Ideas from the workers now flowed, with more than 500 of them sent to a special labor-management screening committee in the first two years; of those, 380 were accepted. Powered by this surge of suggestions, production at Lapointe increased more than 60 percent. And workers took home bonuses averaging about 18 percent, while their job security solidified. "The day that the plan was put in," said Edward Dowd, a Lapointe executive, "there was a definite change in the attitude of the employees toward management, and, in turn, there was quite a change in management's attitude toward its employees."

When everybody is sharing in the good times, getting along is a lot easier.

In late 1955, General Electric stepped up in an area that, arguably more than any other, characterized what was rapidly becoming a private, employer-based welfare system in America: medical insurance for working men and women.

The new GE plan, which supplanted the company's more bare-bones health policies, sought to integrate basic coverage for hospitalization and in-hospital care with added protection against expenses for many out-of-hospital services and for catastrophic illness. GE regarded this "comprehensive insurance" as an important social breakthrough, and it heralded the relief it brought to its employees, who after paying a small deductible (no more than fifty dollars, and often less than twenty-five) could have full confidence that 75 to 85 percent of their medical bills would be paid by the company.

In one case, for example, a GE employee's eight-year-old daughter severely injured her liver after taking a spill on her bicycle. The family faced nearly $4,000 in health expenses, but more than 80 percent of that was picked up by GE's new insurance package, which was underwritten by Metropolitan Life. Under most standard plans, the employee would have been reimbursed less than 50 percent, including being stuck with $1,300 in payments for private nursing and blood. "The steady search for sounder, more effective ways of protecting and restoring human health spawns innovation not only in medical practice, procedures and drugs, but in other fields as well," said Earl Willis, a GE manager of employee benefits. "Insurance is one of these."

Employees were thankful for the company's offering, with eight in ten indicating their approval. "I don't know what would have become of us these last few years if we hadn't had this insurance," said the wife of one GE employee who was hospitalized for more than three months and treated for mental illness. "I don't think that there are many health plans that cover psychiatric care, and if it hadn't been for this care, we would have been destroyed as a family."

GE's generosity pointed up two things about medical coverage in the United States in the 1950s: First, its breadth was quickly widening. And, second, the business community wanted to be sure that the private sector—and not the government—was largely in control of that expansion, doling out health insurance as another artifact of the social contract between employer and employee. This was, after all, the way it had always been.

Through the nineteenth and into the twentieth century, health plans of any variety were a rarity across the nation. Some small immigrant benefit societies, fraternal orders, and unions offered so-called sickness benefits, but relatively few Americans had any buffer against loss of earnings due to illness, and even fewer had insurance that actually paid their medical expenses. Some companies—primarily those operating railroads, mines, and lumber camps—had their own doctors, but their principal duties consisted of examining job applicants and patching up injured employees so that they could get back to work. The federal government, for its part, left it to states and cities to decide the best course on health coverage. And they generally left it up to individuals to acquire insurance, assuming they could even find it. Unlike in Europe, where health care had become a tax-supported function of the state, medical insurance in America remained private and voluntary.

An attempt to change that came at the end of the Progressive Era, but even the reformers were leery of trying to make health insurance a full-on government program. A group of left-leaning academics called the American Association for Labor Legislation led the charge, calling in 1915 for workers and their dependents to receive coverage for medical aid, sick pay, maternity benefits, and funeral expenses. Employers and employees would each pay 40 percent of the cost; the government would chip in the remaining 20 percent. Even this, however, was too much state interference for both management and labor. By this time, many companies were practicing welfare capitalism, hoping that piling on the benefits would win over their employees' allegiance. The last thing business wanted was the government inserting itself into the middle of the relationship. Tellingly, it wasn't just the rigidly conservative National Association of Manufacturers that opposed the state's involvement in the marketplace for health insurance; so did the

National Civic Federation, a forerunner to the more liberal Committee for Economic Development.

In a similar vein, craft unions were positioning themselves as the champions of workers' needs, fighting, above all, for the higher pay that would allow people to buy health insurance on their own. "No remedy is so potent to prolong life and to give help to the individual and to remove poverty as increases in wages," said Samuel Gompers, the president of the American Federation of Labor, as he decried the AALL plan. It was up to unions, he added, "to secure to all workers a living wage that will enable them to have sanitary homes . . . adequate clothing, nourishing food, and other things that are essential to the maintenance of good health." In a strange-bedfellows moment, then, labor and management joined arms to derail the AALL campaign. "Neither unions nor big business at that time wanted any competition from government in social welfare programs," the sociologist Paul Starr has written. "Thus health insurance, rather than pitting labor unions against capital, pitted both of them against the reformers."

By 1917, antagonism to public health insurance was also building among doctors, who feared that the state would cut into their incomes as well as their freedom to practice medicine as they saw fit. "It is a dangerous device, invented in Germany, announced by the German Emperor from the throne the same year he started plotting and preparing to conquer the world," read a pamphlet published by one physicians' organization. The reformers were now in retreat.

By the 1920s, health insurance as a social cause had all but disappeared from the American scene. It would remain mostly moribund throughout the decade, until the issue was revived and reframed by the exigencies of the Great Depression. At this stage, those pressing for expanded access to health insurance viewed rising medical costs as a bigger concern than lost income because of sickness. And they wanted coverage to reach the middle class, envisioning a much wider safety net than the one the progressives had tried to knit together for industrial workers and their families. As one expert put it, the question now was not only how to make sure that blue-collar laborers were protected, but how to "meet the needs and satisfy the demands of the 'white-collar' people of moderate means."

Once again, opposition was vehement, with business and physician groups alarmed at the slightest whiff of any role for government.

When in late 1932 the Committee on the Cost of Medical Care—an independent body of economists, doctors, and public-health specialists—cautiously endorsed the formation of community health centers and proposed that localities contribute a share of the cost of group insurance for low-income individuals, the American Medical Association lambasted these ideas as an "incitement to revolution" and "utopian fantasies." As President Roosevelt rode into office, the political calculus had become perfectly apparent: his administration would need to tread carefully on the topic of health insurance, lest it provoke the fury of the business and medical lobbies.

By 1935, this unease—coupled with the widespread sense that, in the context of the Depression, health coverage wasn't as vital as unemployment or old-age insurance—led Roosevelt to make a fateful choice: medical benefits wouldn't be included in the Social Security Act. An early draft of the bill had contained a provision for a federal panel to study the subject of health insurance, and this prospect alone "was responsible for so many telegrams to the members of Congress that the entire Social Security program seemed endangered," one Capitol Hill staffer would later recall. The line was struck to ensure that Social Security passed.

Pressure for government-backed health insurance didn't go away, however. Among those applying it full bore was organized labor, which had reversed its position since Samuel Gompers first frowned on the notion of public coverage. Now, the AFL favored such a plan, as did the Congress of Industrial Organizations, which saw access to medicine as one piece of a larger social-democratic agenda. "My people are asking that our government take health from the list of luxuries to be bought only by money and add it to the list containing the 'inalienable rights' of every citizen," said Florence Greenberg, a leader of the women's auxiliaries of the Steel Workers Organizing Committee.

Nonetheless, Roosevelt was unable to summon the fortitude to take on the doctors. He toyed with introducing a national health program but never did so. "We can't go up against the state medical societies," the president acknowledged at one point. "We just can't do it."

Others were less daunted. In 1943, Senators Robert Wagner and James Murray, along with Congressman John Dingell, authored a bill that would have made health coverage widely available through changes to Social Security. And President Truman, upon entering office, also advanced a plan for universal federal health insurance. As always, the doctors were unsparing in their assessment of where such a program would lead. "Let the people of our country realize that the movement for the placing of American medicine under the control of the federal government through a system of federal compulsory sickness insurance is the first step toward a regimentation of utilities, of industries, of finance and eventually of labor itself," the *Journal of the American Medical Association* maintained. "This is the kind of reg-imentation that led to totalitarianism in Germany and the downfall of that nation." Other times, the AMA preferred a different bogey-man, alluding to Russia, instead of Germany, in its warnings about government-provided health care. "Would socialized medicine lead to socialization of other phases of American life?" the AMA asked in one piece of literature. "Lenin thought so." It then quoted the So-viet leader—apocryphally, it seems—as having once said, "Socialized medicine is the keystone to the arch of the Socialist State."

By the late 1940s, the doctors—backed by millions of dollars in advertising—had won the day: national health insurance would never gain any real political momentum. At the same time, America's employer-based health system was becoming ever more entrenched, its place secured by a series of actions and decisions rendered by the gov-ernment itself. It began with the War Labor Board, which had capped the amount of pay that companies could offer their employees, but was less stringent regarding benefits. Consequently, businesses used health coverage to attract and keep the best available workers during a stretch when men were off to battle and labor at home was scarce. Group hos-pital coverage nearly quadrupled during the war, to 26 million sub-scribers, with the vast majority enrolled in Blue Cross plans.

In 1949, the Supreme Court's ruling that benefits (and not just pay) were a legitimate issue for collective bargaining helped cast cor-porate America as the nation's leading conduit for health insurance, with organized labor now the prime catalyst in expanding cover-age. That medical benefits "are not a 'fringe' concern to workers has been made clear by the . . . demands for these programs," said Harry Becker, the social security director at the United Auto Workers. Ob-taining a higher standard of health care, he added, "is an integral part of the larger drive for a higher standard of living." By 1954, 12 mil-lion workers and 17 million dependents were enrolled in health plans negotiated by unions—a fourth of all the medical insurance purchased in the country—up from fewer than 3 million workers just six years before. And many nonunion businesses (like Kodak) quickly offered their workers the same deal. The Internal Revenue Service then made it official that people didn't have to pay taxes on their companies' contributions to health-benefit plans, further strengthening this part of the social contract between employer and employee.

As General Electric launched its comprehensive health insurance program, the picture of how medical coverage was distributed in America had crystallized: most people counted on their employer for such protection. The fastest-growing plans were group policies sold by large commercial firms (such as Metropolitan Life), which, unlike the previously dominant, community-based Blue Cross model, didn't allow for people to take their insurance with them should they leave their job; health coverage was becoming a tether to one's place of employment.

From the outset, this configuration prompted several worries. First, tens of millions of Americans remained uninsured. The poor and unemployed often fell through the cracks, as did those with part-time jobs and many of those who worked for smaller companies. The uninsured would continue to be a problem even after the passage of Medicare and Medicaid in the mid-1960s brought expanded coverage to the elderly and indigent. Second, some felt that employees still had to shoulder too much of the cost of their care. Even at General Electric, workers had to pay for much of their routine health maintenance, and maternity benefits were limited. The rank-and-file want "full coverage under the GE plan," said a local union leader in Cleveland.

The final fear was that costs would spiral out of control, especially after GE pioneered comprehensive health insurance—a form of coverage that would grow phenomenally fast, with some 28,000 other employers (including Coca-Cola) taking it up within a decade. "The existence of a fairly generous overall maximum, without any limits on the price of covered services or any specified time limits, has been variously described as an 'invitation to larceny,' a 'blank check inviting higher prices,' and a 'noble experiment challenging the self-restraint of the medical profession and its dedication to voluntary health insurance,'" said a Brookings Institution study.

For some, this risk was just one symptom of a larger threat to the nation—an escalation of employment costs that seemed to have no end. Like health insurance, pensions had also "taken on new meaning" during the 1950s, in the words of *Business Week*. "They're no longer considered a gift bestowed by an employer on his faithful employee," the magazine said, "but rather a sort of deferred wage, which a worker has earned by his sweat and labor." Some wondered how any business, if it fell on hard times, could possibly continue to meet these retirement obligations. "For such a plan to give real security," Peter Drucker wrote, "the financial strength of the company and its economic success must be reasonably secure for the next forty years—the twenty-five years between the beginning of middle-age and retirement during which a man accumulates his pension rights, and the years of his old age during which he receives his pension. But is there any one company or any one industry whose future can be predicted with certainty even ten years ahead?" Although corporations such as General Electric were now pumping tens of millions of dollars a year into their pension plans, they ultimately offered "no more security against the big bad wolf of old age than the little piggy's house of straw," Drucker cautioned.

In general, the increases in benefits through the fifties "have been unprecedented in their magnitude and liberality," General Electric chief executive Ralph Cordiner, told the company's board of directors. "This record, with its disturbing implication for future management planning and for the welfare of employees, public, and the economy as a whole, suggest the need for sober consideration of what underlies this result and what bearing the pattern of the past decade will have on wage and benefit changes during the next ten years." Such admonitions would eventually prove to be correct. But with the 1950s economy roaring and inflation at a quiescent 2 percent, it was probably hard for many to hear what Drucker and Cordiner and any other doubters were saying.

In the meantime, America's burgeoning employer-based health system was—even with its appreciable flaws—having a tremendous effect. In 1950, only 49 percent of wage and salary workers in the United States had hospitalization coverage, 35 percent had surgical insurance, 16 percent had a plan that covered regular medical expenses, and practically nobody had major-medical benefits. By 1965, the ranks of employees covered in these different categories would all increase greatly—to 69 percent, 66 percent, 58 percent, and 25 percent, respectively. What's more, this explosion in health insurance for workers and their families meant that the nation overall was covered as never before: the proportion of Americans with hospitalization benefits would go from 51 percent to 79 percent during the same fifteen-year time frame, while the percentage of those with surgical coverage would double from 36 to 72. "Health insecurity," the historian Alan Derickson has written, "became the exception rather than the rule."

Employer-based medical insurance was a Band-Aid, yes, but it was a mighty big one.

When the 50 millionth car ever made by General Motors came off the assembly line in Flint, Michigan, it was the ideal object to capture the sparkle of America: the 1955 Chevrolet Bel Air Sport Coupe had been swabbed with a golden glint paint, and more than 600 of its parts and accessories had been dipped in a bath of gold cyanide. The interior fabric had been woven together with gold metallic thread, and the seats were upholstered in gold vinyl. "People have money, they have confidence, and they are in a buying mood," said Harlow Curtice, GM's president, who had been picked in 1952 to take over for "Engine Charlie" Wilson.

A lifelong GM man, "Red" Curtice oozed plenty of assurance himself, having pledged in early 1954 to invest $1 billion over two years to expand the production capacity of the nation's biggest corporation, just as some had begun to worry that the economy was losing steam. "There is no more key variable determining our economic future than the climate of business expectations," the *New York Times* wrote in an editorial praising the GM executive for his "statesmanship and responsibility." "Mr. Curtice has shown concretely why that climate should be an optimistic one, and the investment decision General Motors has taken will contribute powerfully to countering the fears of the pessimists." By the end of 1955, Curtice's big gamble had paid off handsomely—for the company, which sold more than $12 billion worth of cars that year, crushing its previous record, while becoming the first firm in US history to ring up $1 billion in profit; for the economy, which produced an all-time high in goods and services, with unemployment holding at less than 4.5 percent; and for Curtice personally, as *Time* magazine enshrined him on its cover as "Man of the Year."

"Curtice was aware that the US, with its growing population, growing bank accounts, growing suburbs, and decentralized industry, could well afford to buy more new cars than it ever had before—if everyone had confidence that the boom would continue," *Time* said. "As head of GM, with more income and more resources at his command than most sovereign nations, he was in the best position to do something about confidence. As a result of his $1 billion bet, confidence spread throughout GM's own sizable world. The 514,000 employees in 119 plants in 65 cities in 19 states quit hoarding for layoffs and began buying—among other things, autos. By midyear most of the 17,000 Chevrolet, Pontiac, Buick, Oldsmobile, and Cadillac dealers in the US were selling more new and used cars than they ever had before."

Like Kodak and GE, GM gave more as it got more. Its 57 officers and directors averaged more than $240,000 in compensation in 1955, about three-quarters of it in bonus income. Harlow Curtice led the way with more than $775,000—the biggest executive payday in America. Equal to nearly $7 million in today's terms, it was a nice haul, to be sure. Still, it would pale in comparison to CEO pay in the decades to come, when executive compensation would become a hot-button social issue.

Even more notable for GM's 100,000-plus white-collar employees, the company in 1955 made available a stock-purchase plan through which they could invest up to 10 percent of their annual salary. Half of the funds would go toward purchasing GM shares, with the company matching this part of the employee's contribution; the other half would be parked in government bonds. "To philosophical economists, the offer—and the sheer magnitude of the dollar figures involved—are proof that the US is moving toward a new kind of capitalism, a system in which the old distinctions between owners and workers—investors and wage earners—will become more and more blurred," *Business Week* wrote. In return for such benefits, GM told its salaried employees, it expected them to live up to their end of the social contract by "maintaining good health and mental alertness, using good judgment, being prompt and regular in attendance, cooperating with your fellow workers, and being loyal to GM—its people and its products."

The company also tried to interest the United Auto Workers in a stock-ownership plan as the two sides sat down in March 1955 to negotiate their first contract since the Treaty of Detroit. But Walter Reuther had other ideas in mind for GM's hourly workers. In the end, the UAW would win the kind of three-year contract that one would expect from a company on top of the world: an increase in the annual improvement factor, a higher night-shift premium, and souped-up pension, insurance, and medical benefits. But the really big prize was one that Reuther had been eyeing for several years now (and that the Electrical Workers attempted, unsuccessfully, to lock in during their own 1955 contract talks with GE): a guaranteed annual wage. "You know," said Reuther, "we go to the bargaining table and management asks: 'Don't you ever get tired of asking for more and more and more?' The answer is, as long as science and technology through the creation of abundance makes more not only economically just, but makes more and more economically necessary—the answer is yes, we are going in year after year and asking for more and more and more because we are entitled to more and more and more."

As proposed by the UAW, the guaranteed annual wage would make it so that once an hourly worker had achieved seniority (something usually reached after ninety days of probation at the auto companies), he would begin to build up protection against future layoffs. By the time an employee had two years of seniority, he would have banked fifty-two weeks of guaranteed income "in amounts sufficient to maintain the same living standards as when fully employed."

Reuther often framed the GAW in ethical terms. A guaranteed income, he said, "would put people above property, men above machines" by ending "the immoral double standard under which the worker, of all those who draw their incomes from industry, has the least protection against economic adversity." But he had other aims as well. One hope was that corporate America would find the GAW put too much of a burden on them, and so business leaders would push the public sector to do more for those who had been laid off. To that end, the union liked to point out that unemployment compensation from the government would also count toward a worker's guaranteed wage, giving companies an enticement to "reduce their liabilities by effectively working toward the improvement of state laws."

Reuther's other intention was to compel employers to provide stable, full-time work; any costs incurred under the GAW were essentially penalties for failing to do so. "The ideal guaranteed annual wage," said Reuther, "would be one that never resulted in payment to any worker for time spent in idleness because the workers covered are kept steadily employed." To show that its thinking wasn't pie in the sky, the UAW cited companies that historically had guaranteed work to its employees during slack times—the consumer-products manufacturer Procter & Gamble, meatpacker Hormel, and shoemaker Nunn-Bush. Printers and brewers had utilized such work-stabilization plans as far back as the 1890s.

At GM, however, not only was there no such policy; individuals found themselves sidelined from work whenever there was a model change. Even during the go-go years of the 1950s, seasonality alone could translate into temporary layoffs for as many as 160,000 between March and August. "GM has never faced up to one responsibility to our people in connection with these production fluctuations," conceded Verne Laseau, an employee-relations official at the company.

Nevertheless, most of those running GM—and their peers across American industry—had nothing but disdain for the GAW. "If we allow ourselves to accede to the principle of 'jobless pay' there is no telling how far such a thing would go in tearing down the spirit of 'working for a living,'" said Donaldson Brown, the GM director. Even Peter Drucker, who advocated a "predictable income plan" to alleviate "the dread of the unknown and the deep feelings of insecurity under which the worker . . . lives," thought that the GAW went too far. "The 'guaranteed annual wage' of union rhetoric," he wrote, "is as empty a promise as one of immortality would be." Quipped John Bugas, the head of industrial relations at Ford: "We'd be very happy if only somebody would come up with a good plan for GAP, or guaranteed annual profits."

The opposition was, ultimately, too great for Reuther to overcome. But 1955 was a very good year, and he was not about to go away empty-handed. What Reuther was able to wring out—first at Ford and then at GM—was a partial version of the GAW. With supplemental unemployment benefits, the companies agreed to contribute five cents for every hour a person worked to a trust fund that could be accessed in case of layoff for up to twenty-six weeks. Combined with state benefits, the SUB provided enough for a worker to receive 60 to 65 percent of his regular pay for as much as half a year. For GM, the cost of the deal was minimal considering what it offered: the promise of three more years of industrial peace.

As was typical whenever GM or Ford took action, other companies followed along: Chrysler and several smaller automakers, along with Continental Can and American Can, the maritime shipping industry, and by 1956, Big Steel adopted the SUB as well. Even so, the SUB would come to protect only 2 percent or so of the American workforce.

Despite the SUB's limited reach, a number of business groups caterwauled. The president of the National Association of Manufacturers suggested that any vestige of the guaranteed wage "could have seriously damaging effects on the American economy, perhaps leading to a socialistic state." The National Economic Council Inc., a conservative group, said "Reuther's GAW-ful fraud" was "uneconomic and can spell only disaster for the worker, for business, and for the nation."

At GM, executives struggled to make sense of the reprobation; in their eyes, it wasn't like they had given in to Reuther's original GAW. "Anybody who draws any conclusions that Ford, General Motors, or others have met the demands for a guaranteed annual wage simply . . . can't read English correctly," said Alfred Sloan. Even Reuther admitted that SUB was no GAW. "You never get everything," he said. (He also was upset that some companies, such as Pittsburgh Plate Glass, had started instituting a new form of SUB that required each worker to fund his own reserve account and "provide for his own security"— an early taste of individual savings mechanisms, like 401(k)s, that would become common in the decades ahead.)

But what shouldn't be lost in all the downplaying was that a national debate over a guaranteed wage had taken place, one that had engaged both business executives and blue-collar workers. It had put Reuther on the cover of *Time* magazine with a story headlined "The GAW Man." And partial plans had been implemented. As with the fight over "full employment" in the mid-1940s, the fact that America would earnestly contemplate a guaranteed wage for workers—one served up not by government but by the private sector—indicated how amazingly far the social contract between employer and employee had come. What was yet to be seen was how far it could go. But few could be faulted in the halcyon year of 1955 if they thought that the Golden Age of American business and, by extension, the Golden Age of America might just roll on forever.

General Electric CEO Ralph Cordiner (at center) helped spark some of the key changes that would roil the American workplace: management's hardened stance against unions, the introduction of new technology, and the rise of knowledge work.

5

STRAINS BENEATH
THE SURFACE

We tend to paint history as a series of sharply defined events, as if someone flicks a switch and one era instantly gives way to the next. Sometimes, these neat blocks are viewed as cause and effect: the Progressive Era, for instance, is seen as a reaction to the political and corporate abuses brought by America's rapid industrialization at the turn of the twentieth century. There is, of course, some logic to this orderly, textbook portrayal of the past; if nothing else, markers help us make sense of things. But in actuality, our collective experience isn't nearly so tidy. Even as one wave of history continues to crest, the undercurrents often start to run in a different direction.

For working America, the social contract between employer and employee would get stronger throughout the 1950s and '60s, with good job security and rising pay and expanding health coverage and pensions. The Golden Age would glitter for many years to come. But by 1958, important changes were already stirring deep below the surface: in management's approach to organized labor; through new technologies being introduced on the factory floor and in the front office; and with the basic profile of the American worker, as ever more people were now being hired to use their heads and not just their hands. As much as anyone, General Electric's Ralph Cordiner was at the center of it all—the extension of a generous deal with his workers and, simultaneously, its early fraying at the edges.

Cordiner, who was elected GE's chairman and chief executive in '58, having served as the company's president for the previous eight years, was a model executive for his time: an Organization Man's Organization Man. He didn't invent the decentralized company (known among business professors as the M-Form, or multidivisional, structure); credit for that would go to DuPont and General Motors under Alfred Sloan. But Cordiner became one of its most enthusiastic practitioners, pushing responsibility for day-to-day decision making—and accountability for results—beyond a small circle of top executives and down to hundreds upon hundreds of third- and fourth-level supervisors spread across scores of operating departments. In so doing, Cordiner helped to introduce "the vast new arena of middle management," as one GE financial analyst put it. Indeed, by 1956, the United States had taken a striking turn: the number of white-collar employees (defined as those in managerial, technical, and clerical jobs) for the first time surpassed the number of blue-collar laborers. This shift away from manufacturing toward "knowledge work," as Peter Drucker was to first call it in 1959, would over time have far-reaching effects on the country's economy and society, transforming the fundamental makeup and character of the American workplace and altering the corporate social contract.

Those entering the ranks of management in the 1950s were in a position to weigh the relationship between employer and employee from two sides: as supervisors overseeing people who reported to them, and as individuals with their own careers to chase. Yet whether they were directing others or being directed, Cordiner's men—and they were practically all men—were expected to stick to the same script: to step up and make good decisions on behalf of the entire enterprise, and to inspire others to do the same. GE had become too large and too complex, Cordiner was convinced, for a top-down system to work any longer. This new alignment, based on encouraging autonomy up and down the chain, was meant to jolt GE out of the state of "security, complacency, and mediocrity" toward which he saw the company drifting. "The manager's work is to lead others by drawing out their ideas, their special knowledge, and their efforts," Cordiner declared, adding that "self-discipline rather than boss-discipline is the hallmark of a de-centralized organization." He wanted those at GE to "lead by persuasion rather than command" and characterized what he was promoting as "a philosophy of freedom." "Decentralization," said Cordiner, "is a creative response to the challenges of our time, a way of preserving and enhancing the competitive enterprise system as it evolves into the new form that has been so aptly named 'the people's capitalism.'"

From most outward appearances, Cordiner was an odd spokesman for "the people's" anything. Colleagues and students of GE have described him as having "as much charisma as a cold fish," with an "aloof personality, Napoleonic in appearance and demeanor." But while he may not have been approachable, Cordiner's beliefs were, in fact, steeped in working-class values, an appreciation for a hard day's effort, and true respect for others. Born in 1900 on a wheat ranch twenty miles outside of Walla Walla, Washington, Ralph Jarron Cordiner—his family called him R.J.—went to work in the fields when he was eleven. His mother, he told his four daughters in a private memoir written in 1958, had imparted "the wisdom of never speaking disapprovingly or unkindly about anyone, which she would not tolerate in her presence. Her contention was that every individual had many good traits, and it was our responsibility to discover these good traits and not be critical of self-evident shortcomings." Over the years, Cordiner picked up a broad range of experience: in addition to being a farm hand, he worked as a janitor for a church, a potato peeler and vegetable preparer at a hotel, a window washer and sidewalk sweeper at a general store, a bookkeeper and salesman for a storage-battery company, and a promoter of college dances. "He never forgot he was from Walla Walla," said Cordiner's son-in-law, Frederick Lione Jr. "He understood the working man."

After graduating from Whitman College in 1922, Cordiner was hired as a commercial manager by a division of Pacific Power and Light, and in less than a year he left to join the Edison General Electric Appliance Company, a GE affiliate. He came to count Gerard Swope and Owen Young, GE's progressive leaders of the Depression Era, as mentors and was promoted rapidly, becoming manager of the company's appliance and merchandise department in 1938. The following year, Cordiner left GE to become president of Schick, the electric shaver company. He lasted three years but was never too happy there. The money was good, but the work wasn't otherwise fulfilling. "I found myself very restive in that there was no challenge in the assignment," Cordiner said, "and my golf handicap was entirely too low because I was bored and did not have enough to do." It was a valuable lesson: "I learned from that experience that one should never work exclusively for financial reward." Cordiner headed to Washington, DC, in 1942 for a stint as a top official of the War Production Board, and in 1943 he rejoined GE as assistant to the president. It was in that role that he began to study the concept of decentralization, and in 1951 he launched his plan for carrying the company into the future.

To make clear exactly what Cordiner was aiming for, GE in 1954 published a hardbound, four-volume series titled *Professional Management in General Electric*. Known as the Blue Books because of their midnight-blue covers, the 1,000-plus pages in these texts sought to spell out how GE's managers should act so as to ensure the company's growth and prosperity, while helping to "fashion an environment where new opportunities for human happiness are abundant." Detailing GE's history and the way it was to be organized, as well as "the work of a professional manager" and "the work of a functional individual contributor," this was serious stuff—easily on par with the most demanding curriculum from the nation's best business schools. The principal author of the Blue Books would have tolerated no less.

Harold Smiddy was a brilliant management thinker who graduated from MIT in 1920, barely a week after his twentieth birthday. He eventually took a job with the consulting firm Booz, Allen, and Hamilton, and in the late 1940s was recruited to GE. He quickly became, in the words of one executive, "the indefatigable formulator and spokesman for the underlying concepts of management that would be necessary to the conversion of the monolithic corporate structure." In Smiddy's eyes, education was a big piece of making decentralization successful. "No longer is it true, in our reasoned judgment, that experience alone can teach the work of managing adequately and in time," Smiddy asserted. "Management is no longer merely an art. It is unlikely ever to be an exact science either. Yet it is fast acquiring the character of a profession. And this means that its principles can be increasingly discovered, stated, verified, and taught systematically." Or, as Smiddy commented in more down-to-earth terms: "No company, no industry, can afford to let managers just happen." To mold them,

Smiddy and his internal team of consultants offered business courses at local GE facilities and drew up individual study plans for managers, serving up selections from a reading list that included Chester Barnard's *The Functions of the Executive*, William Given's *Bottom-Up Management*, and dozens of other tomes.

GE's efforts were part and parcel of a larger push by corporate America to amply prepare its fast-growing crop of managers. "I don't have to tell you that in recent years, training has become one of the most important activities for all major businesses," Coca-Cola president William Robinson told a group of higher-ups in the company's bottler network in 1958. Surveys indicate that right after World War II, only about 5 percent of companies had management-training programs in place; by '58, more than three-quarters did. Kodak, for its part, covered a wide range of topics for new supervisors over twenty-five sessions. Among them: "Getting Ideas Across," "Understanding People," and "The Nature of Fear and Worry." General Motors managers could sign up for a special "Dale Carnegie Course in Effective Leadership," which bore the imprimatur of the self-improvement guru and famed author of *How to Win Friends and Influence People*. "In judging a man's appearance," the GM students were taught, "posture is one of the first things that is noticed." They then learned three exercises to help them stand more erect. They also learned about "acquiring ease and confidence," "thinking on your feet," and "eliminating 'word whiskers'"—those "irritating 'ers' and 'uhs' and 'mmms'" that could mar a manager's message to the rank-and-file.

But no company went further in educating its managers than did GE, which under Cordiner poured $40 million annually into this area, nearly 10 percent of its pretax profit. The center of GE's training universe was America's first corporate university, which the company opened in 1956 in Croton-on-Hudson, New York, after adding two new buildings to the fifteen-acre campus. Crotonville, as the place was called, was no ordinary estate. Along with the physical property, situated about an hour's drive from midtown Manhattan, came intellectual property—specifically, the 7,000-volume management library of the site's former owner, the late Harry Hopf, a leading scholar in the field and a good friend of Smiddy's.

During Crotonville's first five years of operation, some 1,500 GE up-and-comers would go through the advanced-management course held there, staying from nine to thirteen weeks at a time, in groups of fifty to eighty. (The backlog of those nominated to get into Crotonville stretched to two years.) Every participant had the same thing drummed into him—POIM, the company's acronym for four management essentials: planning, organizing, integrating, and measuring work. They also heard from outside experts, including Peter Drucker, consumer-research pioneer Mason Haire, organizational-development theorist Chris Argyris, and others. And though Hopf himself wasn't there, having died in 1949, his spirit certainly was. "Practically every act of management requires for its consummation that cooperative relationships be maintained between two or more persons," Hopf wrote in 1937. "The acid test of the existence of true cooperation is the presence of a two-fold relationship of loyalty—loyalty to his superior on the part of the subordinate and loyalty to the subordinate on the part of the superior."

At its best, Cordiner's decentralized company worked just this way, with managers getting the most out of their people, while giving the most of themselves. When Gerhard Neumann served as general manager of GE Aircraft Engines in the 1950s, he'd hold annual sessions, which he dubbed "Father Neumann's tent revival meetings." He'd erect a circus tent, cram a few thousand employees inside—right down to the floor sweeper—and give them a full report on "what, if everyone does their job, we can accomplish." Managers themselves felt empowered to be bold. One department head, for instance, wanted to manufacture electric toothbrushes. "Everybody he talked to said he was out of his cotton-pickin' mind," remembered Gerald Phillippe, GE's chief financial officer through the fifties, who was among the doubters. "Anybody too lazy to brush his teeth, by gosh, hadn't ought to be alive anyway." But under decentralization, the manager was able to forge ahead—and GE sold more than 1 million units in the first two years alone.

Such triumphs were surely gratifying, and in that way they reflected a general sense of satisfaction among American managers about their jobs. Large surveys of workers in the 1950s found that about three-quarters in managerial positions felt "good" or "very good" about their companies, compared with about 50 percent of hourly employees. An even higher percentage of managers said they liked the kind of work they did. Being in a stable climate had to help. While blue-collar workers were routinely laid off, at least temporarily, when things got tough—a big reason behind Walter Reuther's campaign for a guaranteed annual wage—middle managers across America were typically spared such disruptions. Not that it was uncommon for executives to jump from one company to another during the 1950s to take a better job; many made such moves multiple times. But all in all, managers "were treated as permanent members of permanent enterprises," Charles Heckscher, the director of Rutgers University's Center for Workplace Transformation, has written. Nearly 100 percent of managers in the 1950s believed that their employers provided good job security.

In GE's case, retention wasn't great at first. When Cordiner's plan was first implemented and some of the old guard realized they weren't comfortable accepting the responsibilities that decentralization demanded, the company became plagued with high turnover among managers. Many of these men had worked their way up from the shop floor. Cordiner—and his peers throughout corporate America—wanted a new breed with more years of proper schooling. Increasingly through the twentieth century, "education was the ticket to obtaining a white-collar position," Harvard economists Claudia Goldin and Lawrence Katz have explained. Office workers now needed a high-school diploma; managers, a college degree.

After Cordiner's restructuring had taken effect and things had settled down at GE, the company still had a reputation for being more hard-charging than other corporations that held lifetime employment to be sacrosanct, such as Hewlett-Packard and IBM. "We felt we had lifetime employment with GE—as long as we performed," said Jerry Suran, who joined the company in 1952 and occupied several management positions during his thirty-year career there. Yet even in Cordiner's GE, it was difficult to be fired outright once you were on the supervisory track. You might not advance as far as you hoped. You might be shoved to another part of the company where, it was perceived, you could do less harm. But you had to mess up pretty badly to get tossed out completely. "While there may be promotion of the fittest, there can be survival of all," William Whyte wrote of GE in his 1956 classic about corporate life, *The Organization Man*. "There are exceptions, but one must be a very odd ball to be one."

Despite all of this, being a middle manager had its own particular anxieties. At GE, you still had to fight through piles of paperwork to get anything done. Decentralization might have sounded, on its face, like an assault on the bureaucracy. But the maze of standardized systems and processes set up under Cordiner, along with reams of forms and inch-thick manuals produced, could have put the Politburo to shame. "Our philosophy gives the feel for joy in living, for joy in working, for spontaneity," Melvin Hurni, a senior operations researcher at GE, told Smiddy. "Somehow in practice this gets repressed in dogma, in procedures, in hierarchy."

There was also relentless pressure to produce. Cordiner put in place a new system, called Session C, in which managers met face to face with their supervisor to compare a self-assessment of how well they'd met their annual goals with their boss's evaluation. Such a dialogue was supposed to spur a conversation about each manager's long-term interests and development needs. The intent was less to judge from on high, like a traditional job appraisal, than it was to get individual managers to engage in "self-motivation, self-direction, self-adjustment." Nonetheless, each manager was ultimately rated on a six-point scale from "high potential" to "unsatisfactory" as part of an "individual career forecast." "It was a competitive environment," Suran said.

Not all goals were created equal. GE told its managers that it cared about eight result areas: profitability, market position, productivity, product leadership, the nurturing of personnel, employee attitudes, public responsibility, and the balance between short-range and long-range objectives. But many felt that, in the end, one category was consistently thrust above the other seven. "When the chips are down and their bosses are actually making a determination affecting their compensation," said Donald Webb, a GE manager, "there will be only one measure that counts, and it will be the figure at the bottom of their profit-and-loss statement."

In 1960, GE would face one of the darkest episodes in its long history: the company would plead guilty to colluding with its competitors, including Westinghouse and dozens of other companies, to fix prices through clandestine meetings—the secret roster for which was known as "the Christmas card list" and the gatherings themselves as "choir practice." *Fortune* would call it "The Incredible Electrical Conspiracy." GE was fined $437,500. Fifteen managers from the company were also slapped with financial penalties, and three were sent to jail.

Cordiner fired the employees who'd been convicted and punished others involved, saying that they had exhibited "flagrant disregard" for company policy. He criticized their actions as "a lazy, indolent way to do business." But many were to lay fault for the affair at the feet of the CEO himself, particularly his emphasis that his men must "make their numbers."

Fair or not, there was no doubt that finance as a distinct corporate function had grown in stature under Cordiner. It was the beginning of a bigger trend that was underway at other companies, too, and that would have vast implications for the dynamic between employer and employee decades down the line. At General Motors, for instance, 1958 was a watershed year. Frederic Donner, who had been executive vice president for finance, was picked to replace Harlow Curtice at the top of the company. He kept his office in New York—close to Wall Street; his predecessors had been based in Detroit. They "were auto men, not finance men," *Business Week* noted. Said *Fortune* of Donner: "He has never built an automobile, but he is the companywide expert on cost controls and product pricing."

America's managers carried other burdens, especially as they climbed higher in the corporation. "To me, the job was everything, my whole life," said Arthur Stern, a Hungarian-born survivor of the Bergen-Belsen concentration camp in Germany, who immigrated to the United States in 1951 and shortly thereafter joined GE's electronics laboratory in Syracuse, New York. Three years later, Stern was promoted to be manager of the lab's advanced-circuits group. "I neglected my wife and kids," he said. "I loved my wife and kids—but I hardly ever saw them." Workaholism wasn't unique to GE. In Sloan Wilson's 1955 novel, *The Man in the Gray Flannel Suit*, one of the defining works of the time, the protagonist, Tom Rath, is wary of being sucked into the managerial maw as he considers a new job at a giant broadcasting company. As he tells his wife, Betsy:

> "This sounds like a silly way to put it, but I don't think you can get to be a top administrator without working every weekend for half your life, and I'd just as soon spend my weekends with you and the kids."
>
> "Some good administrators don't work all the time."

"A few—damn few. . . . Why do you think Hopkins is
great? Mainly, it's because he never thinks about anything but his
work. . . . All geniuses are like that—there's no mystery about it.
The great painters, the great composers, the great scientists, and
the great businessmen—they all have the same capacity for total
absorption in their work."

Speaking before the American Management Association in 1956,
Ralph Collins, a consulting psychiatrist for Kodak, ticked off the
headlines of recent articles about executives: "Slow Up or Blow Up,"
"Your Next Promotion May Kill You," "Executive Crackups." "Too
often," Collins said, "the executive finds himself pushed—either by
forces from without or from within—into too much work around the
clock and around the week. He loses his sense of balance, of proportion, between work, hobby, family, recreation, and religion."

Joseph Jones, who served as Robert Woodruff's executive secretary at Coca-Cola, told The Boss that he was constantly "undertaking
to do what you expected and excluding completely family and personal
considerations." Woodruff did not believe, as Jones recounted it, "in
the concept of a 'vacation' as desirable or necessary." And so Jones took
almost none. He had a one-week holiday in 1948 and two weeks in 1956.
But he claimed not so much as a day of vacation in 1946, 1947, 1950,
1951, 1952, 1953, 1955, 1957, and 1959, and he'd take all of three weeks off
from 1960 through 1975. Beyond that, his only vacation was four weeks
in 1949 and three weeks in 1954—and those came on doctor's orders.
Woodruff "did not approve" of the first leave, Jones said, and Jones felt
compelled to cut the second one short; his doctor had recommended
a six-week hiatus. The only other times Jones got away from work was
when he was hospitalized, eight times over a thirty-year stretch. Seven
of those hospital stays were work-related. "After each confinement, especially when surgery was involved, I was told to stay away from work
for a period of two to four weeks," Jones reminded Woodruff. "In each
instance, I returned almost immediately, usually the third or fourth
day, and you were sending me things to do before I left the hospital.
Looking back, I cannot recall a day when I did not have an ache in my
head or in my back or in my legs."

Not all managers worked so hard. Many perched on the middle
rungs earning very nice livings without really knocking themselves

out. "If the organization is good and big," said Whyte, "there will be success without tears." Yet for managers at all levels, there was another price to be paid: a decided loss of individuality. Whyte wrote:

> The younger men are sanguine. They are well aware that organization work demands a measure of conformity—as a matter of fact, half their energies are devoted to finding out the right pattern to conform to. But the younger executive likes to explain that conforming is a kind of phase, a purgatory that he must suffer before he emerges into the area where he can do as he damn well pleases. . . .
>
> Older executives learned better long ago. At a reunion dinner for business-school graduates a vice president of a large steel company brought up the matter of conformity and, eyeing his table companions, asked if they felt as he did: he was, he said, becoming more a conformist. There was almost an explosion of table thumping and head noddings. In the mass confessional that followed everyone present tried to top the others in describing the extent of his conformity.
>
> "A help-wanted ad we ran recently," one executive said, "asked for engineers who would 'conform to our work patterns.' Someone slipped up on that one. He actually came out and said what's really wanted in our organization." And it gets worse rather than better, others agreed, as one goes up the ladder. "The further up you go," as one executive put it, "the less you can afford to stick out in any one place." More and more, the executive must act according to the role that he is cast for—the calm eye that never strays from the other's gaze, the easy, controlled laughter, the whole demeanor that tells onlookers that here certainly is a man without neurosis and inner rumblings.

Kodak hired with this kind of submissiveness in mind. "They actually had a farm system set up with these Midwestern universities—Ohio State and Illinois Tech and so forth—and they'd get their chemists and engineers and some accountants and number-crunchers from there," said Lane Riland, who joined Kodak as an industrial psychologist in 1957. But the company wasn't keen on taking students from more free-thinking institutions, such as Reed College or New York University. "They wanted no boat-rockers," Riland said.

Kodak got what it paid for. During his early years at the company, Riland administered a battery of intelligence and personality tests, including one known as the Edwards Personal Preference Schedule, to about 2,000 Kodakers. He found that the vast majority of managers and professional employees had a very high achievement drive. They were also very orderly—not surprising for scientists and engineers. "They were what would later be called Type As," Riland said. At the same time, they scored exceedingly high in another area: the need to defer to others before making a decision. And their penchant for being independent also ranked below the college average. Riland came up with a phrase to describe these compliant characters populating the company: Midwestern Gothic.

"They were quite willing to take orders," Riland said. "Their autonomy needs weren't that strong to start with. And their primary needs were being filled—their cups runneth over: We had the wage dividend. You got your teeth X-rayed every year, free of charge. There was a swimming pool on the third floor of the recreation center at Kodak Park. Lunch was highly subsidized; every plant had its own cafeteria. Kodak was essentially a monopoly, and these guys were fat and happy. Loyalty was bought and paid for. If you recruit the right people, they're susceptible to that."

GE, which counseled its managers to "never say anything controversial," also used personality testing—one of an estimated 60 percent of big companies that participated in "these curious inquisitions into the psyche," as Whyte called them. Among those sent to have his noggin checked was Arthur Stern. Up to that point, he had been considered an absolute star. He had been involved in the development of GE's first color television, and had spearheaded the design of GE's first transistor radio. In time, Stern was sent to Crotonville to attend the advanced-management course. His prospects seemed unlimited. "I was extremely lucky, and I was treated very well," Stern said.

At one point, however, he committed a sin: in 1956, he turned down a couple of promotions. One was to run a nuclear-related venture in California; Stern thought the business was too risky. The other was to head up a new computer division in Phoenix. But Stern's wife fainted in the desert heat during a visit, and they decided they didn't want to live there. The problem was, no sane Organization Man said no to two big jobs in a row. And so Stern's boss sent him to New York to see the folks at Psychol. Corporation. "They made me fill out a lot of forms—what would you do in this situation?" Stern recalled. When the results came back, Stern's boss called him in. "They say you're not nuts," he told Stern. "You'll stay in the book." And with that, he pulled out a little black notebook. Stern asked him what it was. "This is the list of comers," he replied. True to his word, Stern's boss offered him another promotion in 1957, to manage GE's Electronic Devices and Applications Laboratory. This time, he accepted.

To be a manager in 1950s America was, in many ways, to be something of a robot. All the while, real robots were beginning to make their presence felt as well.

In 1958, America found itself in the midst of its worst economic slump since the Great Depression. There had been other recessions, from 1948 to 1949 and from 1953 to 1954, but they were less severe. The latest downturn, which began in the summer of 1957, turned serious by winter. In January 1958, *Life* magazine visited Peoria, Illinois, and found the mood there to be gloomy. Caterpillar, the heavy equipment maker and the big provider of jobs in town, had already laid off 6,000 workers and cut back to a 4-day week. "Trouble is already here for some people," said one Caterpillar worker. "But it's under the surface for everybody."

In Peoria and across the nation, things got steadily worse. "With relatives and neighbors out of work . . . confidence in the economy's health was still ebbing, and the ebb brought an increasing reluctance to buy and invest," *Time* reported in late February. By July, the national unemployment rate hit 7.5 percent. Some manufacturing industries, including primary metals and transportation equipment, were saddled with jobless rates of 13 or 14 percent. General Electric alone had sent home some 25,000 production workers by the summer of '58; General Motors, 28,000. Studebaker (now Studebaker-Packard) was already in terrible shape when the economy began to contract. The situation then got so bad for the automaker, once proudly led by the CED's Paul Hoffman, that it made a shocking announcement: it would no longer honor its pension obligations for more than 3,000 workers, handing an "I told you so" moment to those who'd been warning about the fragility of retirement promises.

As painful as the recession was, to many it was all part of the natural business cycle: a chance for manufacturers to pare down inventories that had become bloated earlier in the decade, to pull back on investments that had gotten overbuilt, and to adapt to a shrinking export market. The CED called it "one of the long series in the wave-like movement that has been characteristic of our economic growth." Kenneth McFarland, a consultant for General Motors, agreed. "What we have now is normalcy," he said. "The law of supply and demand—the free enterprise system—is working now as it was supposed to work." But some suspected that something else was going on, something structural and not just cyclical. *The Nation* termed it an "Automation Depression."

"We are stumbling blindly into the automation era with no concept or plan to reconcile the need of workers for income and the need of business for cost-cutting and worker-displacing innovations," the magazine said in November 1958. "A part of the current unemployment . . . is due to the automation component of the capital-goods' boom which preceded the recession. The boom gave work while it lasted, but the improved machinery requires fewer man-hours per unit of output." This conundrum, moreover, would outlast present conditions and become even more apparent in an economy that was supposed to accommodate 1 million new job seekers every year. "The problem we shall have to face some time," *The Nation* concluded, "is that the working force is expansive, while latter-day industrial technology is contractive of man-hours."

Questions about what automation would mean for employment were not new. Economists started to explore the issue in the early 1800s, during the Industrial Revolution. Most classical theorists of the time—including J. B. Say, David Ricardo, and John Ramsey McCulloch—held that introducing new machines would, save perhaps for a brief period of adjustment, produce more jobs than they'd destroy. By the end of the century, concern had faded nearly altogether. "Because the general upward trends in investment, production, employment, and living standards were supported by evidence that could not be denied," the economic historian Gregory Woirol has written, "technological change ceased to be seen as a relevant problem."

But fears reappeared in the mid-to-late 1920s, as America experienced two mild recessions and newly published productivity data indicated that machines were perhaps eating more jobs than was first believed. "This country has upon its hands a problem of chronic unemployment, likely to grow worse rather than better," the *Journal of Commerce*, a trade and shipping industry publication, opined in 1928. "Business prosperity, far from curing it, may tend to aggravate it by stimulating invention and encouraging all sorts of industrial rationalization schemes."

The key word was "may." Economists continued to investigate the matter, but reliable statistics were scarce, and no firm conclusion was reached. "The real issue is not whether technological displacement causes workers to lose their jobs," a 1931 Senate report stated. "It undoubtedly does. The real issue is whether over a period of years the continual introduction of new and improved machines and processes is causing a total net increase or decrease in mass employment. . . . On this issue there are two opposing points of view, each held by large numbers of earnest people." By this time, the Depression was in full swing, and many greeted anything that might be keeping people on the unemployment line as an abomination.

"We are being afflicted with a new disease of which some readers may not yet have heard the name, but of which they will hear a great deal in the years to come—namely, *technological unemployment*," John Maynard Keynes wrote in a 1930 essay called "Economic Possibilities for Our Grandchildren." By the midthirties, groups such as the National Organization for the Taxation of Labor-Saving Devices were lobbying to impose a levy on any equipment that was thought to cost jobs. Artist Paul Herzel, who had once worked as a machinist at the American Brake Company in St. Louis, captured the resentment that many were feeling in his 1935 print depicting a throng of men huddled around a construction site, watching a single massive earthmover polish off the whole job. Its title: "The Machine and Unemployment." Still, popular ire aside, numerous studies into the long-run relationship between automation and jobs remained inconclusive. Through the late 1930s, scholarly opinions about technology's net effect on employment were as divergent as ever.

World War II then put the entire debate on hold. But by the 1950s, it was revived again with the stakes seemingly higher than ever, thanks to all the technological advances that had been made by the military and industry during the conflict. Of particular note was ENIAC, or the "electronic numerical integrator and computer." With its 18,000 vacuum tubes and several miles' worth of wiring, it could solve mathematical problems 1,000 times faster than ever before. "Leaders who saw the device in action for the first time heralded it as a tool with which to begin to rebuild scientific affairs on new foundations," the *New York Times* marveled in revealing "one of the war's top secrets" in a front-page story in February 1946. "Such instruments, it was said, could revolutionize industrial engineering, bring on a new epoch of industrial design, and eventually eliminate much slow and costly trial-and-error development work now deemed necessary in the fashioning of intricate machines."

The world was in the throes of what MIT mathematician Norbert Wiener called "the second industrial revolution." And to many, the outlook for employment was suddenly forbidding. "With automatic machines taking over so many jobs," the wife of an unemployed textile worker in Roanoke, Virginia, told a reporter, "it looks like the men may have finally outsmarted themselves." Said *The Nation*: "Automation . . . is a ghost which frightens every worker in every plant, the more so because he sees no immediate chance of exorcising it." Science Service, a nonprofit institution, remarked: "With the advent of the thinking machine, people are beginning to understand how horses felt when Ford invented the Model T." Wiener himself anticipated that "we are in for an industrial revolution of unmitigated cruelty."

Corporate executives largely dismissed these worries, maintaining through the 1950s and '6os that for every worker cast aside by a machine, more jobs were being generated. Sometimes, whole new enterprises sprang to life. "The automatic-control industry is young and incredibly vigorous," John Diebold, dubbed "the prophet of information technology," told business leaders in 1954. Mostly, the argument went, job gains were being realized at the very same companies where new technology was being deployed, as huge increases in output led to the need for more workers overall—office personnel, engineers, maintenance staff, factory hands—to keep up with rising consumer demand. General Motors, for example, added more than 287,000 people to its payroll between 1940 and the mid-1950s. "There is widespread fear that technological progress . . . is a Grim Reaper of jobs," GM vice president Louis Seaton told lawmakers. "Our experience and record completely refutes this view." Those at Kodak made a similar case. "As far as I know, we have not yet laid off anyone who has been with the company five years or more because of improvements made in manufacturing processes," said Ivar Hultman, who oversaw Kodak Park. "Increased productivity has enabled our business to grow, and the growth of the business has allowed us to give more jobs to more people in the community."

No company, however, pressed this point harder than did GE, which was at the fore of automating both its factories and offices: in 1952, it installed an IBM 701 to make engineering calculations at its Evendale, Ohio, jet engine operation. And in 1954 GE became the first company to use an electronic computer for regular data processing, when it bought a UNIVAC I to handle accounting, manufacturing control, and planning at its appliance division in Louisville, Kentucky. "Machines that can read, write, do arithmetic, measure, feel, remember, now make it possible to take the load off men's minds, just as machines have eased the burden on our backs," GE said in one ad. "But these fantastic machines still depend on people to design and build and guide and use them. What they replace is drudgery—not people."

By the late 1950s, GE was offering another justification for its rush to automate: its overseas rivals, having pulled themselves out of the rubble of World War II, were on the rise. Global competition was another trend that wouldn't become wholly ingrained in the national consciousness for another fifteen or twenty years. For now, even most of organized labor discounted the danger of imports, backing free trade as a way to shore up United States access to raw materials from the developing world, advance American exports, and ward off communism across the globe. "The mistaken peddlers of protectionism are selling a poison pill, coated with the saccharin of patriotism," said Guy Nunn, a United Auto Workers official.

Still, the first glimmers of what a resurgent Asia and Europe might mean for American business were starting to emerge. "We have strong competition from highly automated foreign plants paying wages that are only a fraction of ours," said Charlie Scheer, the manager of GE's lamp-equipment unit. "It's a case here of automate or die on the competitive vine." To illustrate the peril, GE showed a film called *Toshiba* to its factory workers in New Jersey, highlighting the Japanese company's inroads into the lamp market. The move backfired, however, when the International Union of Electrical Workers discovered that GE had been investing in Toshiba since 1953, amassing a nearly 6 percent stake in the company. "The purpose of this film is obviously to brainwash you into believing that low-wage competition . . . is a threat to your job security," the IUE told employees. "What GE failed to tell you is that it likes to play both sides of the street at the same time." The union labeled GE's warnings "phony propaganda."

GE wouldn't back down, however. "Automation is urgently needed," Ralph Cordiner soon testified to Congress, "to help individual companies, and the nation as a whole, try to be able to meet the new competition from abroad." More generally, he added, the claim that automation strangled job growth was patently false. "The installation of labor-saving machinery may—and should—reduce the number of persons required to produce a given amount of goods and services," Cordiner said, "but this increase in efficiency is precisely what creates both the attractive values and additional ability to support expanded output, new industries, and new services for an ever more diverse economy." In the broadest sense, he was right. A study by University of Chicago economist Yale Brozen would find that while 13 million jobs had been destroyed during the 1950s, the adoption of new technology was among the ingredients that led to the creation of more than 20 million other positions. "Instead of being alarmed about growing automation, we ought to be cheering it on," he wrote. "The catastrophe that doom criers constantly threaten us with has retreated into such a dim future that we simply cannot take their pronouncements seriously."

But Brozen was too blithe. While automation may have added jobs in the aggregate, certain sectors were hit hard, playing havoc with untold numbers of individual lives. Technological upheaval caused both steelmakers and rail companies, for instance, to suffer drops in employment in the late 1950s. "In converting to more automated processes, many industries found it less costly to build a new plant in another area rather than converting their older factories, thus leaving whole communities of employees stranded," the Labor Department said in one study of the period. In the mid-1960s, the federal Commission on Technology, Automation, and Economic Progress would recognize technological change as "a major factor in the displacement and temporary unemployment of particular workers." The panel pointed out that "employment has been rising most rapidly in those occupations generally considered to be the most skilled and to require the most education," possibly leaving those without adequate training "no future opportunities" for work.

Labor leaders like Walter Reuther and James Carey, cognizant that they couldn't afford to be seen as Luddites, went out of their way to praise the manifold benefits brought by machines. "You can't stop technological progress, and it would be silly to try it if you could," Reuther said. The UAW had already conceded the point in 1950 when, as part of the Treaty of Detroit, it had formally agreed to take a "co-operative attitude" regarding the forward march of technology. Carey likewise said that automation, along with atomic energy, "can do more than anything in mankind's long history to end poverty, to abolish hunger and deprivation. More than any other creation of man's hand and brain, this combination can create a near-paradise on earth, a world of plenty and equal opportunity, a world in which the pursuit of happiness has become reality rather than a hope and a dream."

Then, in their very next breaths, both Reuther and Carey would condemn business for not doing enough to temper automation's ill effects. "More and more," said Reuther, "we are witnessing the often frightening results of the widespread introduction of increasingly efficient methods of production without the leavening influence of moral or social responsibility." With industry having failed, according to Reuther and Carey, it was up to Washington to become much more active in assisting workers idled by machines. They called, among other things, for federal officials to develop more effective retraining programs and relocation services for displaced workers, beef up unemployment insurance and establish early retirement funds, and create an information clearinghouse on technological change to help steer national policy.

For all of the union men's denunciation of corporate America, many companies did try to help workers whose jobs were taken out by technology. The integrity of the social contract demanded as much. Kodak, for instance, left millions of dollars on the table in the late 1950s by holding off on installing more efficient film emulsion–coating machines; by waiting five or so years to make the complete upgrade, the most senior workers who would have been forced out were allowed to reach retirement age. "In this case," Kodak reported, "substantial dollar savings were delayed in order to cushion the effect of mechanization on some of the company's most skilled, experienced, and loyal technicians." Other corporations focused on improving their workers' skills. Some 30,000 General Motors employees were enrolled in various training programs in the late fifties, for example. At General Electric, veteran workers laid off because of automation were guaranteed during a retraining period at least 95 percent of their pay for as many weeks as they had years of service. "This was an effort to stabilize income while the employee prepared for the next job," said GE's Earl Willis. "Maximizing employment security is a prime company goal."

Still, given the pace of change, it didn't take a lot to imagine a day when it wouldn't really matter what companies did to soften the blow of automation. This would become all the more so in the aftermath of the greatest invention of 1958 (and one of the most significant of all time): the computer chip. Then again, having a vivid imagination didn't hurt, either. Kurt Vonnegut tapped his to write his first novel, *Player Piano*, published in 1952. In it, he renders a future society that is run by machines; there is no more need for human labor. Early on in the book, the main character, an engineer named Paul Proteus, is chatting with his secretary, Katharine:

> "Do you suppose there'll be a Third Industrial Revolution?"
>
> Paul paused in his office doorway. "A third one? What would that be like?"
>
> "I don't know exactly. The first and second ones must have been sort of inconceivable at one time."
>
> "To the people who were going to be replaced by machines, maybe. A third one, eh? In a way, I guess the third one's been going on for some time, if you mean thinking machines. That would be the third revolution, I guess—machines that devaluate human thinking. Some of the big companies like EPICAC do that all right, in specialized fields."
>
> "Uh-huh," said Katharine thoughtfully. She rattled a pencil between her teeth. "First the muscle work, then the routine work, then, maybe, the real brainwork."
>
> "I hope I'm not around long enough to see that final step."

Vonnegut, who worked at GE in public relations from 1947 through 1950, had found his muse in building 49 at the company's Schenectady

Works. There one day he saw a milling machine for cutting the rotors on jet engines. Usually, this was a task performed by a master machinist. But now, a computer-guided contraption was doing the work. The men at the plant "were foreseeing all sorts of machines being run by little boxes and punched cards," Vonnegut said later. "The idea of doing that, you know, made sense, perfect sense. To have a little clicking box make all the decisions wasn't a vicious thing to do. But it was too bad for the human beings who got their dignity from their jobs."

In May 1958, the president of the US Chamber of Commerce, William McDonnell, left no doubt as to the cause of the nation's economic woes: the never-ending demand by unions for higher pay. "The surest way to cure a recession," he told a sympathetic business group in Connecticut, "is to get prices down, and you cannot get prices down by raising wages." McDonnell asked management and labor "to work toward halting the wage-price spiral, which has been discouraging consumer buying" and was now poised to "break the country and destroy the free-enterprise system."

A month later, Jim Carey of the Electrical Workers stood before a lectern at Washington's Statler Hotel, addressing his own version of the faithful: an audience of union supporters attending a special IUE Employment Security Conference. There has been "a desperate and despicable attempt to shift the blame for this recession to labor," Carey said, citing McDonnell's speech, as well as recent finger pointing along the same lines by other corporate spokesmen, including General Electric's Lem Boulware. "These profit-obsessed tycoons have not admitted and cannot admit any responsibility—even the tiniest responsibility—for the current recession. . . . Is labor to blame for consumer goods having been priced out of the market? Is labor to blame for industrial overproduction?"

Aspersions aside, Carey was on to something: the industrial peace embodied by the Treaty of Detroit was starting to break apart, and this was very much as corporate America wanted it. In its dealings with organized labor, business had assumed (as many would soon call it) a new "hard line." "Union leaders see management as pressing the labor-saving results of automation to the hilt, over and above management's need to economize on labor costs," said Jack Barbash, an economist at the University of Wisconsin. "They point out that management's demands for work rule changes, notably in steel and railroads, are indeed quite radical and strike hard at the heart of the unions' primary function—protection of their members." What's more, "they point to high-powered public-relations campaigns, which hammer away at wage inflation, 'featherbedding,' and the pressures of foreign competition, as evidence of a freezing of management positions prior to negotiations."

In some ways, unions had weakened themselves. Even Joe Scanlon, the old Steelworkers official who had done so much to improve relations between employers and employees, worried that as labor had become an increasing part of the institutional establishment in America, its core values of fighting for the little guy had somehow been compromised. "Is there a chance to reestablish some of those basic ideals that were involved in the beginnings of this great union of ours?" Scanlon asked an old Steelworkers colleague. "I'm afraid we have lost our way." Others would share these misgivings. "A labor movement can get soft and flabby spiritually," said Walter Reuther. "It can make progress materially, and the soul of the union can die in the process."

In 1957, a Senate Select Committee, led by Arkansas Democrat John McClellan, began to investigate labor racketeering. For more than two years, the panel aggressively publicized all manner of union corruption, particularly among the Teamsters. Although it was unfair to assume that most labor officials behaved this way, in the public's mind unions "came to be synonymous with arrogance and bossism, hand-tailored silk suits, mansions, costly automobiles, violent suppression of workers' rights, and theft of members' money and pensions," James Gross has observed. These stories of graft also helped harden a general perception that, even though the Taft-Hartley Act had to some degree restored the appropriate balance between management and labor, unions still held too much sway. Even the Committee for Economic Development by 1958 was questioning whether unions "have a degree of economic power which is not in the public interest"—a charge that sounded more like it came from the National Association of Manufacturers than the customarily moderate and measured CED.

The NAM, however, wasn't going to be upstaged in terms of vilifying organized labor. "Unions now occupy a dominant position in the economic life of the United States and are reaching out for political dominance as well," said Leo Wolman, chairman of the NAM's so-called Study Group on Monopoly Power Exercised by Labor Unions. "It is the duty, therefore, of every citizen to review—without malice, without prejudice, but with an objective eye—the present status of organized labor and the power exercised by union leadership, and to reflect where this growing accumulation of power will take us if it continues on its present course." Although he was now flying the flag for the NAM, Wolman was not your usual corporate shill. An economics professor at Columbia University, Wolman's path was similar to that of Gerard Reilly, the old New Dealer whose politics moved steadily rightward and who, as a main architect of Taft-Hartley, eventually became a leading force behind limiting the reach of unions. Wolman had spent the 1920s as research director for the Amalgamated Clothing Workers, and in 1933 President Roosevelt named him to the National Labor Board. There he served alongside John L. Lewis of the United Mine Workers; William Green of the AFL; Gerard Swope, GE's liberal corporate chief; and Sen. Robert Wagner, author of the milestone legislation giving workers the right to organize and bargain collectively. Now, some twenty-five years later, Wolman had surrounded himself with souls of a very different sort.

Lem Boulware, who was GE's representative to the twelve-member NAM study group, was as hard-nosed as anybody in arguing that it was time to rein in organized labor. "Union officials . . . long ago erased any inequities in bargaining power between employees and employers," Boulware told a conference of electric industry executives in the spring of 1958. "What's important now is what they've done and are doing to take advantage of their constantly mounting power. I believe it is clear that this unregulated power to persuade and to force is being used and abused in many ways contrary to the interests of those they represent and those others in the whole public they profess to help." Boulware then bashed "the Reuthers . . . and Careys" for a host of alleged sins: fueling inflation though escalator clauses in contracts, favoring wasteful make-work rules over technological changes that would increase productivity, and agitating for "big central government." Nothing, though, got under Boulware's skin more than "compulsory unionism"—the condition under which every worker at a particular place of employment had to become part of a union whether he wanted to or not. "Union insistence on the right to force unwilling

employees to join and support them," Boulware said, is "the most obvious example of the abandonment of concern with individual rights."

With its provision allowing states to adopt right-to-work statutes,
under which no employee could be forced to join or pay initiation fees
or dues to a labor organization, Taft-Hartley had provided a potent
weapon to fight compulsory unionism. More than ever, Boulware and
other businessmen were resolved to use it. Eighteen states—nearly all
of them in the South and West—had passed right-to-work laws by
1958. Six other states were now considering doing the same, and GE
put itself in the thick of the fight, speaking out in California, Ohio,
Washington, and elsewhere. "In this controversy," Ralph Cordiner
told the Dallas Citizens' Council, "the businessman is no disinter-
ested bystander. . . . When an employer says to a workman, 'You can't
work here unless you join this union,' he has asked the workman to
give up one of those fundamental rights which guard American free-
doms." Cordiner's comments may have seemed a little highfalutin, but
they were entirely consistent with the way GE talked about the issue.
"Compulsory unionism is morally wrong," Clarence Walker, a GE vice
president, proclaimed. At Crotonville, Boulware came upon a framed
quotation from Thomas Jefferson: "I have sworn upon the altar of god
eternal hostility against every form of tyranny over the mind of man."
"This," Boulware told his staff, "should fit right into right-to-work arguments and other discussions of compulsion."

The unions had their own case to make, pointing out that right-
to-work states had notoriously lousy records on child-labor standards,
unemployment insurance, workmen's compensation, and the minimum
wage. "Right-to-work laws are designed to exploit workers, to make it
possible to keep workers at the lowest point on the economic scale, to
prevent them from improving their way of life," said the AFL-CIO's
American Federationist. The Electrical Workers said the laws that GE
and other right-to-work advocates were trying to get passed promised
a "return to the sweatshop days." Labor leaders also contended that
their position was a matter of fairness: if workers were benefiting from
a union's activities, it was only just that they join or at least pay dues,
lest they become "free riders."

Throughout 1958, labor groups and right-wing organizations such
as the National Right to Work Committee traded shots and sank
loads of money into mailers and advertising, coalition building, and

grassroots organizing. By one count, the unions outspent their adversaries five to one: $10 million versus $2 million. In Ohio—perhaps the most fiercely contested of the six states considering a "right-to-work" law—"the campaign was bitter and vindictive with charges and countercharges the order of the day," according to one analysis of the scene. "Both opponents and proponents of the amendment frequently resorted to highly emotional appeals; dispassionate, factual presentations were exceptional." At the end of it all, labor claimed victory in five states; only Kansas passed a right-to-work measure.

"Our grandchildren may well read in their history books something of this nature: 'The national forces which sought to destroy trade unions in the mid-twentieth century ultimately met their downfall in Ohio,'" the public relations agency that had helped the unions hone their communications strategy said after all the votes were in. But that kind of gloating was not only premature; it missed the cracks slowly forming beneath the surface. If anyone could discern them, it was Boulware. "Some observers seem to be trying to convince the public and its representatives that the right-to-work movement suffered a devastating defeat in the recent election," he said. "My own feeling is that just the opposite is true since another state voted for a right-to-work law, and in the five other states the old ratio of something like 4-to-1 [against] came down to something less than the order of 2 to 1. This seems to me to be remarkable progress in so unequal a contest where the opponents of right-to-work laws have had a clear field for several decades and where the rapidly rising number of citizens who favor right-to-work laws have only begun to learn to present their story in the face of deep-seated misunderstanding and emotion."

Besides, companies such as GE weren't simply waiting for more right-to-work states to come to them; they were increasingly putting their factories where, as GE phrased it, "the general attitude of the community toward the business" was favorable. By the mid-1950s, GE had located eleven plants in the South and others in the West, and work began moving away from the company's traditional—and heavily unionized—northeastern base. The allure was understandable. During a 1950 train tour of the South arranged by Coca-Cola's Bob Woodruff, himself a General Electric director, GE's board admired the blossoming dogwood, feasted on barbecue, and soaked in the raw economic advantages the South had to offer. Among them, Georgia governor

Herman Talmadge told the GE contingent, was "free enterprise," a thinly veiled reference to the region's positive attitude toward right-to-work laws and the local business community's success (aided by the bald racist attacks of segregationists) in thwarting unionization drives by both the American Federation of Labor and the Congress of Industrial Organizations after World War II. "We hope to continue as a section where capital ventured will be assured a fair return as a profit," the governor said. It was hard to argue with the numbers. In the mid-1950s, a GE carpenter in Newark, New Jersey, made $2.06 an hour; his counterpart in Memphis, Tennessee, made $1.72. An electrician in Schenectady took home $2.14 an hour; his peer in Bloomington, Indiana (which became a right-to-work state in 1957), made $1.78. A crane operator in Pittsfield, Massachusetts, earned $1.86 an hour; in Rome, Georgia, somebody doing the same job pulled in $1.45.

For old-line companies transferring work to low-wage, nonunion states—and this would come to include those in the auto, steel, chemical, paper, tire, and food industries—there was no mad rush to the Sunbelt; it was more of a slow leak. In 1955, GE still had more than 80 percent of its plants and 90 percent of its employees clustered north of the Ohio River and east of the Mississippi. By the late 1950s, GE had created 100,000 new jobs in the Northeast compared with the number of positions that had been there twenty years before. "At a time when charges of 'runaway industry' are loosely made," Cordiner said, "General Electric's department managers have been trying to make their capital investments with a genuine respect for the social and moral factors that bear on these economic decisions. With such investments in the older locations, the company is doing its best to keep them competitive with other communities."

Despite these soothing words, however, the company's long-term intentions were also plain. At a meeting of GE planners in 1954, the company acknowledged that it had only just begun to spread its operations across the country, threatening tens of thousands of jobs in its oldest and most expensive locations—Schenectady, Syracuse, Pittsfield, and four other towns. "As far as decentralization of people," Arthur Vinson, GE's vice president in charge of manufacturing, said, "we have merely scratched the surface." When the Electrical Workers got hold of notes from the meeting, the union protested loudly. "GE is planning a depression" in seven plant cities, the IUE alleged.

GE strenuously denied the charge and even announced big new investments in its old facilities to prove it. But the union wasn't wrong in its dire warnings; it was merely early. In the coming decades, the manufacturing centers of the Northeast would hemorrhage jobs, as ever-stiffer global competition prompted companies like GE to look for lower-cost alternatives, whether they were in the American South or overseas. "The situation is getting worse rather than better," Boulware said a couple of years after the "planning a depression" brouhaha, "with the inevitable result that more and more of the other operations must be taken out of such a high-cost atmosphere."

If you lived in the United States in 1958, you would have had to be unusually farseeing to sense that the labor movement was endangered. Nearly 34 percent of private-sector workers in the United States belonged to a union that year—just a shade under the all-time high. The political landscape also looked promising for labor interests in '58, with Democrats enjoying a landslide in the midterm congressional elections. But even with this, management's "hard line" was no fleeting fad. Though largely imperceptible, a slow but steady dismantling of unions in America was underway. Historian Mike Davis would call the period about to transpire "the management offensive" of 1958–1963. Losers abounded. The United Auto Workers came away in 1958 with its weakest set of contract wins in the postwar period. Protracted strikes against the nation's steelmakers in 1959 and at General Electric in 1960 would yield no real gains for the unions. In 1960, labor won less than 60 percent of representation elections compared with about 75 percent in 1950. On the shop floor, companies were winning more grievance cases and muscling through higher production standards. "There has been a noticeable shift in the balance of power in labor-management relations," George Strauss, a professor of industrial relations at the University of Buffalo, would write in 1962. "Unions are getting weaker and management is growing stronger."

As the recession of 1958 deepened, the Eisenhower administration undertook a series of actions to stimulate the economy: it quickened the rate of procurement by the Defense Department, stepped up the pace of urban-renewal projects on the books, cut loose hundreds of millions of dollars of funds for the Army Corps of Engineers to build roads and other infrastructure, and ordered Fannie Mae to add extra grease to the housing market. The Federal Reserve did its part, too, cutting interest rates four times from November 1957 to April 1958. Some wanted the government to do even more; the Committee for Economic Development, for instance, called for a temporary 20 percent cut in personal income taxes. But President Eisenhower was reluctant to go that far. Instead, he publicly endorsed efforts by business to jumpstart things on its own. "What we need now," the president quoted a Cadillac dealer in Cleveland as saying, "is more and better salesmanship and more and better advertising of our goods."

Many apparently agreed. In Grosse Ile, Michigan, a supermarket owner offered any customer who spent five bucks or more in his store a chance to win a sack of 500 silver dollars. In Hampton, Iowa, seven firms gave their employees surprise bonuses on the condition that they spend the money on nonessential items. Some sought to shake up consumer psychology. A Cleveland realtor hoped to revitalize home sales by accentuating the positive on new signage: "Thanks to you our business is terrific." In Kankakee, Illinois, local businessmen tried to turn residents from economic pessimists to optimists by staging a mock hanging of "Mr. Gloom." The epitaph on his tombstone read: "Here Lies Mr. Gloom Killed By the Boom."

No company, though, did more to try to change the national mindset than General Electric. "A swift and sure recovery cannot be attained by sitting back and relying on government stimulants, deficit spending, meaningless tax cuts, deliberate inflation, or any other economic sleight of hand," Ralph Cordiner told GE shareholders at the company's annual meeting in April 1958. "The solutions to the present difficulties will be found in a common effort by all citizens to work more purposefully, buy and sell more confidently, and build up a higher level of solid, useful economic activity. There is a tremendous business base on which to build." GE called its slay-the-recession initiative Operation Upturn, and the idea was to get every company in America to focus harder than ever on providing its customers with just what they were looking for. "I am not speaking only of sales campaigns or promotional stunts, although they will be important ingredients in the whole picture," Cordiner said. "Nor do I mean a transparent attempt to persuade people to buy things they don't want simply because it is supposed to be the 'patriotic' thing to do so. I am proposing a total effort, by every man and woman who has a job, to concentrate on giving customers the best service and the best reasons to buy they ever had.

"King Consumer needs some constructive attention," Cordiner continued. "He is willing to do his part, if he is convinced that this is the best time to buy. Let's convince him by showing him the best values and giving him the best service he could ask for. This may seem like an old-fashioned prescription to those who are shouting for massive government make-work programs and meaningless tax cuts, but—speaking for myself and the executive officers of the company—we in General Electric are convinced that what happens to the economy in the remainder of the year will be largely determined by what business does to help its customers and itself. This is a do-it-yourself country."

At GE, Cordiner worked to turn the pep talk into policy. He called upon his managers to "eliminate every element of waste that adds to the cost of producing and marketing goods . . . so that the company's customers can be offered the best values possible." The company held down prices and extended new terms of credit in order to help consumers who'd been laid off from their jobs. And GE's marketers kicked into overdrive. "They are reviving the old-fashioned shoe-leather selling that creates business where it does not now exist," Cordiner said. "They are pointing out extra value and features in our products. They are selling hard."

GE also maintained its level of research spending, according to Cordiner, "so that the new products, new industries, and new jobs of the 1960s will not be delayed." It continued to put tens of millions of dollars into recruiting and training scientists and engineers. "This national and company asset must not be allowed to wither during a temporary drought in business," Cordiner said. The company pushed ahead as well with $135 million in capital investments—new machinery and upgrades to plants—in 1958. What's more, said Cordiner, GE was attempting to plan carefully so as to keep production as steady as possible and minimize unemployment.

It's impossible to know just how big a difference was made by GE's Operation Upturn and the other efforts by business to resuscitate the economy, but this much is undeniable: the recession of 1957–1958 didn't last long. The decline was sharper than the recessions of 1948–1949 and 1953–1954, but so was the rebound. The downturn was officially over in just eight months, compared with ten months and eleven months for the other two postwar contractions. The stock market also soared in 1958—proof, said *Time* magazine, that "the US was blessed with a new kind of economy, different from any ever seen on the face of the earth." It was one that "could take a hard knock and come bouncing quickly back," where businessmen could face the "inevitable williwaws of economic life but continue to plan and expand for the long term," while workers found "overall employment more stable." Recession or not, this was still the Golden Age in America, a time where many people could count on finding comfort and safety inside their corporate cocoon. "An enlightened corporation has provided . . . for us in the best way management knows how—by creating a private welfare state," Alan Harrington wrote in *Life in the Crystal Palace*, his late fifties account of being a PR man at a large enterprise.

One could excuse Harrington—or almost anyone, really—for not sensing the stresses that were starting to destabilize America's private welfare state: the historic transition from manufacturing to knowledge work and services; the growing importance of finance; the exponential impact of technology and automation; rising competition from foreign companies; business leaders' increasing revulsion toward organized labor; the shipping of jobs to the South and other low-wage locations. In 1958, it was easy to see when the business cycle turned positive, to cheer about it, and to feel untouchable. "There arrives a day when the corporate sanctuary becomes our whole world," Harrington wrote. "We can't imagine existing outside of it." The larger structural changes that threatened to undermine the social contract between employer and employee would remain mostly in the shadows, hidden from view, for at least a decade more. The Golden Age had stumbled, but it would march on.

PART II
TURBULENT TIMES

The 1964 Rochester riots, which erupted just a few weeks after President Johnson signed the Civil Rights Act, led to a fierce battle for more jobs for African Americans at the biggest employer in town: Kodak.

6

WHITE MALE WANTED

The party that became a riot couldn't have seemed more innocent at the start. A street dance, organized by a Rochester community group called the Northeast Mothers Improvement Association, had been properly permitted. Money collected from the sale of barbecue sandwiches, hot dogs, and punch would go toward buying equipment for a neighborhood playground. Chaperones were present. Police were on hand, too, to help with the crowd and traffic control—but clearly they expected a tame affair; only two cops had been assigned to the Friday night event. By 8:30 p.m., when the dance began, about 200 people from the black part of town had assembled on Nassau Street between Joseph Avenue and Joiner. As night fell on July 24, 1964, the temperature was just shy of eighty degrees, the air was thick with humidity, and a light drizzle came down. But who could pass up the music? Sam Cooke had recently scored a hit with "Good Times" and the Drifters with "Under the Boardwalk." The Dixie Cups crooned "Chapel of Love," Stevie Wonder picked up the beat with "Hey Harmonica Man," and the Temptations got into the groove with "I'll Be in Trouble." The real trouble, though, started about eleven o'clock.

That's when one of the partygoers told a chaperone, "Some boy over there is causing a fuss." The chaperone tried in vain to quiet down the young man, Randy Manigault, and then asked the police to step in. They did. Manigault didn't succumb easily, however. "We walked up to this guy," said Anthony Cerretto, one of the police officers, "and we didn't even get a chance to ask him to leave. He started yelling and resisting and swinging. The next thing, we were all on the ground." The cops finally handcuffed Manigault. But then something snapped. "This crowd that was dancing and enjoying itself turned on us," Cerretto said. "They yelled for us to take off the cuffs and let the guy go." The police radioed for backup, and with the help of a K-9 unit, they eventually hustled Manigault into a paddy wagon, arresting him for public intoxication. That didn't bring much calm, however. If anything, the use of dogs—reminiscent of the way Birmingham public-safety commissioner Eugene "Bull" Connor tried to restrain black protestors in Alabama the year before—only ratcheted up the tension. Rochester's Seventh Ward was poised to explode.

As midnight approached, word raced through the throng, which now numbered about 500: purportedly, a police dog had bitten a little girl, and a cop had slapped a pregnant woman. The rumors were never substantiated, but it didn't matter. Rocks, bottles, and bricks rained down. A mob overturned the police chief's car and set it ablaze. Gangs of white men, some of them armed, rushed into the area, spoiling for a fight. By the early morning hours of July 25, the authorities tried to break up the crowd with tear gas grenades and high-pressure fire hoses. More than fifty people were hauled off to jail. The city manager invoked a state of emergency, and more than 1,500 National Guardsmen were called in to restore order. Yet the violence became more severe and spread before it finally subsided on the evening of Sunday, July 26. In the end, five people were killed: an elderly white man who was hit over the head with a lead pipe and then struck by a car and four others who perished when a surveillance helicopter crashed into a black home. Some 350 were injured, and 250 stores were looted or damaged. In all, 893 people were arrested—720 of them black.

America—which in the coming months, and into the next few years, would witness similar episodes in Philadelphia; the Watts section of Los Angeles; Detroit; Newark, New Jersey; Washington, DC; and elsewhere—had just experienced one of its first race riots of the 1960s. Rochester itself was in shock. "We're so good to our Negroes," said one white citizen. Mayor Frank Lamb said it was "unbelievable that such a thing could happen" in the city. But these views were not only self-serving; they were delusional.

Home to social reformer Frederick Douglass in the mid-1800s, Rochester became a magnet for African Americans in the twentieth century, one of many northern industrial cities that blacks flocked to during their six-decade-long Great Migration from the rural South. From 1950 to 1960, Rochester's total population had declined slightly, from about 332,000 to 319,000. But its black population had risen appreciably over the same period, tripling to nearly 24,000. Those who'd come to Smugtown were hungry for a better life. What they encountered upon their arrival, however, was mainly disappointment. Mirroring trends found across the country, many blacks in Rochester were forced to live in substandard housing as whites fled the urban core. The city's power structure remained almost exclusively white. And many blacks struggled to find decent jobs. Even though the unemployment rate in Rochester had fallen to about 2 percent in the summer of 1964, 14 percent of blacks were counted as without work. "The big Kodak dollar and the lawn sprinklers of the suburbs have seemed both tantalizingly near and hopelessly far to the inner-city man," said an African American barber.

It's not that no advances had been made over the years. Between 1940 and the mid-1950s, per capita income among blacks in the United States had tripled. By 1960, more than 16 percent of African Americans nationally held white-collar jobs, up from less than 10 percent in 1950. Hundreds of corporations signed on as members of Plans for Progress, the private-sector outgrowth of President Kennedy's Committee on Equal Employment Opportunity, and by 1963 these enterprises were hiring nearly ten times the number of blacks that they had at the start of the decade.

But such gains were trivial in the scheme of things. Overall, the Golden Age had left—and was continuing to leave—most black men and women far behind. "The affluence of America, the tremendous economic strides which the society has made in the last fifteen or twenty years have outstripped the strides which Negroes have made," Kenneth B. Clark, the distinguished educator and social psychologist, asserted. By some measures, blacks' financial position had actually worsened since the late fifties. "Negroes have not recovered from the

1958 recession," said a 1964 study on equal opportunity. "First fired and last rehired is still, therefore, an unhappy but apt description of the Negro worker's situation." Only about 2 percent of black men in 1960 were managers—the most secure jobs—compared with nearly 12 percent of whites. Through the midsixties, newspapers ran ads that left no doubt about who stood where in the main of the American economy: "White Male Wanted." If you were a person of color trying to escape such transparent racism, breaking out on your own wasn't much of an option, either. Whites owned more than 97 percent of small businesses in the United States in the 1960s.

Often, there was a disconnect between a company's supposed aims and its day-to-day practices. General Motors, for example, had an unambiguous antidiscrimination policy on the books by the 1960s. But African Americans were routinely consigned to the worst jobs— working in the foundries and as janitors—just as they had been since at least the 1940s, when large numbers of blacks began to enter the auto industry. "The fact that General Motors has expressed its anti-discrimination policy in writing," the Michigan Civil Rights Commission found, "seems to have had little bearing . . . on the extent to which Negroes have been employed or promoted." In the South, where GM was expanding (just like General Electric), the deep roots of racism exercised an especially strong influence on corporate behavior. "We agreed to abide by local custom and not hire Negroes for production work," a GM factory manager in Atlanta acknowledged in the late fifties. "This is no time for social reforming . . . and we're not about to try it." John DeLorean said that when he was a top GM executive in the 1960s, "the corporation was still complaining that there were no hireable blacks," and so he pressed the company to recruit African Americans to study at the General Motors Institute. In the forty-year history of the training academy, not one black had ever been admitted. "GM management went right through the roof," DeLorean recounted. "I was told I was going to destroy the school's standards."

Most of the discrimination at GM, while pernicious, was hidden: individual managers turned blacks away at the plant gate. Some, though, was overt and particularly vile. The few blacks who were eventually enrolled at the General Motors Institute, for instance, were confronted by a student group—sponsored by a faculty member—calling itself the Stoner's Society for the Preservation of White Supremacy.

It handed out what it called a "nigger application for employment," which asked people to name their "motha" and "fatha" if known, the number of children they had on welfare, and other such repugnant questions.

In May 1964, a couple of months before the riot in Rochester, the National Association for the Advancement of Colored People organized protests against GM in forty-two cities, culminating in a mass rally outside GM's Detroit headquarters. "Jim Crow must go! GM Crow must go!" demonstrators shouted. Said Herbert Hill, the NAACP's labor secretary: "We will show GM that while it is a powerful corporation, it is not more powerful than the people. We will show them that it is not a sovereign unto itself." As the company came under fire, executives fell back on their usual line, saying that they had all the right rules in place. After the NAACP contested hiring patterns at a Cadillac dealership in San Francisco, for example, GM issued a statement citing the company's "nondiscriminatory employment policy." But the numbers were the numbers: of the 258 people working at the dealer in 1964, only 9 were black—and all of them cleaned the building or waxed or lubricated the cars. None was a mechanic, salesman, or manager.

The United Auto Workers suffered from its own disparity between rhetoric and reality when it came to race. UAW president Walter Reuther had long championed tolerance and equality, and in August 1963 he stood at the Lincoln Memorial and addressed the March on Washington for Jobs and Freedom. Although Reuther's eloquence that day was easily overshadowed by Dr. Martin Luther King Jr.'s "I Have a Dream" speech, his central message—framed in the context of Cold War politics—was quite compelling. "We can make our own freedom secure only as we make freedom universal so that all may share its blessings," Reuther said. "We cannot successfully preach democracy in the world unless we first practice democracy at home. American democracy will lack the moral credentials and be both unequal to and unworthy of leading the forces of freedom against the forces of tyranny unless we take bold, affirmative, adequate steps to bridge the moral gap between America's noble promises and its ugly practices in the field of civil rights."

The same might well have been said of the UAW itself. The union had set up a fair employment practices department in 1944, but it had been slow to appoint blacks to senior positions, and decades later it still didn't have an effective way to deter prejudice at the local level. "Union representatives show no interest in civil rights violations in the plant," nine black workers at a GM factory in Flint, Michigan, told state investigators. They "are either reluctant to write grievances" or they "compromise with management in cases of racial discrimination." In Detroit, UAW officials systematically kept blacks from entering apprenticeship programs where they might learn to compete for the best factory jobs, such as tool-and-die making. Such attitudes spoke not only to the pervasiveness of racism in America but to a growing fear by white workers that African Americans were a threat to their economic security. "The whites who dominated the auto union's Skilled Trades Department used delay, obfuscation, and harassment of black applicants to defy UAW leaders' frequent—but punchless—calls for reform," the labor historian Robert Zieger has written.

At General Motors, the combination of intolerance from huge segments of the corporation and the union made it all but impossible for black workers to get ahead: out of more than 11,000 skilled positions at GM in the early sixties, African Americans held fewer than 100 of them. James Roche, who became GM's chairman and chief executive in 1967, was personally invested in bringing more blacks into both blue- and white-collar positions. He also recruited the Rev. Leon Sullivan onto the GM board, making him one of the first African American directors at a major corporation. Nonetheless, when federal regulators cracked down on GM (along with the UAW) in 1973 for perpetrating job discrimination "on a national scale," the automaker still faced 1,800 individual complaints.

Circumstances at General Electric—which would find itself charged in the same proceedings, along with the International Union of Electrical Workers—were similar in many respects to those at GM. The liberal-minded Gerard Swope had set forth an antidiscrimination policy at GE as early as 1935, and "Electric Charlie" Wilson had chaired President Truman's Committee on Civil Rights in the late 1940s. In 1961, under Ralph Cordiner, GE became one of the first companies to pledge its support for the Kennedy administration's Plans for Progress. And in 1964, President Johnson named Cordiner's successor as CEO, Fred Borch, to his new national civil-rights committee. GE pointed proudly to these achievements and saluted diversity in those parts of the company where it existed, like at the jet-engine factory in Evendale, Ohio. There, according to GE, "Negro supervisors hold positions of responsibility in many areas of the plant, ranging as high as section manager." Said one GE executive: "We have not been dragged grudgingly into trying to do what is right."

In one publication, *At Work in Industry Today*, GE told the stories of fifty different African American employees: technician Eugenia Edmerson, personnel development specialist Judge Allen, mechanical engineer Ernest Bouey, secretary Georgia Davis, and scores more. "We are telling you about their jobs and their backgrounds to show you the kinds of jobs that capable Negro men and women can hold in General Electric and in industry," the company said. "We are talking about *today*. As these words are written, each of these men and women is at work—designing, typing, drafting, repairing, managing, planning, selling, working standard machinery, or operating some of the most complex equipment the world has ever known." GE distributed some 60,000 copies of the booklet to high-school guidance counselors and at career centers. Yet the unavoidable truth was that the men and women the company profiled were the great exception: in the early sixties, less than 1 percent of salaried employees, and less than 2.5 percent of GE's overall workforce, were people of color.

At Coca-Cola, with its southern heritage, the topic of race was never far from the surface. At a birthday party for Harrison Jones in 1937, a Coke executive arranged to have a special tune sung for him by a chorus of white and black singers at Atlanta's Brookhaven Country Club. "Continue this number with the singers until you see the guests approach their chairs," the instructions to the orchestra leader read. "Then stop this number and go into the Coca-Cola theme song. The colored singers, of course, will not join in on this number." Some lines couldn't be crossed.

Yet it isn't easy to gauge exactly where Robert Woodruff, The Boss, fell on the issue of racial equality. After a brutal murder and hanging at his Ichauway Plantation in the early thirties, Woodruff took a firm stand against lynching—an unusual position considering the time and place—earning him the approbation of the black workers on his farm. In the 1940s, Woodruff began donating money to support educational opportunities for blacks, and he eventually helped to raise tens of millions of dollars for the United Negro College Fund. In 1950,

Woodruff was named to the board of the Tuskegee Institute, and in 1952 he brought a Who's Who of American industry to the South for a tour of black colleges. Among the visitors were Winthrop Aldrich, the chairman of Chase National Bank; John D. Rockefeller III; Robert Wilson, the chairman of Standard Oil; Pittsburgh banker Richard K. Mellon; and Harvey Firestone Jr., the chairman of Firestone Tire & Rubber. Benjamin Mays, the president of Morehouse College, called the visit "the most significant event in Negro education and interracial good will since the War Between the States."

Yet as late as 1960, Woodruff let slip his own bigotry, telling a colleague that he favored "appropriate civil-rights laws" that would protect "the right of a chimpanzee to vote." He also didn't shy away from backing for governor, and later for the US Senate, Herman Talmadge—known as "Klan-loving Hummon," who ran on a platform that "God advocates segregation." As Woodruff toasted the candidate at one campaign dinner, Talmadge political operative Roy Harris told reporters: "The niggers are a little disgusted. They thought they were going to get equality, and now they have found out they are not."

As for business, Coke had spent years all but ignoring the black community, a choice that allowed Pepsi to take a big lead in catering to African American consumers. Woodruff ultimately reversed course, recognizing that he was losing ground to his rival as well as the immense profits to be made from an underserved market. In 1951, the company began to advertise in black weekly newspapers by featuring star athletes—Jackie Robinson, Jesse Owens, the Harlem Globetrotters, and others—along with the slogan, "There's nothing like a Coke." Recruiting and promoting black workers, though, was a whole other matter. Corporate headquarters did not hire many African Americans while Woodruff was alive, and hardly any of those who were brought into the company climbed beyond entry-level jobs.

Through much of Coca-Cola's far-flung bottler network, the racism was just as bad or even worse, inciting a series of boycotts by African American organizations during the 1950s and '60s. While going after bottlers in New York; Omaha, Nebraska; Champaign, Illinois; Atlanta; Chicago; and elsewhere, they leveled two basic complaints: either blacks weren't being hired at Coke bottling operations, or when they were, the jobs they landed were unfailingly "manual or menial," in the words of a group led by Ralph Abernathy, who had helped to cofound the Southern Christian Leadership Conference with Martin Luther King Jr. After King won the Nobel Peace Prize in 1964, Woodruff would pave the way for him to come to Atlanta for a dinner in his honor, all but ordering the city's white business establishment to attend. Woodruff had begun to worry that if Atlanta were seen by the world as a racist stronghold, it would be bad for business. "Coca-Cola cannot operate from a city that is reviled," he said, as he directed the mayor, William Hartsfield, to integrate schools and lunch counters in the early sixties. But even that wasn't sufficient to satisfy King, who in the last speech of his life, just hours before being assassinated, would call on blacks to "go out and tell your neighbors not to buy Coca-Cola" and products from several other companies "because they haven't been fair in their hiring policies."

And then there was Eastman Kodak.

A few weeks before the riot in Rochester, President Johnson signed the Civil Rights Act of 1964. At the ceremony in the East Room of the White House marking the new law, Martin Luther King Jr. sat next to George Meany, head of the AFL-CIO.

"We believe that all men are created equal," Johnson said that day. "Yet many are denied equal treatment. We believe that all men have certain unalienable rights. Yet many do not enjoy those rights. We believe that all men are entitled to the blessings of liberty. Yet millions are deprived of those blessings—not because of their own failures, but because of the color of their skin. The reasons are deeply embedded in history and tradition and the nature of man. We can understand—without rancor or hatred—how this all happened. But it cannot continue. Our Constitution, the foundation of our Republic, forbids it. The principles of our freedom forbid it. Morality forbids it. And the law I will sign tonight forbids it."

If only it were so simple. Although the Civil Rights Act prohibited discrimination in public places, provided for the integration of schools and other public facilities, and made bias in the workplace illegal (while establishing the Equal Employment Opportunity Commission), the conduct at companies such as General Motors, General Electric, and Coca-Cola highlighted how hard it was to bring about a true cultural transformation. Institutional inequity would not ebb instantaneously.

At the same time, blacks' sense of resentment swelled, stoked in part by the passage of a measure intended, as President Johnson put it, "to close the springs of racial poison." Kenneth Clark, the first black to earn a doctorate in psychology from Columbia University, laid it out like this: "The frustration of the Northern Negro was intensified by the alleged victory. . . . There were celebrations on the mall before the Lincoln Memorial. Then, when the Negro looked at his situation, he saw that he was still in housing unfit for human habitation; he was still bitten by rats. The schools to which he was required to send his children were criminally inferior. The tremendous civil-rights progress meant nothing in terms of major observable change in his predicament as a prisoner of the ghettos." Legislative triumphs notwithstanding, Michael Harrington's "other America" stubbornly persisted.

To Clark—whose earlier research had helped lay the groundwork for the Supreme Court's 1954 landmark decision to desegregate schools in *Brown v. Board of Education*—the long-term solution to the plight of blacks lay not with government taking the lead. Despite all the entrenched racism in corporate America, he looked to the private sector as the answer, imploring executives to offer blacks ample on-the-job training, as well as push municipal officials to clean up their cities. "Business should accept this challenge," Clark said, "not for humanitarian reasons, nor for moral or ethical reasons, as is usually stated, but for the kinds of reasons that make sense to business. In eliminating slums and ghettos, business will . . . bring more than one-tenth of the American population into a constructive and profitable role in the economy. In taking present tax-consumers and turning them into tax-producers and contributors to the GNP, business will vitalize and strengthen the economy. Individuals who are now excluded as producers, who are now excluded as distributors, can be made active in the economy and thus provide strength and stability and underpin the dollar."

Over time, although many blacks would continue to suffer from employment discrimination, corporations would in fact open up their hiring and promotional practices to an unprecedented degree. "The decade following the Civil Rights Act would see a concerted effort on the part of the nation's employers to integrate their workplaces," the historian Jennifer Delton has written. By and large, however, these steps were not taken voluntarily, the way Clark had hoped. As Delton has pointed out, "it took the social crisis of the late 1960s—the urban riots, the militant racialism—together with the widespread use of boycotts, an activist EEOC, and court-sanctioned affirmative action" to prompt most employers to move in a positive direction, while "grassroots pressure on the part of black workers and their allies" was also crucial.

In Rochester, it was the black clergy (and their liberal white peers) who brought this grassroots pressure to bear. The ministers felt, in the wake of the rioting, that it was time to start a new dialogue between the black community and the rest of the city. At first, they tried to entice Martin Luther King's Southern Christian Leadership Conference to launch a campaign in Rochester. But after that bid faltered, they opted for a more provocative response, inviting in the Industrial Areas Foundation, headed by Saul Alinsky.

Born in 1909 to Russian Jewish immigrants in the slums of Chicago, Alinsky studied archeology and then criminology in college. Although he had a bookish look, he was drawn to the rough-and-tumble of the streets, and in the course of his studies persuaded Al Capone's men to let him hang out and watch what it was really like to be a mobster—great fodder for the stories that the foul-mouthed, charming, egotistical, truth-stretching Alinsky would delight in telling for decades to come. For a while after school, Alinsky worked with the state of Illinois on juvenile-justice issues. In the late 1930s, as part of his work on a delinquency-prevention program, he allied himself with labor organizers, working for the CIO under John L. Lewis, as they tried to unionize Chicago's meatpacking companies. Alinsky's vision steadily grew broader, and his approach in the neighborhood around the slaughterhouses, an area known as the Back of the Yards, became the template for his life's work.

"What I wanted to try to do was apply the organizing techniques I'd mastered with the CIO to the worst slums and ghettos, so that the most oppressed and exploited elements in the country could take control of their own communities and their own destinies," Alinsky said. "Up till then, specific factories and industries had been organized for social change, but never entire communities. This was the field I wanted to make my own—community organization for community power and for radical goals." Alinsky's tactics were creative and aggressive: rent strikes against slumlords, boycotts against exploitive businesses, sit-downs against the machine politicians at city hall. "Finally," Alinsky said, "the concessions began trickling in—reduced rents, public housing, more and better municipal services, school improvements, more equitable mortgages and bank loans, fairer food prices."

Alinsky, who characterized his M.O. as "rubbing raw the sores of discontent," was a polarizing figure from the start (and he'd continue to cast a shadow long after his death in 1972: the Industrial Areas Foundation trained Barack Obama in community organizing during the mid-1980s, and Hillary Clinton wrote her undergraduate thesis at Wellesley College on Alinsky's mobilizing methods). After Alinsky's victory in the Back of the Yards, Illinois governor Adlai Stevenson praised him, saying his objectives "most faithfully reflect our ideals of brotherhood, tolerance, charity, and the dignity of the individual." The *Chicago Tribune* editorial board, however, had a far less generous opinion of Alinsky. "Rubbing raw the sores of discontent may be jolly good fun for him," it declared, "but we are unable to regard it as a contribution to social betterment." As for Alinsky himself, he couldn't have cared less what anybody thought, one way or the other. "My critics are right when they call me an outside agitator," he said. "When a community, any kind of community, is hopeless and helpless, it requires somebody from outside to come in and stir things up. That's my job—to unsettle them, to make them start asking questions, to teach them to stop talking and start acting, because the fat cats in charge never hear with their ears, only through their rears."

Over time, Alinsky expanded his work—with mixed results—to other areas, including Kansas City, Missouri; Detroit; Buffalo; New York City; the barrios of California; and the Woodlawn district in Chicago. By the time he visited Rochester in early 1965 to consider the invitation of the clergy there, his reputation for rabble-rousing had divided the city's residents. Rochester could "do without hiring an over-priced Chicago 'organizer' who is noted for . . . staging class and race incidents that cause trouble and solve nothing," a full-page ad in the *Times-Union* warned. Alinsky, who accepted the ministers' assignment (and the $100,000, two-year contract that went with it), did absolutely nothing to ingratiate himself to his critics. The more they panicked in his presence, the more he tried to amp up their anxiety. The more they asked him to act with decorum, the ruder he became. "Rochester, probably more than any northern city, reeks of antiquated paternalism," Alinsky said shortly after his arrival in early 1965. "It is like a southern plantation transported to the North. Negro conditions in

Rochester are an insult to the whole idea of the American way of life. I have seen in Rochester people who are sick to death of being treated like chattel, who find themselves regarded as a necessary evil."

By June, an Alinsky-directed organization in Rochester had jelled. FIGHT (which stood for Freedom, Integration, God, Honor, Today) had a long list of stipulations: black representation on city boards, serious efforts at urban renewal, an end to labor-union discrimination, and "direct negotiation" with Rochester's biggest employers to place more African Americans in good jobs. FIGHT first cut a deal with Xerox, which promised to hire fifteen unemployed young blacks. The number was tiny, but Xerox vowed to do more once the pilot program was finished, and the agreement itself was enough of a milestone that by the fall of 1966, FIGHT felt ready to take on the real corporate power in town: Kodak.

Much like GM and GE, Kodak had a fair-employment policy in place by the 1960s and had laid out its own Plan for Progress, which included a commitment to "hold discussions with the employment interviewers in the various divisions to remind them" that "such things as race, creed, color, or national origin" are neither to "help nor hinder in getting a job at Kodak." Yet for blacks trying to work and move up at the company, these assurances didn't mesh with their own experiences. Some of this was a consequence of blacks being poorly educated, especially those who had relocated to Rochester from the rural South. In the company's eyes, they simply weren't qualified. "We don't grow many peanuts in Eastman Kodak," Monroe Dill, Kodak's industrial relations director, said in 1963, adding that the company would start to recruit more from all-black colleges so as to not keep "discriminating by omission." But there was also plenty of discrimination by commission, as individual Kodak managers used their discretion to hire whomever they liked and cast off whomever they didn't. "They would say it blatant, like, 'We don't have any colored jobs,'" recalled Clarence Ingram, who served as general manager of the Rochester Business Opportunities Corporation, an entity formed after the '64 riots to support minority businesses. "They would tell you that." Apparently, they told a lot of blacks that. In 1964, only about 600 African Americans worked for Kodak in Rochester, less than 2 percent of the 33,000 employees based there.

Determined to remedy this was FIGHT, which was led by Franklin Delano Roosevelt Florence, the thirty-one-year-old pastor of the Reynolds Street Church of Christ, a stocky, hard-charging, charismatic man, who called Malcolm X a friend. On September 2, 1966, a delegation of sixteen from FIGHT walked into Kodak's executive suite. Florence, sporting a Black Power button in his lapel, said he wanted to see "the top man." Before he knew it, the minister and his retinue were sitting in front of three top men: Kodak chairman Albert Chapman, president William Vaughn, and executive vice president Louis Eilers. Florence told them about the harshness of life in Rochester's black ghetto and said he wanted Kodak to start a training program for people who normally wouldn't be recruited into the company. Florence braced himself, expecting Kodak to resist. But Vaughn listened carefully and then asked Florence to submit a more specific proposal. Two weeks later, he did. Calling FIGHT "the only mass based organization of poor people and near poor people in the Rochester area," Florence requested that Kodak train 500 to 600 men and women over eighteen months. FIGHT also wanted direct involvement in the process; the group would "recruit and counsel trainees and offer advice, consultation, and assistance."

To Kodak, the proposal was a complete dud. For one thing, the company was loath to commit to a set number of hires, dismissing the target of 500 to 600 as "an arbitrary demand." "Jobs aren't something you turn out on a machine," Vaughn said. He also didn't want FIGHT to recruit Kodak employees, viewing that as an incursion into management's territory—much the way the company had always looked disapprovingly at the prospect of a union butting into business operations. "Florence wanted to . . . tell us what people to hire," Vaughn grumbled. The two sides held a couple more meetings, but Vaughn and the other most senior Kodak executives stopped attending, a not-so-subtle undermining of Florence's status. As the weeks passed, "it became perfectly clear that there was no basis for working with them," said Kenneth Howard of Kodak's industrial-relations staff.

On October 22, Kodak announced that it would bring in a consulting group, the Board of Fundamental Education, to train a hundred disadvantaged people in basic skills. Forty of them already worked at Kodak. Fuming, Florence showed up at the company with forty-five unemployed blacks and insisted they be made part of the program. When Kodak refused, saying that all the participants had been selected, Florence labeled the whole thing "a fraud" and "a trick."

"We can't understand for our lives how a company with their creative ability can . . . create these Instamatic cameras, but can't create Instamatic jobs," he said. Alinsky weighed in, as well. "People talk about General Motors and they talk about this and they talk about that, but you've got yourself one of the most pompous and arrogant and richest corporations with one of the crummiest employment policies as far as the race issue goes."

With Kodak and FIGHT at a standoff—and the company taking the brunt of a lot of bad publicity—Vaughn decided to shake things up. The move came at the behest of John Mulder, a Kodak assistant vice president, who had been active in civil-rights issues and whose wife was a member of a support group called Friends of FIGHT. Mulder, who worked at Kodak Park, suggested that a new delegation be appointed to talk with FIGHT, this time led by managers who were on the front lines of hiring and training. Vaughn agreed and put Mulder in charge of the Kodak team. On December 19, the company and FIGHT met at the Downtowner Motor Inn, and by the next day, they reached a deal. Over a twenty-four-month period, Kodak would recruit 600 people—"the bulk of which would be hard-core unemployed (unattached, uninvolved with traditional institutions)"—so long as there were no "unforeseen economic changes." FIGHT, for its part, accepted that it wouldn't be the sole referral agency for job candidates. Florence questioned whether Mulder could sign the agreement, but he assured the minister that he could; Vaughn had given him the authorization to do so, he said.

Florence immediately hailed Kodak for its "vision." Mulder's bosses, though, had an altogether different reaction when they heard that he had signed a pact promising 600 jobs. "The hell he has!" said Eilers, who the following week was scheduled to take over the company presidency, with Vaughn becoming chairman. By December 22, Kodak had formally repudiated the agreement, saying Mulder never had the authority to sign. "We could not agree to a program . . . which would extend so far into the future," Vaughn said. "Obviously, our employment needs depend on the kinds of jobs available at a particular time." One report indicated that the company also "detected the faint odor" of an organized-labor contract in the FIGHT accord.

Mulder asked if he could relay the news to FIGHT personally. He showed up at a party, where Florence and his wife were celebrating her birthday. The moment Florence saw Mulder's face, he knew. "They've broken the agreement," Florence said quietly. As the FIGHT leader read Kodak's official statement, "the whole thing Brother Malcolm told me about white folks hit me again," Florence later commented. "He said never trust them unless you have the power to make them deliver." The next day, Florence led a rally of 150 ministers, priests, rabbis, nuns, and laypeople at his church. "We are disgusted and angry," he told the congregation. "Kodak's word is no good. Kodak's signature is no good." The company took out two-page newspaper ad saying that it "sincerely regrets any misunderstanding." But it was already too late; the distrust on both sides had thickened and hardened.

By late February—after another six weeks of news conferences full of charges and countercharges; on-again, off-again negotiations; and notice by Kodak of a new job training initiative for 150 unskilled individuals that Florence denounced as "a sham and a disgrace"—the company told FIGHT that it was done talking once and for all. "We believe that there have been enough meetings about meetings," Kodak said. Florence wasted no time in sending back a menacing reply: "Please be advised that the Negro poor of Rochester and the poor throughout the country from Harlem to Watts are not satisfied with your 'see no evil' and 'hear no evil' attitude. Institutional racism as exemplified at Kodak is amoral and un-Christian. The cold of February will give way to the warm of spring and eventually the long hot summer. What happens in Rochester in the summer of '67 is at the doorstep of Eastman Kodak."

Saul Alinsky mostly watched the deepening stalemate between Kodak and FIGHT from the sidelines (though, ever the wise guy, he couldn't resist throwing out the occasional one-liner: "The only contribution the Eastman Kodak Company has ever made to race relations is the invention of color film"). By the time things had reached their breaking point, however, he was already plotting his next maneuver. Before summer even arrived, Alinsky would squeeze Kodak harder than ever.

As discriminatory as corporate America was to blacks through the fifties and sixties, women found themselves every bit as marginalized. "Two things make this business great—one is the product

Coca-Cola, and the other is men," Lee Talley, the president of the beverage maker told a group of company executives in 1957. "We have the product but we shall need more and more good men. Men of character and intelligence. Men who are industrious and hardworking. Men of spirit and ambition. Men of dedication." Women, evidently, need not apply. At Kodak, the language deployed was every bit as masculine. "Many young men have a bright future in the skilled trades at Kodak," the company proclaimed on the cover of one promotional piece. "Are you one of them?" The back of the same brochure stated, "Kodak is an equal opportunity employer," the irony apparently lost on everyone. It's not that major corporations didn't hire women. But their numbers were relatively small, making up less than 20 percent of the workforce at many companies, and the jobs made available to them were sharply limited, with barely any women in management. "Can you tell me why," one frustrated female office worker at General Motors asked in 1956, "none of the corporation's plants have women supervisors?"

Such sexism was bound up in common conventions that had endured for generations. Even the most progressive employers—such as General Electric's Gerard Swope—easily fell prey to them. Like many companies in the 1920s, GE asked women to resign if they got married, and it made certain benefits, such as life insurance, available only to men. Each year, all department heads at GE were required to submit to Swope a PYM List so the company could identify up-and-coming talent. PYM stood for "Promising Young Men." "Our theory was that women did not recognize the responsibilities of life," Swope said. Once they were wed, he added, the company was certain that they "would leave us." Such an attitude both reflected and reinforced prevailing norms about gender: from the late nineteenth century until the 1920s, married women working outside the home were stigmatized; many jobs were dirty and dangerous, and society frowned on the "fairer sex" filling them. Among women in the early part of the twentieth century, the world of work was left mainly to the young and single.

By the early 1930s, with Swope himself now expressing doubts about the "man-run company" he had built, change was afoot. Office work—a type of employment considered "respectable" for females—was suddenly in high demand, and for the first time a big pool of women graduating from high school became typists, file clerks, and secretaries. (The writer G. K. Chesterton wryly observed that "ten thousand women marched through the streets . . . saying: 'We will not be dictated to,' and then went off to become stenographers.") By the 1940s, most companies ended the practice of firing women who got married. And the advent of part-time jobs also drew more women into the workplace.

Then came the war. After Pearl Harbor, women "entered 'men's jobs' in basic industry on a massive scale," the historian Ruth Milkman has written, proving that "they were fully capable of performing such work." The fraction of women working in autos went from less than 6 percent in 1940 to nearly 25 percent in 1944; in the electrical industry, the proportion of women workers jumped from about a third to almost half. Big increases were also seen in rubber, chemicals, and iron and steel. "Women keep piling up evidence that they can do, and do well, a multitude of jobs," the American Management Association reported. One General Motors executive said that, compared with men, women in the factories had shown themselves to be "more precise," "more dexterous," "more conscientious," "less likely to loaf on the job," and "often more loyal to the company." Louis Male, longtime manager of the Schenectady Works at General Electric, became convinced that "women generally were better employees on highly repetitive jobs" because "monotony didn't seem to bother them like it did the men."

But while Rosie the Riveter continues to loom large as an American icon—"All the day long / Whether rain or shine / She's a part of the assembly line," went the 1943 song—Rosie was in reality an ephemeral figure. As soon as the war ended (and in many cases even earlier, as defense contracts were winding down), women were drummed out of the workplace. Some left willingly, content to give up their jobs for men returning from combat. But most women in manufacturing wanted to stay—four out of five, according to surveys—and so employers resorted to numerous tricks to dislodge them: firing them for minor violations that men could get away with; moving them to the midnight shift; assigning them to new jobs and then objecting when they didn't immediately demonstrate enough expertise; and disregarding seniority rules. By 1946, women accounted for fewer than 10 percent of all autoworkers; in electrical manufacturing, their total dipped below 40 percent.

That the ranks of the Rosies shrank this way wasn't merely a matter of companies pushing them out; society was also pulling them in—straight into their kitchens and bedrooms. Among those propounding this position was psychiatrist Marynia Farnham, coauthor of *Modern Woman: The Lost Sex*. "Catastrophic social forces have propelled American women away from femininity and into careers at terrific cost to themselves and society," she said (somehow seemingly immune to such costs herself). "Abandoning their feminine role has made women unhappy because it has made them frustrated. It has made children unhappy because they do not have maternal love. And it has made their husbands unhappy because they do not have real women as partners. Instead, their wives have become their rivals." For the most part, the public agreed. A 1946 *Fortune* magazine poll found that fewer than 22 percent of males and 29 percent of females thought that women "should have an equal chance with men" for any job.

Some came to conclude that commerce, as much at culture, was behind the effort to keep women hemmed in. Among them was Betty Friedan, who would write in her pioneering 1963 book *The Feminine Mystique*: "I am sure the heads of General Foods, and General Electric, and General Motors, and Macy's and Gimbel's and the assorted directors of all the companies that make detergents and electric mixers, and red stoves with rounded corners, and synthetic furs, and waxes, and hair coloring, and patterns for home sewing and home carpentry, and lotions for detergent hands, and bleaches to keep the towels pure white, never sat down around a mahogany conference table in a boardroom on Madison Avenue or Wall Street and voted on a motion: 'Gentlemen, I move in the interests of all, that we begin a concerted $50 billion campaign to stop this dangerous movement of American women out of the home.'" Nonetheless, while Friedan rejected such conspiracy theories, she did believe that "somehow, somewhere, someone must have figured out women will buy more things if they are kept in the underused, nameless-yearning, energy-to-get-rid-of state of being housewives."

In spite of the obstacles, ever more women joined the labor force through the 1950s and '60s, owing to a variety of factors: rapid growth in part-time work; the passage of antidiscrimination laws, including the Civil Rights Act of 1964; and the introduction of the birth-control pill, which allowed women to delay having children and focus instead on their careers.

The first factor—the surge in temp jobs—had the muscle of industry behind it. Temp agencies had gotten their start in the late

1940s, and in the 1950s they kicked into full expansion mode, backed by millions of dollars in advertising and other promotions. By 1961, more than half of US companies had used their services, and by '63 about 1,000 temp firms operated across the country, employing some 400,000 workers.

With names such as Western Girl Service, Workman Girl Service, American Girl Service, White Collar Girl Service, Right Girls, and Kelly Girl Service, these firms masterfully positioned themselves in a way that would mollify a society still ambivalent about married women (especially white, middle-class married women) being employed outside the house. Temp jobs, they claimed, gave women a much-needed sense of self-fulfillment and adventure without destroying the sanctity of the family. They could look forward, in effect, to leading "a double life," said a 1965 ad from Manpower, the industry leader, whose "Girl in the White Gloves" became a ubiquitous image. Or as sociologist Erin Hatton has written: "Rosie was working only until her soldier came home from the war; Kelly was working only until her kids came home from school."

Yet temp work had plenty of pitfalls. Manpower, Kelly Girl, and the other agencies circumvented many of the standards and regulations protecting full-time workers—such as health benefits, unemployment insurance, and equal-rights laws—while they also avoided being organized by unions. In the decades ahead, these subpar conditions would wind up affecting far more than just female temps, as "contingent work" would become increasingly common throughout the American economy.

In the meantime, all those women entering the labor force constituted a steady wave that would, by the 1970s, lead to a total makeover of American society. "The radical consequences of incremental change" is the way historian Alice Kessler-Harris has described it. But it would also prove a very bumpy ride, as companies shortchanged women on pay, relegated them to particular jobs stereotyped as female, and subjected them to all manner of harassment.

General Electric was typical. On the factory floor in the 1950s and into the '60s, GE explicitly offered two wage rates—a higher one for "men's jobs" and a lower one for "women's jobs." At the company's Fort Wayne, Indiana, plant, for instance, female group leaders, who had been trained for eight to ten months, earned about $2.35 an hour—6 cents less than a male motor assembler whose job required just six weeks of training. GE also used double seniority lists so that, during downturns, men with short stints of service were kept on while women with ten or fifteen years at the company were laid off. The Electrical Workers—which, like other unions, including the United Auto Workers, fought much harder for women than it did for blacks—succeeded in eliminating some of these practices over time. Still, many things remained the same straight through the sixties, with female factory workers at GE put into the lowest-paying jobs; regularly passed over for better positions, like drill-press operator and material handler; and shut out of company courses where they could learn new skills, such as reading blueprints.

Some women at GE held higher-level jobs—but they were few and far between, and advancement was painfully slow. Consider Adelaide Oppenheim. When she looked for a job at GE in the spring of 1941, having graduated from the State University of New York with a master's degree in education, there was a separate hiring process for female applicants. The person in charge, an unwavering conventionalist named Mary Holmes, "only thought that women were capable of doing secretarial work," Oppenheim recalled—and she wasn't interested. So Oppenheim navigated her way past Holmes and directly into the accounting department, only to be told, "Well, we don't hire any women here." She began to argue with the manager, saying that war was imminent and GE better start hiring women as a kind of insurance policy. Insistent (and just this side of impertinent), she got the job. It came, though, with a warning: if the emergency petered out and war didn't come, Oppenheim would be fired. Three months later, many of GE's best men were departing for the military, and Oppenheim was suddenly put in charge of unbilled inventory for the whole company.

It was a bad match. Oppenheim didn't hesitate to voice her ideas for how to better organize the work of the department, and her boss didn't appreciate her outspokenness. "I was reprimanded . . . for making all these suggestions," she said. By March 1942, she was ordered to find work elsewhere within GE. "They said, 'We're reorganizing our group, and we're not going to have any women, and you'd better look for a job.'" When Oppenheim questioned why this was happening, her boss left little doubt that the decision was final. "Oh, we'll give you a very good recommendation because you're very aggressive and very ambitious and very intelligent," he said. "But we don't want you in the department. Ta-ta."

Oppenheim got bounced back to Holmes, the woman in charge of female hiring at GE, who again tried to shove her into the secretarial pool. As before, Oppenheim refused, and she talked her way into a technical job, doing calculations in a company laboratory. This time, she fit right in. "I was just one of the guys, you know," she said. "At noontime, when some of the other women would be sitting eating their lunch and so on, I'd take a sandwich and go down the line and poke around in the shops, watching the guys with the machines. . . . I would just talk to everybody, and I kept asking questions." She filled a notebook with every detail she heard. And the more she learned, the more her confidence grew.

Eventually, Oppenheim received advanced training in engineering and went to work on the Manhattan Project. "At the end of the war, they told us, 'Gee, thanks a lot, you wonderful women. You did wonderful things. Now go home.' But I didn't go." Instead, in the late 1940s, Oppenheim became head of a new twenty-five-person planning and program-management department—a breakthrough at the time. "Although it's not our policy to give any kind of supervisory position to women," Oppenheim was told, "we're going to let you try it." She did well. Yet it would take many more years, all the way until 1962, before Oppenheim was officially designated a manager—one of only six women inside GE to then hold such a title. The climb for women in most big companies was similarly arduous. Looking across the corporate arena at the time, a *Harvard Business Review* report on women in management found that "there is scarcely anything to study."

Women in major technical roles were just as rare. A 1959 ad by GE in the *Cincinnati Post* showed four "girl engineers," as the company called them, working at its aircraft-engine plant in Evendale, Ohio. "We're mighty pleased to have them and only wish there were more than four," the ad said. The piddling numbers at GE were no anomaly: in 1960, women accounted for just 6 percent of doctors, 3 percent of lawyers, and less than 1 percent of engineers in the United States. "The problem for a girl in this business," said Loren Ingraham, one of those at Evendale, "is that people are afraid there will be a problem."

Locked out of white-collar professions, most women at GE were shoehorned into what would come to be called the "pink-collar ghetto" of clerical work. Steering them in this direction, and then leaving them trapped there, was par for the course in corporate America, where the first question that women—even college graduates—were typically asked during a job interview was, "How well do you type?"

Yet companies seemed to care about the sartorial as much as the secretarial. In one 1950s guidebook, GE laid out this advice: "As a business girl you will want to maintain a certain professional appearance. You will want to look as if you belong in the office and not at a cocktail party or on a date. Most business gals find that the most suitable clothes for the office are tailored dresses—skirts worn with blouses, jersey tops, or sweaters—pretty suits. It's wise to avoid such things as too sheer blouses, too tight sweaters and too much jewelry. However, just because you are a business girl, you will not be expected to wear dark colors only. Every gal should select colors that are flattering to her own skin tones, eyes, and hair."

The company advised women not only on what to wear but on how to walk. "It is not necessary to rush when you walk," the guidebook said, "but you don't want to drag yourself around either. A person who has a brisk walk, which says she's going someplace and has something to do, usually does get somewhere. If you have trouble with your posture and find that you get tired often, there are many good foundation garments on the market that will help you to achieve better posture and keep you from being fatigued. They will help you to look better in your clothes, too." No detail was overlooked: GE's counsel extended to selecting lipstick, powder, and rouge; applying nail polish; choosing the right hairstyle ("Loose flowing hair . . . has a tendency to muss easily"); and encouraging the use of "body deodorants and mouth antiseptics."

The guidebook also informed its readers how essential it was to eat right and get enough sleep. It discussed the need for women in the office to display "an even temperament," while reminding them to be "cheerful," "open-minded," "reliable," "thoughtful," and "discreet." It urged them to show "initiative" and "resourcefulness" and "cultivate tactfulness and courtesy." And it asked what GE asked of every employee, whether male or female: "We hope that you will be loyal," the guidebook said, "not only to your boss but to General Electric, too."

But it was a woman's looks that seemed to carry inordinate weight. "This winsome lass is Carol Goff, a clerk-typist in shipping,"

GE's distribution transformer department in Oakland, California, announced in the "Who's New" section of its internal newsletter in late 1961. "Another pretty lil' gal, Joyce A. Tate, is our new mail girl." GE ogled its professionals in the same way. When Betty Lou Bailey, one of the four female engineers from Evendale, visited GE's Everett, Massachusetts, factory to check on some production parts, the company newsletter noted what a fuss she stirred up. "Not even a visitor from Mars could have attracted more attention than Betty Lou Bailey," it said. "Not that the visitor had any of the characteristics of a Martian—in fact, with her blue-eyed, blonde-haired attractiveness she would have been an eye-catcher anywhere."

By the 1970s, with the women's liberation movement in full flower, GE toned down the language. It also took steps to ensure that job postings and upgrades were blind with regard to race or gender. This "really opened up the door for both men and women," said Helen Quirini, who took a job doing piece work at GE's Schenectady, New York, plant in 1941 and spent decades fighting for the equal treatment of female employees and minorities.

But the company still isolated women in other ways. In 1971, a pregnant GE factory worker named Martha Gilbert challenged the company's disability policy, under which she was advised to take three months off without pay before giving birth and then mandated to take six weeks of unpaid leave after her child arrived. This was standard practice for US companies, which held that women shouldn't receive a benefit—namely, paid leave—that men didn't get. Gilbert, who was soon joined in a lawsuit against GE by six other employees, countered that if a man were injured off the job, he would receive disability pay; a pregnant woman, they said, should be entitled to the same thing. The case, which evolved into a class action for the 100,000 women working at GE at the time, was watched with great anticipation throughout corporate America. In 1976, it reached the Supreme Court, where GE won.

Two years later, President Carter signed into law the Pregnancy Discrimination Act, which overrode the Supreme Court's decision. The measure required that if an employer offered disability pay to men, it had to do the same for women "on the basis of pregnancy, childbirth, or related medical conditions." For GE, though, the passage of the law was moot; the company had already overhauled its policy.

Specifically, GE did away with compulsory maternity leave, allowing a woman and her doctor to decide whether she should take a break. The company also began awarding partial pay to women beginning six weeks before they gave birth and continuing for six weeks after. "We saw that the mindset of our workforce had changed and certainly we have to change as a company to attract the most talented people," a GE spokesman said.

It was a remarkable admission for a corporation that just a few years earlier, when it wasn't battling women in the courtroom, was engaged in even more invidious behavior: acting as if they didn't exist. With its advertising tagline from the early 1970s, GE had casually erased half the planet's population. "Men Helping Man," it said.

As the winter of 1967 melted into spring, Saul Alinsky mulled ways to break the logjam between FIGHT and Eastman Kodak. He thought about organizing a national boycott of the company's products but quickly concluded that such a campaign wouldn't get very far. "You couldn't ask the country to stop taking pictures," he said. Having heard that Queen Elizabeth owned Kodak stock, Alinsky and the other FIGHT leaders batted around the idea of picketing Buckingham Palace. But this plan, too, was dropped. Ultimately, Alinsky seized on an even wilder notion: FIGHT would march straight into the lion's den of capitalism—the company's annual meeting, set for April 25 in Flemington, New Jersey.

The concept was pretty simple at first: FIGHT would buy some Kodak stock, giving it access to the shareholders' meeting for purposes of "harassment and publicity," Alinsky explained. But Alinsky soon realized that if he and Franklin Florence could induce other owners of Kodak stock to assign their proxies to FIGHT, they could put even more heat on the company. And so they began contacting church organizations that held Kodak shares in their investment funds. Alinsky wasn't trying to wage a battle for control of the board. He wasn't even attempting to elect a director or two who would represent FIGHT's interests inside Kodak. But by amassing enough shares to potentially threaten the board's agenda, Alinsky felt he could acquire "the razor to cut through the golden curtain that protected the so-called private sector from facing its public responsibilities."

In the weeks leading up to the annual meeting, Kodak executives became nervous. If nothing else, if FIGHT pulled in enough proxies, it might be able to grab the government's attention and prompt congressional hearings or even a Justice Department investigation into the company's hiring practices. Meanwhile, Alinsky would go on to endorse the use of this stratagem far beyond Kodak. It was a means to impose "social and political pressure against the megacorporations" and "a vehicle for exposing their hypocrisy and deceit," he said. It is "also an invaluable means of gaining middle-class participation in radical causes. . . . Proxy participation on a large scale could ultimately mean the democratization of corporate America."

Even with Alinsky's cunning, FIGHT didn't wind up controlling very many Kodak shares—just 40,000 out of more than 80 million outstanding. Yet that didn't stop Florence from barging into Flemington like he owned the place. Outside Hunterdon Central High School, where Kodak's annual meeting was about to begin, some 600 FIGHT supporters milled about. Most had been bused in, and many held signs: "Kodak is negative." "Kodak is out of focus." "Kodak Snaps the Shutter on the Negro." Inside, about forty people in the FIGHT camp sat alongside Florence and Alinsky. At one o'clock, Kodak chairman William Vaughn began the meeting. Immediately, Florence jumped to his feet. "Mr. Chairman, Mr. Chairman," the minister shouted. Vaughn called him out of order, but Florence would have none of it. "I'll be heard as long as I'm on the floor!" he said. Florence then said he would give Vaughn one hour—until two o'clock—to honor the agreement that Kodak assistant vice president John Mulder had made with FIGHT the previous December to hire 600 "hardcore unemployed." Some among the 1,000 shareholders in attendance booed while others yelled, "Throw him out!" But nobody needed to. Florence and his entourage then left the high-school auditorium.

At two o'clock, they returned. "Point of order! Point of order!" Florence repeated over and over, demanding the microphone. Vaughn asked him to wait for his turn to speak, which only roused the FIGHT sympathizers. "White arrogance!" one cried. After a few minutes, Florence was recognized. "Just a yes or no if you are going to honor the agreement," he said, pointing his finger straight at Vaughn. The chairman paused and then replied in a firm voice: "No, sir, no we are not." With that, Florence and the others with FIGHT got up and started to leave the meeting once again. Shareholders screamed, "Get out of here!" while some in Florence's party lobbed slights at Vaughn on their way out the door: "Coward!" "Liar!"

From that point, FIGHT became even more confrontational. "This is war," said Florence, "and I state it again—war." He raised his requirement from 600 to 2,000 jobs. He intimated that FIGHT might picket the home of Kodak's beloved founder, George Eastman, or hound the company's president, Louis Eilers. "Everywhere he goes, we go," Florence said. Or perhaps, he suggested, FIGHT would stage an "eat-in" at the Eastman School of Music, downing beans "while our white brothers pass by in their silks and satins." Finally, Florence announced that a candlelight pilgrimage to Kodak headquarters would be held on July 24, the anniversary of the Rochester riots—a move so inflammatory that it caught even Alinsky by surprise.

By June, however, FIGHT had started to lose support among the churches, and the group became weary. It was time to settle. Alinsky called in a mediator: Daniel Patrick Moynihan, the former assistant secretary of labor and future US senator, who was then the director of the Joint Center for Urban Studies at MIT and Harvard. "We won't hold Kodak to a contract," Alinsky told Moynihan. "But we want something." What it got was a statement from Kodak acknowledging that the company "recognizes that FIGHT, as a broad-based community organization, speaks on behalf of the basic needs and aspirations of the Negro poor in the Rochester area." Kodak also agreed to work with FIGHT to send job interviewers into inner-city neighborhoods. Importantly, however, Kodak hadn't actually agreed to employ anyone. Yet that didn't stop Franklin Florence, who was set to step down as FIGHT's president, from claiming otherwise. "We have a deal for jobs!" he told the FIGHT faithful at the organization's annual convention. In any event, he added, the biggest thing was that Rochester's African Americans had earned the respect of one of the nation's largest corporations. "Black men today," Florence said, "can walk taller in this community."

Whether because of FIGHT's tenacity or its own sense of what was right, Kodak did provide new employment for blacks. In December 1967, the company said it would "combat poverty in Rochester" by assisting in the formation of small businesses in the city's slums. And in January 1968, it expanded on the idea by establishing the Rochester

Business Opportunities Corporation "to promote and encourage independent business enterprises in and for the inner-city." Kodak, for instance, was able to get a black-owned plastic mold shop off the ground by granting it a $150,000 contract. It also funded Teens on Patrol, an initiative in which young minorities were paid to help supervise playgrounds, recreation centers, and swimming pools.

Within Kodak itself, the company developed intensive training programs for those lacking in education and skills, a system that other companies (including Coca-Cola, Ford, McDonnell-Douglas, and Mobil) would later follow as part of a federally subsidized effort known as the National Alliance of Businessmen. And in April 1967, shortly before its annual meeting, Kodak had helped to start a program called Rochester Jobs Inc. through which local industries would hire 1,500 poor minorities over the next year and a half. Though Florence scoffed at the plan, Kodak's share was estimated to be 600 jobs—exactly the amount that FIGHT had been calling for. "I believe we at Kodak are trying to do what we should do," said William Vaughn.

By 1968, 2,000 blacks worked for Kodak in Rochester. This was more than triple the number at the time of the riots. Looked at another way, it was only about 4 percent of the company's total local employment.

The headway achieved by African Americans at Kodak was emblematic of that made by blacks and other minorities across corporate America: it wasn't as if they hadn't gotten anywhere, but there was still a terribly long way to go.

Measures of occupational segregation by race, for example, would fall dramatically between 1960 and 1970, but they would in no way disappear. In 1967, full-time African American workers made, on average, 35 percent less than their white counterparts. By the end of the 1970s, that differential would narrow—but still stand at 27 percent. The proportion of African Americans in white-collar jobs soared by 80 percent from 1960 to 1970, but blacks still held a miniscule fraction of managerial positions. And unemployment among blacks would remain stuck at twice the rate experienced by whites. The "quest for 'Freedom Now,'" *Ebony* magazine said of the "decade of struggle" following passage of the Civil Rights Act, "has produced mixed results."

The same was true for women. More and more entered the workforce, especially those who were married, with females taking two-thirds of all new jobs created in the 1960s. But women would continue to be paid considerably less than men (about sixty cents on the dollar), and even the most ambitious would find that they could get only so far in their careers before hitting a "glass ceiling"—a term that would enter the American lexicon in the late seventies. "Women's rising labor force participation . . . has not resulted in women getting a chance at the higher paying and more powerful jobs," Rosabeth Moss Kanter wrote in her 1977 study, *Men and Women of the Corporation*. "The title of William H. Whyte's . . . bestseller, *The Organization Man*, did not reflect an unwitting failure to use a better generic term for all of humanity. There were then and still are so few women in management that 'the organization *man*' meant exactly what it said."

Women and people of color had finally been admitted to the party that was the nation's postwar economic boom. But they were put at the worst table. And by the time they'd been let in, the bash was about to come to an end.

President Nixon, seen here in 1971 announcing
wage and price controls, tried to tamp down inflation. But he had a hard time holding unions in line,
as they pressed for higher pay for their members, in
part to keep up with the rising cost of living.

7

THE UNRAVELING

In September 1967, General Electric's Virgil Day stepped to the podium at an industry conference in Chicago to discuss the state of labor relations in America. In a matter of no time, he widened his lens. "The twentieth century is two-thirds over this year," Day told the group, his low voice filling the room. "Today's kindergarten class will still be in its thirties when the year 2000 rolls around. What will be the dominant forces and trends during the final third of the century that lies ahead?"

Day, who as a private pilot was naturally inclined to take a high-altitude view of things, went on to pick out ten big-picture developments that he saw on the horizon. He talked, for instance, about the fate of poor minorities, noting that "the War on Poverty, not to mention recent riots, have quite properly absorbed the nation's attention and revealed deep and unsolved problems." He spoke of the need for learning to become a "lifelong process" for all adults. And he contemplated "greater mobility in every phase of American life"—not just in terms of the ascent of air travel and a huge expansion of the interstate-highway system, but the "enormous job mobility" and "changes in once-stable institutions" that were beginning to show themselves. In one community after another, Day said, "people have few lifetime ties anymore. Most of their experiences take the form of 'passing through.' . . . They are not disturbed by not having roots. Loyalties to a hometown or a company or a union or a profession . . . are watered down or even nonexistent for many."

It's unclear whether Day's audience realized how incredibly far-sighted his remarks were. But if they had trouble imagining the future, there is little question that they would have understood what Day described as one of the most "important pressures on management decision making" facing them in the moment: a sharp rise in inflation.

Concern about mounting costs was nothing new, of course. It was a burst of inflation immediately after World War II that had led to the introduction of cost-of-living adjustments in labor contracts. And executives had long decried the "wage-price spiral" that unions were supposedly generating as workers continued to see large jumps in their earnings through the late 1950s and into the '60s. But the reality was that inflation had been docile for many years, topping 3 percent just once since 1957 and averaging less than 1.5 percent a year from 1960 through 1965. Meanwhile, save for a mild recession from mid-1960 into early 1961, the economy remained strong—and, in fact, for years seemed to be getting even stronger.

President Kennedy had come into office arguing that the Golden Age of the 1950s hadn't actually been golden enough, and he promised to "get the country moving again." The "New Economics" put forth by his administration (and later advanced by President Johnson) sought to ramp up economic growth through tax cuts and spending increases and a more relaxed stance at the Federal Reserve—all of it carefully engineered by the biggest brains in government, who would fiddle with the dials at their disposal and "fine-tune" things to ensure the nation's continuing good fortune. "With proper fiscal and monetary policies," said economist Paul Samuelson, a Nobel laureate and an adviser to Kennedy and Johnson, "our economy can have full employment and whatever rate of . . . growth it wants."

Although such assertions highlighted the hubris of the president's men—convinced that they were "effectively abolishing the business cycle," as historian Wyatt Wells has put it—their master plan worked, for a time anyway. From 1961 through 1966, the economy had expanded at an average rate of more than 5 percent a year, a very healthy pace. The unemployment rate, which had hit more than 6.5 percent in the early part of the decade, had fallen back to less than 4 percent by '66. *Time* even put John Maynard Keynes, patron saint of the New Economics, on its cover in late 1965. "In Washington," the magazine declared, "the men who formulate the nation's economic policies have used Keynesian principles not only to avoid the violent cycles of prewar days but to produce a phenomenal economic growth and to achieve remarkably stable prices. In 1965 they skillfully applied Keynes's ideas—together with a number of their own invention—to lift the nation through the fifth, and best, consecutive year of the most sizable, prolonged, and widely distributed prosperity in history." Indeed, by the time Day made his remarks, the United States was in the midst of an economic expansion that would span 106 months—a record at the time.

"Now, however," Day warned, "we face a new ballgame"—one that, if not mitigated, could well prove "ruinous." He rattled off the statistics: Wage increases negotiated with the major unions had been on a steady upward march, climbing from a shade under 3 percent in 1961 to 4.5 percent in 1966. Some industries, including the airlines and telephone and electrical companies, had seen upsurges of 5 percent. And in rubber and railroads, the gains had been more like 6 percent. Arthur Burns, who had served as chairman of President Eisenhower's Council of Economic Advisers, expressed fear that America was on "the threshold of a wage explosion."

Practitioners of the New Economics hadn't been oblivious to these dangers. In 1962, the president's Council of Economic Advisers had issued guideposts that urged business to hold down prices and labor to be sensitive that wages didn't go up any faster than productivity. (General Electric went even further, saying that heightened "challenges of competition from abroad . . . call for compensation increases that are *less* than the increase in the nation's productivity, rather than increases that are simply noninflationary.") Some complied. Early in '62, after an appeal from the Kennedy administration, the United Steelworkers agreed to a new contract that contained only a modest improvement in fringe benefits and no across-the-board bump in wages—the first time that had happened in two decades. Kennedy praised the union's "high industrial statesmanship," and it was generally presumed that the steel companies would now do their part and keep the lid on prices.

Less than two weeks later, however, Kennedy got a surprise visit from Roger Blough, the chief executive of US Steel. The company, he informed the president, was raising prices by six dollars a ton, or

3.5 percent. Kennedy erupted. "You made a terrible mistake," he told Blough. "You double-crossed me." As Kennedy paced the Oval Office after Blough had left, he got even hotter. "He fucked me," the president told Arthur Goldberg, his labor secretary. "They fucked us, and we've got to try to fuck them." The incident would lead, as well, to one of Kennedy's most notorious comments: "My father told me that all businessmen were sons-of-bitches. But I never believed it till now." (In response, some began wearing buttons that said "S.O.B. Club" for "Sons of Business.")

Bethlehem Steel and four other companies followed US Steel's move, and Kennedy retaliated. "In this serious hour in our nation's history," the president said in a televised appearance, "when we are confronted with grave crises in Berlin and Southeast Asia, when we are . . . asking union members to hold down their wage requests, at a time when restraint and sacrifice are being asked of every citizen, the American people will find it hard, as I do, to accept a situation in which a tiny handful of steel executives whose pursuit of private power and profit exceeds their sense of public responsibility can show such utter contempt for the interests of 185 million Americans." Kennedy's scolding was the least of it. He ordered the Justice Department and Federal Trade Commission to investigate possible antitrust violations, and government agents raided corporate offices to search through executives' records. The Pentagon cancelled its contracts with US Steel. The president also approached Inland Steel, Kaiser Steel, and others in the industry that hadn't yet raised prices, coaxing them to hold the line and undersell their rivals. Just three days after Blough had called on the White House, word came down that US Steel and Bethlehem were rescinding their price hikes. The steel barons had been broken; Kennedy had won.

For all of the political theater, Kennedy seems to have dug in against the steel companies more because he felt personally slighted than because of some firmly held conviction about inflation. Compared with President Eisenhower, who truly believed that the federal budget should be balanced so as to keep the economy from overheating, Kennedy and his counselors were far more focused on promoting growth and stifling unemployment. "Inflation," said James Tobin, a member of Kennedy's Council of Economic Advisers and another Nobel Prize winner, "is greatly exaggerated as a social evil. Even while prices are rising year after year, the economy is producing more and more the goods, services, and jobs that meet people's needs. That, after all, is its real purpose."

By the second half of the 1960s, though, inflation was becoming too severe to shrug off—the result, in large part, of an economy over-stimulated by copious amounts of government spending on Great Society social programs as well as the Vietnam War. "The famous debate between 'guns and butter' was left unresolved," the journalist William Greider has observed. "The people got both." President Johnson did his best to corral prices. Taking a page from President Kennedy, he waded into contract negotiations between the Steelworkers and management in 1965 and pressed the two sides into a deal that fell within his wage-price guideposts. Later, he successfully bullied Bethlehem Steel into pulling back on a price increase, and then he did the same with aluminum and copper companies. No part of the economy was too small or too obscure for Johnson to insert himself. When the price of lamb rose, the president told Defense Secretary Robert McNamara to order cheaper meat from New Zealand for the troops in Vietnam. When egg prices shot up, Johnson had the surgeon general speak out on the hazards of high cholesterol.

Still, even the steamroller that was LBJ could flatten inflation only so much. In the summer of 1966, in an attempt to settle an airline industry strike, Johnson ignored his own guideposts, which called for wage-and-benefit increases of about 3 percent. Looking past that cut-off, the president endorsed a package of more than 4 percent. In the end, the carriers and machinists union settled on 5 percent. The head of the machinists, Roy Siemiller, insisted that the agreement "will not cause inflation." If anything, he added, "there should have been more." Yet Siemiller also acknowledged that the accord "effectively and thoroughly shreds the so-called wage guidelines."

And so it did. Suddenly feeling more confident, the steel industry increased prices—and the White House could do little this time but frown. "No one can force them to do something they don't want to do," said Bill Moyers, the president's press secretary.

The top had popped off the kettle. In 1967, consumer prices ticked up by more than 3 percent, and then they rose by over 4 percent in 1968—and were headed higher still. Virgil Day's trenchant assessment in Chicago was looking, more and more, to have been right on the mark: "Whether or not Washington's New Economics may have been successful in minimizing unemployment," he'd said, "it has been conspicuously deficient in coping with the new phenomenon of rising prices."

As President Nixon took office in 1969, inflation was the nation's biggest economic malady. But much like his Democratic predecessors, the Republican was more intent on keeping unemployment low than attacking rising prices. "When you talk about inflation in the abstract, it is hard to make people understand," Nixon explained. "But when unemployment goes up one-half of one percent, that's dynamite." And so Nixon opted for a policy of "gradualism" in which the new administration sought to put the brakes on the economy by cutting the budget and increasing taxes while the Federal Reserve tightened the money supply—but all of it executed with a touch light enough that the country wouldn't veer into recession. "We want to level things off," Nixon said, "not shake them up and down." At the same time, Nixon pledged to stay out of labor disputes, saying that he didn't want to "jawbone" business and labor into submission, as Presidents Kennedy and Johnson had done.

By the fall, Nixon and his men, along with officials at the Federal Reserve, were claiming that their approach was now kicking in. In the third quarter of 1969, wholesale and consumer prices both accelerated less quickly than they had before. And it looked like inflation would continue to moderate, what with government spending going down, taxes staying up, and credit harder to come by. The nation, Federal Reserve chairman William McChesney Martin told Congress in September, was "at the tail end" of its inflationary frenzy. "We're making slow and steady progress," he said. *Life* relayed that "a consensus is now developing among economists that Nixon's . . . medicine is beginning to have its intended effect. . . . They are on the right course, and it's no time to change it."

But for all that optimism, the administration's handle on wages and prices was tenuous at best, and Nixon leaned on corporate and union leaders to remember that "inflation is everybody's problem"—not just Washington's. The president emphasized that he wasn't planning to institute wage and price controls, which he said were "bad for business, bad for the workingman, and bad for the consumer." He didn't even want to go so far as to reestablish formal government guideposts.

Nonetheless, Nixon impressed upon the private sector that it must join his administration in combating the high cost of living. "The business that commits errors in pricing on the up side, expecting to be bailed out by inflation, is going to find itself in a poor competitive position," the president cautioned. As for labor, he said, "it is in the interest of every union leader and workingman to avoid wage demands that will reduce the purchasing power of his dollar and reduce the number of job opportunities."

Getting either side to fall in line was tough. The rate of inflation may have slowed, but prices were still going up. The same week that Martin, the Fed chair, offered lawmakers his hopeful reading of the economy, General Motors said it would raise the sticker price on its 1970 models by an average of nearly 4 percent—the largest spike in more than ten years. Also that week, GE increased the price of its ranges, refrigerators, freezers, and washing machines by about 3 percent. The nation's airlines announced higher fares, as well, and coffee producers boosted the price of beans. With workers continuing to lag behind, no labor leader felt as if he could compromise at the bargaining table, regardless of what Nixon had to say about inflation starting to wane. If anybody were to pull a punch based on the prospect of better days in the future, "he isn't going to be the head of that union very long," said George Meany, president of the AFL-CIO. Walter Reuther of the Auto Workers was typical: "We are going to . . . get our equity," he said, "and we don't care what business's attitude may be or what the attitude of the Nixon administration may be." Another union official broke it down like this: "Our people can know all they need to know about inflation at the supermarket. Nixon tells them he is licking inflation and the next day prices take another big jump."

And so labor pushed—and often prevailed. Unit labor costs (the amount of money needed to pay employees to make one unit of output, a single widget) began to escalate: after edging up less than 1 percent on average from 1960 through 1965, this critical measure leaped by nearly 3 percent in 1966, more than 3.5 percent the following year, and more than 4.5 percent in 1968. By the end of 1969, it was on track to increase by 7 percent. When it came down to it, corporate America was still taking care of its employees. But "perversely," the business columnist Robert Samuelson has written, the "social contract became a conveyer belt for higher inflation."

Whether wages were chasing prices or prices were chasing wages, neither business nor labor was ready to back down—and each side accused the other of the same deadly sin: greed. "The source of the problem is not the fact that American workers are fighting for their legitimate wage claims," said Reuther, but it's the "giant corporations of America who control the marketplace and . . . keep raising prices to maximize their profits." To corporate executives, however, fault resided with union officials who were trying to maximize their members' incomes beyond reason. "What is happening," said *Fortune* magazine, "is that organized labor is overreaching."

Desperate to reverse the tide, business in 1969 took aim at a key catalyst for inflation: construction costs. Because of the vast influence of unions in the industry—the US Chamber of Commerce slammed them as "the most powerful oligarchy in the country"—compensation in the building trades was rocketing upward at an annual rate of 10 percent. In turn, unions in other sectors felt compelled to keep up with the hard hats. As George Morris, director of labor relations at General Motors, recounted: workers in construction would see their brethren in the auto plants and "irritate them, so that our electrician goes down to his UAW local and says, 'Goddamn. How come that guy gets $8.50 an hour and I get $5.80?'" The Construction Users Anti-Inflation Roundtable was formed to counteract all of this by coordinating labor relations across corporate America and by lobbying for changes in public policy that might rein in "runaway wages." The group swore that it had no "antiunion" bias, but its statements and activities indicated otherwise.

Roger Blough, who had recently retired from US Steel, was the head of the group, which became known among executives as "Roger's Roundtable." But it was hardly a one-man show. Representatives from more than one hundred top companies were involved, including Eastman Kodak, Coca-Cola, General Motors, and General Electric. GE's Virgil Day—a protégé of Lem Boulware and a fan of his firebrand variety of conservatism—demonstrated particular enthusiasm for the cause, speaking on the organization's behalf when he labeled the union hiring hall "the root of all evil in the construction industry."

At one point, President Nixon would suspend the Davis-Bacon Act, a Depression-era law mandating that workers on federal public-works projects be paid prevailing local wages and benefits—a way to prevent contractors from bringing in cheap labor. Blough took credit for the president's action, but there was really only so much impact that this kind of government intervention could have. "We've made progress, but too little," Blough conceded.

The real fight against higher inflation was to unfold company by company, contract by contract. And the next year was set to bring one trial after the next: a series of expiring labor agreements covering more than 1 million workers in construction, 450,000 in trucking, 70,000 in the rubber industry, 75,000 among the nation's meatpackers, 100,000 making farm equipment, and 600,000 in autos.

The first proving ground, though, lay right outside Virgil Day's door: in October, GE made its opening offer in negotiations with a group of unions representing 147,000 workers at 280,000 plants in 33 states. The *New York Times* called it "an acid test for Nixon's plea for 'restraint.'" Any pact eventually reached, the paper said, was bound to have "a crucial effect on the success or failure of President Nixon's" program for "checking the wage-price spiral." Yet for the unions involved, especially the International Union of Electrical Workers, squaring off against GE carried additional stakes that were every bit as high. Played right, this was their chance to finally put an end to Boulwarism.

G eneral Electric's 1955 labor contract—celebrated as a "splendid settlement" by both the company's Lem Boulware and James Carey of the IUE—was, in retrospect, a clear aberration, a single flower that had bloomed during America's short season of industrial peace. It had then wilted fast.

In the years since, big business had taken its "hard line" against organized labor, with many companies inspired by Boulware's bargaining tactics: going directly to the rank-and-file to hear workers' wishes and to lay out the views of management; subsequently making an offer that GE unilaterally proclaimed was "feasible and fair"—and more or less firm and final; and doing away, wherever possible, with the back-and-forth that typified most union negotiations. GE called its process "truthful and forthright." The IUE termed it "brainwashing." And by the next contract talks, in 1960, Carey and his union colleagues were more determined than ever to force GE to change its practices. "From our viewpoint," the IUE said, "this is a struggle for the survival not only of our union but for the union movement in America."

The two sides were far apart from the start in '60. The IUE was looking for a two-year contract, with annual wage gains of 3.5 percent, a supplemental unemployment benefits program, and a renewal of the cost-of-living escalator that it had secured in 1955. GE had offered a three-year deal featuring a wage increase of 3 percent immediately and another 4 percent down the line, along with a job retraining initiative and some improvements in benefits. The COLA, GE argued, had become too expensive to continue.

The company had presented its proposal in August and, as was its wont, hadn't altered its offer since—even with an October strike deadline fast approaching. "You think there is something else coming," Philip Moore, GE's chief negotiator, told Carey as talks broke down. "Well, there isn't now, next week, next month, or any other time. Now get that through your thick head." Whether Carey was thickheaded or not, he was as hotheaded as ever. At certain points, his screaming in the negotiating room got so loud, he could be heard through a double-block wall that supposedly had been soundproofed.

The IUE went out on strike a minute after midnight on Sunday, October 2. It was the first major walkout at the company since 1946—the event that had precipitated the advent of Boulwarism. GE said that it would keep its plants open and that anyone who came to work would receive the pay and benefits that the company had offered back in August. On the picket lines, things degenerated in a hurry. At a GE factory in Ohio, pickets jabbed those who dared to enter the facility with hat-pins. At the company's Electronics Park complex in Syracuse, New York, union loyalists broke automobile windows and scattered nails. Outside two GE factories in Massachusetts, IUE members tried to form human barricades and block people from entering. In Pittsfield, six people were arrested and charged with assault and battery as fistfights broke out. In Lynn, police made space for carloads of nonstrikers to get through, and the pickets menaced those who passed. "You are marked men," they shouted. "We'll remember you." They also deflated their tires.

But it was the IUE that soon saw the air rush out of things. Support for the strike among various union locals had been lukewarm at best, most notably at the largest of them all: IUE Local 301 in Schenectady, New York, which represented nearly 9,000 workers. Leo

Jandreau, the head of Local 301, at first refused to join the strike, saying that Carey "did not have the issues or the organizational strength or the other economic factors that are necessary" to make a work stoppage effective. After a few days Jandreau did agree to participate—but then in the midst of the strike he pulled an about-face and his members returned to their jobs. "Carey," he said, "is on a suicidal expedition that will weaken the IUE." Back-to-work drives began to materialize in other locations around the country as well. Just as he had during the early 1950s, Carey was losing his grip over the IUE.

Carey called Jandreau a "Benedict Arnold" and predicted that "to decent union members his name will be a symbol of infamy." But the dressing down didn't have any consequence. Three weeks into the walkout, Carey caved. In spite of his insistence to GE before the strike that "all of our demands are musts," the union chief settled for what the company had been offering all along—a total yielding. GE was careful not to brag. "Nobody ever wins this sort of thing," Moore said. But the *New York Times* characterized it as "the worst setback any union has received in a nationwide strike since World War II."

Carey, however, wasn't done. The IUE filed a complaint with the National Labor Relations Board, alleging that GE had violated the law by refusing to bargain in good faith. The union had tried to bring such charges in the past, but they'd never stuck. This time they did. In 1961, the NLRB's general counsel took up the case as his own, scouring for evidence that GE had engaged in unfair labor practices. He didn't have to dig far. The transcript of the 1960 negotiating sessions between the IUE and GE was filled with passages like this:

> JANDREAU. Mr. Moore, can I ask a question? Is it possible to change the company proposal one way or another? I ask this because you said to me and McManus that this is it. It is all on the table. Is there any chance of changing your position one iota?
>
> MOORE. There are two things, Mr. Jandreau. After all our month of bargaining and after telling the employees . . . that this is it, we would look ridiculous to change it at this late date; and secondly the answer is no. We aren't changing anything come a strike or high water.

GE had stonewalled in other ways, too. An IUE request for an estimate on the portion of the workforce that was to be covered by a certain benefit program, for example, brought the following reply from Moore: "Somewhere between zero and 100 percent."

Yet the case against GE was not only that the company was obstinate. At issue was the essence of Boulwarism—the way GE would go straight to its employees to gauge how they felt regarding wages and benefits and other workplace concerns, and then spell out for them in a barrage of articles, editorials, cartoons, radio and television broadcasts, telephone messages, and letters home why they were going to get what they were going to get.

In April 1963, an NLRB trial examiner ruled that the company had broken the law, citing, among other things, its outreach to workers. "The very massiveness of the communications" undertaken by GE, he found, "is itself a measure" of the company's "determination to deal essentially, not with the employees through the union, but with the union through the employees." GE's goal, he concluded, was "to undercut not only the union's bargaining position, but its authority as bargaining agent."

GE appealed, and in December 1964, the full NLRB upheld the trial examiner's decision. By this time, Lem Boulware was retired from GE. But his successors—above all, Virgil Day—were more than ready to defend Boulwarism. The way they saw it, the NLRB had erred on the facts. Plenty of times over the years, they pointed out, the company had revised a contract offer, at least at the margins. There is a "common misrepresentation which portrays us as starting with a proposal, which we then allegedly refuse to alter," Day said. "We do modify and have made various concessions . . . in light of discussion with the union or new information a union may provide—but not just to 'prove' that we are bargaining." Even more fundamentally, GE was horrified that the NLRB would seek to interfere with the company communicating "fully and frankly" with its own workers.

The media rushed to GE's defense. The *Detroit Free Press* said that the NLRB had "gotten onto dangerous ground" with its decision. The *St. Louis Globe Democrat* accused the labor board of "arbitrary censorship." The *New York World Telegram* asked: "Do you know that free speech is guaranteed to everyone in the United States by the First Amendment of the Constitution—except managers of business?" The

Washington Post said that the NLRB "has gone far beyond the boundaries of the Wagner Act and is, in effect, telling parties how they must bargain."

Yet while GE found instant comfort in the court of public opinion, it would get no swift answers in a court of law. The company's appeal of the NLRB's ruling made its way slowly through the federal judiciary, in part because the IUE and the company clashed over which circuit the case should be litigated in. That took more than a year to sort out. Another year and a half went by as the parties tried unsuccessfully to settle. At last, arguments were heard by the federal Court of Appeals in New York in June 1969—just as the latest round of contract talks between GE and the IUE were about to get underway.

Much had occurred since the controversy began. The IUE and GE had agreed on two other contracts, one in 1963 and another in 1966, without nearly as much furor as before. What's more, in addition to Lem Boulware now being out of the game, so was Jim Carey—only he hadn't been sent off in nearly as flattering a fashion as his nemesis from GE. As Boulware headed into retirement, he was not only held in high regard inside the company; he had also become something of a legend within conservative circles. "If it's the last thing I do," the *National Review*'s William Buckley told Boulware a few months before he left GE, "I'll build a statue with your name on it." Carey's undoing had come in 1965, with the IUE racked by ever more infighting. For a while, the longtime union president was able to fend off his opponents—the "Judas element," he snarled—who protested that Carey had turned into a reckless dictator. Then Paul Jennings, the executive secretary of the IUE district encompassing New York and New Jersey, challenged Carey for the union leadership. Initially, it appeared that Carey had squeaked out the election by about 2,000 votes. But a Labor Department investigation found a miscounting of ballots and the false reporting of results by five pro-Carey union trustees. Jennings, it turned out, had won by more than 23,000 votes.

Although the forty-seven-year-old Jennings had helped Carey cofound the IUE when it split in 1949 with the Communist-led United Electrical, Radio, and Machine Workers of America, the two men were nothing alike. A voracious reader of everything from Churchill and Sandburg to detective novels—known to devour several books in a single night—Jennings was as even-tempered as Carey was irascible.

He said that the IUE had made a mistake in letting contract negotiations become "personalized" in the past; from now on, tantrums would not be thrown at the bargaining table.

But none of this meant that Jennings was soft. Associates often referred to him as "tough-minded," and he was a shrewd tactician. During the 1966 talks with GE, Jennings had pioneered the concept of bringing multiple unions together—in that case, ten of them, in addition to the IUE—to bargain with the company as a single bloc. Observers said that the unions' ability to coordinate was instrumental in them obtaining a generous contract, with annual 5 percent advances in wages and benefits over the next three years.

Also noteworthy in '66, the union coalition had swayed GE to raise—by just a tad—its original offer, cracking ever so slightly the bedrock of Boulwarism. But GE was a long way from forsaking its methods. It's still a "paternalistic, father-knows-best attitude," John Shambo, the IUE's lead negotiator in 1969, said a month and a half into talks with the company. "They have this lousy damn position. . . . They won't negotiate. They say they are going to do right voluntarily." Bargaining with GE, he said, was just like "shoveling smoke."

Despite President Nixon's request to both labor and management to help curtail inflation, it was obvious what the IUE and the dozen other unions allied with it were out to accomplish in '69: "GE's workforce—pinched by soaring prices—is hungry for a substantial raise," *Business Week* noted. And Jennings and the other union leaders in his coalition were committed to feeding their members.

By the end of September, GE officials were becoming anxious. "It is our conviction that if a strike does occur it will likely be a long one," Phil Moore told the company's managers. "The IUE-coalition strategy seems aimed only at getting a strike started, and apparently has given little thought as to how it may end—especially if we don't come through with the kind of concessions they need to claim they have destroyed 'Boulwarism.'" Moore added, "I hope my analysis is wrong."

It wasn't. With negotiators on entirely different pages, union members walked off the job on October 27. The IUE and the others wanted a contract with hourly wage gains of 35 cents the first year, 30 cents the second, and 25 cents the third—a total jump of nearly

28 percent for workers then making, on average, $3.25. On top of that, they were asking for cost-of-living protection and bigger benefits. GE's offer—which it hadn't wavered on since originally serving it up, a la the precepts of Boulwarism—rested on a 20-cent-per-hour wage increase the first year, with a call to reopen negotiations on pay during each of the next two years. The company stressed that wages would be increased in 1970 and 1971, but it wanted to leave the size of the increase open until later, since both sides would then be in a better position to judge what was happening with inflation. The company's chief negotiator, John Baldwin, said it was "the best offer ever in GE history." Paul Jennings said it was among "the worst."

Just like in 1960, violence flared right away on the picket lines. In Schenectady, about 3,000 union members linked arms and encircled the GE plant, trying to keep anyone from entering; 18 people were arrested. At a GE factory in Cicero, Illinois, police cleared out demonstrators with Mace and clubs. But the biggest blow—at least as far as the company was concerned—was delivered just a couple of days into the strike by the federal Appeals Court in New York: the judges affirmed the NLRB's finding that GE had failed in 1960 to bargain in good faith.

The company, the court said, had exhibited "a pettifogging insistence on doing not one whit more than the law absolutely required, an insistence that eventually strayed over into doing considerably less." Throughout the contract talks, the judges found, GE had "displayed a patronizing attitude towards union negotiators inconsistent with a genuine desire to reach a mutually satisfactory accord." And they concurred with the NLRB that the company's direct communications with employees on contract issues had led to a lack of honest give-and-take with the IUE. "We hold that an employer may not so combine 'take-it-or-leave-it' bargaining methods with a widely publicized stance of unbending firmness that he is himself unable to alter a position once taken," the court said. "Such conduct, we find, constitutes a refusal to bargain 'in fact.' It also constitutes . . . an absence of subjective good faith, for it implies that the company can deliberately bargain and communicate as though the union did not exist, in clear derogation of the union's status as exclusive representative of its members."

The IUE pounced on the ruling, contending that it obligated GE to raise its existing offer. The strike of '69 Jennings said, "has been provoked by the same methods condemned by the court as unlawful." To no one's surprise, GE interpreted things much differently. "We can't conceive of anything out of the court ruling that would require us to enlarge our current proposal," said a spokesman for the company, which nonetheless vowed to appeal. The court may have wounded Boulwarism, but it was plain that the union was going to have to persevere on the picket lines to finish it off. Jennings, who had rid the IUE of its internal strife, seemed ready. "We'll hold out as long as we have to to get what we deserve," he said.

On November 7, the Federal Mediation and Conciliation Service pulled company and union negotiators back to bargaining for the first time since the strike began. Yet neither side was ready to give an inch, and the talks promptly broke off. When they resumed more than a week later, a GE official hoped that things would now go better. They didn't. "We got twenty-two no's," said a union spokesman.

The strikers hunkered down—and, unlike in 1960, the solidarity among the 130,000 strikers was impressive. Groups of workers bought meat in bulk and stored it in commercial lockers that they rented together. At IUE Local 301 in Schenectady, a posting on the wall advertised "immediate job openings" for part-time work at area retail stores gearing up for the holidays, giving union members a way to supplement their twelve dollars a week in strike benefits. Mohawk National Bank spotted a chance to be a good neighbor—and to generate a little business. "Need Help? See Us For a Loan," read the sign it placed atop a building on Erie Boulevard. At Bond's clothing store, the manager said he'd allow strikers to wait until ninety days after a new contract was reached to pay their bills. A dentist in town said that his patients who were GE employees were seeking a similar reprieve, while others were missing their checkups altogether. "They prefer to eat first and worry about their teeth later," he said.

Despite the hardships, the IUE gave no hint of relenting. At an emergency convention, 500 delegates voted unanimously to ensure that the IUE's strike fund wouldn't go dry by having the union's hundreds of thousands of members at companies other than GE contribute an amount equal to an hour of their pay every week while the walkout lasted. "The union has come of age," Jennings said after the vote, "and we're going to win." This wasn't baseless boosterism. The longer the strike dragged on, the rougher that things got for GE, where production was running at only about a quarter of its normal rate.

In late November, the AFL-CIO tried to further tighten the screws on the company by calling for a national boycott of its products. GE dismissed the ban as "public posturing," while simultaneously stewing over the negative effect that it could have vis-à-vis the fast-gaining Japanese and Germans. "Foreign goods," said Chief Executive Fred Borch, "will flow into any vacuum." GE reminded its workers that, in this way, scaring off customers in the short run might lead to fewer jobs in the long run. A boycott "almost always hurts the very people it is supposed to help," a company official said. Merchants around the country, for their part, stated that the AFL-CIO's campaign wasn't cutting into business very much; the whole thing was kind of a flop.

But as the GE strike stretched into its seventh week, the economies of the 135 cities across the United States where the company had factories were starting to sputter. "Sales are way down," said the manager of a department store in Erie, Pennsylvania, where thousands of GE strikers lived. "The banks are starting to feel the pinch, too, I hear." In Lynn, a car dealer said the stoppage had caused a 15 percent falloff in sales. In Pittsfield, where GE workers were foregoing about $1 million in total payroll each week to stay on strike, some store owners said the walkout was responsible for a 25 percent decline in business. Over time, the pain would only get worse, with suppliers and customers also affected. Carrier Corporation, an air-conditioner manufacturer, laid off 350 employees, or about 10 percent of its hourly workforce in Syracuse, because it couldn't procure equipment normally produced by GE. Consolidated Edison told New York City residents to brace for summer blackouts because the gas-fired generators it had on order with GE weren't being delivered. For GE itself, the strike was also now taking a stiff toll, wiping out most of the company's profit for the fourth quarter.

On December 6, GE blinked. It scrapped its original idea of reopening negotiations on wages in 1970 and '71 and instead said that it would increase pay at least 3 percent in each of those years—and as much as 5 percent, depending on the cost of living. Although Borch was adamant that this was "the maximum economic package GE can make" and no third offer would be forthcoming, some saw it as an extraordinary gesture, a historic backpedaling from Boulwarism. "A strong argument can be made that the company has junked the most basic elements of the take-it-or-leave-it approach GE unions always found so infuriating," said A. H. Raskin of the *New York Times*. But the IUE and the other unions didn't rejoice. Rather, they rejected the company's new proposal as "a hoax" and came back with a fresh offer of their own: a sixteen-month contract with an immediate 11 percent wage increase, built-in adjustments after that based on inflation, and a host of other benefits crammed into this tighter time frame.

The two sides then met for a few days, but old habits die hard: the unions charged GE with refusing to bargain and ended the negotiations, while the company said the unions were being "irresponsible." The union coalition "is so locked in that we can't make any real progress," said a GE executive. "They are out to beat us down." Wrote Raskin: "Boulwarism may be dead, but the end of the strike is no closer."

Even as the holidays drew near, the unions' resolve never flagged. "The company has sought to lure strikers back" to work "on grounds that their families should not suffer a dreary Christmas," the Associated Press reported. But "the strategy," the AP said, "appeared to backfire." The AFL-CIO was about to write a $1 million check to replenish the GE strike fund. And the picket lines were fuller than ever. "People think this is a strike for a few cents an hour," said Ralph Boyd, a GE worker in Schenectady. "But it is about human dignity. It is about the workingman's right to organize, and it is about an employer's duty to bargain. . . . For those issues, I would rather starve than surrender." Christmas came and went; so did New Year's.

Then, on January 7, 1970, the head of the Federal Mediation and Conciliation Service entered the fray. For three weeks, he shuttled between GE and the unions before, finally, ninety-five days into the strike, he announced that the two sides had come to terms. The agreement would give GE workers a 25 percent wage increase over forty months, plus additional cost-of-living adjustments, if needed. Boulwarism had been defeated not only at the bench (the Supreme Court would decline to hear the unfair labor-practices case, letting the earlier ruling against GE stand) but in the trenches, too. Union leaders were jubilant, saying that this was the first contract that had been legitimately negotiated with GE since Boulwarism was born. Everything prior had been "articles of surrender, like the Japanese signed on the battleship *Missouri*," said one labor official. Exclaimed another union staffer: "We did it. They said we couldn't, but we damn sure did it."

GE executives denied that they'd given up much between their first and final offers. "We stayed in the ballpark," said one. "We just moved the fences a little." But even they had to confess that an era had come to an end. "Boulwarism just does not work today," admitted a company official. Boulware himself, now retired in Florida, said privately that he had "a deep sense of guilt that I did not—with all the opportunity I was given—leave behind a better preventative against" a long strike.

Still, the unions' triumph was double-edged. Slaying Boulwarism meant winning a contract that was, by most accounts, inflationary. "The Nixon administration and the national economy are among the losers," said *Time* magazine. "Such an increase, granted by one of the nation's hardest-bargaining employers, may well embolden other union leaders to hold out for hefty increases in different labor negotiations later this year." That scenario would help to bring about more inflation, just as economic growth was slowing down. And that toxic mixture—high prices and high unemployment—would do far more to grind down America's workers than Boulwarism ever did.

The year 1970 was rotten for the United States economy. The recession, which had begun in December 1969 and would last until the following November, would end up being the mildest of the five slumps since World War II. But it was a recession nevertheless. Output shrank. The unemployment rate increased from just over 4 percent in the first quarter to nearly 6 percent in the fourth. Productivity lagged. Corporate profits shriveled. Even with all of this slowing, inflation remained elevated, barely abating from the year before. Big labor agreements, like the one reached at General Electric, put workers ahead—but hardly. They were forever catching up to rising prices; the treadmill wouldn't stop. Many of those monitoring the numbers, including those inside the Nixon administration, were baffled. "We underestimated the inflationary expectations," said Charls Walker, the undersecretary of the treasury. "We didn't expect that it would be so tough."

Working families got by the best they could. Women smeared their faces with vegetable shortening, instead of expensive cold cream, to remove makeup. When Hunt-Wesson Foods published a booklet of cheap recipes titled *We'll Help You Make It*, the company received 850,000 requests for copies. Personal-finance columnist Martha Patton of the *Chicago Daily News* had an even simpler solution. "Never market when hungry," she advised her readers. In New York, some put on "Beat Inflation" parties with menus that recalled World War II rationing: canned tomato soup, cheese on Ritz crackers, and sweet-and-sour Spam.

If this winding down of the nation's postwar boom were somehow lost on anyone, the tragic death in May of Walter Reuther surely served as a sign of the fall. The United Auto Workers president and his wife were killed with several others in a plane crash in the woods of northern Michigan. He was sixty-two years old. A large group of luminaries—Golda Meir, Cesar Chavez, Coretta Scott King, General Motors CEO James Roche, and Henry Ford II, among them—sent their condolences and paid their tributes. But the most poignant outpouring came from thousands and thousands of men and women without any fancy titles or speeches to make. "We felt so close to him because of how much he had done for workers like us," said Clarence Rydholm, a GM retiree who filed along the royal blue carpet inside the Veterans Memorial Building next to the Detroit River where the Reuthers lay in state. Outside, a light rain fell. "He bargained for the broom pushers like me," said Sam Smith, who came to pay his respects on his way to work, carrying his metal lunch pail past Reuther's oak casket. "He wanted the laboring man to live good and make money like others with prettier jobs."

That mission—to help the laboring man live good—was to be taken up by Reuther's replacement, Leonard Woodcock. He had been with the UAW for thirty-five years, and until now, he'd held the most important post next to the presidency: directorship of the union's General Motors Department. As one might imagine, as soon as he took the top job at the UAW, Woodcock was constantly being compared to Reuther. He managed to hold his own. Intelligent and articulate, Woodcock showed an excellent command of the long-term trends jeopardizing the financial security of his members and working folks in general, including overseas competition and automation. "It's easy to be for free trade when you don't have a problem," Woodcock said. "The test comes when it begins to impinge upon the jobs of our people." To forecast what technology might mean for employment, he proposed creating a National Department of the Future.

But it was here, in the present, where Woodcock, a man known affectionately inside the union as "Timber Dick," was being asked to really show his stuff, as the UAW prepared to face off with GM and the other automakers over a new three-year contract. Union members' wages had gone up by 6 percent a year under their 1967 agreement— but that was all on paper. Inflation had consumed the entire increase and more, so that workers' purchasing power was now nearly 7.5 percent behind where it started. Part of the reason for this slippage was that Reuther had agreed in '67 to cap the cost-of-living formula, giving away the union's unlimited defense against higher prices. Before he died, he said this was the biggest mistake of his life.

Besides fighting for higher pay and restoration of the full COLA, the UAW had one other main demand: after thirty years of service, no matter their age, the union wanted workers to be able to retire at a pension of $500 a month. "Thirty-and-out" became the rank-and-file's mantra. Behind this sentiment for many older workers was a yearning to get past the dead-end dullness and degradation that had long been the fabric of factory life. In 1964, to the surprise of the union leadership, the rank-and-file had forced a strike at General Motors over conditions in its plants. "The strike is not about money," Reuther told GM. It is "about the human use of human beings. . . . It is a revolt against the concept, implicit in the corporation's attitude, that it owns the workers whom it employs—that they are mere extensions of the production process." The contract reached after the month-long walk-out gave workers some comfort, such as more relief time on the assembly line. But it wasn't enough to quash the feelings of ill temper among the industry's old-timers. They were worn out and ready to be done.

Younger hourly employees, under the age of thirty, were also restless, maybe even more so. They now made up more than 40 percent of the UAW's membership, and they'd been stricken with what became known as "blue-collar blues." Many drowned themselves in drugs or alcohol. "I knew a lot of guys they'd never make it home Friday nights from the bars," said James Beeman, a GM worker. "They'd spend their whole check on the way home, then on Monday morning they didn't even have coffee money. It was a problem . . . but I don't blame the people. I blame the type of job."

Yet blue-collar employees didn't just drink up; they also pushed back, exerting what historian Stephen Meyer has identified as a "youthful working-class militancy." Conflicts between the UAW and the automakers at the plant level—over the speed of the line, the cleanliness of bathrooms and cafeterias, the manner in which supervisors would discipline people, and assorted other particulars—proliferated. At GM alone, local demands went from fewer than 12,000 in 1958 to 24,000 in 1964 to 39,000 in 1970. Then, too, there were the workers' unofficial actions: many played hooky, as the rate of absenteeism in auto factories rose to 5 percent in 1970, double where it had been in the 1950s and most of the '60s. On Mondays and Fridays, it was not uncommon to have 10 to 15 percent of the workforce as no-shows. When they did report, they behaved badly. Some even sabotaged the vehicles being built, slashing seat covers, scratching paint, bashing in radios, and tearing out glove-box doors.

The General Motors plant in Lordstown, Ohio—a sleek new structure that produced the Chevy Vega, a subcompact designed to compete with the rapid influx of foreign cars—would emerge in the early seventies as the national poster child of these tensions. (The alternative name for "blue-collar blues" was "Lordstown syndrome.") Attendance at the factory was atrocious and discipline poor. "These workers reflect the changing lifestyle of today's youth," the *Akron Beacon Journal* told its readers. "Many wear their hair shoulder length, have grown mustaches or beards, and come to work in hip-hugging, bell-bottomed trousers. They are probably better educated than any generation of workers in the history of American industry. They were taught to question traditional values and encouraged to stand up and be counted."

In answer to the disgruntlement, GM got tough. The company ordered time-and-motion studies, furloughed hundreds of "unproductive" workers, and introduced mandatory overtime. Then, GM cranked up the line, so that it spit out at least one hundred cars per hour, more than twice the number that workers back in the fifties thought was oppressive. A Lordstown laborer said that the company had "taken away the time to scratch your nose." Some were left black and blue from trying to keep up the pace. For other workers, it wasn't just their bodies that were beaten. "It felt like I was losing my mind," said one.

The blue-collar blues weren't being sung only at GM or the other auto companies. "This place is more mentally depressing than physically," said John Shindledecker, who worked at Coca-Cola's Chambersburg, Pennsylvania, bottling plant. "They should make each employee feel important and needed." At Kodak, workers in Rochester started skipping out on their jobs so frequently that the company issued a bulletin saying it "must have employees who can be depended upon." At a General Electric facility in Erie, Pennsylvania, distrust led management to install closed-circuit TV cameras and open microphones. The local union was livid. "There are institutions in which the inmates are kept under constant surveillance—jails and mental hospitals," it said. "Animals in a zoo are likewise exposed against their will to the gaze of others. But the employees involved here are human beings, not animals. . . . We repeat, they are human beings—not monkeys or jail birds, or nuts."

Production workers weren't the only ones so distraught. "The blue-collar blues is no more bitterly sung than the white-collar moan," Studs Terkel wrote in his 1972 book *Working*. "'I'm a machine,' says the spot-welder. 'I'm caged,' says the bank teller, and echoes the hotel clerk. 'I'm a mule,' says the steelworker. 'A monkey can do what I do,' says the receptionist. 'I'm less than a farm implement,' says the migrant worker. 'I'm an object,' says the high-fashion model. Blue collar and white call upon the identical phrase: 'I'm a robot.'"

Yet it was on the auto assembly line, where the alienation seemed to be greatest, that many employees—the younger ones especially—were all too happy to give their employers less than their all. "The young men and women workers saw no reason to work to the bone," William Serrin, who covered the scene for the *Detroit Free Press*, has written. "Their fathers hated the drudgery, the repetition of the assembly line, but they were older men and older men are not rebellious; they had seen the Depression and they remembered it; they also knew what it had been like in the plants in the days before the union; and they had, in their years in the plant, come to accept plant life as the way plant life was meant to be. The younger workers had not; often, they quit or stayed home, or harassed the foremen. Fuck this, the younger workers said."

For GM, the problem wasn't so much their workers' outrage as it was their output. All of this agitation translated into low productivity. And low productivity was seen as the culprit for high inflation. "It is important to recognize that the basis—the only basis—for a rising standard of material well-being is rising national productivity," James Roche, GM's CEO, told a business luncheon in St. Louis in February 1970. "This is a fact of economic life. It is as true when, as in the recent past, we were caught in an inflationary spiral, or when we were enjoying relative price stability."

Between 1959 and 1965, Roche said, output per man-hour and compensation per man-hour had increased in lockstep—each rising about 25 percent over that period. But from 1965 to 1969, the two decoupled: compensation kept going up at the same clip but output slackened to less than 10 percent. According to Roche, as unit labor costs rose, prices followed. "Although some groups of workers may have pushed up their compensation faster than others," he said, "no one really gained from this inflation: not the employees, not the companies, not the consumer. Inflation is really nobody's friend."

For Roche, the blue-collar blues had to be cured—though he put the burden for doing so almost entirely on those who manned the line. It was as if the company had no role whatsoever in its workers' disaffection. "Absenteeism lessens the effectiveness of all employees," Roche said. "It undermines the foundation on which efficient production depends. It cuts into the quality standards of the product. It carries a price for all workers—the present and the absent alike—and ultimately the consumer. . . . As we face up to our national crisis of cost, American industry continues to be willing to make the investment and take the risk necessary to a continued rise in productivity. . . . The vital question is: Are the unions and the individual employees willing to live up to their end?"

Roche ended his speech by looking at the contract bargaining ahead—and reiterating the need to have wages conform to output. "In the negotiations of 1970," he said, "unions and management must strive together to achieve regular attendance, eliminate unnecessary work stoppages, and cooperate in improving quality. We must restore the balance that has been lost between wages and productivity. We must receive the fair day's work for which we pay the fair day's wages. For upon this balance rests our national ability to cope with inflation."

In September, GM and the UAW exchanged proposals. They went nowhere, and the usual choreography commenced: more than 340,000 workers walked off the job. Days on the picket lines dissolved into weeks. Morale among the strikers held up even as they collected food stamps to scrape by. Tens of millions of dollars in losses piled up for GM. The financial fallout extended to the company's suppliers and showrooms. The union strike fund drained. Talks suddenly intensified. And then, fifty-eight days into the stoppage, an agreement was hatched.

In between the strike and the settlement, GM and the UAW sparred primarily over wages and who should pay for inflation—past and future. The company proposed a nearly 10 percent increase in wages in the first year, to be rounded out by a gain of 3 percent in each of the next two years. Woodcock called GM's tender "less than equitable." Only in 1970s America would 10 percent be scorned as the offer of a skinflint.

The union wanted a 15-plus percent pay increase out of the gate. (Nearly half of the total, it suggested, was essentially back pay owed to employees because of increases in the cost of living since 1967.) The UAW said it couldn't yet ask for second- and third-year raises until it knew whether it was going to win another demand that the company opposed: a COLA with no ceiling. Earl Bramblett, GM's top negotiator, called the UAW position "extreme." But the union had no interest in Bramblett's critique or Roche's sermons on productivity. It favored reaching back to Charles Wilson's words in 1948, as he put in place GM's first COLA and thus made possible the Treaty of Detroit two years later: "The working people did not make . . . inflation. They only want to catch up with it in order to pay their grocery bills." With the union now invoking old "Engine Charlie," it's safe to assume that he was no longer the most revered figure in the GM pantheon, if ever he had been. "We would like to go out and piss on his grave," said one executive.

The final contract split the difference on pay. The first-year raise was about 13 percent, with annual 3 percent increases after that. But on the COLA, the UAW scored big: the unlimited escalator was reinstated. The union also received much of what it wanted on "thirty-and-out." The company had hoped to limit the full $500-a-month retirement benefit to those fifty-eight and older. But it agreed to drop the age requirement to fifty-six and opened the door to it being lowered even more in future years. For many workers, early retirement was their prime motivation for having gone out on strike. "All I have to look forward to is 'thirty-and-out,'" said Pete Tipton, a welder at Cadillac.

For the company, however, the policy was troubling in a couple of respects. First, it threatened to hasten the exit of some of GM's most skilled and experienced people—a potentially "crippling blow," Bramblett had said at the start of negotiations. And, second, it heaped more expense on the company in an area that seemed to be lurching out of control: "fringes." Over the previous ten years, hourly wages at GM had gone up by about 55 percent. But the cost of fringe benefits, for insurance and pensions, had swelled by more than 230 percent. GM was no outlier, either. Over the next few years, worries would grow that the employee-benefits system being created across much of American industry was unsustainable, especially for pensions. "There is a distinct possibility that the economy in the future will not be able to support all of the retirement benefits which are being promised," said Dan McGill, of the University of Pennsylvania. "It is possible to promise too much."

In the short term, though, GM had bought three years of calm on the labor front; to pay, the company jacked up the price of its cars for 1971 by the largest amount in a decade. For its part, the UAW had gotten most of what it wanted—arguably a "fantastic victory," said the *New York Times*. But neither side had done much, if anything, to heed President Nixon's entreaty to quell inflation. Woodcock maintained that the multibillion-dollar agreement wasn't really inflationary. And Bramblett, having evidently forgotten Roche's lessons about what happens when labor costs outrun productivity, said that inflation "evolves out of the pressures in our economy which are beyond the control of either party."

The White House didn't accept any of that. It denounced the contract—and fretted over what it might portend. "If everyone in his turn gets as big a wage or price increase as the biggest obtained by others during the height of the inflation," said the Council of Economic Advisers, "the inflation will go on endlessly." The GM agreement did set a pattern, not only at Ford and Chrysler and other auto companies, but in copper and aluminum, in aerospace, at the US Postal Service, at American Telephone and Telegraph, at US Steel, and elsewhere. By the end of negotiations in 1971, the number of employees covered by COLA clauses had doubled to nearly 60 million. Many of those working at nonunion companies also saw big nominal gains in pay—the spillover of organized labor's battles—as did white-collar employees.

On the face of it, American workers were doing better all the time, just as they had since the end of World War II. But things were very different now. With the cost of living rising perpetually higher and the economy stalling, the Golden Age was fast losing its luster. Instead of sharing in their employers' riches, employees were now grabbing furiously for whatever they could. Instead of being built up on a foundation of strength, the social contract was resting on a wobblier and wobblier frame.

By 1971, the United States had technically pulled itself out of recession. But high prices were still rampant, even though unemployment lingered at 6 percent. "The rules of economics are not working the way they used to," Arthur Burns, now the chair of the Federal Reserve, told Congress in July. "I wish I could report that we are making substantial progress in dampening the inflationary spiral. I cannot do so." In August, believing that he had nowhere left to turn (and with a bunch of voices bellowing in his ear, including that of the Committee for Economic Development), President Nixon went back on his word and ordered a freeze on wages and prices. Washington hadn't meddled in the marketplace this much since the New Deal. Business and labor were both dumbfounded. So were many in Nixon's own administration. As one high-ranking official reflected, "The president made a new economic policy out of all the things we had been saying weren't needed and couldn't work."

At first, the so-called Nixon Shock did work. After an initial ninety-day freeze, the president established a Price Commission and a Pay Board, the latter of which consisted of appointees from the public, labor (including the UAW's Leonard Woodcock), and business (with GE's Virgil Day chairing that part of the panel). The board aimed to keep annual wage increases to 5.5 percent, and though it didn't always succeed, it challenged more than a hundred labor contracts and its presence helped to ease "the psychology of inflation," as Day said. Consumer prices edged down. The other bold features of the president's plan—to end the automatic convertibility of the dollar into gold, a mainstay of international finance since 1944, and to levy a surcharge on imports—helped to make American companies more competitive against foreign firms (if only artificially so).

The Nixon administration also upped its spending, and the Fed lowered interest rates, pumping more money through the economy. Output took off. The nation was finally making real headway against both inflation and unemployment. It was a masterful steering—some would say manipulation—of the economy, helping the president win reelection in 1972 in a landslide over George McGovern. "People can see an improvement," said Harvard's Otto Eckstein, a Democrat who had served on President Johnson's Council of Economic Advisers. His own grade on Nixon's handling of the economy, he told the press, had gone from a D to an A minus.

But it wouldn't be long before Nixonomics flunked. In early 1973, worried that wage and price controls might become a permanent crutch, the administration scaled them back. Big business was pleased. "It is time to return to the self-regulating discipline of a competitive marketplace," said Richard Gerstenberg, who had taken over for Roche as GM's chairman and CEO in 1972. "It is time to give our economy's built-in system of checks and balances a chance to work again." It didn't. Inflation went straight through the roof, reaching nearly 9 percent for the year. In October, reacting to the demise of the gold standard and Nixon's devaluation of the dollar (as well as, most immediately, US support for Israel in the Yom Kippur War), the Organization of Petroleum Exporting Countries put in place an oil embargo, and the cost of crude quadrupled, adding still more inflationary pressure. Consumer prices rose more than 12 percent in 1974; wholesale prices bounded upward more than 21 percent.

Tripped up by OPEC, the economy also tumbled back into recession, a much longer and more calamitous downturn than the last one. The stock market crashed. The official unemployment rate would reach more than 8.5 percent this time around, though the actual figure was probably twice that big. (Nixon himself was out of a job by August 1974 in the wake of the Watergate scandal.) The one-two punch of historically high inflation and joblessness became known by many different names: "slumpflation," "infession," "inflump," and, most of all, "stagflation." Arthur Okun of the Brookings Institution added up the two rates to create a new economic indicator: "the Misery Index."

For America's workers, it was miserable indeed. Outplacement services, a new industry dedicated to helping companies reduce head count, caught on. By late 1974, GE had laid off half of the employees at its sprawling Appliance Park in Louisville, Kentucky, or about 12,000 people. GM had idled about 100,000, or 20 percent of its entire labor force. Several thousand more salaried employees took early retirement under a new program to lower costs. Watching those at his facility bid farewell "was the most emotionally charged experience I had with GM," said Walter Huppenbauer, a personnel administrator at the company's South Gate, California, plant.

Time, which just a decade earlier had put a smiling portrait of John Maynard Keynes on its cover while it sang of the seemingly limitless virtues of the New Economics, now asked this on the front of the magazine: "Can Capitalism Survive?" While the question was a bit hyperbolic, what was ailing the nation couldn't be fixed with a simple jolt of confidence, a push for companies to size up the consumer and sell more, the way that General Electric had advocated in 1958 with Operation Upturn. The problems of business ran much too deep for that.

Corporate profit margins were sinking fast—from more than 15 percent through the 1950s and 1960s to less than 11 percent in the 1970s. "Profits are to free enterprise what oats are to the racehorse: essential both as a reward and as a fuel for continued competition," said GM's Gerstenberg. "Every American should be concerned about the ability of American business to continue to prosper." The forecast wasn't promising. Growth in productivity, which had started to slow in the late sixties, was now at a crawl. Looking back, economists would pinpoint 1973 as a defining marker—the beginning of a two-decade stretch in which productivity gains at US companies were less than half of what they had been after World War II. In due course, this drop-off would eat away at wages and benefits and job security, tearing into the social contract between employer and employee. Experts have put forward all sorts of possible explanations for the productivity collapse: the rise in energy prices, shortcomings in public education, a ballooning federal budget deficit, the weight of government regulation, a depletion of mineral resources.

Others have suggested that the wounds were self-inflicted: many American companies had stopped investing in new equipment, leaving their factories to rust well before the term Rust Belt came into use. They also cut back on research and development through the 1960s, so that they merely "coasted off the great R&D gains made during World War II," said C. Jackson Grayson, president of the American

Productivity Center. As often happens to hegemons, any number of US corporations had gotten stupid, fat, and lazy. "Especially in large organizations," said one executive quoted in *Harvard Business Review*, "we are observing an increase in management behavior which I would regard as excessively cautious, even passive; certainly overanalytical; and, in general, characterized by a studied unwillingness to assume responsibility and even reasonable risk."

Whatever the case, other nations could now exploit America's weaknesses. Countries such as Japan and Germany, which were flat on their backs after the war, had become economic powers. At the outset, America welcomed their revival, as they provided expanding markets for US companies to export their goods. But in time, America's trading relationships got spun on their head. Foreign companies borrowed technical insights and management techniques from the United States and made them their own. In some instances, they made them much better. Germany and Japan leapfrogged America in steel, automobiles, machine tools, consumer electronics, and other industries. Other countries and regions, including Hong Kong, Korea, Singapore, Brazil, and Spain, also stepped up their exports through the seventies. In 1971, imports into the United States exceeded exports for the first time since 1888. By 1976, the United States would swing to a trade deficit that remains unbroken to this day.

This flood of goods from overseas presented a paradox for American households. On the plus side, it gave them access to cheaper items of superior quality. For example, by the early 1970s a Japanese sedan cost 45 percent less than a comparable model built in the United States. American autos were likely to have more of only one thing: defects— twice as many as their Japanese counterparts. As a customer, all of this was so delightful that 100,000 Hondas would be sold in the United States in 1975, up from fewer than 1,500 in 1970. As an employee, though, such intense competition was disconcerting. Or at least it should have been. One reason Japan had a leg up, GM was quick to point out, was that the total compensation received by its factory hands was far less than the pay and benefits for American autoworkers—about 60 percent less in 1974. In coming years, the car companies would use this differential to pull concessions from the UAW.

Other unions were similarly put on the defensive. For a moment in the early seventies, it seemed as if organized labor might be given an injection of vitality from new members who had been radicalized in the antiwar, civil rights, and feminist movements. The discord at GM's Lordstown facility had been a signal to some that a more combative expression of unionism was taking hold. But it wasn't to last. "The unrest of the early decade was based on the most successful economy in American history—simply put, in terms of class power, most workers never had it so good," Vanderbilt University's Jefferson Cowie has written. "Once the rug of economic success was pulled out from underneath workers during the bitter recessions that began with the first oil shock in 1973, they lost their footing in their fights for solutions to their discontents." At that point, "the economy drifted toward stagnation: Industrial capacity plummeted, unemployment rose to its (then) postwar high, foreign competition eroded market position, rising interest rates prevented plant modernization, and holding down wages and benefits became the central goal of corporate strategies as inflation eclipsed unemployment as political enemy number one."

In 1974, an ominous milestone was reached: Americans' wages declined. It was the first time that this had happened since the end of World War II. Even during previous recessions, wages had gone up. But no more. Although no one could have foreseen it at the time, this 2 percent dip would mark what commentator Harold Meyerson has called "a fundamental breakpoint in American economic history"—the onset of a forty-plus-year period in which people's paychecks would barely get any bigger once inflation was taken into account.

Through the 1970s, companies also shifted work to less costly countries, driven in part by a long-standing set of US trade policies that sought to open up American markets to goods made overseas. Washington's aim was to stitch together a world that was economically interdependent and, as such, would stand as a bulwark against Soviet aggression. In 1965, American businesses invested less than $50 billion in foreign factories, offices, and equipment. Ten years later, that number increased to more than $120 billion, and by 1980 it would rise to more than $210 billion. GM, for one, had operated plants abroad since the 1920s to serve those local markets. But now, its international factories began to make parts and cars to sell back in the United States. GE spread its operations overseas as well—and then tried to enlighten its workers on why any other path was imprudent given the globe's growing interconnectedness. "Stop foreigners from flooding US markets with their goods?" the company asked in an employee newsletter. "Stop US companies from setting up shop overseas? Stop exporting US technology? Stop world trade?" Putting a halt to any of this, GE said, would be counterproductive for the company, its workers, and the nation. As if to prove the point, GE added 30,000 jobs abroad during the 1970s—though over the same period it cut 25,000 positions at home.

Other jobs were, by their nature, more resistant to being sent offshore. And these service occupations accounted for a larger and larger share of the US economy, overtaking manufacturing as the primary way that people across the country made a living. By the midseventies, about 60 percent of Americans worked in services, as the nation transitioned into what sociologist Daniel Bell dubbed a "post-industrial society." But these jobs had a real disadvantage. "It happens to be the poorest-paid sector," Gus Tyler, a top official of the International Ladies Garment Workers Union, told a symposium of business leaders gathered in Washington in the summer of 1974.

Paul Austin, the CEO of Coca-Cola, had invited Tyler—along with former commerce secretary Pete Peterson, the Urban League's Vernon Jordan, Trilateral Commission chairman Zbigniew Brzezinski, and others—to try and help make sense of the turbulent times. According to Tyler, the "new class" of employees replacing those in manufacturing included some who would do just fine: college-educated knowledge workers. But many others would have a hard time keeping up. Behind the hotel manager, Tyler said, are "all those little people that do the sweeping and making of the beds. In a hospital, it's the doctor, but behind the doctor stand twenty or thirty people who are not doctors at all. They just scrub and wash and move dirty pans. At an educational testing service you have a few brainy professors, and you have several thousand little ladies who just punch holes into little cards."

Actually, even those with knowledge jobs were being buffeted by change. There is "a need for less structured offices throughout our organization to enable quick decisions with full participation in an increasingly competitive world," a young Coca-Cola manager told Austin when asked for his biggest takeaways from the symposium. "The world of tradition and loyalties is rapidly disappearing." It was, without question, a different environment than the one in which Austin had come up. He had joined Coca-Cola in 1949 with a Harvard Law degree and the can-do spirit of someone who had been an oarsman on the 1936 US Olympic rowing team and the commander of a PT boat during the war. For the next twenty years, he had climbed steadily up the corporate ladder. But this young manager was very perceptive. The kind of linear career that Austin had was about to become a relic. The Organization Man was dying.

Alvin Toffler, in his bestselling 1970 book *Future Shock*, prophesied that the companies that would do well in the years ahead were those that were most nimble, paring back their bureaucracy and fostering an "ad-hocracy." "Instead of being trapped in some unchanging, personality-smashing niche, man will find himself liberated, a stranger in a new free-form world of kinetic organizations. In this alien landscape, his position will be constantly changing, fluid, and varied. And his organizational ties, like his ties with things, places, and people, will turn over at a frenetic and ever-accelerating rate."

In the meantime, the title that Austin had picked for his little confab couldn't have been more perfect: "The World We Know No Longer Is."

The chairman of the Committee for Economic Development, Philip Klutznick, stood before his trustees and invited guests in New York City in January 1975 to talk about the economy. It was still performing dreadfully. "In Talmudic fashion," the wealthy real-estate developer said, "we argue over which is worse, an inflation or a recession, and which is best, a tax increase or a tax cut. Policies designed to deal with one set of problems may serve only to exacerbate another. We need to unlock the conundrum of simultaneous inflation and recession. But to do so, we are turning instinctively—almost nostalgically—to past policies and precedents."

The fact was, few cared what Klutznick had to say. The CED had lost its glow.

A few years earlier, due in large measure to Virgil Day's prompting, the Anti-Inflation Roundtable had merged with two other associations to become the Business Roundtable. The new lobby had by now surpassed the CED to become the leading voice of corporate America.

The changing of the guard had big implications. Industry was in a much different spot than when the CED had, in 1943, set forth its vision for all citizens "to work, to live decently . . . to provide against sickness and old age." And the positions staked out by the Business Roundtable bore little resemblance to what had come before. "If the group did not completely abandon all concern about the larger public interest," Mark Mizruchi, a sociologist at the University of Michigan's business school, has written, "it certainly paid considerably less attention to it than the CED had." Instead, the Business Roundtable concentrated on shrinking the role of government and organized labor—efforts, Mizruchi has said, that "led to a weakening of these two forces" and "increased the ability of corporations to act without the pressures of . . . their workers." This new, more narrowly self-interested agenda would hasten the unraveling of the social contract between employer and employee.

A telltale moment came in 1976 when Sen. Hubert Humphrey and Rep. Augustus Hawkins introduced the Full Employment and Balanced Growth Bill. It was a virtual copy of the Full Employment Act that had been introduced in 1946, in the CED's early days. Back then, the CED had broken with the Chamber of Commerce and the National Association of Manufacturers to support the idea that full employment should be a public objective. Now, however, the Business Roundtable joined with the Chamber and NAM to gut the latest legislation.

Their principal argument, which they marshaled successfully, was that unless it were killed or completely overhauled, the bill would fan inflation. "While all Americans desire 'full employment,' it is unrealistic and less than honest to promise such a result simply through installation of a complex new national planning system, or through the symbolism of legislating an unachievable unemployment goal," the roundtable's Lewis Foy told Congress. For any business leader to embrace the CED's notion that "full employment" should, "like 'liberty' and 'justice' . . . stand as "a goal of democratic government" had become, in just thirty years, utterly unthinkable.

Reg Jones, CEO of General Electric (at right), found in Jack Welch the ideal successor to shake things up in the face of increasing global competition. Welch would transform GE into a striking combination—part meritocracy, part meat grinder.

8

GOING BACKWARD

Being a Georgia boy, President Carter had long had a close relationship with Paul Austin and Coca-Cola—to the point of barring Pepsi from White House vending machines. "You know, ma'am, our crowd likes a good old Democratic drink: Coke," Bert Lance, the budget director, told a secretary when he came upon her sipping the rival soda. But as the US economy continued to sag in the late 1970s, Carter turned for guidance to an ever-wider group of executives, including DuPont's Irving Shapiro, AT&T's John deButts, and Thomas Murphy of General Motors, who in 1974 had replaced Richard Gerstenberg as the automaker's CEO. No business leader, though, had more influence on the president than did Reg Jones of General Electric, his first name pronounced with a hard *g*, it was said, as in "God."

Jones, who had become GE's chief executive in 1972, following Fred Borch, had a most dignified bearing—a CEO straight out of Central Casting. This was not a posture that he came by naturally. Reginald Jones was born in Stoke-on-Trent, England, into a blue-collar clan. His father was a steel-mill inspector. Their outhouse was in the back. When Jones was eight years old, the family moved to New Jersey, where his dad became an electrician at Acme Rubber. After high school, Jones attended the University of Pennsylvania on a scholarship. He earned a little cash by stuffing a classroom full of kids and helping them cram before exams, charging two dollars a head. He also washed dishes at his fraternity.

Jones joined General Electric in 1939 in Schenectady, New York, and after a management training course, he became a traveling auditor, providing him a glimpse inside nearly every GE plant in the country. Through the years, he picked up the social graces that one needed to make it big in corporate America: Jones dressed immaculately and learned to play a respectable round of golf (though he retained one habit of the working class—chain-smoking). By 1961, he'd become a GE vice president and in 1968 the company's chief financial officer. "It's really the Horatio Alger story on steroids," said Jones's son, Keith.

By the late 1970s, Jones was the most admired businessman in the country, gladly giving advice to President Carter on taxes, trade, and training. The president needed whatever help he could get. The economy had brightened since the 1973–1975 recession, but it still wasn't doing very well. Inflation and unemployment hung on at high levels; stagflation was a virus that America just couldn't shake. And by early 1979, the nation was getting sicker again. The downturn was caused partly by another energy crisis—this one set off by the Iranian revolution.

But gasoline lines or not, Americans' attitudes had already undergone a basic shift. After a decade of sharp price increases, with very little pause, people now assumed that high inflation was here to stay. And why wouldn't they? The government calculated the Consumer Price Index, its representative market basket of goods and services, at a baseline of 100 in 1967. In 1970, the CPI had climbed to 116. In 1975, it was at 163. By 1979, it had increased to 217—a nearly 90 percent rise in prices in less than ten years. Paying more had become rooted in families' expectations, in their daily choices about buying and borrowing. As long as wages kept going up, there was no reason to restrain one's self from purchasing new things or, better yet, putting them on credit before prices could go up again. "Inflation doesn't slow people down the way it always has," said Jay Schmiedeskamp, research director at the Gallup Economic Service. "That's a rather historic change. There used to be a brake—inflation came along and people stopped buying. That isn't happening now."

Yet unlike during the Golden Age of the 1950s, the consumerism of the late 1970s was freighted with anxiety. Beneath all of the buying, people were unsure where the country was going, unsure how long inflation and unemployment could remain so high without terrible consequences. "For the first time, we actually got numbers where people no longer believed that the future of America was going to be as good as it was now," recalled Carter's pollster, Patrick Caddell. "And that really shook me, because it was so at odds with the American character."

The president tried his best to reverse this "crisis of confidence," as he called it. On July 15, 1979, he spoke to the country in a tone befitting one of the Sunday school classes he loved to teach at church. "In a nation that was proud of hard work, strong families, close-knit communities, and our faith in God, too many of us now tend to worship self-indulgence and consumption," Carter said. "Human identity is no longer defined by what one does, but by what one owns. But we've discovered that owning things and consuming things does not satisfy our longing for meaning. We've learned that piling up material goods cannot fill the emptiness of lives which have no confidence or purpose.

"The symptoms of this crisis of the American spirit are all around us," the president went on. "For the first time in the history of our country a majority of our people believe that the next five years will be worse than the past five years. Two-thirds of our people do not even vote. The productivity of American workers is actually dropping, and the willingness of Americans to save for the future has fallen below that of all other people in the Western world."

Carter got a brief bump in the polls from his solemn address. But the pundits—labeling it the president's "malaise speech," even though he didn't actually use that word—came down hard. They accused him of blaming the public for all the things that Washington couldn't fix. Whether or not that was a fair assessment, one thing was undeniable: the president and his aides were at a loss for how to cure the economy.

In early 1980, Carter submitted his new budget to Congress. But the financial markets had no faith in the administration's projections, and investors fled from bonds. "In the executive offices of most securities firms," the *Wall Street Journal* reported, "the atmosphere of apprehension and doom is as thick as the carpets." The Federal Reserve added to the fretfulness. The strong-willed Paul Volcker, who now led the central bank, was out to attack inflation in a more serious way than had previous Fed chairs. But stage-managing the money supply was quite difficult. And well before Volcker could engineer inflation to fall, interest rates raced to their highest point since World War II. Economic activity was choked off. Builders, facing construction loans of more than 20 percent, stopped digging new holes. Appliance dealers, unable to afford financing at 19 percent to carry inventory or to meet other working capital needs, stopped placing orders from factories.

In March, still trying to beat back inflation, the president and the Fed pushed forward with a program of emergency credit controls. The scheme worked—only too well. In a perverse sort of patriotism, people cut up their credit cards and mailed them in to the White House. Visa lost half a million accounts. Retail spending screeched to a halt, much to the dismay of Sears, J.C. Penney, and other national chains. "The idea was not to make the economy go into the tank," said Fred Schultz, the Fed's vice chair. "It was supposed to allow the economy to grow but without excesses. Instead, the consumer got it into his head that the government was telling him not to use credit. The darned economy just fell off the cliff." America was now in the midst of another recession; by the summer, the jobless rate was near 8 percent. Inflation, meanwhile, was still sky high, with consumer prices soaring at a 13 percent pace.

Many of the other alarming trends that had begun in the late 1960s and had festered through the seventies were worse than ever. "US business finds itself challenged by aggressive overseas competitors," Reg Jones said in his letter to GE shareholders in 1980. "National productivity has been declining and, in industry after industry, product leadership is moving to other nations. Companies that refuse to renew themselves, that fail to cast off the old and embrace new technologies, could well find themselves in serious decline." In reality, many corporations were already in decline—inexorable decline.

Among them were the one-time industrial stalwarts along the Mahoning River in the "Steel Valley" of eastern Ohio. Youngstown Sheet and Tube had announced in 1977 that it was shutting down its Campbell Works and laying off 4,000 employees. Many directed their anger at President Carter for not doing enough to keep out the foreign-made metal being imported from Asia and elsewhere. "We helped put him in office and look at this," said William Maskell, one of the steelworkers who was let go. "Maybe he ought to run for President of Japan." Within the next three years, some 10,000 people in the Youngstown area would lose their jobs due to mill closures;

during the next decade, 50,000 jobs there would disappear. Cities like Youngstown were being hollowed out by "deindustrialization," a dry euphemism for the mothballing of some 1,000 factories across America in the 1970s. One study estimated that large manufacturers were cutting jobs at a rate of more than 900,000 a year.

This ruination, which would gain steam through the eighties, resulted in a kind of writerly ritual: reporters would visit these once-vibrant sites and then author their obituaries. One said of Youngstown: "The dead steel mills stand as pathetic mausoleums to the decline of American industrial might that was the envy of the world." In Dundalk, a blue-collar section of Baltimore, it was noted: "Older folks mourn the passing of not only prosperity but the strong sense of pride and self-sufficiency that once defined" the place. The wreckage in Homestead, Pennsylvania, brought this: "America uses things—people, resources, cities—then discards them." Similar fates befell dozens of other locations, leaving them struggling to catch up for decades on end: Warren, Ohio; Allentown, Pennsylvania; Newark, New Jersey; Buffalo, New York; New Bedford, Massachusetts; Decatur, Illinois; Port Arthur, Texas; as well as large parts of Philadelphia, Milwaukee, Cleveland, St. Louis, Detroit, and other spots. Because they were disproportionately concentrated in inner-city neighborhoods where many plants were being closed, black workers were often the hardest hit.

In the title track of his 1975 album *Born to Run*, Bruce Springsteen spoke of a working-class desire to escape from all the desolation: "We gotta get out while we're young," he wailed. But by 1980, with the release of his new record *The River*, the singer had determined that there was nowhere to go:

> *I got a job working construction for the Johnstown Company*
> *But lately there ain't been much work on account of the economy*
> *Now all them things that seemed so important*
> *Well, mister, they vanished right into the air*
> *Now I just act like I don't remember*
> *Mary acts like she don't care*

For Carter, the timing of the economy's collapse couldn't have been worse. 1980 was an election year, and, as opposed to President

Nixon, who had pulled out every expedient he could in 1972, right before people entered the voting booth, Carter seemed totally helpless. "Only Herbert Hoover, whose name is forever linked with the Great Depression of the 1930s, carried into an election economic problems as severe as those that burdened the thirty-ninth president," Georgia Tech professor W. Carl Biven has written.

At one point, Reg Jones had offered Carter his own plan to fight inflation. It was a rather unimaginative agenda—a typical corporate wish list. Jones, for instance, proposed tax cuts and new incentives for companies to invest in facilities and equipment, and he urged lower government spending and reductions in regulation. He also suggested that the president ask businesses to "exercise a decent restraint" in pricing their goods and serves, unions to avoid pressing for wages that would cause inflation to "spread like a cancer through the economy," and consumers to comparison shop for the best prices.

None of Jones's ideas, or anyone else's, were enough to save Jimmy Carter. On November 4, 1980, he was trounced in the election by the old host of *General Electric Theater*, Ronald Reagan. But Jones wasn't done leaving his imprint on the economy. Two weeks later, on November 20, he did something that would have a much greater impact on the lives of thousands of workers than anything he'd recommended to President Carter: he formally told the GE board that his preferred choice to succeed him as the company's chairman and CEO was Jack Welch.

If Reg Jones was a starched Brooks Brothers button-down, Jack Welch was a loud Hawaiian top—brash, colorful, informal, in your face.

Welch had been raised in a working-class section of Salem, Massachusetts, the son of a railroad conductor (and active union man) on the Boston & Maine commuter line. Though he'd grow to be only five foot eight, he was a good-enough athlete—and scrappy enough—to captain his high-school hockey team. He also excelled at golf, a game that he learned by caddying at the local country club. Welch went to the University of Massachusetts and then landed a fellowship at the University of Illinois, where in just three years he earned his PhD in chemical engineering.

In 1960, Welch joined GE. Yet he almost left just a year into his job, when his boss gave him a $1,000 raise. That seemed plenty generous on top of the $10,500 he was earning at the time—until Welch learned that he'd received the same pay increase as the three other guys who shared his office. Welch felt that he deserved more because he had done better work, helping to design and build a pilot plant for a new type of plastic, PPO. It was a perspective that would guide him for the next forty years. "Winning teams come from differentiation," Welch has said, "rewarding the best and removing the weakest, always fighting to raise the bar." Giving everyone a standard amount was what bureaucrats did, and Welch had no tolerance whatsoever for bureaucrats. "Dinks," he called them.

GE persuaded Welch to stay by upping his raise to $3,000 and giving him more responsibility. He advanced rapidly from there—to general manager of the plastics business; then vice president of the chemical and metallurgical division; then group executive overseeing medical systems, appliance components, electronic parts, and more—a $2 billion chunk of GE's business. At every stop, Welch waged what he liked to call "constructive conflict" while, as one review of him put it, he displayed "an antiestablishment attitude toward General Electric." But no one could argue with the performance of each of his units, which was consistently excellent and sometimes better than excellent. In 1977 Welch was placed in charge of the company's $4 billion consumer sector. And in 1979, he was made one of three GE vice chairmen, setting up the horserace for who would succeed Jones.

Welch never lost his edge as he climbed the ranks. But he was politically savvy enough—and, by the early 1970s, ambitious enough to be thinking about running GE some day—to stay just on the right side of a rigid system. "I was a renegade," Welch said. "But I wasn't stupid."

Still, when Welch claimed GE's top position, it was a surprise. He was only forty-four, and his reputation for what many perceived as arrogance and rudeness preceded him. Welch's two competitors for Jones's job were older and cut more in the traditional company cloth. Welch had a bad temper and a voice that became shrill when he got wound up, which was often. He chewed gum, at times stuffing most of a pack of Wrigley's into his mouth at once. He stammered and bit his nails, once referring to himself as a "stuttering overachiever." If he didn't like a report he'd been given, he'd send back a fax with a single image drawn on it: a fist with its middle finger raised.

Yet Reg Jones, who had championed Welch for years, to the chagrin of many of GE's hidebound executives, saw something special in him. Maybe it was the working-class background that they shared—though Welch loved to play up his "Irish street kid" persona while Jones suppressed his proletarian past. Whatever it was, Jones had become convinced that Welch's passion, intensity, and irreverence were just what the company needed to make it in a fast-changing, cutthroat world. Jones was very much part of the old GE, having just a couple of years earlier declared that the corporation's "distinctive set of traditions, values, and beliefs . . . inspires great loyalty" and "is one of our most valuable assets." Yet he'd clearly concluded that, going forward, these attributes would no longer suffice. And in Welch, Jones had found the rarest of creatures: a leader who had managed to ascend to the apex of a century-old corporate giant (where one's rank in the hierarchy was measured by how many ceiling tiles he had in his office) but who, nevertheless, thought and behaved more like someone at a start-up, dying to buck the status quo. Harvard business professor Richard Vancil has remarked that, in effect, "GE was able to select an 'outsider' from inside."

Welch wasted no time in breaking with the past. Governments, he said, were likely to combat the high inflation of the early eighties by keeping the supply of money tight. That, in turn, promised slow economic growth. GE also faced tougher and tougher foreign competition—a fact that Welch acknowledged by making sure that statistical comparisons prepared for the board no longer be made just to Westinghouse, as was the company's custom for many years, but to Siemens, Hitachi, and Toshiba. In this kind of climate, Welch asserted, "there will be no room for the mediocre supplier of products and services—the company in the middle of the pack." Welch's mandate, then, was for GE to be first or second in every one of its markets. If the company couldn't achieve that in a particular line of business, it needed to get out: Welch's famous "fix it, close it, or sell it" strategy.

Yet being number one or number two wouldn't happen automatically. In a 1981 speech to securities analysts, Welch called for "an atmosphere where people dare to try new things—where people feel assured in knowing that only the limits of their creativity and drive, their own standards of personal excellence, will be the ceiling of how far and how fast they move."

At this early point, Welch's words sounded like nothing more than the usual corporate blah, blah, blah. It would take many years of repeating himself for Wall Street, and even his own employees, to truly fathom what Welch was getting at—the degree to which he was going to blow up the old GE and put in place a new structure, which was far leaner and quicker to make decisions, and where people would be rewarded for the strength of their ideas, no matter where they happened to fall on the company org chart. In due time, thousands and thousands of those who worked for GE under Welch would come to love the wide-open culture that he built. "Power may corrupt," said Bill Lane, Welch's longtime speechwriter, "but it also can liberate, and he began to instinctively conceive ways for us to free ourselves from the corporate crap that had enslaved and bored" lots of employees for many years.

There was another side to it as well, however. While many at GE reached for the ceiling, others felt the bottom drop out on them. To achieve the level of agility that Welch demanded meant first flattening the organization as much as possible. GE wasn't the only American company that had gotten puffy around the middle. By 1980, managers made up 10 percent of the US workforce, compared with just 4 percent in Japan and 3 percent in Germany. But GE had more flab than most. Upon taking office, Welch was stunned at all the paper-pushers that the company had accumulated over the years, like barnacles on the underside of a boat. "We had layer on layer on layer," he said. "They added no value. I didn't need those people, all those armies."

Worst of all, perhaps, the reports that they endlessly churned out were, as often as not, terribly abstruse. Said Walter Wriston, the chairman of Citicorp and a GE director: "You'd take the size of the guy's shirt collar and divide it by the Gregorian calendar and multiply it by the square root of pi, and you'd come out with a number that was totally meaningless." Ralph Cordiner had created the network of middle managers that generated all this paperwork. Fred Borch and Reg Jones had refined the system but hadn't changed the guts of it. Jones, in fact, seemed to luxuriate in the bulging briefing binders that, as

Fortune magazine described it, "had grown to . . . dense impenetrability." Welch, by contrast, was completely sickened by the red tape. Nor did he trust the information being presented. In a world that was moving faster, five-year business forecasts no longer made sense.

At GE's main office, in Fairfield, Connecticut, one group had been assigned to evaluate and grade the corporation's strategic-planning book. "It was crazy," Welch said. "I fired them all." He then dismantled the strategic planning department itself. He dumped the corporate economists, too. He pared the finance staff and the company's band of internal management consultants, which Harold Smiddy had once led. Individuals who couldn't get in line with Welch's vision were culled as well. From his third-floor office, it was not uncommon to hear Welch yelling something like, "You asshole! You're in deep shit! You get this cleaned up or you're outta here." Or this: "We've got to get rid of this fucking idiot. Do you want to do it, or should Glen do it?" Welch never cared for doing it himself; firing employees directly wasn't in the chairman's job description. What's more, in spite of his confrontational style, Welch wanted people to like him. Many did. Many others didn't. In the winding corridor running through the east and west buildings at HQ, somebody in the mid-1980s defaced an art exhibit of wildlife portraits by scrawling "Jack Welch" on the frame of a shark painting. The security guard said that the vandalism had been committed by an executive vice president whom Welch had "sent home"—his preferred term for sacking somebody. In all, the head count at GE headquarters dwindled to about 900 from more than 2,000.

The real cutting, though, came outside of Fairfield: in Schenectady, GE eliminated 22,000 jobs; in Louisville, Kentucky, 13,000; in Evendale, Ohio, 12,000; in Pittsfield, Massachusetts (Welch's old home, when he ran the plastics business), 8,000; in Lynn, Massachusetts, 7,000; in Erie, Pennsylvania, 6,000; in Fort Wayne, Indiana, 4,000. "GE is where our fathers and grandfathers worked," said Pete Pallescki, a machine operator in Schenectady. "We didn't expect them to let us down so badly." All of a sudden, it felt like the doomsday scenario laid out during that 1954 session at GE—the one where the union had gotten a copy of the meeting notes and warned that the company "is planning a depression" by proposing to wipe out most of the jobs in these old industrial centers—was coming true.

G E was hardly the only company that reduced its workforce through the early 1980s. Another recession—this one even worse than the contraction of 1973–1975—began in the summer of 1981 and lasted until the fall of 1982. Normally, the Federal Reserve would have injected money into the economy at such a time. But Paul Volcker, hell-bent on finally killing off inflation, did just the opposite, adding greatly to the recession's severity. President Reagan was fully supportive. "I'm afraid," he said, "the country is just going to have to suffer two, three years of hard times to pay for the binge we've been on."

It paid dearly. By late '82, the unemployment rate had reached almost 11 percent, a postwar high. In autos, some 23 percent of the labor force was jobless; in steel and other primary metals, the figure was 29 percent. Overall, about 20 million Americans were now either out of a job, working part-time when they wanted a full-time position, or had stopped looking for employment altogether. Thousands of small enterprises went bankrupt. Homebuilders sent two-by-fours to the Fed to symbolize all the houses that they weren't constructing. Auto dealers mailed in keys to unsold cars.

Despite the pressure, the Fed held steady. And by late 1982, high prices had finally been slain. Inflation for the year rose just a bit over 6 percent—4 percentage points less than in 1981. In 1983, they increased about 3 percent. "The long nightmare of runaway inflation," Reagan proclaimed, accurately, "is now behind us." The recovery was also finding its momentum; what would turn out to be the longest economic expansion since the Kennedy-Johnson years was now beginning.

For many workers, however, the "Reagan economic miracle" came with an asterisk. It would take until 1987 for the annual unemployment rate to fall below 7 percent. High-paying factory jobs were still being shed, with US manufacturing employment having peaked in 1979. The unions, which had their strongest presence in these blue-collar industries, were now in full retreat. In 1978, a big attempt by the political left to strengthen labor law had failed in Congress. Then, President Reagan broke the air-traffic controllers in 1981, legitimizing the replacement of strikers in the eyes of most companies. "In ninety days," said a former antilabor consultant, "Ronald Reagan recast the crimes of union busting as acts of patriotism." Deregulation, which President Carter initiated and Reagan accelerated, was another gut-punch to the unions. That's because many of the companies suddenly able to enter and compete in previously closed markets weren't organized. For example, the portion of the workforce in the trucking industry that was unionized would go from 46 percent to just 23 percent in the two decades following deregulation. At telecommunications companies and the airlines, similar declines would hit labor.

But government action and inaction could explain only so much. The "hard line" that management had taken against unions since the late 1950s had gotten progressively harder. More and more employers used a combination of tactics—legal and also illegal—to stifle unionization efforts. "Unions responded predictably, by filing an increasing number of unfair labor practice charges against companies and demanding back-pay and the reinstatement of workers unlawfully terminated during election drives," the sociologist Jake Rosenfeld has written. "They won a lot of these legal battles, but would lose the war." Whereas labor was still successful in a majority of representation elections through the mid-1970s, they were victorious in fewer than 50 percent now. Wage concessions in various industries followed, and pay continued to decline across the economy. In 1985, 40 percent of unionized employees lost cost-of-living adjustments from their contracts; the great stabilizer of purchasing power, popularized by General Motors and the United Auto Workers after World War II, was now being aggressively killed off.

In 1988—while President Reagan spoke of the "economic and social revolution of hope based on work, incentives, growth, and opportunity" that his administration had brought about—inflation-adjusted weekly earnings hit their lowest point since 1960. The percentage of private-sector workers with pensions fell during the 1980s, the first time that had happened over the course of a decade since World War II. The portion of workers with company-provided medical coverage also began to go down for the first time since the war. In terms of the social contract between employer and employee, things were now going backward. The political economists Bennett Harrison and Barry Bluestone would call this "The Great U-Turn."

Certainly, the economic "boom" of the 1980s was far different from anything that had come before. Even as the United States economy took off, it seemed to be falling behind—to the Japanese, in particular, who now dominated the world stage. The Reagan administration tried to help American businesses, imposing tariffs, quotas, and surcharges on imports of steel, electronics, autos, and other products. But these interventions didn't have much effect. By the mideighties, Japan's industrial output had nearly caught up to that of the United States. And at the end of the decade, the Japanese seemed to have totally vanquished US industry, when Mitsubishi purchased a majority stake in one of America's great landmarks—Rockefeller Center. "New York, a subsidiary of Mitsubishi," a voice intoned as the opening credits rolled on *Late Night With David Letterman*.

Within a few years, Japan's economy would enter a long period of stagnation; America's "Japan Problem," as *Foreign Affairs* called it, had in many respects been overstated. But the underlying danger that Japan Inc. seemed to pose would never go away. Whether it was because of competition from Japan, India, China, or some other country, American executives felt besieged as never before. To measure up, they needed to be as efficient and cost conscious as possible—and the social contract for US workers became more ragged as a result.

In the past, American companies would routinely recall many, if not most, of their laid-off workers as business recovered after a recession. Now, they decided that they couldn't afford to bring back their employees anymore; they opted to restructure instead, terminating positions for good. By 1984, so many businesses had gone this route that the federal Bureau of Labor Statistics began tracking "displaced workers" for the first time, distinguishing them from those who had been furloughed temporarily and got their old jobs back. Another sign of the times: by decade's end, Washington had enacted the Worker Adjustment and Retraining Notification (or WARN) Act, requiring companies to provide advanced, sixty-day notice of plant closings and mass job cuts. "Virtually all workers are now subject to displacement at some time during their working lives," cautioned a panel put together by the National Planning Association. Its very name was haunting: the Committee on New American Realities.

Even the most unstinting employers felt the need to do more with less. Kodak, which was being taken on by the Japanese film manufacturer Fuji Photo, offered an early retirement package to 5,000 workers in 1983. Three years later, in a move unheard of for Rochester's "Great Yellow Father," it laid off nearly 13,000 people. The company also cut its cafeteria hours and got rid of free medical checkups. At General Motors, a reorganization was announced in 1984 that was meant to streamline things by putting all of its automobile design, engineering, and manufacturing in the United States and Canada into two groups: one for large cars, the other for small cars. As part of the reshuffling, GM did away with its Fisher Body division, which had been established in 1908. "We were destroying some long-lived loyalties," conceded John Debbink, a GM veteran who had helped plan the overhaul. "Here was Fisher Body celebrating its seventy-fifth anniversary, and within a year we come around and say, 'Fisher, you are no more.'" GM, however, believed it had no alternative: "The automobile market has become a global market," the company's chairman, Roger Smith, told top company executives. "Demand has shifted away from our traditional strengths into areas where foreign manufacturers now hold significant advantages. . . . We need to do things differently." Under its new setup, GM hoped to make gains in efficiency as it consolidated duplicate staff jobs and trimmed white-collar employment.

The list went on and on. One out of every five jobs that existed at DuPont at the beginning of the 1980s was gone by the end. The number of production workers at US Steel declined to 30,000 from more than 100,000 during the decade. AT&T slashed 24,000 positions at its information-systems division in 1985. The next year, the telecommunications company announced that it was eliminating another 27,000 workers, or nearly 9 percent of its total. Ford jettisoned 10,000 white-collar jobs. Chevron shrank to about 52,000 workers in 1986 from 79,000 two years earlier.

Nobody, though, chopped deeper or faster than Jack Welch. By the early 1990s, nearly 170,000 jobs had been lost at GE due to layoffs, attrition, and other cuts—most of them by 1986. That's about as many people as who live in Fort Lauderdale, Florida, or Providence, Rhode Island. And this didn't count the 135,000 employees who were in parts of the company that Welch sold to others.

Welch was playing in a mergers-and-acquisitions market that had heated up tremendously in the early 1980s. For his part, he divested 117 business units in total. Some of these sales, like the unloading of the company's small-appliance lines (with their signature GE monogram logo) to Black and Decker in 1984, demoralized employees. But at Welch's GE, there were "no sacred cows." He also bought tens of billions of dollars worth of businesses, including a majority stake in the Wall Street investment bank Kidder Peabody in 1986 and RCA in 1987—and swiftly put his stamp on these new acquisitions.

After Kidder cut 1,000 jobs, or about 15 percent of its workforce, it was obvious where the orders had come from. "Prior to GE's investment in Kidder, the firm was one of the most paternalistic on Wall Street, one that paid out high bonuses and found it hard to let people go," said one industry watcher. "I don't think Kidder would have moved to the extent they have without a lot of prodding from General Electric." As for RCA, once its radio and TV manufacturing operations were merged into GE's consumer-electronics business, the plan was to winnow the number of factories from twenty-three to fourteen, while cutting the ranks of salaried personnel by 44 percent and hourly employees by 18 percent. That all changed in a hurry, though, when Welch suddenly decided to abandon consumer electronics—one of six RCA businesses that GE sold or closed in just eighteen months—and swap it for a medical-imaging-equipment business that had better prospects not only in the United States but outside of it as well. "You have to be global in this business to survive," Welch said, a comment that would prove prophetic, as nearly every American corporation would soon be compelled to start thinking on a worldwide scale.

Not long after the bloodletting at GE got underway, the media started calling Welch "Neutron Jack," a nickname meant to convey that he took out all of the people but left the buildings standing. (Actually, this wasn't quite right. Bill Lane, the speechwriter, remembered being with Welch one day while a wrecking ball and a bulldozer razed some of GE's locomotive-manufacturing facilities in Erie. "A time-tested management technique," Welch said to him.) Welch wasn't the first to be stuck with such a sobriquet, and he wouldn't be the last. In the 1960s, Chrysler's John Riccardo was christened "the flame thrower" for his ruthless demeanor. Al Dunlap, the CEO of Scott Paper and then of Sunbeam, would come to be called "Chainsaw Al" and "Rambo in pinstripes" for his cold-blooded focus on the bottom line. But while those other executives reveled in their notoriety, Welch never thought "Neutron Jack" was fair or accurate.

In many ways, it wasn't. Welch preached "soft landings—give them soft landings" whenever people were shown the door at GE. And, by all accounts, that's what most of his soon-to-be-ex-employees received. Lane recounted the time that GE's vice chairman, Larry Bossidy, fired three senior vice presidents in the same day, hopping on and off the corporate jet to dismiss one executive at the company's lighting business in Cleveland, another in Fort Wayne, and the other in Columbus, Ohio. Inside the company, this trip became known as the "Midwest Massacre." Lane could only imagine that after Bossidy delivered each fatal blow, the fallen executive "staggers away from his desk and slumps facedown into a huge pile of cash, options, pension, supplemental pension, and free appliances."

The rank-and-file weren't treated nearly so well. Most, though, got substantial exit packages. "We're trying to be lean and compassionate," not lean and mean, Welch said. When he sold GE's Utah International mining subsidiary for nearly $2.5 billion in 1984, for instance, Welch set aside more than $1 billion of that to fund large severances for the tens of thousands of people who lost their jobs because of the deal. In general, "we gave people a lot of notice," Welch said—up to six months, compared to just one week at many companies. "We gave them health care. We weren't in a crisis. We had a nice cushion. So we could be tough but fair; in our minds, fair."

Welch also hated being tagged "Neutron Jack" because it made it seem like he took some wicked pleasure in firing people when, as he saw it, he had no other choice. To survive in the 1980s and beyond, GE had to have a big boost in productivity. The only way to get there was to become more agile. And the only way to do that was to cut loose those who, for whatever reason, couldn't keep up. "Any organization that thinks it can guarantee job security is going down a dead end," Welch said. "Only satisfied customers can give people job security. Not companies. That reality put an end to the implicit contracts that corporations once had with their employees. Those 'contracts' were based on perceived lifetime employment and produced a paternal, feudal, fuzzy kind of loyalty. . . . I wanted to create a new contract, making GE jobs the best in the world for people willing to compete. If they signed up, we'd give them the best training and development and an environment that provided plenty of opportunities for personal and professional growth. We'd do everything to give them the skills to have 'lifetime employability,' even if we couldn't guarantee them 'lifetime employment.'"

Sometimes, Welch's rewriting of the social contract worked out wonderfully well for individual employees, as it did for Michael Watson. Other times, it didn't work out at all, as was the case with Wilbur Hany.

In the early 1940s, when Hany was six years old, his father walked out on his mother, and the family lost their 80-acre farm in central Illinois, about 125 miles southwest of Chicago. "It was devastating," he'd later recall. From then on, his mom had to work two jobs, cleaning houses and babysitting. As he grew up, Hany excelled at sports, but his mother told him that he couldn't participate because if he got hurt, she'd have to skip work to take care of him; they'd be out on the street. Hany was so gifted, however, that the coach at Gridley High School assured her that he'd find someone to tend to her son should he ever get injured. Hany went on to win sixteen varsity letters—in football, basketball, baseball, and track—and the local newspaper would later call him "arguably the finest all-around athlete in school history."

As he got ready to graduate in 1955, Hany thought about pursuing a scholarship at Bradley University, Western Illinois University, or the University of Wisconsin. But he decided to take a job at General Electric and earn a little money instead. His plan was to work at GE's nearby factory in Bloomington, Illinois, for a year and then suit up in a college football or basketball uniform and get his degree. He never did. He threw himself into his work and remained at GE for the next twenty-nine years.

Over that time, Hany was a solid employee, and he was promoted on several occasions at the plant, which produced a variety of electrical equipment, including on-and-off switches for industrial motors. He starred on several company-sponsored sports teams. He became president of the local General Electric Employees Club, an expanse of parkland where blue- and white-collar workers and their families would swim, play tennis, fish, and shoot trap. He made a good living and raised two kids.

Hany ended up in purchasing, where he bought aluminum, copper, brass, chemicals, and other materials to make the factory go. Then, in 1982, things started to change. A new boss took the reins of GE's general-purpose control department, which oversaw the Bloomington plant and a handful of other facilities. Jesse Lawrence had been at GE since 1960, but he wasn't beholden to the old way of doing things, not in the least. "We had a lot of people who had . . . gotten into some bad habits, who had forgotten the sense of urgency, had forgotten customers, were really on a treadmill, doing the same thing over and over and over every day," he said. As an executive, Lawrence was a ball of fire, a junior Jack Welch. "He was autocratic," said Ken Sampen, who ran the Bloomington factory under him. "He believed in results."

Results were hard to come by when Lawrence stepped in to his new job. The entire department was losing money, and Bloomington would ring up a deficit of about $12 million for the year. Like many other parts of GE, the factory had become wildly inefficient. It had too many products chasing too few customers. And it had too many employees for the amount of revenue being brought in. "We had to restructure the business," Lawrence said. "It couldn't afford the numbers of people that it had. It couldn't afford the things they were doing. They were all busy. That was not an issue. They all worked, and they worked hard. . . . But the business couldn't afford it."

Over the next four years, Lawrence had one goal: "to fix the business and fix it as quick as possible." And eventually, he would turn things around. "He simply saved the plant," Sampen said. But doing so was extremely painful. The department discontinued eighty different product lines, mostly low-volume items that carried inordinately high overhead. Lawrence invested in new technology, but the enhancements "meant that we needed less people catching errors at the end of the line," he said. Most of all, Lawrence reduced costs by cutting the number of salaried workers from about 400 to less than 200, beginning with a big round of layoffs just a few weeks after he arrived—an action that workers in Bloomington called "Bloody Thursday."

Deciding who would get to keep their jobs and who wouldn't was not for everyone. Frustrated at the pace of change, Lawrence replaced his operations manager, Bob Montgomery, with a less squeamish executive. "Bob Montgomery was as nice a person as you'll ever find," Lawrence said, "but didn't have the heart to do the job that had to be done." Doing the job required looking at things differently than during the pre-Welch era. Before, length of service with the company was often the determining factor as to whether someone would be laid off. But Lawrence made clear that "ability . . . counted for more," said Marilyn Rebmann, who handled employee relations in Bloomington.

To help gauge people's abilities, managers in Bloomington were given a matrix to assess those who reported to them. This grid took into account someone's record of service, but also relative performance, essential skills, and overall contribution to the company. Each employee would then get a total score, making it easy at a glance to see how one stacked up against the other.

Ranking people this way was right in step with Welch's ethic of "differentiation": the idea that the only way for a company to constantly improve was to prune its least effective employees. Even in Ralph Cordiner's day, GE had rated workers and didn't cosset underachievers. But "Jack turbocharged the process," said Bill Conaty, who worked for Welch as his senior vice president of human resources. "The word 'complacency' was blown out of the GE vocabulary by Jack Welch. We absolutely employed angst in the system, but a healthy angst. I never thought I could put my feet up on my desk and say, 'I've given you thirty-nine and a half good years.'" Later in his tenure, Welch would introduce the "vitality curve"—a bell-shaped distribution by which GE supervisors sorted those who worked for them into three camps: the top 20 percent, the "vital 70" percent in the middle, and the bottom 10 percent.

Welch regarded the majority who fell into the middle as "the heart of the company," and thought they should receive increases in pay and some stock awards to recognize their contributions—all while their managers sought to help them get even better at their jobs and vault into the top part of the curve. Those who were already at the top of the heap, the "A players," were to be showered with higher salaries, loads of stock options, and promotions. "Losing an A is a sin," Welch said. "Love 'em, hug 'em, kiss 'em, don't lose them" to another company.

The 10 percent who were graded lowest and unable to improve quickly were to be let go, a regular purging of the weakest from the herd. "Some people think it's cruel or brutal to remove the bottom 10 percent of our people," said Welch. "It isn't. It's just the opposite. What I think is brutal . . . is keeping people around who aren't going to grow and prosper. There's no cruelty like waiting and telling people late in their careers that they don't belong—just when their job options are limited and they're putting their children through college or paying off big mortgages. The characterization of a vitality curve as cruel stems from false logic and is an outgrowth of a culture that practices false kindness."

Despite Welch's reasoning, and the adoption of similar "forced-ranking" frameworks by a slew of large corporations that followed his lead, many considered the vitality curve to be horribly flawed. Peter Drucker, who thought that Welch was a brilliant strategist, disapproved of this method. Many derisively called it "rank and yank"—another name that Welch detested. Some worried that its Darwinian nature could lead employees to try to sabotage one another. Others said it was too formulaic: after a few years of driving out the genuinely poor performers, the bottom 10 percent would then be made up of good workers who were making a positive contribution; with no fat left, the only choice was to cut into muscle and bone. Rather than do so, some supervisors tried to cheat the system. Still others said that the model was ripe for abuse by managers who were racist, sexist, or ageist. Ranking people, one against another, gave the process a patina of objectivity; putting a hard number to something, or to someone, tends to do that. But the scores given to employees at GE were utterly subjective. Often it boiled down to the opinion of a single manager as to who should stay and who should go.

In 1982, HR targeted Wilbur Hany to be laid off, but his supervisor fought it, and the lot fell on one of his coworkers instead. It seemed like a wise decision. The next year, the company applauded Hany for being a top contributor to the department's cost-cutting program. And Hany's performance review that year praised him for his intelligence and knack for innovating. In early 1984, the following was added to Hany's file: "Wilbur responds favorably to the demands of his job. Readily recognizes cost improvement opportunities, takes necessary steps to implement same. Is responsive to new assignments. Has assisted in implementation of purchasing system. His performance trend is favorable."

That is, until it wasn't. Just a few months later, in April, the forty-eight-year-old Hany was handed a "lack of work" notice and told he was being fired. "I wasn't overly impressed with Mr. Hany as an employee," Sampen said. "I didn't feel that he performed at the level that was really up to our expectations." All of the laudatory evaluations that Hany had received apparently meant nothing. Said Hany: "I was just dumbfounded." His immediate supervisor again tried to fight for him, arguing that Hany should be kept on and someone else laid off. But this time, it was no use. In what amounted to a high-stakes game of musical chairs, Hany was out—though not before he was asked to train a younger man, a computer whiz named Mike Meronek, to take over much of his material-purchasing job. Like others who'd received a "lack of work" notice at the plant, Hany was offered a different position if he wanted to stay, but it would have meant a 27 percent cut in pay and a lousy work schedule. He declined to accept.

On his final day in Bloomington, Hany wished his colleagues in purchasing good luck and told them good-bye. It was "one of the saddest days I ever had in my life," he said.

As unforgiving as Welch's GE could be for some, others, like Michael Watson, appreciated the way that the company gave them a chance to push themselves and learn new and exciting things.

Watson was born in 1959 in New York, and raised by his grandparents in New Brunswick, New Jersey. They had been laborers in the South before they couldn't work anymore and were left to collect government disability checks. Watson's grandmother knew that college would be his way out. "She didn't want me to end up in the kind of jobs that they had to do," Watson said, "because in those kinds of jobs you work until your body just breaks down and you can't do them anymore." He was an outstanding student and got a scholarship to Yale, where in 1981 he earned a degree in economics.

After graduation, Watson went to work at IBM, which clung to the old social contract that Welch disparaged. Even though the country was in a deep recession, IBM seemed impervious to the tough times. Revenue was growing and profits were strong. Watson was among the 135,000 new people that the company hired between 1980 and 1985. "You didn't get the sense that IBM was going to be threatened in any fundamental way," Watson said. But there was also something else that made those working for Big Blue, as the company was called, feel untouchable: the steadfast assurance that if the business did flounder, everybody would be protected. "You got told stories about how even during the Depression, they didn't lay off employees—that if you performed well, you basically had a job for life," said Watson, who entered a corporate training program and over the next four and half years sold computer systems and PCs from Florida. "It felt like one of the safest places in the world."

Since the early 1900s, IBM had seen its no-layoffs policy as an extension of what it held out to be its "most important" core value: "respect for the individual." "As businessmen, we think in terms of profits, but people continue to rank first," the company's CEO, Thomas Watson Jr. (no relation to Michael), wrote in 1963. In the 1980s, IBM made a point of highlighting the way it would retrain and reassign employees, rather than send them packing: "Jobs may come and go. But people shouldn't." It was quite a contrast to what was happening at GE, where Jack Welch was asked by some of his own workers about the IBM campaign. "At a time when I was being routinely assaulted with the Neutron tag," he admitted, "those ads really pissed me off."

Michael Watson did well at IBM, winning the company's coveted Golden Circle Award as a top salesman. But he also felt stuck. Since college, Watson had been interested in human resources, and after several years he was ready to make the jump from sales. Yet HR was already overstaffed, and with such little turnover at IBM, Watson didn't see a way to break in. The downside of job security was stunted mobility. "If I kept waiting, I didn't know how long it was going to be," Watson said. "That kind of a job may have taken me five or ten years to get at IBM."

And so he started looking around for a different opportunity, and in 1986 accepted an HR job at GE Capital in Stamford, Connecticut. Before long, he was charged with setting up a college-recruiting program—exactly the work he wanted to be doing—and managing training efforts for the whole unit. "This was my dream," Watson said. He was then sent to Canton, Ohio, to build an HR function from scratch at a GE Capital collection center with hundreds of employees. Watson was still only in his twenties. "GE," he said, "was willing to take bets on people." For his exemplary work, Watson was awarded a spot in GE Capital's Pinnacle Club and sent on a ten-day, first-class, all-expenses-paid trip to Japan and Thailand—an example of the fantastic perks that Welch's A players enjoyed, even while the Cs were being fired.

For all of Watson's success, however, GE never left him with the illusion that he'd be at the company forever. This was no IBM. One day, Frank Doyle, a senior vice president at GE, addressed more than a hundred HR staffers, including Watson. Doyle's message was unvarnished—and Watson would never forget it. "Over time, as a society, we're going to be moving away from the things that tie people to a company for thirty years," Doyle told the group. "At GE we're going to have to make a system where we guarantee you'll have a very good experience, where we'll make you more valuable whatever you go and do. If I were all of you, I'd do good work, work hard, and always have a copy of your resume ready." A hush fell over the room.

Notably, GE didn't see this as something unique to the company. The entire labor market was changing, and GE was merely reacting to a fluid situation. "What I'm advocating," Doyle told lawmakers in 1987, "is the basic premise that people will change jobs, upgrade skills, and switch industries, not once but several times in their careers." GE, he said, was striving be a place where employees were "ready to go and eager to stay."

Watson fit this mold perfectly. He eagerly remained at GE Capital for seven years before getting an itch to move into an HR role in a different part of the company. "It was time to get some different experiences," he said. His plan was to slide over to one of GE's manufacturing businesses, but then the cable company Time Warner started to court him. Ultimately, Watson felt that being exposed to a whole new industry would teach him the most, and so in 1993 he left GE. In 1999, after three good years at Time Warner as a corporate human-resources manager (a period in which he also picked up a master's degree in organizational behavior) and a stint back at IBM, Watson made another move—this time to the nonprofit sector. For the next thirteen years, he would serve as the top HR executive for Girl Scouts of the USA. Later, he would become the senior vice president of talent and culture at the National 4-H Council.

His experience was exactly as Welch and Doyle had said it should be: GE didn't guarantee him lifetime employment, but it did give him lifetime employability—or at least Watson would always credit the company for doing so. "I'll be an advocate for working at GE as long as I live," he said. "I never felt this sense of risk because of what I was getting in terms of skills and confidence. I felt I could always find a job. I have a set of skills that can never be taken away by anybody."

Others, like Wilbur Hany, were left with a very different impression. After he was fired from GE, he found work as a sales representative for a company called Sueske Brass and Copper. But it paid 20 percent less than he'd made at General Electric—$24,000 compared with $30,000. The job didn't last long anyway; Hany was out of work again after about eight months, when Sueske restructured. He then

applied for jobs at more than a dozen employers: International Tape
Electronics, Furnace Electric, Bendix Corporation, Danville Metal
Stamping, and more. But he didn't catch on anywhere. After a while, he
took to doing yard work and other odd jobs under the name Hany Jan-
itorial Service. He was just trying to get by. "I never thought it would
come to this," he said. At GE, there was "no doubt I was a company
man. I built a house within two miles of the job so I could be closer to
it. Now I got house payments and no job." Finally, Hany became a win-
dow-installer at Diamond Star Motors, a joint venture between Chrysler and Mitsubishi, where he earned about $11.50 an hour.

In the meantime, he became one of fifteen people from the
Bloomington plant to sue GE, alleging that the company had engaged
in a pattern of age discrimination. In 1989, after a lengthy jury trial in
federal court in Springfield, Illinois, Hany and his coplaintiffs won. A
second jury subsequently found that Hany had been individually dis-
criminated against on account of his age. The judge ordered GE to re-
instate Hany to his old position at a salary of about $37,000 a year. The
court also directed GE to pay him more than $117,000 in lost earnings
and benefits. The company appealed, and Hany settled for an undis-
closed sum. The other former GE workers also settled.

As it happened, though, nobody was immune to GE's axe, regardless of how old they were. Mike Meronek, then age thirty-three,
whom Hany had trained to buy materials for the factory, was supposed
to be something of a miracle worker in Bloomington. He had an engineering degree from the University of Illinois, Jack Welch's alma
mater, and had been in a special management-studies program. His
boss, David Vanover, viewed him as a "top technical talent"—a guy
who had the capacity to modernize the plant's purchasing group. "His
job was to go in there and be a change agent," Vanover said, "to do
things differently to help this business survive." But in about a year, he
was gone, too. "As soon as we got to the point of recognizing that his
value wasn't as great as what we had hoped it would be . . . we ended
up giving him a 'lack of work'" notice, Vanover said. "Away he went."

Perhaps no group of people experienced the two faces of GE—one
part meritocracy, one part meat grinder—as intensely as the company's unionized workers.

By the late 1980s, only about 35 percent of GE's hourly employees were members of organized labor, down from 50 percent twenty years before. The drop reflected, in large part, the manner in which Welch had retooled the company: on balance, GE was now making most of its money through nonunionized businesses—services, high-tech, and finance—as it turned away from many of the blue-collar lines that had long been its lifeblood. Across the rest of corporate America, much the same thing was happening, as the US economy continued its transition to a postindustrial age.

The difference was that, at many companies, executives continued to manage through the same command-and-control systems that they had always relied upon. Welch wanted everyone—including, and even especially, those on the shop floor—to have real input as to how GE could perform better. This desire went way beyond anything that Ralph Cordiner had envisioned in the 1950s, when he characterized corporate decentralization as "a philosophy of freedom" and called upon GE's managers to lead "by persuasion rather than command." For all of Cordiner's good intentions, GE had remained mostly a top-down culture. Welch was dead set on flipping it.

Among his more senior people, he fostered an open dialogue by giving a face-lift to GE's Crotonville management-training facility, which had fallen into disrepair during the seventies. Critics did not understand how Welch could spend tens of millions of dollars to spruce up an education center when he was laying off tens of thousands of people. They began calling Crotonville "Jack's Cathedral." But Welch thought it was vital to make Crotonville a world-class destination—a place that would attract the company's best and brightest to think through some of GE's biggest challenges. The intent was for them to walk in with a vexing problem and walk out with a bold plan of action, often by mixing it up with Welch himself. "Thanks to Welch, GE's 'people factory' at Crotonville has no rival," said Warren Bennis, the leadership scholar. Welch, he added, personally enjoyed spending "a lot of time there, standing in the auditorium—he called it the 'pit'—with his sleeves rolled up, encouraging tough questions, barring no holds, loving the percussive to-and-fro he thrives on."

Lower down the ranks, Welch wanted the same to-and-fro. "The idea was nothing more than trying to recreate Crotonville in a thousand different places," he said. In the late 1980s, with this in mind,

GE launched a process that it called "Work-Out," a series of town-meeting-style gatherings in which employees were empowered to make suggestions directly to higher-ups—who were then required to make instant, real-time decisions on every proposal. Once a plan was approved, it was to be executed right away, with no interference from the bureaucracy. "The people closest to the work knew more about it than their supervisors did, so we wanted to hear their ideas," Welch said. "We wanted people at the bottom of the hierarchy to talk to people at the top." Within five years, more than 200,000 GE employees had participated in Work-Out, resulting in all sorts of solutions for reducing waste and improving productivity.

For Welch, Work-Out had another plus as well: it made at least some union members and their leaders feel like they were finally being heard. During a Work-Out meeting at the Lynn plant, for example, an hourly employee scratched out on a brown paper bag the design for a new protective shield for grinding machines. What he proposed was so smart and cost-effective, Lynn's rank-and-file were able to keep the work in-house rather than watch it be contracted to an outside vendor. Before Work-Out, "we had the feeling they were trying to phase us out," said Vic Slepoy, a Lynn electrician. "Now at least we have an avenue to make a pitch for our jobs."

Welch won favor with the union in other ways, too. His predecessors as CEO wouldn't dare sit down with their counterparts from labor. To do so would have indicated that GE put them on an equal plane. But Welch was different. He got a kick out of inviting top union officials to dinner a couple of times a year, capping the evening with cognacs back at his New York office. "Our relations were good," Welch said. "We knew their kids." When Welch heard that the wife of a negotiator for the International Union of Electrical Workers, Bob Santamoor, had gotten cancer, he made sure that she was treated at the best hospital around—Sloan Kettering. "Somehow it got taken care of," Santamoor said. "I was surprised as hell."

It wasn't that Welch had any love for organized labor. Like those who ran GE before him, he felt that the union was a needless obstacle between management and the frontline workforce—and he told the IUE as much. "I wanted to get rid of them," Welch said. He paid close attention to each labor contract and pressed GE's lead negotiator,

Dennis Rocheleau, to drive a hard bargain. "Are you here to tell me that you're going to let those fucking guys run all over us again?" Welch would ask him. Through the 1980s, many of the threats that the union feared most—robots replacing workers, certain tasks being outsourced to cheaper vendors, jobs getting sent to Mexico and other foreign countries—were becoming more and more common. As one GE executive said, any plant that wasn't sufficiently profitable was expected to "automate, emigrate, or evaporate."

Yet Welch would contend that the close connections he made with the union's leaders had the desired effect: through his entire twenty-year run as CEO, the IUE never struck nationally. How much this serenity could be attributed to Welch's charm is debatable. Beginning in the 1980s, as unions lost most of their power, the number of walkouts by organized labor plunged across the country. The strike was no longer a viable weapon. Still, Welch's personal ties with the IUE surely didn't hurt. "I considered him a friend, even though he was ready to put all the jobs on a boat to China," Santamoor said, adding that with Welch, you at least always knew where you stood. "Jack's a straight-shooter. If he tells you it's going to rain, you grab an umbrella."

Under Welch it poured. The IUE resigned itself to obtaining relatively meager wage gains through the eighties—less than 3.5 percent a year. Other big unions settled for the same or even less, as the contracts reached in 1988 across all of industry contained pay increases averaging less than 2 percent annually. Two decades earlier, with inflation running at about the same rate, the yearly wage bump was nearly 6 percent. For the IUE and others, the dramatic downsizing of corporate America had forced them to fight less for compensation and more for job security. But that fight didn't go very well, either, as the percentage of unionized workers continued to go down, down, down—both at GE and at most other employers. In 1980, more than 20 percent of private-sector workers in the United States were still members of organized labor; eight years later, fewer than 13 percent were. For many, bitterness set in. At the IUE, "union meetings were angry affairs," the journalist Thomas O'Boyle, who is perhaps Welch's harshest detractor, has written. "Workers denounced their leadership for not being more militant, for not standing up to the company, even though there was little if anything the union could do but capitulate."

In January 1988, *Los Angeles Times* writer Harry Bernstein published a piece that compared Lem Boulware's infamous take-it-or-leave-it construct in labor negotiations with what he termed "Welchism"—a "system of drastically eliminating union jobs without openly fighting with unions." Should Welch establish "a pattern for other corporate executives faced with domestic and international competition," Bernstein said, "it may make Boulwarism look like a picnic for the labor movement. . . . Boulware at his worst never managed to weaken GE unions" as much as Welch had. When Boulware, then in his nineties, saw the article, he couldn't hide his delight. "I judge . . . that I can move over and let you take the hot seat I have enjoyed for forty years as the tough guy of General Electric," he told Welch. "Congratulations and thanks!"

If Welch's workers didn't always come out ahead, one group seemed to: GE's stockholders. Welch had taken a profitable company and made it far more profitable in an ever more challenging world, with earnings rising steadily from $1.5 billion dollars in 1980—Reg Jones's last year as CEO—to more than $4 billion by 1990. The market genuflected. And by the midnineties, Welch would find himself on the cover of *Fortune*, hailed for having "unlocked the secrets of creating shareholder value." At GE, the magazine said, some $52 billion in investor wealth had been produced during Welch's time as CEO. Next to him on the cover was one other corporate chief, who was credited for conjuring even more in shareholder riches—$59 billion. That was Coca-Cola's Roberto Goizueta.

PART III

THE ERA OF
SHAREHOLDER
SUPREMACY

Coca-Cola CEO Roberto Goizueta (at right), seen here with his top lieutenant, Donald Keough, put one aim above all others: "I wrestle over how to build shareholder value from the time I get up in the morning to the time I go to bed."

9

LIVING AND DYING
BY THE NUMBERS

Given his expertise, age, and accent, Roberto Goizueta's rise to the top of Coca-Cola was every bit as unexpected as Jack Welch's climb to the chief executive's office at General Electric.

Goizueta had joined Coke in 1954, overseeing production processes in the three bottling plants that the company ran in his native Cuba. He was twenty-two at the time, the son of a Havana family that had made its fortune in sugar, and had just earned a chemical-engineering degree from Yale. He immediately showed himself to be a tireless worker, willing to do whatever it took to keep the line moving, even if it meant sleeping through the night at the factory so that he could be on hand to troubleshoot problems. He impressed, as well, with his devotion to quality, trying to ensure that every Coke sold was, as he said in a 1957 report, "pure and wholesome."

With Goizueta's ambition and intensity, it was likely only a matter of time before higher-ups in Atlanta would have plucked him from Cuba and assigned him to bigger and better things. Before they could act, however, Goizueta's upper-crust existence was shattered. In February 1959, Fidel Castro was sworn in as prime minister of Cuba after his guerrilla campaign forced right-wing dictator Fulgencio Batista into exile. It wasn't long before Goizueta found himself harassed by the new regime. Soldiers stopped him one night and searched his brief-case, evidently trying to make sure that he wasn't hiding any company documents from the government. The following year, with tensions flaring between the United States and Cuba and Castro threatening to seize American interests on the island, the moment had come for Goizueta and his wife to leave.

They landed in Miami with just enough clothes for a supposedly short "vacation" and only $200 between them. They left everything else behind—their house, their cars, their bank accounts, their books and art. Goizueta did, however, still own one other notable asset: a hundred shares of Coca-Cola stock that he had bought with $8,000 lent to him by his dad. "You shouldn't work for someone else," Goizu-eta's father had told him when he first took the job with Coke. "You should work for yourself." Keeping a close eye on the company's share price—and, in the end, doing absolutely everything that he could to help it go up—would become Roberto Goizueta's obsession.

After coordinating technical operations for Coca-Cola in Latin America—a job that had him shuttling between Miami and a base in the Bahamas—Goizueta was summoned in 1964 to Atlanta for a spe-cial assignment: helping to reorganize the company's engineering and research activities. Whatever mixing of the elements went on in the lab, the real chemistry occurred between Goizueta and Coca-Cola's senior leaders. Now ensconced at headquarters, and with his responsi-bilities steadily widening to include issues related to general manage-ment and the allocation of capital, Goizueta worked closely with CEO Paul Austin and, before long, Robert Woodruff—The Boss—who, from his seat as chairman of the board's Finance Committee, was still very much in control of the company.

In 1966, at age thirty-five, Goizueta was promoted to vice president of technical research and development—the youngest vice president in Coca-Cola history. In 1974, he was named a senior vice president, and in 1979 he was elevated to be one of six new vice chairmen of the corpora-tion. At forty-seven, Goizueta was three to twenty years younger than anyone else in the "vice squad," as the group came to be known. In many respects, his meteoric ascent was similar to Jack Welch's. Yet as coarse and hyperkinetic as Welch could be, Goizueta was just the opposite:

reserved, refined, and flawlessly put together, with his Guccis, tailored suits, and silk handkerchiefs tucked in his breast pocket. He was also adept at sucking up to Robert Woodruff. And he padded his credentials, claiming falsely that he'd graduated tenth in his class at Yale.

As it entered the 1980s, Coca-Cola was in a bad spot. Austin had expanded into a bunch of areas, including water purification, shrimp farms, carpet shampoo, plastic straws, and more, diverting the company's attention away from its core business: selling soft drinks. There couldn't have been a worse time to stray, either. Coca-Cola's biggest rival was aggressively offering blind taste tests across the country—the Pepsi Challenge—and stealing market share. Coke's cash reserves dwindled and its stock price lagged. "Executives were paralyzed by indirection," one journalist has noted, "and the company's operations and financial policies were outmoded, in some cases medieval."

At the same time, Coke's bottlers had "no confidence in what Austin tells them," Joseph Jones, Woodruff's right-hand assistant, warned The Boss. "They have no respect for him, they don't trust him." Neither did Woodruff, who had lost all patience with Austin after he made some questionable personnel moves and built a fancy new headquarters tower that the old man hated. Austin then tried to pay for the building with something that the financially conservative Woodruff hated even more: $100 million in debt. As the company lost its focus, Austin lost his, fumbling through speeches and forgetting things and otherwise behaving erratically. Some of Austin's longtime colleagues figured that he'd developed a drinking problem. Only later would it be revealed that he had been suffering from a crippling combination of diseases—Alzheimer's and Parkinson's.

As company insiders and outsiders began to speculate on who would replace Austin, few gave Goizueta a shot. He was relatively young, had no branding or marketing experience in a company that was all about branding and marketing, and "was a foreign national" at an institution "heretofore led by dyed-in-the-wool Georgians," as one commentator remarked. But Goizueta's every-other-day visits to Woodruff's Tuxedo Road mansion, sipping vodka and tonic in the sitting room with the old man, apparently paid off. Goizueta emerged as Woodruff's choice to take charge of his company; everyone else in the running was knocked out. The *Financial Times* called Goizueta's selection "one of the most surprising executive appointments in US business this year." Most of those working for him couldn't even pronounce his name (Goy-SWET-ah).

It wouldn't take any time at all, however, for Goizueta to make
plain what he intended to accomplish. Just like Welch at GE, he declared that there would be "no sacred cows" at Coca-Cola, and he set
out to impose a new degree of discipline for a new day. "It has been
said that the fifties, the sixties, and even into the midseventies were
the years of determinism in the corporate world—a period when predictable, satisfactory earnings growth records could be achieved without a great deal of management input or careful attention to details,"
Goizueta told employees in May 1981. "Since the midseventies, however, we have been in a period of uncertainty. In this environment, the
finest test of management competence will be the management of productivities: productivity of money, of physical assets, and of people."

To make Coke more productive, Goizueta pressed executives to
execute with a level of rigor that was never before required of them.
Under Austin, they had been able to make five-year plans that were
full of vague promises. Under Goizueta, they were compelled to lay
out precise three-year plans—and then they'd better be sure to nail
their targets. "I want you to tell me what you need to do to expand
your business, what kind of capital you need to do it, and what kind
of net return you're going to get," Goizueta instructed his seventeen
division chiefs. He insisted on answers that were clear and smart and
grounded in data that was accurate. "Facts are facts," Goizueta would
write again and again on his executives' budget submissions, sending
them scurrying back to revise things.

"People have got to believe they are living or dying by these
numbers," Goizueta told Coke's president, Donald Keough, a highly
respected company veteran who had wanted the CEO job but, after
being passed over, agreed to stay on as the second-in-command.

"Yes," Keough responded. "We've got some toilet training to do."

For those who hadn't done their homework, Goizueta gave no
forbearance. His questions were so sharp that an early session when
he prodded and probed his managers became known as "The Spanish
Inquisition." Goizueta's aim in all of this was, in many ways, a mirror
of what Welch was trying to do at GE: take an organization that had
become tired and slow-footed and rejuvenate it by spreading more responsibility and accountability throughout the ranks. "It would take a

long and difficult battle to mold Coke into a world-class company at every level of operation in every market around the globe," Goizueta's biographer, David Greising, has written. "But his job, as he saw it, was to shrink the time line, to jolt Coke into the future abruptly, to shake up the managers and make them understand. It was time for these people to get on board or get out."

Like Welch, Goizueta wanted employees who would dream big and take risks, so long as those risks panned out more times than not. "The needs of our business demand that we look for and develop entrepreneurs rather than just caretakers," he said. Most companies, Goizueta added, like to "reward the 'team player' who doesn't rock the boat or step out of line. I'm all for loyalty and team spirit—but only if they do not discourage innovative thought and action."

Goizueta led by example, taking a series of bold steps throughout his time as CEO. Although he held a dim view of his predecessor's fondness for diversifying—"cats and dogs," he called the assortment of businesses that Austin had branched into in the 1960s and '70s— Goizueta purchased Columbia Pictures in 1982, giving Coke a taste of Hollywood. The acquisition couldn't have gone down any smoother. During that first year, on the strength of the box-office smashes *Gandhi* and *Tootsie* and a successful joint production deal with Home Box Office, Coke's entertainment subsidiary rang up a hefty $90 million in operating profit, 50 percent more than Goizueta had predicted. (Seven years later, Goizueta would sell Columbia to Sony for a net gain of half a billion dollars.) He also introduced Diet Coke, a runaway hit. The company was now booming.

"I have been racking my brain to figure out what to give you" for a ninety-fifth-birthday gift, Goizueta wrote to Robert Woodruff in December 1984. "After much thought, I have come to the conclusion that what you probably would enjoy the most is knowing how well your company is doing." Goizueta then ticked off "a few facts and figures": Earnings for the first nine months of the year were up 17 percent. Operating profit was poised to pass the billion-dollar mark for the first time ever. And Coke's stock price was at an eleven-year high. "For the last three years," Goizueta told The Boss, "the value of the shareholders' interest in your company has increased from $4.6 billion to about $8 billion. . . . This year alone, the total return on your investment in the company will likely end up being at least 20 percent." For his part, Woodruff was pleased. "My company is being run very well," he told an associate.

In March 1985, Woodruff died while holding his nurse's hand and listening to the gospel song "Just a Closer Walk with Thee." Although he could be a tough S.O.B., Woodruff left $1 million in his will to Joseph Jones, who had denied himself all those years of vacation so as to faithfully serve The Boss.

The following month, Goizueta made his biggest bet yet: he replaced the company's flagship product with a reformulated version of the ninety-nine-year-old cola. The backlash against New Coke, as it was called, was overwhelming, as some 400,000 phone calls and letters poured into the company. The buying public abhorred the change. So did Coca-Cola's bottlers. Pepsi pounced, too, saying that Coke had sweetened its soda to mimic the taste of its closest competitor. "The other guy just blinked," Roger Enrico, the president of Pepsi-Cola USA, proclaimed in an open letter that appeared in newspapers across the country. But even one of the greatest blunders in business history couldn't slow down Coke for long. The company soon reintroduced its original formula, now dubbed Coke Classic. Consumers were so thrilled by the reversal that some wondered whether the company had concocted the entire crisis. "Some critics will say Coca-Cola made a marketing mistake," Keough told reporters. "Some cynics will say that we planned the whole thing. The truth is we are not that dumb and not that smart." In any case, by early 1986 Coke Classic was once again outselling Pepsi, while New Coke faded away.

Through all of the successes and occasional failures, Goizueta remained firmly fixated on the company's financial health. Increasing sales was crucial, he believed, but not at the expense of profitability, and he stipulated that every line of business at Coca-Cola must generate at least a 20 percent return. For some of the old-timers, this new emphasis left them cold. "We moved into the eighties and everything seemed to change," said Charlie Bottoms, a marketing manager who worked at Coke for forty years. "Financial engineers run this company."

It wasn't surprising that employees felt this way. For one measuring stick had come to stand above the rest at Coca-Cola: the company's stock price.

"It is easy in the rush of our day-to-day routines to forget for whom we are really working," Goizueta had said when he first became

CEO. "There are 79,305 shareholders—mostly individuals like you and me—who own the Coca-Cola Company. After all is said and done, our primary responsibility is the long-term enhancement of their investment in this company."

By 1988, Goizueta had wrapped Coke's strategy around this one main objective: "to increase shareholder value over time." "I wrestle over how to build shareholder value from the time I get up in the morning to the time I go to bed," he said. "I even think about it when I am shaving." If such an orientation sounded different than that favored by previous CEOs, that's because it was. Typical of the old guard was Coca-Cola president William Robinson, who told a group at Fordham Law School in 1959 that it was a mistake for executives to put "the stockholders first, last, and all the time." Rather, he said, a corporation had to serve four constituencies: the stockholder, the community, the customer, and the employee—Coke's version of GE's "balanced best interests" doctrine. But for Goizueta, the shareholder was the undisputed king. "There are plenty of . . . missions upon which a company could focus: serving customers . . . providing the highest quality of products and services; creating jobs and job security," he said. "But I would submit that in our political and economic system, the mission of any business is to create value for its owners."

Under Goizueta's leadership, Coca-Cola split its stock and bought back billions of dollars of its shares—a maneuver that became popular throughout corporate America in the 1980s—in an effort to nudge the price higher. He also hectored securities analysts who dared to disagree with his vision for the company. One analyst, from Merrill Lynch, was essentially blackballed for a year after raising questions about Coca-Cola's foreign currency exposure. Goizueta personally kept close tabs on the company's share price as well. Constance Hays, who covered Coca-Cola for the *New York Times*, captured the scene that played out in a conference room in Atlanta, at a time before the gyrations of a company's stock could be followed on any PC, laptop, or smartphone.

> The room, down the hall from the top executives' offices on the twenty-fifth floor of the Coke tower, held a machine capable of tracking moment-by-moment changes in trading volume, index performances, and specific share prices. A squat-looking little thing, it sat on a table all by itself, powered up nearly all the time.

During the day, at any given hour, people passing by that conference room might see a dark-haired man standing before the table. His back would be to the open door, his hands stuck inside the pockets of his suit jacket. Even from behind, everyone knew who he was: the chairman and chief executive of the Coca-Cola Company. And they knew what he was doing. He was watching the market move. Unaware of the employees passing down the hall behind him, undisturbed by conversations wafting in from other rooms, he was oblivious to everything but the green light coming from the screen.

Roberto Goizueta was hardly the only corporate executive in America so transfixed.

There was a time in the United States when few businesses were owned by anyone outside of their founders (and their families) and perhaps small pools of investors. But that was long ago. Starting in the early nineteenth century, companies in one sector after another began to disburse their shares widely: textiles, railroads, banking and insurance, mining and quarrying, and finally, by the first few decades of the twentieth century, many other types of manufacturing and service operations. As corporate stock found its way into more people's possession, another development followed: new crops of professional managers were hired and left to determine the day-to-day direction of these ventures. Ownership, now diffuse, became more distant and passive.

Not everyone was pleased by this shift, fearing that it opened up the possibility of widespread abuse by executives and directors who, while not acquiring so much as a single share of their own companies, would put their selfish interests first. "It is . . . evident that we are dealing not only with distinct but often with opposing groups: ownership on the one side, control on the other—a control which tends to move further and further away from ownership and ultimately to lie in the hands of management itself, a management capable of perpetuating its own position," attorney Adolf Berle and economist Gardiner Means wrote in their seminal 1932 book, *The Modern Corporation and Private Property.* "The concentration of economic power separate from ownership has, in fact, created economic empires, and has delivered these empires into the hands of a new form of absolutism, relegating 'owners' to the position of those who supply the means whereby the new princes may exercise their power."

Yet, for all of their concerns, Berle and Means did see one way that management might have a positive impact—even if its agenda diverged from that of shareholders. "Should the corporate leaders . . . set forth a program comprising fair wages, security to employees, reasonable service to their public, and stabilization of business, all of which would divert a portion of the profits from the owners of passive property, and should the community generally accept such a scheme as a logical and human solution of industrial difficulties, the interests of passive property owners would have to give way," they wrote. Ideally, Berle and Means continued, corporate management should be attuned to "balancing a variety of claims by various groups in the community and assigning to each a portion of the income stream on the basis of public policy rather than private cupidity."

One could argue that "balancing a variety of claims" is exactly what happened as the social contract between employer and employee evolved during the twenty-five years after World War II, with rising wages and benefits, dependable job security, and sound businesses built on the prosperity of America's growing consumer class. It wasn't a flawless system. Not even close. But many of the country's biggest corporations found themselves working for "the larger interests of society," as Berle and Means had imagined they might, even if they did so unevenly and at times begrudgingly.

Then, as the US economy languished and the weaknesses of many American corporations began to be unmasked, the old debate about the proper role of business reignited. One of the first to weigh in was Milton Friedman, the influential University of Chicago economist, who contended in a 1970 essay in the *New York Times Magazine* that a corporation had but one legitimate "social responsibility": "to increase its profits so long as it . . . engages in open and free competition without deception or fraud." A company that was pursuing anything else, including trying to "take seriously . . . providing employment," was in Friedman's mind doing little more than "preaching pure and unadulterated socialism." By this reasoning, the obligation of executives placed in charge of a company was straightforward. "The manager is the agent of the individuals who own the corporation," Friedman wrote. And it was up to him "to conduct the business in accordance with their desires" as shareholders, "which generally will be to make as much money as possible."

Friedman's thesis was one part of a broader intellectual movement, which extolled the cool rationality of the marketplace and ascribed to it an almost preternatural ability to sort out a vast range of social problems. By the early 1980s, the Princeton historian Daniel Rodgers has observed, "the proposition that the free play of private interests might better promote maximum social well-being"—more so than would a government program or traditional welfare capitalism—had "moved closer and closer to the default assumption" in American life. A collection of scholars (including Robert Lucas, Richard Posner, Kenneth Scott, Gary Becker, Eugene Fama, Frank Easterbrook, Daniel Fischel, and others) joined Friedman in carrying this thinking deep into the fields of economics and law, while Ronald Reagan and his supply-siders applied it to politics and policy. "You know," the president said, "there really is something magic about the marketplace when it's free to operate."

Among those who understood the publication of Friedman's article to be a major event—not just for business, but for the whole of American culture—was Michael Jensen, a professor at the University of Rochester's Graduate School of Management, who in 1976 coauthored his own paper on the relationship between corporate executives and shareholders. The piece was written with his Rochester colleague William Meckling, who, along with Jensen, had been trained in neoclassical economic theory at the University of Chicago. Filled with mathematical equations, it would find its home in an outlet far more obscure than the *New York Times*—namely, the *Journal of Financial Economics*. Nonetheless, "Theory of the Firm: Managerial Behavior, Agency Costs, and Ownership Structure" would go on to become the most cited academic business paper of all time.

Like Berle and Means, Jensen and Meckling saw an inherent conflict between managers and shareholders. The manager, they wrote, has a natural "tendency to appropriate perquisites out of the firm's resources for his own consumption"—in other words, to feather his own nest. He may also be disinclined to search out "new profitable ventures . . . simply because it requires too much trouble or effort on his part." Unlike Berle and Means, however, Jensen and Meckling saw nothing redeeming about executives who provided good wages or security to their employees. Just as Friedman had, they characterized corporate leaders as mere agents of the shareholders; their sole function, then, was to maximize shareholder value.

For those who weren't up to the task, Jensen encouraged that they be driven out of their companies through hostile takeovers—a comeuppance for entrenched executives. "The takeover process," he wrote, "penalizes incompetent or self-serving managers whose actions have lowered the market price of their corporation's stock." Loading up corporations with debt was praised as a way to bring profligate executives to heel.

A group of buyout artists were the heroes of Jensen's narrative. As Roberto Goizueta and Jack Welch were remaking their companies from the inside, a gaggle of corporate raiders—Carl Icahn, T. Boone Pickens, Victor Posner, Harold Simmons, and others—were taking aim from the outside, trying to squeeze more value out of what they maintained were inefficient and mismanaged businesses. Even those who were wary of the financiers' tactics had to concede that the case they were making couldn't be dismissed out of hand. Peter Drucker, for instance, was no fan of Milton Friedman's framing of corporate responsibility. "Altogether far too much in society—jobs, careers, communities—depends on the economic fortunes of large enterprises to subordinate them completely to the interests of any one group, including shareholders," he wrote. But Drucker also recognized that "what made takeovers and buyouts inevitable . . . was the mediocre performance" of American companies through the 1970s and early '80s.

"Whatever the reasons or excuses," Drucker said, "the large US company has not done particularly well on professional management's watch—whether measured by competitiveness, market standing, or innovative performance. As for financial performance, it has, by and large, not even earned the minimum-acceptable result, a return on equity equal to its cost of capital. The raiders thus performed a needed function. As an old proverb has it, 'If there are no grave diggers, one needs vultures.'"

They circled hungrily. By one count, nearly half of all major US companies received an unsolicited takeover offer in the eighties, much of it greased by new financial instruments such as "junk bonds." Many of the deals that unfolded during the decade were so-called bust-up takeovers in which diversified companies (many of them assembled during the 1950s and '60s, when conglomerates were hot) were targeted and then dismembered, with the component pieces sold off.

Some, like Boone Pickens, pointed to Jensen's work to justify their methods, while executives and boards of directors began to talk and act as if maximizing shareholder value was their legal duty. As a factual matter, this was wrong; the law has never mandated any such thing. But that didn't stop "agency theory" from permeating the realm of practice. "Under the sway of the new economic orthodoxy," Harvard's Rakesh Khurana has written, "any suggestion that the corporation was subordinate to any societal institution other than shareholders was increasingly regarded as soft-minded and suspect."

For many years, the Business Roundtable held fast to a concept that seemed as if it came straight from the glory days of the Committee for Economic Development. "Corporations are chartered to serve both their shareholders and society as a whole," the group said in a 1990 statement. "Some argue that only the interests of shareholders should be considered by directors. The thrust of history and law strongly supports the broader view of directors' responsibility to carefully weigh the interests of all stakeholders." By the late 1990s, however, the Roundtable would parrot the prevailing sentiment. "The paramount duty of management and boards of directors," the organization now said, "is to the corporation's stockholders. . . . The notion that the board must somehow balance the interests of other stakeholders fundamentally misconstrues the role of directors."

So much for the "thrust of history and law."

None of this was advantageous for workers. It wasn't that the push to maximize shareholder wealth was the central cause of the social contract crumbling. New competitive realities brought by globalization, the decline of organized labor, the reach of technology— all of these were already altering the compact between employer and employee before the cult of the shareholder was established. And yet, with agency theory embraced so fully, each of these trends was amplified. "During the postwar boom, American corporations had taken on the provision of stable careers, health insurance for employees and their dependents, and retirement security," the University of Michigan's Gerald Davis has written. "Now corporations increasingly saw employment as an avoidable expense. Creating shareholder value was in tension with creating stable employment."

Indeed, takeovers were frequently followed by layoffs as new owners expected executives to reduce redundancies and cut out anything—or anyone—that might be deemed waste. Meantime, many top managers didn't wait for a Carl Icahn to storm the gates or for an institutional investor to initiate a proxy fight and attempt to oust them. They tried to get ahead of things by making their organizations leaner and flatter, hoping that such proactive behavior would help their companies, as well as their own careers, live on. "It is important to distinguish between the causes of layoffs and the CEOs who as agents of change respond to ensure the competitiveness and survival of their companies," said Northwestern University's Alfred Rappaport, who is credited with coining the term "shareholder value." "Spare the messenger."

Sometimes, they got eliminated regardless. More than a quarter of the country's biggest corporations—those in the Fortune 500—received tender offers during the eighties. Two-thirds of them were unsolicited, and by the end of the decade a third of the names that had been on the magazine's list no longer existed as independent entities. A good bit of this turnover was undoubtedly for the better. Economies thrive and grow over time as companies whose products and services become stale and obsolete are unseated by more innovative upstarts—a never-ending cycle of renewal that economist Joseph Schumpeter called "creative destruction." In this context, "destruction does not mean 'death' in the Judeo-Christian tradition, but rather 'transformation' in the Hindu tradition," consultant Richard Foster and management professor Sarah Kaplan have written.

Yet even proponents of this economic churn, which was now happening at a much faster pace than it did during the 1960s and '70s, could see that such regeneration came with significant social costs—specifically, "the number of people 'left behind,'" to use Foster and Kaplan's words. By 1990, the number of employees among Fortune 500 companies had dropped to fewer than 12.5 million from nearly 16 million a decade before. When Jack Welch had started out, vaporizing tens of thousands of jobs was still seen as scandalous. Pretty soon, it was common across corporate America—a wholesale realignment of who stood where in the eyes of management. "It used to be that companies had an allegiance to the worker and the country," said Jim Daughtry, local leader of the International Union of Electrical Workers in Fort Wayne, Indiana. "Today, companies have an allegiance to the shareholder. Period."

Well, not exactly. Through the 1980s and '90s, at least one category of employee was making out better than ever: the CEO.

Top executives in America had always done quite well for themselves. In the 1950s, gadflies started to show up at corporate annual meetings to deplore the excesses of executive pay—a scene satirized in the comedy *The Solid Gold Cadillac*, starring Judy Holliday and Paul Douglas:

> THE WOMAN. I'm sorry, I—I've never attended a stockholder's meeting before. Maybe I'd better sit down.
> BLESSINGTON. Just as you wish, Madam.
> THE WOMAN. Thank you.
> BLESSINGTON. Now, there is a motion—
> THE WOMAN. On the other hand—it says here that the salary for the chairman of the board next year will be $175,000. Tell me—is that true?
> BLESSINGTON. Well—uh—wherever did you get a notion like that, Miss—uh—
> THE WOMAN. Mrs. Partridge. It's on page ninety-six. Right here.
> BLESSINGTON. I see. Uh—Mr. Snell, as treasurer, would you care to answer that question?
> SNELL. Yes, indeed! Happy to oblige. . . . The—uh—could I hear the question again, please?
> MRS. PARTRIDGE. I don't want anyone to think I'm nosy, but is it true that the chairman will get $175,000 next year? It seems such a lot of money.
> SNELL. Why—Madam. In a company of this size, that is not considered a large salary. Not a large salary at all. I believe that answers the question.

Actually, in 1956, the year that *The Solid Gold Cadillac* hit the big screen, $175,000 (equal to about $1.5 million now) was considered a large salary, though dozens of executives made more than that—some much more. The highest earner among corporate chiefs in '56 was Eugene Grace, the chairman of Bethlehem Steel, whose compensation topped $800,000 (more than $7 million in current terms). Harlow Curtice of GM netted more than $695,000. General Electric's Ralph Cordiner brought home about $260,000, while Kodak's Thomas Hargrave commanded more than $210,000. Coca-Cola's president, Bill Robinson, was paid just over $112,000 for his services.

At the midpoint of the range, top executives made about $150,000 a year during the 1950s—the same amount that they'd earned since the 1930s (when adjusted for inflation). Their pay would remain at a similar level through the 1960s and '70s as well. There were lots of exceptions on both the high end and the low end, but overall, executive compensation held remarkably steady for five straight decades. Then, in a flash, everything changed. Median CEO compensation climbed more than 50 percent during the 1980s, and it more than doubled from there during the 1990s. By 2005, it would more than double again, so that a large-company CEO in the middle of the pack on pay was now making more than $9 million a year.

A big reason for this surge was agency theory. As companies sought to align the interests of managers and shareholders, they began to issue ever more stock options to top executives. Granting stock to CEOs was prevalent through the 1950s and '60s, but it wasn't a major part of their remuneration; salary and cash bonuses accounted for about 90 percent of total executive compensation through those years. Then, in the 1980s, stock awards became far more prominent. In 1993, Congress changed the tax code so as to further stimulate this trend. By 2001, shares of stock would account for 85 percent of CEO pay, by some calculations. Compensating top executives this way made exquisite sense if you bought into how Jensen and Meckling said the world should work, which by now nearly every corporate board of directors, executive team, and business consultant had accepted. The idea was shorthanded as "pay for performance": if a company performed well for its shareholders, the CEO would rightfully get his piece.

But what looked so cogent on paper turned out to be problematic when implemented. To begin with, the expansion of stock-based pay coincided with the longest bull market in American history—a 1,500 percent jump in the Dow Jones Industrial Average from August 1982 to January 2000. "Despite the fact that the rising stock market was making options far more lucrative than boards likely anticipated when they issued them, directors couldn't seem to break themselves of the habit of giving options to CEOs," law professor Michael Dorff has written. "To the contrary, they kept issuing more."

In turn, executives were incentivized to behave in perverse ways. Many stinted on investments in research and development, as well as on new factories and equipment, in order to hold down expenses. Such choices, along with creative accounting and other machinations, had the desired effect: they inflated current profits, which goosed the company's share price—for a little while anyway—and allowed the CEO to make off with millions. Presumably, the CEO also stood to lose a bundle if he didn't perform. But the rules and norms governing executive pay proved far less reliable than the law of gravity: what went up didn't come down, at least not nearly to the same extent. CEOs "can make huge amounts of money," the compensation watchdog Graef Crystal complained in 1991, "but it is hard for them to lose much money. . . . No matter how many times I have touted them, negative bonuses—the kind where the CEO writes a check to the company— have just never caught on."

Of course, none of this created much value for stockholders, at least over the long haul. "Improving real-market performance is the hardest and slowest way to increase expectations" among investors and lift a company's shares, the University of Toronto's Roger Martin has explained. "The company has to build facilities, hire employees . . . and wait for these all to convert to real sales and profits increases." It's much easier "to hype your stock on Wall Street by providing aggressively high guidance on the company's projected earnings" and then hit those numbers, down to the penny, by driving short-term results. In such an atmosphere, according to Martin, "companies focus more on their stock market analysts than on their customers," and "employees feel ever less loyalty to their company, knowing that their company has precious little loyalty toward them."

Roberto Goizueta wasn't unmindful that maximizing shareholder value was being "vilified by many critics," as he put it, especially after "huge layoffs at certain companies." But none of that fazed him, as he dressed his preoccupation with Coca-Cola's share price in a cloak of morality. Only by putting its stockholders first, last, and all of the time, he said, could the company hope to "contribute to society in meaningful ways." Investment firms handling "the retirement funds and savings of teachers, public employees, and other citizens," Goizueta pointed out, owned nearly 40 percent of Coke's shares. The company's employees owned another 20 percent or so, and some had become millionaires because of their Coke holdings.

Others rode the market wave, as well. When Jack Welch became CEO at GE, about 500 executives were awarded stock in the company every year. But Welch opened the spigot, so that by the time he retired, about 15,000 employees, or 5 percent of GE's workforce, were awarded options worth more than $2 billion. "What a kick!" Welch would later remember. "Every Friday, I got a printout listing all the employees who exercised stock options and the size of their gains. The options were changing their lives, helping them put their kids through college, take care of elderly parents, or buy second homes."

At Coca-Cola, for anyone who had bought $100 worth of stock the day Goizueta became CEO, its value was nearing a thousand bucks (with dividends reinvested) by his tenth anniversary in the job. The market now valued the company at $35 billion, up from $4 billion when he took over.

Nobody, though, would fare as well as Goizueta himself. Over his seventeen years as CEO of Coca-Cola, he would receive more than $1 billion in compensation—an extraordinary payout for someone who wasn't the founder of a company but, rather, merely hired help. After Goizueta was gone and Coca-Cola slumped, some business experts would question whether he had really built the company for sustained success, though he always stressed the need to think years and years into the future, censuring leaders who slashed and burned their companies or played games to manipulate the stock. "Focusing on creating value over the long term keeps us from acting shortsighted," he said. There was also a flap in the media when it was discovered that Coke's board in 1991 had given Goizueta 1 million stock options, worth more than $80 million, and then obscured the fact in the company's financial filings. Instead of spelling out "1,000,000 shares" in the part of its proxy statement that listed the CEO's salary and bonus, the company wrote out "one million shares" and buried it in a thick paragraph three pages later. More condemnation from good-governance advocates came when it was revealed that Coca-Cola had agreed to fork over more than $100 million to cover Goizueta's entire federal and state tax bill.

Yet, despite the outcry, one group didn't seem to care much at all: Coke's shareholders. As long as Goizueta was making them rich—and he was—they cheered him on. Before Goizueta's arrival, Coke's stock had been stagnant for twenty years. "They could have put their money in a drawer and done as well," Keough said. Now, the stock was soaring—and so was their sense of gratitude. A group called "the Coca-Cola widows," which was made up of Georgia women whose working-class husbands had bought a few Coca-Cola shares and held on to them until they became worth millions, thought of Roberto Goizueta as their savior. "I never sold a single share," one elderly woman said, "and I just wanted to tell you Coca-Cola has put my six children and seventeen grandchildren through college." At the annual shareholder meeting in 1992, Goizueta worried that he might be confronted about his exorbitant pay. Instead, those in attendance interrupted his remarks four times with their applause.

Coca-Cola was, in this way, a microcosm of America as a whole. The generation of executives that had entered the workplace in the 1950s and '60s was steeped in an ethic of commitment and community that arose out of the shared struggle and sacrifice of the Depression and World War II. "The old giving/getting compact," the great pollster and trend-spotter Dan Yankelovich wrote in his 1981 book *New Rules*, "might be paraphrased this way: 'I give hard work, loyalty and steadfastness. I swallow my frustrations and suppress my impulse to do what I would enjoy, and do what is expected of me instead. I do not put myself first. I put the needs of others ahead of my own. I give a lot, but what I get in return is worth it. I receive an ever-growing standard of living, and a family life with a devoted spouse and decent kids. . . . I have a nice home, a good job, the respect of my friends and neighbors; a sense of accomplishment at having made something of my life.'" Through the eighties and nineties, however, such attitudes all but disappeared.

The "do your own thing" spirit of the 1960s and '70s counterculture had gone mainstream and taken on a harder edge—mutating into a "culture of narcissism," to use the title of Christopher Lasch's 1979 bestseller. "Tens of millions of Americans have grown wary of demands for further sacrifices they believe may no longer be warranted," Yankelovich reported, based on a plethora of social-science research. "They want to modify the giving/getting compact in every one of its dimensions—family life, career, leisure, the meaning of success, relationships with other people, and relations with themselves." Inside many companies, the refashioning of the compact came down to this: managers were thirsting to get more and give less; they began to think about themselves rather than the larger group. "A crude individualism reasserted itself; that is, the largely mythical, nostalgic, and debilitating view that in America, people pulled themselves up by their own endeavors, acting heroically and alone, as Jay Gatsby had in F. Scott Fitzgerald's 1925 novel *The Great Gatsby* or as Howard Roark did in Ayn Rand's 1943 novel *The Fountainhead*," the journalist Louis Uchitelle has written.

Among CEOs, this propensity was particularly pronounced. "The logic is, 'What's good for me is good for everybody,'" Yankelovich said. In point of fact, it's difficult to see how what's been good for CEOs has been good for almost anybody else, especially the 90-plus percent of employees who don't hold any stock options. Until the 1970s, the pay of the average worker was going up faster than that of top executives. By the 1980s, however, CEOs were galloping ahead while most everyone else was standing still or falling behind. And the gap was getting exponentially wider. In 1965, CEOs at big companies made 20 times what the average worker did. By 2000, they'd make 376 times more. Never mind that it's exceedingly debatable how much of a company's performance is due to the talent of any single individual—even the CEO—as opposed to the collective efforts of the entire enterprise. Stock options are also rarely indexed to the market or the industry as a whole, so executives often benefit from a general rise in economic conditions, not from anything they've done personally. Some refer to this as "lucky dollars."

As the years rolled on, many rank-and-file workers were to discover that they too were becoming more dependent on the stock market—or, more particularly, their retirement security was. They, however, weren't nearly so lucky.

America's pension revolution began more or less by accident, when Rep. Barber Conable, a New York Republican, tried to help out some people back in his home district: the employees of Eastman Kodak.

In 1958, Kodak had started giving its workers a choice: they could take their wage dividend as they always had—as a cash bonus—or they could have the company add it to their pension plan. One advantage of the latter was that they wouldn't have to pay any taxes on the money until it was tapped during retirement. Through the 1970s, however, the Treasury Department kept eyeing that pool of protected income and making noise about taxing it as a way to raise revenue. Conable, a senior member of the House Ways and Means Committee, felt as if the bureaucrats at Treasury—"running dogs," he called them—were trying unfairly to change the rules midstream. And so he looked to shut them down by adding new language to Section 401 of the Internal Revenue Code. Thanks to subsection (k), Treasury would no longer be able to go after profit sharing that had been placed into a retirement account.

When the Revenue Act of 1978 passed, Conable's contribution to the legislation was considered largely inconsequential—a neat way to assist the men and women of Kodak, as well as others who participated in profit-sharing plans. "There was absolutely no discussion in '78 that if you do this, the world is going to change," said Daniel Halperin, a Treasury official at the time. Conable himself had all but forgotten that he'd even authored that part of the law when in early 2000 he was shown a copy of *Pensions & Investments* magazine, which had just named him as one of its top picks for "person of the century." Long retired from Congress, Conable was at a board meeting of the insurer American International Group when someone pulled out a copy of the trade publication, which had paid tribute to Conable alongside Andrew Carnegie, Warren Buffett, Benjamin Graham, and a handful of others who'd left an everlasting mark on finance and investing. "Everybody was saying, 'Oh, Barber, you did such a wonderful thing!'" he later recounted. "I said, 'I don't think I did.'" Finally, he phoned the Ways and Means staff, and someone there confirmed it: Conable had most certainly been responsible for the 401(k)—and, lo and behold, it had changed the world.

In the two decades between Conable's seemingly modest act of constituent service and his coronation by *Pensions & Investments*, the 401(k) had gone from being a narrowly conceived instrument to promote profit sharing to becoming the most popular pension vehicle in the country. Yet the 401(k) wasn't only widely used; it was also widely criticized. The principal reason: it allowed companies to transfer the risk for retirement savings from their own books onto the shoulders of their employees.

Even in its heyday, the private pension system in the United States was far from perfect. Although it had expanded rapidly through the 1950s and continued to grow during the '60s, due mainly to bargaining-table victories by organized labor, employer-sponsored retirement coverage never reached more than about half of the private-sector workforce. Those employed by small businesses usually had no pension plan at all, except for Social Security. Some workers who thought they were covered—perhaps as many as a third of them—wouldn't actually wind up receiving any benefits when they retired because they hadn't met the vesting requirements. Others objected that their company's pension payouts were so miserly that they couldn't possibly keep up with inflation. "It must be evident to you that due to soaring medical expenses, spiraling costs of living, food prices, taxes, etc., your average GE retiree is sinking deeper and deeper into debt," Alfred Articolo, who'd been retired from the company for a dozen years, wrote to General Electric's HR department—one of hundreds of protests made over decades. "Many have exhausted their life savings and don't know where to turn." Still others watched their pensions vanish altogether when their employer hit the skids, as Studebaker had. "There is this myth that we once had a wonderful retirement system," said Ted Benna, who sold pension plans to companies. "That's just a bunch of nonsense."

Nevertheless, even with all of these shortcomings, for most of the 25 million or so workers who had traditional retirement benefits through the mid-1970s, it was an excellent deal—in many regards, the fullest expression of how the corporate social contract in America was built on an expectation of lifelong loyalty between employer and employee. Before the 401(k) took off, pensions at most large businesses consisted of "defined-benefit plans," which gave workers a set annual income upon retirement for the rest of their days, typically equal to a percentage of their average salary multiplied by their number of years of service to the company.

With the 401(k), which is a type of "defined-contribution plan," it was now up to the employees to decide what portion of their salary they wanted to sock away for retirement. The majority of employers matched at least some of what their workers put in. But there was no dependable return. If you saved enough in your 401(k) account and that money was invested wisely, you could do just fine. But if you didn't save adequately or couldn't afford to, or if you invested poorly or were the victim of bad timing—so that you retired right when the stock market happened to tank—you were sunk. The conventional wisdom was that "all you have to do is contribute to your 401(k), keep it there, and invest in stocks. You're going to strike it rich," cautioned Karen Ferguson, director of the Pension Rights Center, a Washington-based nonprofit whose goal is to make sure that Americans have enough money to live on when they are too old to work. "The reality is that you may strike it rich, but the odds are excellent that you will not." It didn't take long before the 401(k) was the punch line of a joke among businesspeople: "What begins with an F and ends in K and means screw your employees?"

It wasn't supposed to be like this. Originally, the 401(k) was designed to help workers add to their retirement savings, but they'd still rely on their defined-benefit plan and Social Security for the bulk of their pension income. "It was to be a three-legged stool," said Benna, who was a pioneer in creating 401(k) plans. Yet corporate America had other ideas. By 1985, workers in defined-contribution plans outnumbered those with guaranteed pensions, and over the next decade the trend greatly accelerated. Hardly any new companies put defined-benefit plans into place anymore, choosing to offer only 401(k)s instead. Eventually, it became routine for older corporations to freeze their long-established retirement funds rather than keep building them up. And many—including Kodak, Coca-Cola, General Electric, and General Motors—would in time just replace them with defined-contribution plans or other alternatives that were cheaper for the corporation. The three-legged stool was now teetering on two.

Several factors spurred the headlong rush by businesses into 401(k)s. To start with, they contained some features that were genuinely well-liked by workers, including the ability to easily move the money that had accumulated in these accounts whenever someone switched companies. In an era when fewer and fewer people could count on anything approaching "lifetime employment" anywhere, many viewed such portability as a plus. By contrast, defined-benefit plans were often back-loaded so that some of the largest pension gains came in an employee's last years—an arrangement that incentivized people to stay with the same company all the way through the end of their career and thus bring continuity to an employer's payroll. By the mid-1980s, when corporate downsizing had become commonplace, a framework that rewarded such loyalty no longer seemed very relevant.

Companies had other motivations, as well, for substituting their old pensions with 401(k)s. In 1974, President Ford signed the Employee Retirement Income Security Act, which was intended to prop up the country's private pension system. Among other things, ERISA established a new agency—the Pension Benefit Guarantee Corporation—to step in and pay retirees at least a portion of their plans when their employer faltered and could no longer meet its obligations. With the PBGC in place, the thinking went, there would be no more disasters like the one that had struck thousands of workers at Studebaker. For some people, this safety net would surely make all the difference. As the years went on, the PBGC would assume responsibility for the current and future pensions of about 1.5 million Americans. Yet ERISA also had unintended consequences. Businesses with defined-benefit pensions now had to pay an insurance premium to the PBGC, and they faced new funding requirements and other regulatory burdens. Companies that offered only 401(k)s escaped this hassle and expense. And so more and more elected to do just that.

Besides costing companies a third to half as much as defined-benefit plans, 401(k)s were attractive to top executives for another reason: using them to supplant traditional pensions became another means to enrich themselves. In 1987, a new accounting standard went into effect requiring companies to report pension liabilities on their balance sheet. The rule, FAS 87, was meant to increase transparency for investors. But as a byproduct, companies found that if they cut workers' old pension benefits, they would get to record a paper gain and fatten the bottom line. "Unfortunately for employees and retirees," the investigative reporter Ellen Schultz has written, "these newfound tricks coincided" with tying executive compensation to short-term financial results. "Thus, deliberately or not, the executives who greenlighted massive retiree cuts were indirectly boosting their own pay." By the late 1990s, hundreds of companies had effectively transferred large amounts of wealth from frontline workers to the CEO via FAS 87.

All in all, the advent of the 401(k) would turn into a big mess for most American workers. While private pension coverage had never been very complete, it didn't get any better as defined-benefit plans died out and 401(k)s proliferated; about half of all US workers were still left with no retirement cushion outside Social Security. As for the families that did have 401(k)s, the numerous pitfalls in these plans would leave most of them with the tiniest of nest eggs—less than $400 a month, on average. The societal implications of this deficiency were enormous: from the end of World War II until the 1980s, the share of older Americans in the labor force had fallen every year. But by the mid-1990s, in large part because of the paucity of income provided by people's 401(k)s, that reversed itself. For many, their retirement dreams were now broken. They had no choice but to keep working.

And still, for all of its egregious faults, the 401(k) was very much a product of its time, in no small measure because it "comports so well with American cultural norms about private property and individual ownership," as law professor Edward Zelinsky has written. The big unions that in the 1950s had fought to set up defined-benefit plans for their members had a very different sensibility—one of group solidarity. "Unions cover workers who would not otherwise choose or be able to save, such as garment workers, coal miners, and construction workers," labor economist Teresa Ghilarducci has said. "They would never have the kind of pensions they do if it weren't for unions. They need, like most workers, a collective solution." By the 1980s, collective solutions were fast falling out of favor across much of the country. 401(k)s, which Ghilarducci and others have called "do-it-yourself pensions," were well suited for a nation that now prized self-reliance over other values.

The biggest difference between Jack Welch's revamping of General Electric and what Roberto Goizueta was doing at Coca-Cola was that the body count was so much lower at Coke. Goizueta "has done it without the scars of heavy-handed restructuring evident at many other big corporations," *Fortune* gushed in 1987. "There have been no layoffs."

Yet while Goizueta was not anything close to a "Neutron Roberto," his tenure atop Coke wasn't as bloodless as it may have seemed. He fired dozens of executives who couldn't meet their numbers—though, like Welch, he never did the deed personally. And he wound up pushing out thousands of others, albeit more indirectly, as his quest to maximize shareholder value filtered down to where most of the people in the Coca-Cola system actually worked: at the bottling plants.

Goizueta knew that if Coca-Cola was going to succeed to the degree he wanted, he needed to improve the operations at many of the more than 150 independent Coke bottling companies spread across the United States. At first, his approach was to have the parent company buy up the weakest bottlers, turn them around, and then sell them back to stronger members of the system; he called this "refranchising." A small portfolio of corporate-owned bottlers was to be kept to a minimum. But in 1986, Goizueta was presented with opportunities to purchase two giant bottling franchises, one in the South and one in the West, for about $2.5 billion. He jumped at them.

These weren't fixer-uppers but well-run businesses that Coke wasn't about to quickly resell. The problem was that Goizueta now needed to clean up Coca-Cola's books, which all of a sudden were overloaded with debt. And so he turned to his chief financial officer, Doug Ivester, for the answer. Through his alchemy, Coke would spin off its now big bottling arm into a new publicly traded company, Coca-Cola Enterprises, and retain 49 percent ownership. Coke's stake in CCE was large enough to ensure that the main company was still really in charge. But because it technically held a minority position, Coke could now dump billions of dollars in debt from its balance sheet, as well as have CCE absorb its old plants and equipment—depreciating assets that didn't fit the picture Goizueta was trying to paint to Wall Street. Coke would sell lots of soda concentrate at its desired price to CCE, and CCE would send dividends back to the corporation. For Goizueta, Ivester's "49 percent solution" was a money machine. "Coca-Cola has margins that would make a cocaine dealer blush," was how Jack Bergstrand, a then-young manager who would rise up the ranks, liked to describe it.

But things weren't so pleasant for many of those inside the factories where Coke was bottled and packaged and from which red and white trucks loaded with the stuff fanned out along routes that had been worked for generations by salesmen who knew the names of every shop owner in town, and the names of their kids, too. For them, being swept under the CCE umbrella was painful—the culmination of a decades-long shakeout.

In the late 1950s, more than 1,000 Coca-Cola bottlers were scattered across America, many of them family-owned businesses employing anywhere from several dozen to a few thousand people. Over the next twenty-five years, as competition from Pepsi intensified and the profile of customers changed from mom-and-pop groceries to supermarket chains and big-box retailers, the number of bottlers would shrink by more than 80 percent. But even so, many of the survivors were still being managed as they'd always been—without the sophistication needed to make it in this new, less forgiving world. "The business was moving fast and moving beyond some of these guys," said Bill Casey, a former senior executive at Coca-Cola who ran several bottling operations during his thirty-two-year career at the company.

Jack Bergstrand was among those brought in to help rectify the situation. Coca-Cola had hired him in 1979, right after he got his master's in advertising from Michigan State. But instead of being given a marketing job in Atlanta, he was sent off to Boston to be an operations analyst, and soon a manager, at one of the few bottling plants that the company then owned. With his advanced degree, Bergstrand stood out; most of those at the factory hadn't gone to college. "I didn't meet anybody else who was in management in the bottling business who hadn't started on a truck and worked their way up," Bergstrand said. "They'd put in a lot of time slinging cases of Coke. It was freezing cold in the winter and hot and windy in the summer. And then here comes this twenty-one-year-old kid into management. It wasn't something that people were used to."

Bergstrand was sensitive to the misgivings of those around him, having grown up in a blue-collar home in northwest Illinois, the son of a tool and die maker at Ametek Incorporated, a maker of electronic components. He'd always remember the union newspaper that his dad had laying around, with the black circle and defiant message on the front page: "Blow on this dot. If it turns blue, company promises may come true." Bergstrand did his best to blend in at Coke, playing blackjack and drinking beers with the guys at the pubs around Needham and Worcester. "I'd spend about ten or eleven hours working and another five hours socializing," Bergstrand said. "I tried to endear myself to the old regime." He won over almost everyone—though, because of his position, he had things that they didn't, like a company car. And they had things that he didn't, like calluses on their hands. But that would change. For a while, Bergstrand drove a sales route, learning the business from the ground up, and eventually he lugged enough cases of soda to toughen up his palms.

After a series of management jobs, Bergstrand was pulled in to help form CCE. From an operating standpoint, "CCE was brilliant," he said. "Now, overnight, you've got this massive publicly traded company that does nothing but bottling. You have all this synergy." Processes were made consistent from plant to plant; KBIs, or key business indicators, replaced backslaps and shots at the local tavern as the basis of decision making. "We were running off information instead of instinct and personality," said Ted Highberger, another longtime Coca-Cola bottling executive who went to work at CCE. "Everything got upgraded."

Yet for those who had come up under the old system, this blast of "professionalization" was jarring—and not everyone made it through. "Some people wound up with better jobs than they'd had because the size of the company afforded greater opportunities," Bergstrand said. "But other people got cut out completely."

As CCE grew through a string of acquisitions, the company found new efficiencies by combining different aspects of the bottling business—from manufacturing to IT to sales to warehousing to distribution. "One of the purposes of bringing these companies together was to gain some economies of scale," said Jean Michel Bock, the assistant to the president of CCE. "There were a lot of functions which were redundant."

The man behind much of the consolidation was an executive named Larry Smith, who had been recruited to CCE from Pepsi. Smith was actually the one who had thought up the blind taste tests that became the Pepsi Challenge, making his presence at CCE difficult for many to bear. "He was reviled, partly because he came from Pepsi," Highberger said. But that wasn't the only reason. Smith was also "totally numbers-oriented. He couldn't give a shit about people." Said Bergstrand: "He was like the anti-Christ to the old Coke system"—notorious for supposedly telling employees, "I'll laugh with you. I'll joke with you. I'll fire you." Prior to CCE, Bergstrand recalled, "I never really heard a lot about head count" at the bottlers. "It was much more of a family orientation. It became much more of a business orientation."

One of those who felt the sting was Bill Maiocco. His father, George, had run Coca-Cola bottling plants in Boston and Baltimore. Bill began to work full-time at the company in 1958 at age seventeen, fresh out of high school. His first job was making the Coca-Cola signs—"Delicious and Refreshing"—that merchants would hang in their stores. Soon, Maiocco got a sales route out of Boston, and then out of the plant in suburban Braintree, donning his orange uniform with green stripes as he filled vending machines at offices and college dorms.

By the mid-1960s, Maiocco had become a sales manager, often putting in eleven- or twelve-hour days, topped off by a Red Sox game or a boxing match with some of his best customers. He would continue to advance over the next two decades until he was made a vice president of Coca-Cola New England, supervising a hundred people in sales and clearing a six-figure income between his salary and bonus. "I loved it," Maiocco said. "I had a good job, and I thought I did a good job."

But once Coke New England was folded into CCE, Maiocco was in for a fall. First, the new leadership took away his vice president title. And Maiocco found himself being bossed around by a new top manager who had worked previously at United Parcel Service—a background that Maiocco, who bled Coca-Cola, just couldn't understand. "The guy had never even seen a Coke bottle in his life," Maiocco said. "Why would you hire a person to run your business who has never been in the business?"

For several years, Maiocco kept most of the same responsibilities that he'd had before CCE. But then, in 1994, the company brought in a younger manager from Europe. "He had a doctorate in something," as Maiocco remembered it. Maiocco trained him—and then he replaced Maiocco. "He was with me for three months, side by side," Maiocco said. "The next thing I know, I'm being demoted, and he's being promoted into my job. I had no inkling whatsoever."

Maiocco was offered a lower-level job as an account manager. He decided to retire. He was fifty-five and would live out the next twenty years comfortably, though not lavishly, by drawing down his 401(k). He'd have regrets from time to time, wondering if he'd retired too soon, particularly when the stock market wasn't doing very well. But Maiocco had seen enough to know that CCE didn't much care for the opinions of those who'd risen into management from behind the wheel of a delivery truck. "We weren't appreciated," he said. "Why they thought we were lousy, I have no idea."

Jack Bergstrand had an idea. Executives like Maiocco—hard-working, personable, loyal—were exactly what was needed when there were scores of independent bottlers, each managed according to its own idiosyncrasies. But CCE was all about standardization and rationalization. Maiocco wasn't so good with that. "I'm fine with you centralizing—as long as I can do whatever I want," he once told Bergstrand, apparently only half in jest. If CCE hadn't adjusted, if it hadn't brought in all of those MBAs and others with the skills to make the system more responsive to the changing demands of the market, most of those bottlers never would have lasted anyway. "The model was not sustainable," said Bergstrand, who in the late 1990s would become the chief information officer of Coca-Cola.

Yet Bergstrand also realized that something was now missing—a way of life in which someone with only a high-school diploma could go from blue-collar employee to manager to vice president. Even making soda had become knowledge work. "There's a bit of Bill Maiocco that's been lost in every company," Bergstrand said, and that would always make him sad.

In September 1997, Roberto Goizueta checked into Emory University Hospital, pale and fatigued. In no time, doctors found a malignant tumor on one of his lungs. Hardly anyone who knew him was shocked. Goizueta had smoked cigarettes since he was a schoolboy in Cuba—sometimes as many as three packs a day.

After sixteen years as the CEO of Coca-Cola, he already had been contemplating who would succeed him. Doug Ivester, who had been promoted from CFO to chief operating officer, was Goizueta's heir apparent. Still, the passing would come much quicker than anyone was really ready for.

Goizueta, then sixty-five, would live only about six weeks after his diagnosis. "He loved this company and the associates because of what we were able to accomplish together," Ivester told employees in a recorded message sent around the world on the morning that Goizueta died. For Goizueta, that list of accomplishments was no doubt led by this: Coke's stock was now valued at about $180 billion—an increase of 3,500 percent since 1981.

He was true to himself to the very end. While he was hospitalized at Emory, in the same penthouse suite where Robert Woodruff had breathed his last breath, Goizueta would regularly check the machine that had been hooked up in the adjoining room. There, he could see Coke's share price pulsate.

Workers hung a banner saying, "For sale due to poor corporate judgment" outside the General Motors plant in Tarrytown, New York—one of dozens of factories that the company shuttered through the 1980s and '90s.

10

THE BETRAYAL

In January 1998, the federal court of appeals in Chicago handed down a ruling in *Sprague v. General Motors*—the climax of nine years of litigation so labyrinthine that the case file contained more than 1,000 exhibits and a trial transcript that filled nineteen thick volumes. For Sprague's lawyer, though, the whole thing could be summed up very simply: "The court decided that American industry no longer needed to keep its promises." When it was pointed out that this was a rather curt way to recap a matter of such great importance, the attorney retorted: "It doesn't take a lot of words to explain that you got fucked."

Robert Sprague had joined GM in 1943 when he was just sixteen. His father also worked at the company, a union man on the crankshaft line who had taken part in the 1937 sit-down strike at the Chevy plant along the Flint River. The junior Sprague, who worked at the same factory complex as his dad—"Chevy in the Hole," it was called—took after the old man in many ways. He was as strong as an ox and as tough as one, too. "He wouldn't take crap from anybody," said his son, Robert Jr. In the late 1950s, Sprague entered the lower rungs of management, becoming a maintenance supervisor. His work ethic bordered on the pathological. He routinely put in seven days a week at Chevy's metal-fabrication division, all while growing soybeans, corn, and wheat on his family's forty-acre farm. Somehow, he found time for fun, as well, hunting pheasants, fishing, and kicking back with his buddies and a splash or two of Black Label on Michigan's Upper Peninsula.

In spite of the pace, Sprague never missed a day at GM. Well, that's not exactly true. He once had appendix surgery on a Friday and was back to work by Monday. On another occasion, when he was really sick, he got sent home after half a day. But that was it—a day and a half of work missed (aside from vacations) through thirty-eight years on the job.

In March 1982, Sprague's boss, Sam Rodnick, approached him about taking early retirement. The offer came as part of a series of cost-cutting initiatives that GM had been undertaking for several years, though at this early stage, the belt-tightening was hardly noticeable. As late as 1979, GM was still the biggest company in America, whether ranked by revenue (more than $63 billion) or employment (nearly 620,000 US workers). Its profit stood at $3.5 billion—also tops in the nation—and many GM executives felt as if the company were unassailable. When Ron Hartwig, a public-relations manager for GM on the West Coast, started to see a profusion of Japanese-made cars on the road, he sent a note back to Detroit, alerting his boss. "Clearly their popularity here means they are going to be popular across America," Hartwig told him. The reply that Hartwig received was pure brass: "I just looked out my window in the GM Building, and I don't see any Japanese cars." Of late, however, the pressure on GM to trim its payroll had increased considerably.

The back-to-back recessions of the early eighties were killing America's Big Three automakers, as Chrysler and Ford recorded huge losses. In 1980, GM posted its own net loss—its first annual deficit since 1921. The following year, the company eked out a profit, but only by whacking more expenses; sales were still slumping. The company also saw its prized AAA credit rating evaporate. And GM's attempts to take on Toyota and other Japanese producers with its new subcompact, the J-car, were going nowhere. Things were so bad that even the United Auto Workers agreed to "givebacks" in early 1982: a two-and-a-half-year wage freeze, a delay in cost-of-living adjustments, and the elimination of certain paid holidays. (The union seethed when it discovered that GM had simultaneously, under a new compensation scheme, made it easier for its executives to collect big bonuses. Chairman Roger Smith quickly backtracked.)

At the same time, as Sprague would tell it, the deal that GM offered him and other white-collar managers to retire before the normal age of sixty-five sounded awfully sweet. Rodnick "told me I would get all benefits I was presently receiving, for life, with no strings attached," Sprague recalled. Plus, "he said I could get another job and make as much money as I could without any penalties." A plant personnel manager, Sprague added, subsequently confirmed those details about taking an "early out." To Sprague, it felt like the right moment to jump. His youngest son, Bill, had gone to work at the Chevy plant in Flint in 1977, and so the family's proud connection to GM would continue. Sprague himself had just turned fifty-five and was beginning to feel worn down by hypertension and arthritis. He was also conscious of the heart disease that ran in his family. And so he agreed to hang up his wrench.

Over the next several years, GM struggled more. The big reorganization that Roger Smith had instituted in 1984—the one that included the dismantling of Fisher Body—was a fiasco. The new org chart drove GM "into a corporate nervous breakdown," the journalists Paul Ingrassia and Joseph White have written. "Disoriented and fearful for their jobs, many lower-level managers simply ducked. They waited to be told what to do, bucked critical decisions up the line, and suppressed problems in numbing rounds of interdivisional meetings. . . . Smith had hoped the reorganization would allow for shrinking GM's army of paper-pushers. Instead, the bureaucracy got more complex." The company was in such a state of confusion that the running joke was about a manager who walked out of his office and told his secretary, "If my boss calls, please get his name." Said one GM executive: "It is tough to operate when the structure isn't right. It just stops you cold."

The cars stopped cold, too. Filled with malfunctioning parts, Buicks and Oldsmobiles and other makes began coming to a standstill without warning. Between late 1985 and 1991, GM would be hit with more than 2.5 million warranty claims for stalling cars. The company's Pontiac Fiero, for its part, had the unfortunate tendency to catch on fire. And its GM-10 cars, a family of midsized vehicles designed to vie with the Ford Taurus, Honda Accord, and Toyota Camry, were so inefficiently built that the company lost thousands of dollars on every one it manufactured. MIT researcher James Womack would call the GM-10 program "the biggest catastrophe in American industrial history." In-congruously, GM was building many of the auto industry's most abys-mal products just as Smith was investing in all kinds of new technology. But this movement to modernize became a farce, with automated sys-tems mistakenly sticking Buick bumpers onto Cadillacs and robots spray-painting each other instead of cars. GM's market share plunged, from 45 percent in 1984 to 37 percent in 1987. "We have vastly underesti-mated how deeply ingrained are the organizational and cultural rigidi-ties that hamper our ability to execute," Elmer Johnson, GM's executive vice president, told his senior colleagues in a January 1988 memo.

For all of his inventiveness, Smith at some point concluded that, in order to regain control of his sinking enterprise, he had no choice but to slash jobs. In late 1986, GM announced that it would shut down eleven factories and get rid of 29,000 positions, including 23,000 hourly employees. Even though that represented more than 5 percent of GM's workforce, officials tried to play down the weight of the move, saying that the company had built six new assembly plants since the late 1970s, and so it was only natural that these older facilities would be closed now. Yet others read the cutbacks as a tacit admission by GM that it couldn't imagine a way to regain the business that it had lost to the Japanese as well as to Ford and Chrysler, which had pinched their production and were showing signs of financial and op-erational improvement.

Besides, even if GM did rebound, it didn't mean that those 29,000 spots were ever coming back. Neither were the 35,000 salaried jobs that the company earlier in the year had said it was phasing out, mostly by offering early retirement incentives similar to what Robert Sprague had opted for. The imperative to do more with less because of global competition—and the ability to do more with less because of technological progress—presaged a steadily contracting workforce. "There's no longer a direct link between prosperity in the marketplace and jobs," labor economist Harley Shaiken said after GM spelled out its plan to fold up the eleven factories. "No matter how the market performs over the next five years, General Motors will end up em-ploying fewer workers. This announcement is not the end of the layoff process for General Motors. It's the beginning."

Actually, for some it seemed more like the last straw, given that GM had been shedding jobs since 1979, leading to the disintegration of communities like Flint, Michigan. Nearly 30,000 Flint residents had departed the city between 1982 and 1987, many for the Sunbelt, where their prospects for employment were brighter. Stores in Flint even began stocking newspapers from Houston and Dallas so that locals could peruse the classifieds. Michael Moore, a Flint native whose dad worked on a GM assembly line making AC spark plugs, watched with grief as his hometown decayed. Now the editor of an alternative weekly called the *Michigan Voice*, Moore wrote in late 1984:

> Two more friends moved away from Flint today, two more in a long string of friends, family, and coworkers who have left Flint in the last five years. Either for lack of a job or lack of any signs of a quality life, they've moved downstate, down south, out west, or out of the country.
>
> They're the lucky ones. The rest of us here are either unemployed, expecting to be unemployed, or living amongst the two, sort of like Father Damien in the leper colony of Molokai; sooner or later you feel like you'll end up, job or no job, as one of the walking dead.

Two years later, as Moore heard about the eleven factories slated for closure—an action that threatened to eat into Flint's total employment by another 15 percent—his heartache gave way to anger. "You're a fucking terrorist," Moore remembered thinking of Roger Smith when the news was broadcast. "I can't take this anymore. I have to do something. I'm going to make a movie." The result was *Roger & Me*, an acid film that ended with Smith's sappy Christmas greetings to GM employees ("We smell the pine needles on the trees and the turkey on the table") interspersed with footage of a laid-off GM worker's family being evicted from their home in Flint because they couldn't make the rent. Although some critics skewered Moore for taking liberties with the facts, there was no denying that he had captured a larger truth about the devastation pouring down upon tens of thousands of people. "The hardships associated with plant closings are both pervasive and persistent," a team studying the situation from the Michigan Health and Social Security Research Institute found. "Workers whose plants close suffer financial losses, marital strains, and symptoms of poor mental health."

It was no wonder that those left jobless were scarred so severely. "People feel as if they are being thrown away," said Richard Price, a University of Michigan psychologist. To many, it felt as if their entire heritage was being thrown away, too. "A manufacturing plant can become a moral bedrock, an institution that anchors a town's special character, weaving the fortunes of many generations together," the anthropologist Katherine Newman wrote in her 1988 book *Falling from Grace: The Experience of Downward Mobility in the American Middle Class.* "When something so fundamental to a community's sense of self disappears, the consequences are more than economic—they call into question deeper commitments of loyalty, stability, and tradition. . . . Thus, in the midst of coping with the practical, personal consequences of economic dislocation (the familiar litany of occupational degradation, income reduction, economic insecurity), blue-collar workers also face the question of where (or whether) they belong in postindustrial America."

Even amid so much distress, those working in autos had it much better than their peers in many other industries, thanks to the historic strength of their union. Hourly employees who were let go by GM could still count on the supplemental unemployment benefits that the UAW's Walter Reuther had fought so hard for in the mid-1950s, and that had been enlarged in the late 1960s. Depending on how long laid-off employees had been at the company, they could now collect 95 percent of their take-home pay for anywhere from a few months to two years under the SUB. There was also a "guaranteed income stream," which kicked in after the SUB ended. For those with ten or more years of seniority, this provided 50 to 75 percent of their pay until age sixty-two—so long as the idled worker hadn't turned down an open job at GM or through the local unemployment office.

What's more, GM and the UAW had agreed in 1984 to create a Jobs Bank to help dull the effects of automation. Under the system, which the rest of the Big Three would also adopt, up to 5,000 or so GM workers who had been displaced by machines or other efficiencies were to be retrained or allowed to take part in some other company-approved activity, all while receiving 95 percent of their wages. As the Jobs Bank expanded in future years, it would come to be seen as a gross perversion of the social contract—the corporate equivalent of the mythological "welfare mother who drives a Cadillac," Harley Shaiken said—after it was reported that those in the program were being paid to do crossword puzzles, watch cartoons, and take naps.

But the fact was that none of the job-security measures won by the union could offer any real security in the end. Shaiken was right: the American auto industry—and especially General Motors—was getting smaller and smaller. And nothing could reverse the trend.

In April 1988, GM executives finally conceded as much, telling securities analysts that the company would pare its production capacity over the next five years so that its American factories would operate at 100 percent, two shifts a day, five days a week—something that it hadn't been able to do since 1984. The *Wall Street Journal* called it "a strategic retreat that will significantly shrink the largest industrial concern in the world for the first time in its history." GM president Robert Stempel, the company's top executive behind Smith, vowed that the consolidation would be "handled in an orderly manner" and that the carmaker would cooperate with the UAW on a plan. The union, though, would hear none of it. "They sure as hell aren't working hand in hand with me on eliminating plants," said Don Ephlin, a UAW vice president.

Meanwhile, the company looked to bring down costs in every other way it could. Its greatest expense was medical care, with GM shelling out 13 percent more annually, on average, from the mid-1960s through the 1980s to cover its hourly and salaried employees and retirees. Its health bill totaled about $3 billion a year by decade's end. One effect of this, said Gregory Lau, an assistant treasurer at the company, was that it put GM "at a serious disadvantage" relative to the Japanese companies that had opened factories on American soil because they had much younger workforces and very few retirees. "The spiraling increase in health-care costs places a special burden on mature industries like ours," Lau said. Ever richer retirement benefits, which the UAW had continued to wangle from the automakers through the late 1970s, also added to the Big Three's uncompetitive position. The Japanese could now manufacture and ship a car to the United States for $1,600 less than it cost the Americans to make one at home. It wouldn't be long, as the writer Roger Lowenstein has expressed it, before GM would be seen as little more than "a pension firm on wheels . . . an HMO with a showroom."

And so GM desperately tried to get out from under, at least on the health-care front. In January 1988, following the lead of others in the industry, GM made its salaried workers responsible for meeting certain copays and deductibles—up to $750 in annual out-of-pocket costs per family. (By the early 1990s, that number would rise to $2,600.) This wasn't the first time that GM had altered its health-care plans. But there was a major difference: practically every modification that GM had implemented in the 1940s, '50s, '60s, and '70s—often through collective bargaining with the UAW, which then set the course for what would happen with the company's salaried staff—broadened workers' benefits. Now, it was cutting them. "The changes made in '88 were inconsistent with past practice, past policy . . . and to an extent violated the trust that employees had granted to General Motors over the years," admitted Doug Eavenson, a GM benefits manager. One hundred and ten thousand white-collar employees were affected, along with 84,000 salaried retirees.

Robert Sprague was among those blindsided by GM's new direction. "Had I known that General Motors was going to change my health-care benefits," he said, "I would not have taken the special early retirement." Sprague said he'd relied on what his boss and other GM officials had told him: that "I would have these benefits for the rest of my life." Like other GM managers, Sprague had also been given a stack of benefit booklets, which appeared to summarize the company's commitments. "Your basic health care coverage will be provided at GM expense for your lifetime," one said. The others conveyed the same thing—a pledge that GM had been giving its workers since the Golden Age of the 1960s, when it had first expanded medical coverage for salaried retirees and their spouses.

In the summer of 1989, 114 early retirees, including Sprague, filed suit against GM for denying them no-cost health-care benefits. Eventually, the court certified the case as a class action, ruling that 50,000 other early retirees could join the suit.

GM's defense came down to this: whatever the retirees were told in person or in writing, the company had always made clear that nothing was set in stone. "The corporation retained the right to modify, terminate, or suspend the programs," said Richard O'Brien, a GM vice president. And, indeed, many of the summary booklets—as well as the company's health-care plans themselves—said as much, even if this proviso wasn't put front and center. Many of the retirees said they never really noticed any such admonition, focusing instead on the "for your lifetime" language. As for the possibility of out-of-pocket costs being imposed, "I never gave it a thought," said Sprague.

When Sprague brought his lawsuit, his son, Bill, was still working for General Motors. He was now in human resources. "That was somewhat uncomfortable," Bill said. "People would ask, 'Do you know this Sprague guy?'" But Bill never spoke up on his dad's behalf. "Sometimes, being in HR, there's a path that you have to walk," he said. And he genuinely appreciated the cost constraints that the company was under. "When you looked at the financial problems we were having, something had to be done," he remarked. Yet Bill also felt for this father. It wasn't that he couldn't afford the medical expenses suddenly thrust upon him. "He was luckier than others in that way," Bill said. It was the principle of the thing. "I could understand what my dad was standing up for," he said. "A promise is a promise."

In December 1991, as the Sprague case worked its way through the courts, General Motors announced that it would need to cut costs much deeper. Over the next few years, the company said, it would close 21 of its 125 North American factories, wiping away 74,000 jobs in the United States and Canada, about 18 percent of the total. Twenty-four thousand of those positions would be gone within a year. "GM," said Robert Stempel, who had become chairman after Roger Smith retired, "will become a much different corporation."

That was undeniable—but not everyone viewed such a gigantic scaling back as being for the better. Sen. Donald Riegle, a Michigan Democrat, called it "an economic Pearl Harbor." Owen Bieber, the UAW president, said that for his members, "once again the reward is anxiety and dislocation at best or unemployment at worst." Others had a more favorable take. "Management is finally rolling up its sleeves and attacking its problems aggressively," said John Casesa, an analyst with the investment firm Wertheim Schroder. Even billionaire Ross Perot was impressed. GM had bought his company, Electronic Data Systems, in 1984, giving him a seat on the automaker's board. Within a couple of years, he was making no secret of how little he thought of Roger Smith and his tolerance for limitless layers of red tape. At his company, EDS, the first person "who sees a snake kills it," Perot said. "At GM, the first thing you do is organize a committee on snakes.

Then you bring in a consultant about snakes. Third thing you do is talk about it for a year." But this time seemed different, and Perot praised Stempel for "facing reality."

Whatever one's perspective, Stempel had not come to this place easily. He had started at GM in 1958 as a junior engineer and got his big break in the early 1970s when he helped to oversee development of the catalytic converter, a device that curtails pollution by filtering a car's exhaust. When he was named GM's chairman in August 1990, Stempel looked to be distinct from his predecessor in every way. Smith was short in stature with a high, squeaky voice. Stempel was a full-throated baritone and built like he used to play college football, which he had. Most notably, he was the first "car guy" to inhabit the chairman's office in more than thirty years, following a steady run of executives whose backgrounds were all in finance. As such, Stempel seemed to identify with those workers who actually got their hands greasy, and he immediately established a good relationship with the UAW. He liked to speak in terms of "we" more than "I."

In September 1990, during contract talks with the union, the company agreed to lay off its hourly employees for thirty-six weeks at most; if there was no possible way to call them back to work because there wasn't anything for them to do, they'd still receive unemployment benefits equal to nearly full pay for up to three years. Stempel said he hoped that the accord would "provide the basis for a new level of trust" between the company and its blue-collar workers.

As optimistic as Stempel could sound, he didn't sugarcoat GM's need to be smaller—a lot smaller. But more than many of the executives who had led GM previously, he was sensitive to easing the misery for the men and women on the line. Before, "this was a company run by financial guys who said people are expendable," asserted Joseph Phillippi, the auto industry analyst at Lehman Brothers. Under Stempel, he surmised, GM would be more inclined to "take care of the people." Even after Stempel announced seven plant closures in November 1990, the union was forgiving, thanks to the safety net that had been constructed. When Smith used to walk into a GM factory, the workers would boo him; for Stempel they cheered.

But the comity wouldn't last. After Stempel dropped the bombshell in late 1991 about closing twenty-one additional plants, there seemed to be no way for employees to evade real pain. The simple fact

was that GM's workforce was on track to be half the size in 1995 that
it had been ten years earlier. And the magnitude of the retrenchment
triggered fears that the funds GM had set aside to ensure that its laid-
off workers would receive virtually full pay—some $3.5 billion—would
now be drained prematurely.

Still, for Stempel, there was no other option. On August 2, 1990,
just one day after he had assumed GM's chairmanship, the economy
had buckled: Iraqi dictator Saddam Hussein invaded Kuwait, helping to further weaken an American economy that had just fallen into
recession. Oil prices spiked and consumer confidence plunged, dragging down car sales. GM would lose $2 billion in 1990, followed by
an astonishing loss of nearly $4.5 billion in 1991—the biggest pool of
red ink in the history of corporate America. Some on GM's finance
staff worried that the company might go bankrupt. Of course, the economic downturn only compounded a more basic problem confronting
GM. As Sean McAlinden, an automotive researcher at the University
of Michigan, stated: "They made a lot of cars that people don't want
to buy." Ford and even Chrysler were, relatively speaking, doing better
with those shopping for autos.

In the meantime, GM's outside directors—the members of its
board who were not part of management—were leaning on Stempel to
act more swiftly and boldly. The board itself was feeling the heat from
large institutional investors who had begun to exercise their growing
power in this new era of shareholder capitalism. For companies that
were "nonperformers," said Richard Koppes, the general counsel of the
California Public Employees Retirement System, which held a large
block of GM stock, "the status quo doesn't do." Yet rather than pacify
the outside directors, who were led by former Procter & Gamble CEO
John Smale, Stempel's plan to downsize GM only made them more
perturbed. Some of this was due to Stempel's style: he hadn't bothered
to consult with the board before he announced the twenty-one factory shutdowns. And some was more substantive: instead of specifying
which factories were going to be cut, Stempel decided to punt those
difficult calls until later, adding to the impression that he was still
dithering and grasping for answers, not putting in place a thoroughly
thought-out strategy.

For his part, Stempel believed he was being considerate by not
naming names right before the holidays. But for GM's workers, the

lack of specificity about which plants would be closed tossed them into a horribly stressful guessing game, as tens of thousands of lives were now in limbo. "It's like putting six people in a room and saying, 'Well, one of you has AIDS,' but not telling them right away," Michael Moore commented in his inimitable way. "Why would you do that to somebody?" The UAW accused the company of pitting union locals against each other, with those willing to make concessions presumably enhancing the chances of seeing their factories survive. Stempel insisted that he wasn't engaging in any such "whipsawing." But two months later, when GM disclosed a dozen of the locations where it was going to halt production, few missed that its plant in Arlington, Texas, was spared while its Willow Run factory in Ypsilanti, Michigan, wound up on the company's hit list. Both places made larger cars. But the union in Texas had been open to amending certain work rules, allowing GM to run the facility around the clock and thereby boost efficiency. The UAW at Willow Run had been slower in consenting to such changes.

Still, the 4,000 employees at the Michigan site were stunned by the news, having believed that Willow Run's place in history—it built B-24 bombers during World War II—and proximity to GM's main supplier base would save the plant from being targeted. Workers had even bought hot dogs and sodas in anticipation of celebrating; instead, many were left weeping. "It's like they took a knife and stabbed me in the back," said Homer Wiley, a twenty-eight-year GM veteran.

In Texas, by contrast, workers stood up and applauded when they heard that their jobs had been preserved. But they quieted down fast. "It got reverent because we got something somebody else had to lose," said Lloyd Parker, a union official in Arlington. "There are a lot of sad people up north."

They were reeling as well in Tarrytown, New York, where another GM plant was tagged for closure.

"It's tough and aggravating and hard to accept," said Tim Shore, one of the nearly 3,500 workers at the factory, which had started building Chevys in 1915. He and his two kids had settled a couple of years earlier in Tarrytown, which lies about an hour up the Hudson River from New York City, after the Fiero plant in Michigan where he had been working ceased operations. In relocating across the country, Shore had joined a group known as "GM Gypsies"—hourly employees forced to move from city to city, chasing diminishing amounts of work. But now, Shore couldn't help but think that his chances of finding another gig within GM may have run out. "With all the other plants shutting down around the country," he said, "there's not going to be a lot of places to go."

The curtain coming down in Tarrytown was particularly hard to take because the plant had become the embodiment of so many things that GM was doing right, after years of having done so many things wrong. Back in the late 1960s, Tarrytown was one of the company's worst factories. Efficiency and productivity were crummy, and labor was not so much led as lorded over. "I am the goddamn boss, and you'll do as I say!" was a customary response whenever a supervisor perceived that he was being challenged in any way. Management "thought we were scum," said Bill Marmo, who came to work the assembly line in Tarrytown in 1952. The UAW didn't think any better of management, and the antagonism between the two sides was constant. "My job . . . was to respond to any complaint or grievance regardless of the merits, and just fight the company," one union committeeman recounted. "I was expected to jump up and down and scream." Said Bill Slachta, the plant manager: "The whole pattern was destructive to the best interests of both parties and absolutely provided no middle ground."

By 1971, those in charge of Tarrytown figured that they had to try something different—or the plant might well be put out of business. Over the next few years, top managers and their local union counterparts unveiled a program that was meant to raise the "quality of work life" throughout the factory. Under QWL, as it was known, workers were trained to learn more about what managers actually did. And managers were trained to learn more about the functions of the union. Hourly employees and their supervisors then sat down together to generate solutions to problems, as well as to make suggestions for heading off other problems before they even cropped up.

Initially, at least some employees were skeptical of QWL. If you give a worker "the opportunity to share with you the responsibilities of his job, he'll meet you more than half way," Ray Calore, the president of UAW Local 664 in Tarrytown, told a group of GM managers. "But you've got to come that half way first because he's a suspicious person because of what's happened to him for so many years." Really, who could blame him? "When you hired an autoworker off the street, you bought his hands, his feet, and his back—and you cut him off at the head," Calore said. "Shame on you because you lost an awful lot. Because that same person, when he goes to church, he's asked to share in the responsibilities of running the church. He belongs to the Elks or the Eagles, and he serves on committees, and he belongs to the volunteer fire department and the community chest. So for sixteen hours a day, he's a parent. He's a person in the community who's respected. And people are using him for his mind. And you're not. Shame on you."

Such fist shaking notwithstanding, Calore was sold completely on QWL. So was Slachta, the plant manager, who was willing to acknowledge that, for the most part, "management must be the bearer of the olive branch" to the rank-and-file. In time, most of the Tarrytown workforce embraced QWL. By the end of 1978, more than 3,000 employees were participating, working closer with management than ever before. "We were a team," said John Inzar, an hourly employee who'd come to Tarrytown in 1965. The impact was enormous: Gauges of product quality rose substantially. Absenteeism declined by more than 50 percent. Worker grievances were down to a few dozen; seven years earlier, some 2,000 such complaints were in the hopper. "More generally," said Robert Cole, a management professor who examined what was transpiring in Tarrytown, "workers now felt that they were being treated like human beings, and that someone was listening to them; there was a newfound dignity."

In the coming years, GM would extend QWL to other factories all over the country. The company's Fleetwood plant in Detroit, for instance, was a lot like Tarrytown had been: churning out second-rate products at a high cost while nobody seemed to get along. "Our job was to screw the union; their job was to screw management," said one supervisor. "It was a way of life." But in the late 1970s, a new plant manager introduced QWL, and within a few years, things had totally turned around. Now, managers actively solicited their workers' input. Tensions decreased and performance increased, both greatly.

Not everyone was in favor of such togetherness. In some factories, managers were reluctant to yield their authority. Workers would be trained to have more involvement in planning. But then—in the words of a manager at the GM factory in Linden, New Jersey, where the adversarial atmosphere lingered—"they'd go back down to the floor, and . . . they'd get a superintendent who said, 'That stuff you learned up there in that ivory tower, leave it up there, because this is the real world down here.'" Some union officials were also resistant to QWL, especially the hard-liners who thought it was a ploy intended to undermine organized labor. Others simply dismissed it as a bunch of malarkey. "Management says, 'joint, joint, joint,' but if they want to do something, they just go ahead and do it," said Fred Myers, president of UAW Local 599 in Flint. Despite all the talk about blue- and white-collar employees finally seeing eye to eye, GM through the 1980s maintained the ultimate symbol of separateness at many of its factories: A "salaried men's rest room" sat right next to the "hourly men's rest room."

Nevertheless, GM and the union continued to promote QWL, hopeful that a flowering of trust and collaboration between management and labor would enable every person in the plant to contribute to his or her fullest. Before long, other vaunted company programs would advance the same philosophy. One of them was a joint UAW-GM Quality Network, launched in 1987. An identical spirit also animated New United Motor Manufacturing Inc., or NUMMI, a venture that GM opened in 1984 in Fremont, California, with Toyota. "The key to NUMMI's early success," *Newsweek* reported in 1986, "is Japanese-style 'participatory management.'" And Saturn Corporation, which GM formed as a stand-alone subsidiary in 1985, was built on such values as well. Saturn was able to thrive, said the UAW's Don Ephlin, a trailblazer for employer-employee partnership, because GM had agreed "to push the decision-making power down to the lowest possible level."

Surely, few, if any, of those behind these efforts knew that "Engine Charlie" Wilson had in the late 1940s put forward a similar notion—that blue-collar workers should have a bona fide voice in GM's affairs—only to be rejected by both Alfred Sloan and Walter Reuther, each of whom considered the plan to dangerously distort the rightful duties of management and labor. That Wilson's vision was now coming to pass (at least to some degree) said a lot about how the relationship between employer and employee had evolved over the ensuing thirty to forty years. Some companies, such as those with Scanlon Plans, had long sought their workers' insights, but they were very much in the minority. By the 1980s and into the '90s, with executives willing to try new things to make their operations more productive and competitive, that began to change.

More than a third of businesses, according to surveys, had backed away from using strictly command-and-control models and moved toward more flexible arrangements, like quality circles and self-governing teams. All sorts of corporations, beyond those in the auto industry, took up the cause: Corning Glass, Xerox, J.C. Penney, Texas Instruments, and thousands more. General Electric had Work-Out, while parts of the Kodak and Coca-Cola empires set up Total Quality Management systems in which frontline employees were given more of a direct say in how work should get done. Among America's best companies, it had become common wisdom that they should not "foster we/they labor attitudes" and instead see every worker "as a source of ideas," Tom Peters and Bob Waterman wrote in their runaway bestseller from 1982, *In Search of Excellence*.

But if this was a valuable upgrade to the corporate social contract—and programs like QWL certainly did provide many workers with more fulfillment and meaning in their jobs—it was impossible to ignore how much other, more concrete aspects of the employer-employee compact had fallen apart. Yes, "many workers have been empowered to play a greater role in designing their jobs," MIT's Paul Osterman submitted, but "wage levels have stagnated . . . and employment security is eroding," often "at the same companies that are trying to restructure their workplaces" by forging these innovative alliances between management and labor. Said Harley Shaiken: "There's going to be a problem on how these fit together."

At Tarrytown, they didn't fit at all. On February 24, 1992, the workers there were told to take a break from building Chevy Lumina APVs, Pontiac Trans Sports, and Oldsmobile Silhouettes and to gather around to watch a special telecast. That's when they learned that the factory was going to be closed. "It was the worst thing in my life," said Bill Marmo. "When I think about it, I get tears in my eyes." The New York *Daily News* blared a two-word headline on the front page, "GRIM MONDAY," over a picture of the Tarrytown plant. The

very next day, a Washington think tank—apparently unaware of the
death sentence that GM had just issued—released a report exalting
the QWL program at the factory. "Labor and management were able
to establish mutual trust where before it had never existed," the Employment Policy Foundation declared. "Both sides became convinced
of the other's sincerity and commitment." If words ever seemed empty,
it was now. Compared with other plants, GM said, the cost of recon-
figuring Tarrytown to produce the company's newer-model minivans
was too high to carry on.

In 1996, the last vehicle at Tarrytown rolled off the line—number
11,889,266. Two years later, the factory was demolished. All that was
left behind, besides the memories, was a ninety-seven-acre, weed-
strewn, apocalyptic landscape. Down the street at the old UAW hall,
a sign read: "Parking Only For Union Made American Cars." The lot
sat empty.

Bob Stempel didn't last even that long. In April 1992, upset that
the CEO was still not displaying enough alarm over GM's dire condition, the company's directors dislodged him as head of the board's
executive committee—a clear signal of their loss of faith in him as
a leader. The directors also demoted Stempel's right-hand man, GM
president Lloyd Reuss, who epitomized the company's lethargic, head-
in-the-sand ways. Through the summer, as Reuss's replacement, Jack
Smith (no relation to Roger), resolutely pursued a turnaround plan
called "Fundamental Change," Stempel found himself isolated. Rumors swirled that he was being pushed out.

By late October, Stempel had had enough. He resigned, and Jack
Smith became CEO. The board's coup was now complete. Stempel
would go down in the opinion of some as one of the most wretched
CEOs in the history of the auto industry. Others would say that it was
Roger Smith who deserved such opprobrium; Stempel was just a victim of the wreck that he'd inherited. Either way, Stempel's departure
had a galvanizing effect on other boards: going forward, chief executives who didn't cut it were more likely to be shown the door. Shareholders demanded nothing less. By some estimates, average CEO
tenure would fall to seven years in the 1990s from ten in the 1980s. It
was hard, however, to feel too sorry for most of those who got the axe.
Their severances were unquestionably a lot better than most workers'.

Stempel, for one, was awarded an $800,000 annual pension and a two-year consulting deal worth $1 million.

In March 1993, General Motors was back in the news: *Time* magazine informed its readers that, with its workforce down to 367,000, GM wasn't the biggest employer in America anymore. The real story, though, was that it wasn't General Electric or Exxon or some other industrial giant that now claimed the top spot. As *Time* tallied it (and as would be repeated again and again), the crown belonged to Manpower, the temp agency, which had 560,000 workers.

Truth be told, that number was spurious. More than half a million employees was accurate only if you counted them over the course of a year. On any given day, Manpower had about 110,000 people working for it. That's because they would typically spend just a few weeks in the company's employ before moving on—which, really, was the whole point. "The US is increasingly becoming a nation of part-timers and freelancers, of temps and independent contractors," *Time* said. "This 'disposable' workforce is the most important trend in business today, and it is fundamentally changing the relationship between Americans and their jobs. For companies large and small, the phenomenon provides a way to remain globally competitive while avoiding the vagaries of market cycles and the growing burdens imposed by employment rules, antidiscrimination laws, health-care costs, and pension plans. But for workers, it can mean an end to the security and sense of significance that came from being a loyal employee. One by one, the tangible and intangible bonds that once defined work in America are giving way."

This unwinding was not by chance. Well before Manpower was said to have one-upped GM, corporate America was being sold on the advantages of using temp labor—and not just the "Girl in the White Gloves" variety that had become so recognizable through the mid-1960s. By late that decade and into the '70s, the temp industry pivoted to include men in its marketing, and the message now had less to do with giving women a way to balance work inside and outside the home, and more with giving businesses a way to pump up their bottom lines. "You May Have a Severe Swelling of the Payroll," Olsten Temporary Services proclaimed in a 1968 ad, which showed a sick-looking fellow lying in bed, a thermometer protruding from his mouth. It went on:

A very painful condition, this.

As you add new people to your staff things get worse. Up go your fringe benefit costs, overtime costs. Down go your profits.

That's when it really hurts. After all, new people are supposed to help add to profits, not reduce them. So what should you do?

First, don't buy, rent. Second, come to Olsten Temporary Services. . . .

You have nothing to lose. We'll take care of the payroll and fringe benefit nonsense.

That makes us practically painless.

Businessmen. Take the cure.

For workers, this wasn't necessarily all bad. Some people were pleased to be employed as temps because they were in school, taking care of a child or an elderly parent, or looking to cut back on their hours but not fully retire. Others wanted to check out a job before committing to it. "The peripheral worker in our society provides the economy with a very important part of the flexibility which it must have if it is to be efficient and dynamic," Columbia University's Dean Morse wrote in 1969, in one of the earliest assessments of how traditional employment was starting to fracture.

More than 80 percent of independent contractors were glad to be their own boss and not work for somebody else. Others argued that because those in "alternative work arrangements"—freelancers, temps, on-call employees, and contract-firm workers—were dispensable by definition, they gave companies a ready means to shave costs during slow times, helping to insulate their longtime employees from being laid off. "A major function of the contingent workforce is to buffer core workers from the vagaries of the market," said Cornell law professor Stewart Schwab. "It is one thing for a temporary worker to lose a job early when job loss was foreseeable from the outset. It is quite another for someone on a career track for fifteen years, for example, to lose a job."

Yet as more and more Americans found themselves in "alternative" or "contingent" positions, other experts became concerned. Only a fairly small portion of the labor force fell into these categories— somewhere between 10 and 30 percent, depending on how you sliced it. But the ranks of temp-agency workers were rising especially fast, and these employees were by and large unhappy. There were exceptions, including those white-collar workers who enjoyed being able "to go to the Caribbean when you want," as one laid-off General Electric marketing executive turned temp put it. However, some two-thirds of temps wished they had a regular job—and for good reason. They tended to make less per hour than did permanent employees for the same work. They usually received no sick pay or vacation pay and had no insurance or retirement plan. All too many failed to be given proper safety training before being told to take on hazardous tasks. And some were made pawns as companies battled unions, with temps deployed to help beat back organizing drives or endure strikes. Temps could also take a toll on a company's other workers by serving "as a subtle reminder . . . of the precarious nature of their own job security," as one study has characterized it.

Troubling, too, was that since about 1970, nearly all of the growth of part-time work in America was taken up by those who preferred to have a full-time job instead—a reversal of earlier years when women and others streaming into the workplace grabbed up part-time positions because they were actually seeking such a schedule.

"These contingent workers . . . quickly are becoming a second class of workers within many large US firms," warned Kathleen Christensen of the Sloan Foundation. Their subpar status earned them their own publication, *Temp Slave!*, with biting articles such as "Working Poor," "Hello, My Name is Temp 378," and "Ignorant Dumb Shitwork." The inspiration for the 1999 cult classic *Office Space* was filmmaker Mike Judge's stint as a temp, when he alphabetized purchase orders. The job was "soul-sucking torture," he said, making plain that the temp had replaced Charlie Chaplain's assembly-line worker as the serf of modern times. Many stuck around so long at the same employer that they became known as "permatemps." Pushing back, employment agencies defended themselves as responding to the needs of a new America. "We are not exploiting people," said Manpower's chairman, Mitchell Fromstein. "We are not setting the fees. The market is. We are matching people with demands. What would our workers be doing without us? Unemployment lines? Welfare? Suicide?"

Through the 1990s, companies didn't just bring more temps in to take pink-, blue-, and white-collar jobs; they also farmed more work out. Businesses had always depended on various contractors and suppliers. But now they were starting to off-load jobs that, in prior periods, they had handled exclusively themselves. One of the pioneers in this new age of outsourcing was Kodak, which in 1989 decided to turn over the running of its data centers to IBM. The move saved Kodak money—5 to 15 percent of its information-technology budget. But its primary aim was to better focus on its film business. "We were a photographic company, not a computer company," said Kathy Hudson, who was then Kodak's chief information officer. "We were not thinking about it in a cost-cutting way but in a strategic way."

The plan caused a stir nonetheless. Hudson assured the hundreds of Kodak employees who would soon see their jobs sent away that they'd have every opportunity to move right along with the work; IBM was going to hire them all. But "no matter what you do or how employee-friendly you try to be, there's not a lot of trust between management and companies on something like this," Hudson said. At one point, she went out to dinner with some key members of her group, along with their husbands and wives. "If you thought the employees were nervous," said Hudson, "that paled in comparison with their spouses. They were all asking, 'What are you doing?'"

If anybody was well suited to answer and inject a measure of calm, it was Hudson. Not only had she been with Kodak since 1970; she had been brought up in its protective bubble. Her father, Edward, had joined the company in the early 1930s, running errands and cleaning inkwells. He went on to become an information-services manager, sitting in the very same office where his daughter later kept her desk. "In Rochester, you did not go to work for Kodak," Hudson said. "The phrase was 'you got in'—because you got in for life." The world was changing now, and changing fast, but Hudson did all she could to uphold this legacy. The reason she selected IBM to operate Kodak's mainframes, instead of going with a technically impressive bid from Electronic Data Systems, was that Big Blue still had a defined-benefit pension plan and would let her employees transfer over their years of service. "We were moving our people from a paternalistic Kodak culture into an equally paternalistic IBM culture," she said.

As executives at other companies began to copy what Hudson had done—in those early days, the outsourcing of IT was known as "doing the Kodak"—the transitioning of work wasn't always so gentle. Most of the time that jobs were absorbed by outside contractors, employees were let go without a second thought. The cafeteria crew, the maintenance staff, customer-service agents, security guards, and janitors were among those most at risk. The UAW tried to fight outsourcing in the auto industry, but it was now too weak to win, and the practice spread rapidly. Manufacturing a host of parts once made in-house by the car companies, US auto suppliers added more than 100,000 jobs from 1987 to 1996, while employment at GM, Ford, and Chrysler dropped sharply.

For many of those in the employ of these outsiders, their circumstances were less than ideal. Most auto contractors were nonunion shops, and they paid 30 to 40 percent less than the Big Three. Janitors and guards who worked for contractors were likewise paid relatively little compared with those who were employed directly by the companies where they scrubbed the floors and checked the locks. The same was true for food-service workers and those at call centers. In some cases—including at many warehouses—the contractors, in turn, subcontracted with temp agencies. At each step, as they got more distant from the big corporations whose customers they were serving, employees became more vulnerable to violations of law and other abuses.

The outsourcing wave didn't stop at the nation's borders, either.

A mong the fiercest proponents of searching out the most cost-efficient suppliers—wherever they happened to be, almost anywhere across the globe—was a General Motors executive named Jose Ignacio Lopez de Arriortua.

Lopez had first caught the eye of Jack Smith, now GM's CEO, when Smith was running the company's European division. On a visit to GM's factory in Zaragoza, Spain, Smith found the engineer in his office, with components piled everywhere: on the desk, the chair, every other stick of furniture, even the floor. Lopez had disassembled a subcompact car, the Corsa, looking for all of the innards that could be removed or substituted without compromising quality. Over the next few hours, Lopez went through each single piece, showing Smith how he could carve out a sizable percentage of the costs. Smith would never forget Lopez's brilliance or his bravado.

Lopez—"Inaki" to his friends—was soon promoted to GM's main European outpost in Rüsselsheim, Germany, where he was asked to take apart something much bigger: the entire purchasing operation.

Lopez did whatever he needed to obtain the best prices from those manufacturing parts for GM in Europe, even if it required him to break long-standing relationships with local contractors in Germany by sending the work to Spain, Italy, Turkey, or some other country that could do it cheaper. This concept of "worldwide purchasing" was revolutionary. Suppliers in Germany began calling him "Lopez the Terrible," "The Rüsselsheim Strangler," and "The Spaniard Who Makes the Germans Tremble."

Now, Smith wanted Lopez to bring his methods to the heart of GM: the company's North American operation, which spent $35 billion a year on 10,000 different parts for its trucks and cars. Ever the swashbuckler, Lopez referred to those on his purchasing staff as "warriors," and the man who liked to work fifteen-hour days pressed them to adhere to his "Warrior's Diet" of fruits and whole grains and finicky food combinations because, he said, "there was a direct correlation between nutrition and professional efficiency, between health and the warrior spirit." The real diet, though, would come for GM's suppliers, from whom Lopez extracted billions of dollars in costs by subjecting them to as many as six rounds of bidding for a single job.

At first, Lopez framed his actions in patriotic terms. "We are fighting to save the auto industry and our lives," he said. "If we lose the battle . . . our sons and daughters will become second-class citizens, and the US will have a second-class economy." He swore that he'd work with the UAW, as well. "I love the union," he said. But such statements became harder to believe as Lopez whipped up his warriors to find the best deals wherever they could, regardless of whether the supplier was unionized or even located within the United States.

In addition to Lopez's quest for the lowest-priced components, GM also opened up more of its own factories in Mexico to supply parts to its assembly plants in the United States. By 1998 it owned more than fifty facilities south of the border, employing 72,000 Mexican workers. The migration didn't go unnoticed at home. "There's hardly anybody at this plant who hasn't seen machinery moving out in a crate with an address on it that says 'Mexico,'" Larry Mathews, a UAW official in Flint, related.

The pull to go elsewhere was strong. "By the early 1990s, the Big Three paid around eighteen dollars an hour—plus generous benefits such as fully paid health care—to unionized workers at parts plants," the automotive writer Micheline Maynard has noted. "By contrast, workers at nonunion plants averaged about eight dollars to nine dollars an hour, and few had anything approaching UAW-style benefits. And plants based in Mexico or Asia paid workers just a fraction of nonunion US wages. Workers there took home in a week what UAW members earned in a day." Given this gap, it was no surprise what happened next. In 1990, automakers in the United States imported about $30 billion worth of components from abroad; ten years later, that had soared to more than $50 billion in foreign-made parts.

Other industries similarly built global production networks, often over decades, helped along by advances in technology and logistics. US multinational corporations had been around for a long time—General Motors, General Electric, Kodak, and Coca-Cola among them. But the speed and scope of what was happening now was unprecedented. "What is new," said the political economist Robert Reich, "is that American-owned multinationals are beginning to employ large numbers of foreigners relative to their American workforces, are beginning to rely on foreign facilities to do many of their most technologically complex activities, and are beginning to export from their foreign facilities—including bringing products back to the United States."

For those making computer hardware and consumer electronics, Taiwan became a crucial base of supply. For many other American brands—whether in appliances, toys, cameras, shoes, or apparel—Chinese factories emerged as a main source of production through the nineties. American companies directly employed 11 percent of Ireland's industrial workers by the late 1980s; they manufactured a whole range of products, many of which were shipped back across the Atlantic to be sold in US stores.

From the mid-1980s through the late '90s, General Electric chopped its US workforce by half (to about 160,000) while nearly doubling its foreign workforce (to 130,000). In some instances, this was because the company wanted to be nearer to its overseas customers. The hottest market for GE's power generation business, for example, was in Asia, and so in 1992 Jack Welch reassigned the lead sales office for the unit to Hong Kong from Schenectady, New York. "Psychologically," said Welch, getting "away from 'Mother Schenectady' . . . shocked the system. Suddenly we heard people say: 'They really mean it. Globalization is for real.'" In other instances, GE changed countries just to pay less for labor. "Ideally," said Welch, "you have every plant you own on a barge." The company also prodded its suppliers to drive down costs—Welch called it "squeezing the lemon"—by picking up and reopening in Mexico.

All of this put blue-collar laborers in the United States, especially those in certain sectors, in particular jeopardy, whereas those with more education and skills seemed better poised to make a go of it. "Some Americans, whose contributions to the global economy are more highly valued in world markets, will succeed, while others, whose contributions are deemed less valuable, fail," Reich wrote, shortly before he became labor secretary in the new Clinton administration.

But no employee was immune from new competition, Reich hastened to add. By 1990, Texas Instruments wasn't just doing most of its manufacturing in East Asia, but also its research, development, and design. W.R. Grace, Du Pont, Merck, Procter & Gamble, Upjohn, and Kodak had all opened R&D labs in Japan. And Hewlett-Packard was tapping talent in West Germany, Australia, and Singapore for breakthroughs in fiber optics, computer-aided engineering software, and laser printers.

For those trying to save money on IT staff, accountants, and software programmers, India was becoming the place to turn. One of the first to spot the opportunity there was GE, which first consolidated its own "back-office" operations in India in 1997, and then offered these services to other companies interested in hiring "legions of English-speaking, college-educated workers . . . on the cheap," as the New America Foundation's Barry Lynn has described it. Even Kathy Hudson, who had taken so much care to ensure that her Kodak employees didn't lose their IT jobs, couldn't fault companies that now sent work far away, across the ocean. "When I can bring on an engineer in Bangalore for what it costs just for health care for a US employee, who am I going to hire?" she asked. "It's the way it goes."

As unnerving as globalization started to become for American workers in the 1980s and '90s, many economists and policymakers contended that the subject was prone to a fair share of sophistry. The number of jobs being outsourced, they said, was pretty tiny all in all, accounting for perhaps a few percentage points of lost employment in the United States over the years. Automation, some indicated, posed a much graver danger. Also largely overlooked was that since at least the late 1990s, many American companies opened overseas factories and offices not to ship low-cost goods to the United States, but to serve local markets; the foreigners employed in those cases didn't swipe jobs from US workers. Nor did "offshoring" happen only in one direction; foreign-owned companies operating in the United States during the nineties increased their hiring of Americans as well. Increased trade gave US companies new access to export markets that they could sell into, and a panoply of goods (many of them inexpensive) were now available for US consumers to buy.

Looked at in the right light, then, the greater interconnectedness of the world's economies could seem a big net plus. Some even maintained that for every person an American multinational employed abroad in the nineties, this growth in business spurred it to hire two people in the United States—a "win-win" formula if ever there was one.

Such was President Clinton's mindset when he advocated passage of the North American Free Trade Agreement, which was to ease the flow of products and services among the United States, Mexico, and Canada. "We seek a new and more open global trading system not for its own sake but for our own sake," he said. "Good jobs, rewarding careers, broadened horizons for . . . middle-class Americans can only be secured by expanding exports and global growth."

But while Clinton enthusiastically endorsed NAFTA and pooh-poohed Ross Perot's prediction that there would be a "giant sucking sound" because of all the US jobs flooding to Mexico, he was always careful to acknowledge the darker side of a world with more open borders. "For a high-wage country like ours, the blessings of more trade can be offset, at least in part, by the loss of income and jobs as more and more multinational corporations take advantage of their ability to move money, management, and production away from a high-wage country to a low-wage country," Clinton had said when still a candidate for the White House. "We can also lose incomes because those companies that stay at home can use the threat of moving to depress wages, as many do today."

As he signed NAFTA into law in December 1993, putting him in conflict with fellow Democrats and organized labor, Clinton again recognized that there would be losers as well as winners—and the losers were likely to be those who already had lost a lot. "We have an obligation to protect those workers who do bear the brunt of competition by giving them a chance to be retrained and to go on to a new and different and, ultimately, more secure and more rewarding way of work," the president said. "In recent years, this social contract has been sundered. It cannot continue."

Nobody was really sure, however, how to stop the contract from ripping further.

O fficially, the one recession to sting America during the 1990s didn't last too long, having ended in March 1991, just eight months after it had begun. But the economic expansion to follow was different than any upturn that had come before it, at least since the end of World War II.

"Even though business profits are up, output is growing, and the economy is recovering," Michael Mandel, the chief economist at *BusinessWeek*, said in 1993, "help-wanted ads are still scarce, and private job growth is plodding along at a measly 75,000 per month—with many of these temporary or part-time positions." Corporate America, he added, "has developed a deep, and perhaps abiding, reluctance to hire."

After the eight previous recessions, it had taken only ten months on average to recoup the number of jobs that had been lost during the downturn. It would now take twenty-three months. The "jobless recovery" was born.

No one knew for certain why the labor market was lagging, but in many industries, especially manufacturing, employers were not behaving as they had historically. Companies in the past would hold on to more workers than necessary during slack periods—a practice termed "labor hoarding"—so that they didn't have to retrain new people once business picked up. Now they were letting people go without any intention of ever filling those positions again.

Around the same time that GM had announced it was abolishing 74,000 jobs, many others said they were terminating multitudes of workers as well: Unisys, Xerox, McDonnell Douglas, Sears, Tenneco, Westinghouse, TRW, Chemical Bank, Manufacturers Hanover, and more. "Do not confuse cyclical fluctuations with powerful structural forces that are now affecting the very fabric of our social order," Morgan Stanley economist Stephen Roach told a congressional panel. The

Federal Reserve Bank of New York said that, unlike before, a recession for many wasn't "an event to be weathered," but "an opportunity—or even a mandate—to reorganize production permanently, close less efficient facilities, and cull staff."

For Kodak, the culling commenced in 1993, in a scene that played out very similarly to the one at GM with Bob Stempel. Like Stempel, Kodak CEO Kay Whitmore seemed overly cautious just when the company needed an assertive leader—in its case, to keep Fuji and private-label film manufacturers in check and to make the leap to digital photography. It didn't help that Whitmore, a chemical engineer who had been at the company since 1957, would fall asleep in meetings; once, he even dozed off during a session with Microsoft cofounder Bill Gates.

Kodak did have one big advantage over GM: it was still making money; there was no real crisis in Rochester—not yet anyway. But institutional investors and the company's outside directors were frustrated that Whitmore wasn't delivering much higher profits. Kodak's stock price was as listless as Whitmore himself. "Kay may be the right guy to be the pilot of a glacier," said Robert Monks, whose firm had bought millions of dollars in Kodak shares and was now calling for change. "The trouble is, the water has gotten hot."

Although Kodak had lowered its head count some in the 1980s, when Whitmore had been the company's president and he had recently eliminated another 2,000 jobs, the board wanted him to cut harder and faster. Whitmore said the right things: "There's a shared sense of urgency at Kodak." In January 1993, he had even recruited a chief financial officer, Christopher Steffen, who'd earned a reputation at Chrysler and Honeywell as an unapologetic cost-cutter. But Steffen abruptly quit Kodak after less than four months, irked that Whitmore and other senior executives kept trying to slow him down.

Whitmore was now sitting right in the crosshairs. This was, as Steffen had labeled it, a "post-Stempel world." In August, Kodak's board voted to oust Whitmore. The value of the company's stock went up by a billion dollars that day.

Even as they booted him, the directors said they still expected Whitmore to keep working on a plan to bolster Kodak's finances. Two weeks later, he announced that by 1995 the company would cut 10,000 jobs, or about 10 percent of its workforce. Wall Street, hoping for 20,000 positions to melt away, was disappointed. Employees, however, were shaken. The paper in Rochester ran a cartoon of Whitmore, his head being served up on a platter, that said: "Only 9,999 to go."

It would be left to the new CEO, George Fisher, to preside over the layoffs. Fisher, who had been lured away from Motorola, which he'd led to great acclaim, had a little Jack Welch in him. He wasn't as prickly as Welch. But like the GE chief, he was intent on smashing the snail-paced bureaucracy that had built up over many decades at Kodak, making it so that, as one business partner complained, the company would "have 1,000 people in the room and couldn't make a decision." Breaking this stultifying system, thought Fisher, was the only way to make real headway on the strategy he was honing: capturing more foreign markets and winning in digital imaging.

From the first day, Fisher regularly strolled Kodak's offices and factories—even the employee cafeteria—asking questions, welcoming opposing views, seeking ideas from everyone about how to increase productivity, improve quality, and expunge waste. David Swift, who had been Whitmore's executive assistant and was now Fisher's, never forgot the first senior staff meeting he attended with the new boss. Swift entered and took his seat at the edge of the room, the way subordinates in the Kodak hierarchy had always done. Fisher stared at him, befuddled. "Why are you sitting over there? If you're part of my team, you need to sit at the table." (If Fisher ever surrendered the aura of the Everyman it was with his pay package, which included a $5 million signing bonus and the potential to make more than $100 million in compensation if Kodak's stock price climbed high enough.)

Also like Welch, Fisher was insistent on holding employees accountable for achieving results. Just showing up wasn't good enough anymore. He even overhauled Kodak's wage dividend policy so that it would now be tied to specific corporate financial objectives—return on net assets, to be precise; no longer was a payout all but guaranteed. "When I joined Eastman Kodak out of high school" in 1964, said Mike Morley, the company's director of human resources, "it was a real . . . entitlement mentality. We are trying to change that culture to be much more performance-based."

And although the new CEO was determined for Kodak to grow its way to bigger profits—and not hack its way there—he reined in benefits where he felt it was essential. Much to the displeasure of Kodak's employees, for example, Fisher pulled back on pensions and

retiree health care. He also went forward with the 10,000 layoffs that
Whitmore had set in motion, though he tried to do it in a way that
would complement his strategy, directing a small team of executives to
make pinpoint reductions rather than cutting across the board. Swift
was part of the group that huddled in a room on the sixteenth floor
of the Kodak building, choosing who would stay and who would go.
"It was unbelievably gut-wrenching," he said. "It was one of the hardest things I've ever had to do." Fisher, too, hated having to dismiss so
many people. "You don't like to do it, but you've got to do it," he said.
"You agonize about the impact, the personal impact on families."

Al Waugh, an engineer who received one of the 10,000 pink
slips, had worked at Kodak for twenty years. "One of my beliefs has
been dashed to pieces," he said. "People worked hard, got a decent living, and made a good enough wage to raise a family. The whole thing
came tumbling down." For Waugh and his wife, Mary, it was tough
to know what to do now. Kodak was everything to them. Generations
of their families had worked at the company. Waugh's grandmother,
Bessie, had even been a secretary to George Eastman. "It's interesting
to think that she met him," Al said. Mary had a different reaction:
"He's probably turning over in his grave a hundred times a day."

Perhaps. But this was now George Fisher's Kodak, not George
Eastman's. And Fisher didn't hide that the company could not—and
would not—give its workers all that it had given them in the past. He
even put in place what he called, explicitly, a "new social contract,"
which echoed Jack Welch's promise of "'lifetime employability" as opposed to "lifetime employment." At Kodak, employees were to receive
forty hours of training and career development per year. That way,
if another round of layoffs were to come, workers would at least be
"more marketable," as Fisher said, raising the odds that they'd be able
to land another job somewhere else. The hope, too, was that this kind
of investment would lead to a fresh relationship between management
and Kodak's workforce, one in which trust would replace the jitters
and contempt that all the cuts had provoked. But overcoming the em-
bitterment wasn't going to be easy. "The majority of employees still
craved the security blanket that used to come with a Kodak job," Alecia Swasy, a *Wall Street Journal* correspondent who covered the '93 layoffs, observed. Only 30 percent of employees, internal surveys showed,
now thought that Kodak had a "sincere interest" in their future.

By 1997, harboring such doubts seemed more sensible than cynical. Kodak announced another series of layoffs that year: 3,000, then 6,000, then 10,000—a Chinese water torture of sackings. "Everyone there is again saying, when . . . will it be me; when are the job cuts going to end?" said Eugene Fram, a marketing professor at the Rochester Institute of Technology.

As disturbing as it was for many to witness Kodak's cultural conversion, perhaps even more unsettling were the job cuts that IBM initiated in 1993. The company had been shrinking its payroll since the mid-1980s, going from more than 400,000 workers to about 250,000, but this had been done through attrition and voluntary retirement (though the company, exhibiting a sharper edge, had also stepped up its firings for poor performance). In principle, IBM's no-layoff policy had remained intact—and, more than that, it was still looked upon as "one of the factors that give the company its soul," Harvard's D. Quinn Mills wrote in 1988.

But once IBM lost money—nearly $8 billion in 1991 and '92—its soul was lost, too. A new CEO, Louis Gerstner, had been brought in from RJR Nabisco to do what George Fisher at Kodak had been brought in to do: transform a sluggish company into a supple one. "If IBM is as bureaucratic as people say, let's eliminate bureaucracy fast," Gerstner told his most senior managers during his first meeting with them. "Let's decentralize decision making wherever possible. . . . If we have too many people, let's right-size fast."

That he did. Four months into his job at IBM, Gerstner revealed plans for 35,000 layoffs, which were to come on top of another 25,000 early retirements already announced.

Within a year, IBM would return to profitability and soon thereafter it would begin a seismic, and exceedingly successful, shift from the mainframe business into computer services. Gerstner would go on to become one of the more venerated leaders in business history—one who could, to use his famous metaphor, make an elephant dance. But the "paternalistic IBM culture" into which Kathy Hudson had felt so good about placing her workers was no more. In the years ahead, as IBM took over the IT operations of many other companies, including those of J.P. Morgan Chase and AT&T, many of the workers it acquired were eventually laid off as their old departments were made more efficient. Those who were kept on the IBM payroll often faced cuts in their income and benefits. "It sometimes looks as though IBM is hired to be the hatchet man," said Michael Smith, a Washington attorney retained by a group of high-tech workers who had lost their jobs. IBM also started to utilize another tactic that became an employer favorite during the 1980s and '90s: firing a person one day and then bringing him back as an independent contractor, at lower compensation, the next.

One person who kept an eye on the job cuts at IBM was Jack Welch at General Electric. He had never liked IBM's holier-than-thou advertising campaign in the 1980s: "Jobs may come and go. But people shouldn't." Now, he couldn't help himself. When he'd run into IBM executives at some business or charity event, he'd smile and ask, "Why isn't he 'Neutron Lou?'"

Less amused were people like Michael Cunningham, whom IBM fired in 1993 after he'd been with the company for sixteen years. Everything about it bugged him, including the way that a group of security guards—unfamiliar faces all—kept watch as his supervisor escorted him out of the Poughkeepsie, New York, lab where he'd worked. He also felt demeaned by the language in IBM's dismissal letter: "You have been designated a 'surplus employee' effective immediately." Cunningham was one of nearly 8,000 IBM employees in New York's Mid-Hudson Valley who'd been "surplused," as the job cuts came to be known. "That word was the most disgusting word I ever heard," he said. "It told me I was excess baggage, junk, garbage."

"Surplused" was far from the only weasel word that employers used during the 1990s. There was also Gerstner's expression, "rightsizing," as well as "de-hiring," "slivering," "retooling," "downshifting," and "reengineering," among many others. That last term grew out of *Reengineering the Corporation*, a blockbuster bestseller by former MIT professor Michael Hammer and consultant James Champy, which was published in 1993. It would long be cited as one of the most influential business books of all time—and not because it had been good for workers. "Hammer and Champy's 'manifesto' obliterated the implicit social contract between employers and employees," said *Inc.* magazine. "Gone were the notions of lifetime employment and corporate loyalty, replaced by an endless regimen of downsizing, rightsizing, outsourcing, and offshoring."

In all fairness, that was a terrible misreading of the book, which called for reorganizing business by breaking down activities into small steps and then finding new efficiencies by reassembling these processes with a "clean sheet" approach. Although the authors did anticipate that some jobs would be combined through reengineering, mass lay-offs were never part of their prescription. That, however, didn't stop executives and consultants from using the book as intellectual cover for wholesale downsizing. "It is astonishing to me the extent to which the term reengineering has been hijacked, misappropriated, and mis-understood," said Hammer. Added Champy: "At least half of the work that was going on out there under the name of 'reengineering' was really just shedding bodies."

The 1990s wasn't only about losing jobs. It was also about adding them—in record quantities, actually—which can make the pe-riod seem more than a bit bipolar. Some have called it "The Downsiz-ing Decade," others "The Roaring Nineties."

Pointing to his long list of accomplishments, you could make a persuasive argument that Bill Clinton's guiding of the economy was the best of any president who has ever served. During his eight years in office, the United States netted nearly 23 million new jobs. Unemploy-ment reached a thirty-year low, falling below 4 percent. Productivity jumped, and real wages rose at their fastest rate since 1972. Income gains were widespread, including for African American and Hispanic families. Poverty declined. Inflation was stable. "America," Clinton said, "again has the confidence to dream big dreams."

But for lots of workers, it was hard to dream big when they were feeling so fitful, and understandably so. Most concerning, perhaps, was that during the nineties job opportunities for Americans became increasingly split, reinforcing a trend that had started in the late 1970s. Employment was rising in high-education professional, technical, and managerial occupations, as well as in low-end service work: food pre-parers, health-care aides, security guards, and so on. But both blue-collar and white-collar jobs in between—the work of factory hands, sales assistants, clerks, and low-ranking administrators who could once build a middle-class life, even with little formal education—were now vanishing. David Autor, an MIT economist who has documented this hollowing out of "middle-skill" jobs, has fingered the automation of routine work and globalization as prime causes.

For many, this meant that when they did find a new job after being laid off, it paid less than the one they'd had before. For millions of others, especially men without a college degree, this absence of demand for what they had to offer was so dispiriting that they stopped looking for work. As they dropped out of the labor force, with a good many now collecting government disability checks to get by, Washington didn't count them anymore in its official tally of the unemployed. "Overall," wrote David Leonhardt, the Pulitzer Prize–winning columnist for the *New York Times*, "the rise in the number of missing workers calls into question the great achievement of the 1990s economy: the best job market since 1970."

Even for those who were working in "good jobs," the nineties could be disquieting—a lot like the 1980s, when the social contract really began to pull apart, only more so. Through the first few years of the Clinton recovery, companies forced workers out of their jobs at a greater rate than during the brutal recession of the early 1980s. "It is difficult to imagine more compelling evidence that the nature of the employment relationship has changed than this," the University of Pennsylvania's Peter Cappelli has written.

Most corporations made no bones about it. A 1997 survey from the Conference Board, a business group, found that two-thirds of employers acknowledged that while they once had an "employee compact" that gave their workers job security, this wasn't the case any longer. "Hidden behind America's low official unemployment rate," Yale University's Jacob Hacker has said, was the "specter of workplace insecurity," beckoned by a "growing recognition that no worker, no matter how educated, no matter how well trained, is free of the risk of sudden and large economic losses—when the economy is racing along as well as when it is struggling."

Eager to become ever more efficient, many companies were now purging people not only when they were doing poorly but also when they were financially sound. And as organizations became flatter, white-collar employees were often the first ones to be let go. During the 1990s, in fact, managers were more likely to be taken out in a large-scale layoff than were lower-level workers—a switch from earlier periods. For those coworkers still employed after a big lay-off—the "survivors"—it was not unusual to experience low morale and high stress as they endeavored to cope with shock, grief, fear, a heavier workload, and a loss of institutional knowledge. Jill Andresky Fraser, an editor at *Inc.*, announced the birth of the "white-collar sweatshop."

It is easy to turn the portrait of downsizing in America into a caricature and miss the tremendous complications inherent in the issue. Many times, for example, companies would lay off large numbers and then follow up with a burst of new hiring within a few years, leaving them with more employees than they'd originally had. Others would announce a downsizing and continue to hire new employees at the same time. Moreover, while companies talked about "delayering" and set out to dismiss many of their managers, the percentage of the American workforce in managerial positions grew through the nineties. Outside of manufacturing, retailers and service-sector businesses were mostly "upsizing," not downsizing. And even among manufacturers, while big companies lost jobs, smaller producers added them. "With big firms growing smaller and small firms growing larger, the script is clearly not one of universal decline, as the most obvious interpretation of downsizing might have us believe," economists William Baumol, Alan Blinder, and Edward Wolff have explained.

But even with all of these qualifications, there was no escaping it: throughout the Clinton boom—an economic expansion that would run longer than either Kennedy's or Reagan's—the dissonance of downsizing could be heard constantly in the background. As the "jobless recovery" bowed to vigorous job growth, there was by historical standards extraordinary churn in the workforce. "Downsizing has taken on a logic of its own—has lost its connection to takeovers or to financial problems or even to genuine business need," G. J. Meyer, who'd been laid off from executive jobs at aerospace manufacturer McDonnell Douglas and heavy-equipment maker J.I. Case, wrote in 1995 in his melancholy memoir about being jobless. In 1998, despite the zooming economy, there were nearly 680,000 job cuts in America—10 percent more than 5 years earlier.

Employees felt the social contract continuing to deteriorate in other ways as well. Wages grew solidly in the late 1990s, as the labor market tightened. But this upswing would turn out to be brief, and across the whole of the decade, hourly earnings for the typical worker

would rise only about half a percent a year on average—a quarter of
what was seen during the Golden Age. One thing that kept wages
from moving higher was downsizing. Apprehensive about losing their
own jobs, some employees were evidently reticent to ask for even bigger raises.

Companies continued to put less money into pensions, too—
nearly 30 percent less, on average, than they had in the late seventies.
By the close of the nineties, even IBM had given up guaranteeing retirement security, saying that the defined-benefit model was appropriate when "thirty-year careers were the norm," but not any more.
Thousands of IBMers, scared that the changes the company was making would destroy a third or more of the value of their pensions, weren't
as ready to brush off the past. "These are employees who, throughout
their careers, rejected job offers from other companies because of their
loyalty to IBM," said Bernie Sanders, a then-congressman from Ver-
mont who counted many of the workers among his constituents. "And
these are the same employees who woke up one day, not so long ago,
to discover that all of the promises IBM made to them were not worth
the paper that they had been written on."

Health care was also slipping. President Clinton rode into office resolving to tame medical inflation while covering the 37 million
Americans who didn't have health insurance. He also wanted to end
"job lock": people wary of leaving one employer for another for fear of
losing their insurance. The 1,300-plus-page piece of legislation that his
administration produced was M. C. Escher-like in its complexity and
New Deal-esque in its ambition—"the Social Security Act of this generation," as Hillary Clinton, then the president's wife, who was placed
in charge of the plan, called it.

At first, it looked like big business, concerned about escalat-
ing health costs, might rally behind the proposal. But gradually, one
lobby after another—the National Association of Manufacturers, the
Chamber of Commerce, and the Business Roundtable—peeled off and
opposed the president. They just couldn't accept the amount of government regulation in the Clinton bill, and even if they could have
been persuaded on the fine points, they never truly trusted the administration. In some eyes, they also lacked a concern for the common
good that their corporate forebears had possessed. "In the past, elites
within the business community had intervened to prevent the most

venal interests from dominating Congress," the political commentator John Judis has written. "In 1946, the Committee for Economic Development, acting not as another business group but as an elite organization committed to the national interest, rescued the Employment Act. There were, however, no comparable organizations and no comparable leadership that could have rescued health-care reform from oblivion."

With the demise of the Clinton measure, businesses tried to hold down medical costs on their own. Companies directed their employees away from fee-for-service plans and into HMOs, PPOs, and other forms of managed care, where expenses could be more tightly controlled but where patients had less choice over their doctors. And many became stingier with their benefits. By 1998, only 28 percent of workers with employer-provided health coverage had the full cost of their insurance premiums paid by their companies, down from 44 percent in the early 1980s. When it came to their retirees, many companies yanked health coverage altogether—or, as with Bill Sprague and tens of thousands of others who'd worked for GM, they began to make them cough up more of the costs.

The majority of the appeals court in the Sprague case didn't dispute that GM had told its white-collar retirees, time after time, that the company would continue to provide them with the same medical benefits "for your lifetime." But because GM also apprised them that it could possibly revise those terms in the future, it hadn't violated the law—regardless of whether this note of caution was essentially buried in the fine print. "GM's failure, if it may properly be called such, amounted to this: the company did not tell the early retirees at every possible opportunity that which it had told them many times before—namely, that the terms of the plan were subject to change," Judge David Nelson ruled in his 1998 opinion. "There is, in our view, a world of difference between the employer's deliberate misleading of employees . . . and GM's failure to begin every communication to plan participants with a caveat."

But for Boyce Martin, one of three dissenting judges, the company had betrayed its employees, plain and simple. "When General Motors was flush with cash and health-care costs were low, it was easy to promise employees and retirees lifetime health care," Martin wrote. Decades later, "rather than pay off those perhaps ill-considered promises, it is easier for the current regime to say those promises never were made. There is the tricky little matter of the paper trail of written assurances of lifetime health care, but General Motors . . . has managed to escape the ramifications of its now-regretted largesse."

In the aftermath of the decision, corporations all over America cited the Sprague case as they defended their own cutting of retiree health benefits from lawsuits. More often than not, the companies won. GM, which had been so instrumental in building up the social contract, was now pivotal in pulling it down.

As scholars have thought about what company epitomizes American capitalism in the twenty-first century, many have settled on Wal-Mart, which has kept prices low for consumers in part by keeping wages low for workers.

11

THE NEW FACE OF
CAPITALISM

As America slipped toward, and then settled into, the early 2000s, it was only natural to look back upon the preceding one hundred years and take stock of those people and institutions that had exerted the most influence on the country and the world. *Time* magazine named Albert Einstein its Person of the Century. National Public Radio came out with its list of the hundred greatest American musical works of that span—a catalog whose eclectic nature was reflected in a sequence of tunes found in the middle of the Ss: "Singin' in the Rain," "Sittin' on the Dock of the Bay," "Smells Like Teen Spirit," and "Stand by Your Man." *Popular Mechanics* proclaimed the car the "defining device" of the era. And in the business world, many saw one company as the paradigm of the period (or a good chunk of it, anyway): General Motors.

But as edifying—or at least as entertaining—as it was to look back, it also made sense to look ahead. And as the new century began, commentators were eager to identify the company that was now positioned to be, in the words of one group of scholars, "the face of twenty-first-century capitalism." Their choice, and the choice of many others, was Wal-Mart.

In terms of scale, Wal-Mart was the obvious successor to GM. In 2002, the retailer became the biggest corporation in America, topping the Fortune 500 list for the first time. By 2005, its revenues exceeded $285 billion, and profits surpassed $10 billion. It was the nation's leading seller of toys, furniture, jewelry, dog food, and scores of other products. It was also the largest grocer in the United States through its so-called Supercenter stores. To peddle all this merchandise, the company employed more than 1.3 million US workers. But there was a massive difference between GM and Wal-Mart. While the former had put most of its workers on a secure route to the middle class, the latter was placing many on a path to impoverishment.

For decades, Wal-Mart had enjoyed a reputation as the most wholesome kind of company, steeped in American values and a down-home culture captured in the cheer that Wal-Mart employees would do, gathering in a circle at the start of every shift change: "Give me a *W*! Give me an *A*! Give me an *L*! Give me a squiggly! (followed by a shaking of the butt) Give me an *M*! Give me an *A*! Give me an *R*! Give me a *T*! What's that spell? Wal-Mart! What's that spell? Wal-Mart! Who's number one? The customer! Always!" Wal-Mart, said David Glass, who'd joined the company in 1976 and had served as its CEO from 1988 until 2000, was "sort of like motherhood and apple pie."

Nobody did more to enhance this image than Sam Walton, better known inside the company as "Mr. Sam," who liked to swing his muddy boots into the cab of an old pickup truck and drive around Bentonville, Arkansas, where in the early 1950s he'd started Walton's 5&10 on the town square. The first actual Wal-Mart was opened in 1962 in Rogers, about eight miles to the east. From the beginning, whenever Walton would deal personally with his workers—"associates," in Wal-Mart's communal-sounding parlance—he went out of his way to be as nice as nice could be. "This is a man who . . . treated his associates well as persons, not just as clerks and salespeople," said Walter Loeb, a retailing consultant. Signifying this trait, Walton renamed the personnel department the "People Division" and put forth a management philosophy that was all about motivating each and every employee to give his or her best. Wal-Mart "believes management's responsibility is to provide leadership that serves the associate," the company asserted in the 1991 edition of *Sam's Associate Handbook*. "Managers must support, encourage, and provide opportunities for associates to be successful. Mr. Sam calls this 'Servant Leadership.'"

But there was another aspect of Walton's belief system—an extreme tightfistedness—that rubbed up against this creed of caring. The idea was that by doing absolutely everything possible to minimize costs, Wal-Mart would be able to deliver consistently low prices to its customers, giving hardworking people more money to spend on other things. For the company, serving up bargains was more than just a business strategy; it was practically a religious calling. "If we work together," said Walton, "we'll lower the cost of living for everyone. We'll give the world an opportunity to see what it's like to save and to have a better life." Consumers ate it up. By 2005, more than 90 percent of American households could be counted on to shop at Wal-Mart at least once a year; about a third of the nation shopped there every week.

For Wal-Mart's folksy founder, his CEO successors, and their executive teams, the company's parsimony translated into having tiny offices, emptying their own trash, flying coach, even sharing budget hotel rooms with colleagues when traveling on business. For Walton, who had a net worth of more than $100 billion, making him the richest person in the world, these were minor gestures. For Wal-Mart's hourly workers, though, the company's determination to pinch every penny was anything but minor: it left many of them scrambling to get by.

In the 1960s, Mr. Sam set up his stores as separate corporate structures—all linked back to a single financial partnership that he and his family controlled—so that revenues would come in at less than $1 million apiece, a threshold that permitted each location under government rules to pay less than the minimum wage. (A federal court eventually found this arrangement, while undeniably clever, to be improper.)

As the decades passed, the pressure to extract more from the workforce increased. Wal-Mart managers around the country forced employees to work off the clock and skip breaks; broke child-labor laws; and used illegal immigrants to clean its stores. It also locked workers inside overnight. The company maintained that this was to keep employees safe in high-crime neighborhoods, but former store managers said that the real purpose was to discourage workers from stealing anything or sneaking out for a smoke. Steven Greenhouse, the

New York Times reporter who documented these and other such practices, has characterized them as "downright Dickensian."

Some Wal-Mart managers tried to make conditions insufferable for their highest-paid employees so that they'd quit and could be replaced by others earning less. Others made sure that their workers never logged quite enough hours to reach full-time status since, as part-timers, they wouldn't qualify for certain benefits. "I knew what I had to do," said Melissa Jerkins, who oversaw a staff of 120 at a Wal-Mart in Decatur, Indiana. "I had to meet the bottom line or my ass was in trouble. They didn't care how I got to that bottom line . . . so long as I got there."

Even for those employees who weren't victims of manipulated schedules or outright abuse, it could be tough to scratch out a living. In 2005, most Wal-Mart workers took home less than ten dollars an hour, compared with more than thirty dollars for a nonskilled assembly line worker at General Motors. This added up to a yearly income at Wal-Mart of about $18,000—below the poverty line for a family of four. Wal-Mart liked to talk up its profit-sharing plan. But because of high turnover, typical of most retailers, relatively few employees ever got to take much advantage of it. And even Wal-Mart acknowledged that a full-time worker might not be able support a family on a company paycheck. The health benefits that Wal-Mart offered were also lacking. As a result, many of its employees had to turn to public relief: food stamps, Medicaid, and subsidized housing.

In *Nickel and Dimed*, her 2001 modern classic about what it was like to take up a series of low-wage jobs across America, Barbara Ehrenreich recounted how when she went to work at a Wal-Mart in Minneapolis, making seven dollars an hour, she soon found herself about to run out of money. She wound up seeking help through a human-services agency called the Community Emergency Assistance Program, which recommended that she move into a homeless shelter until she could save enough for a deposit and first month's rent on an apartment. Wrote Ehrenreich:

> At one point toward the end of the interview, the CEAP lady had apologized for forgetting almost everything I said about myself— that I had a car, lived in a motel, etc. She was mixing me up with someone else who worked at Wal-Mart, she explained, someone

who had been in just a few days ago. Now, of course I've noticed that many of my coworkers are poor in all the hard-to-miss, stereotypical ways. Crooked yellow teeth are one sign, inadequate footwear is another. My feet hurt after four hours of work, and I wear my comfortable old Reeboks, but a lot of women run around all day in thin-soled moccasins. Hair provides another class clue. Ponytails are common or, for that characteristic Wal-Martian beat-up and hopeless look, straight shoulder-length hair, parted in the middle and kept out of the face by two bobby pins.

But now I know something else. In orientation, we learned that the store's success depends entirely on us, the associates; in fact, our bright blue vests bear the statement "At Wal-Mart our people make the difference." Underneath those vests, though, there are real-life charity cases, maybe even shelter dwellers.

One reason that Wal-Mart workers have always had difficulty improving their lot is that they've never been able to form a union. At its core, Wal-Mart's rationale for being against organized labor was not unlike that of Kodak, say, or General Electric under Lem Boulware: management had an open door policy, by which any worker could ostensibly walk in and discuss anything. Therefore, as Wal-Mart laid out in its "Manager's Toolbox to Remaining Union Free," "we do not believe there is a need for third-party representation. It is our position every associate can speak for him/herself without having to pay his/her hard-earned money to a union in order to be listened to and have issues resolved."

Yet unlike Kodak, which tried to frustrate union organizers by keeping its workers happy with good wages and princely benefits, Wal-Mart has been reliably ungenerous. And unlike GE, which fought tooth and nail against the International Union of Electrical Workers but ultimately honored its right to exist, Wal-Mart has never allowed so much as a single one of its stores to be organized. Indeed, ever since Mr. Sam's time, the company has done everything it can to crush the unions, painting them in the most Manichean terms. They are "nothing but blood-sucking parasites living off the productive labor of people who work for a living!" said attorney John Tate, an iron-willed right-winger whom Walton had hired to help beat back the Retail Clerks in the early 1970s and who then stuck around at Wal-Mart where he developed an array of antiunion techniques.

In the early 1980s, when the Teamsters attempted to represent employees at two Wal-Mart distribution centers in Arkansas, Walton himself showed up with a warning—US labor law be damned. Recalled one worker: "He told us that if the union got in, the warehouse would be closed. . . . He said people could vote any way they wanted, but he'd close her right up." The Teamsters lost the election.

But it wasn't just top executives who were expected to resist being organized. "Staying union free is a full-time commitment," read a manual given out at a Wal-Mart distribution center in Indiana in 1991, the year before Walton died. "Unless union prevention is a goal equal to other objectives within an organization, the goal will usually not be attained. The commitment to stay union free must exist at all levels of management—from the chairperson of the 'board' down to the front-line manager. Therefore, no one in management is immune from carrying his or her 'own weight' in the union prevention effort. The entire management staff should fully comprehend and appreciate exactly what is expected of their individual efforts to meet the union free objective. The union organizer is a 'potential opponent' for our center."

The main thing that a Wal-Mart manager was supposed to do when he or she caught even a hint of union activity was to contact corporate headquarters via a special hotline. Immediately, a "labor team" would be sent from Bentonville to the store where union organizers might be gaining even the slightest toehold. This squad from HQ would then take over the running of the place, putting workers on a steady diet of antiunion propaganda videos; weighing whether local managers were too timid or sympathetic to labor and should be ousted; and keeping a close eye on any employees agitating for a union or simply disposed to having one. "As soon as they determine you're prounion, they go after you," said Jon Lehman, who was a Wal-Mart manager in Kentucky for seventeen years. "It's almost like a neurosurgeon going after a brain tumor: we got to get that thing out before it infects the rest of the store, the rest of the body."

Much of this strategy evoked the way that GM and other companies deployed Pinkertons to bully the unions way back in the 1930s. "I had so many bosses around me, I couldn't believe it," said Larry Adams, who worked in the tire and lube express department at a Wal-Mart in Kingman, Arizona, which grabbed the labor team's attention in the summer of 2000. With temperatures soaring well above a hundred degrees, Adams and some of his fellow automotive technicians got angry when their boss wouldn't spend the $200 needed to fix a broken air conditioner. So they reached out to the United Food and Commercial Workers union. Within forty-eight hours, twenty outside managers were crawling all over the store. "It was very intimidating," said Adams. The UFCW's organizing push in Kingman would end in defeat; within a year or so, nearly every one of the union supporters would be fired or compelled to quit.

At a Wal-Mart Supercenter in Jacksonville, Texas, a group of meat-cutters had better luck at organizing—though not for long. A week or two after they voted to join the UFCW in February 2000, the company announced that it would cease cutting meat and switch instead to selling prepackaged beef and pork at all of its stores. Wal-Mart said that the butchers' seven-to-three vote in favor of the UFCW had nothing whatsoever to do with its decision to stock "case-ready" meat. Yet it was all but impossible to miss that the move essentially eviscerated the union's first ever victory at the company, as Wal-Mart successfully argued that the changes to the meat department made it so that collective bargaining wasn't appropriate going forward. The UFCW challenged the company's stance before the National Labor Relations Board, but after eight years of rulings by the agency and the courts, the union could claim only a partial win; Wal-Mart would escape being unionized.

The dust-up in Texas was far from unusual. In all, unions filed 288 unfair-labor-practice charges against Wal-Mart between 1998 and 2003. Most alleged that the company had engaged in improper firings, threatened employees if they tried to organize, carried out surveillance, or illegally interrogated workers to determine their views on labor-related matters. Of these charges, the NLRB found ninety-four of them to be substantive enough to issue a formal complaint against the company. Still, none of it was enough to shake Wal-Mart's conviction that organized labor needed to be stopped at all costs. "I've never seen a company that will go to the lengths that Wal-Mart goes to, to avoid a union," said consultant Martin Levitt, who helped the company hone its attack before writing a book titled *Confessions of a Union Buster*. "They have zero tolerance."

But if Wal-Mart was particularly strong-minded in its opposition to organized labor, most other companies weren't too far behind. For example, at a Coca-Cola bottling plant in Yuma, Arizona, a manager told employees in 2002 that they'd lose their 401(k)s if they voted to be represented by the United Industrial, Service, Transportation, Professional, and Government Workers of North America. The union lost the election by a vote of eleven to ten. At a General Electric subsidiary in Muskegon, Michigan, which hadn't been organized, a machine operator named Michael Crane began to hand out literature promoting the Electrical Workers and wear a union T-shirt on the job, only to find his manager repeatedly asking him, "Don't you have a better shirt to wear?" If this was overly subtle, the company's subsequent action wasn't: it fired Crane on a bogus accusation of substandard workmanship.

It wasn't always like this. In the 1960s, when some 30 percent of the private-sector workforce in America was still unionized, employers were generally cautious about how far they'd go in trying to repel organized labor. "They were as nervous as whores in church," said one corporate adviser. "The posture of major company managers was, 'Let's not make the union mad at us during the organizing drive or they'll take it out at the bargaining table.'" By the 1980s, a whole industry had sprung up to assist business: "union avoidance" consultants, lawyers, psychologists, and strike-management firms. The more enfeebled the unions became, the more forcefully employers then acted. By the 1990s, even companies that had once accepted unions as a fact of life were now totally defiant.

"The most intense and aggressive antiunion campaign strategies, the kind previously found only at employers like Wal-Mart, are no longer reserved for a select coterie of extreme antiunion employers," Cornell University's Kate Bronfenbrenner wrote in an analysis of how business conducted itself during representation elections from 1999 through 2003. Specifically, she discovered that companies threatened to close the facilities where employees were trying to organize in 57 percent of elections, raised the possibility of cuts to wages and benefits in nearly half, and went so far as to actually discharge workers a third of the time. Over the years, employers also became adept at delaying union elections so that they had more time to coerce workers to see things their way.

All of this proved highly effective. Even if the NLRB ruled that a company had illegally dissuaded employees from organizing, the price to pay was typically small—about $200,000 in penalties—compared with the many millions of dollars that could be saved by ensuring that union negotiators never got a shot to bolster workers' earnings, retirement plans, and health-care benefits.

Unions hurt themselves as well. Apparently carried away by the power that they were able to maintain through the 1950s and '60s, labor leaders by the 1980s were dedicating less than 5 percent of their budgets toward recruiting new members. By the time that they woke up and realized that it was crucial to expand their rolls, the composition of the economy had been recast. During the 1930s, when the Auto Workers were first signing up members inside the nation's car factories, it was possible to pull in large pools at once because each plant averaged between 2,000 and 3,000 blue-collar employees. By contrast, organizers were likely to find a tenth that many workers under the roof of a big-box retail outlet and far fewer at a fast-food joint, making it much more expensive and daunting to pick off sizable slices of the service sector. The growing use of temps and other contingent workers also complicated union organizing.

Labor did notch some significant triumphs through the 1990s, such as the Service Employees International Union's Justice for Janitors campaign, which propelled more than 100,000 building workers in various cities into collective bargaining, and the election that saw 74,000 home-care aides in Los Angeles County join the SEIU. But such advances were extremely rare. By 2000, the portion of private-sector workers across the United States who were union members stood at just 9 percent—less than half of what it had been in 1980. By 2010, this figure would dip below 7 percent, even though surveys showed that a majority of nonunion workers desired representation.

The drop was rough on employees across the economy. While the ascension of unions helped to lift pay and benefits for tens of millions of workers in the first few decades after World War II—not only at those companies that had been organized, but at many others that felt the need to keep up—the fall of organized labor was now dragging down people's compensation. Researchers have found a connection between the decline of unions and the rise of income inequality in America; without the added clout that comes with collective bargaining, a good many employees have seen their compensation stagnate or even get set back. "Deunionization," Lawrence Mishel of the

Economic Policy Institute has written, "has strengthened the hands of employers and undercut the ability of low- and middle-wage workers to have good jobs and economic security."

For many people, this reality has had a perverse effect: it has incentivized them to do their shopping at one destination above all others—Wal-Mart. It is tough to fault them. In the early 2000s, the prices on groceries at a Wal-Mart Supercenter were running 8 to 27 percent below those of a traditional supermarket. All in all, the company's prices have been so low—and its reach so vast—that some economists have credited it with singlehandedly helping to hold down inflation for the entire country.

Even union members, who are keenly aware of the company's two-fisted tactics against organized labor, have been tempted by the discounts. "Ten bucks," said Glenn Miraflor, an ironworker and a father of four, as he lowered a twenty-inch box fan into his cart at a Wal-Mart in Las Vegas in 2003. "You can't beat that." Eyeing a new PC, he added: "Where else are you going to find a computer for $498? Everyone I work with shops here."

The clamp that Wal-Mart put on workers didn't stop with those on its own payroll.

Most every time it opened a new store, other retailers that charged their customers more—but also paid their employees better—would find that they couldn't compete. For many of them, the only way to survive was to imitate the Wal-Mart model, cutting back on their own workers' wages and health care. "Socially," said Craig Cole, the chief executive of Brown & Cole Stores, a supermarket chain in the Pacific Northwest, who was wary of Wal-Mart coming into his area, "we're engaged in a race to the bottom."

In October 2003, members of the United Food and Commercial Workers struck Vons and Pavilions markets in Southern California. In a show of solidarity, Ralphs and Albertsons locked out their union members the next day. In all, 59,000 workers were idled. Although the grocery chains and the union were the only two sides actually facing off at the negotiating table, another presence hovered over the talks: Wal-Mart, which was on the verge of opening dozens of Supercenters in the region. "They are the third party now that comes to every bargaining situation," said Mike Leonard, director of strategic programs for the UFCW.

As the supermarkets depicted it, the union would have to make concessions—or Wal-Mart would use its low-price formula to snatch away a substantial amount of their business, causing them to close many of their stores and costing many thousands of jobs. After all, what else could anyone expect to happen when Wal-Mart paid its grocery workers about nine dollars an hour in wages and benefits, compared with nineteen at the big supermarkets? Already, from 1992 through 2003, Wal-Mart's leap into groceries had led to the closure of 13,000 supermarkets in other parts of the country and the bankruptcy of at least twenty-five regional chains. Yet for the UFCW and its allies, this was precisely the time to hold the line and not let Wal-Mart dictate that the entire sector would subject its workers to the lowest common denominator. "If we don't as labor officials address this issue now, the future for our membership is dismal, very dismal," said one California union representative.

For nearly five months, the UFCW rank-and-file walked the picket lines from San Diego to Bakersfield. Finally, a settlement was reached—and it marked a big step backward for the union and its members. Central to the accord was the introduction of a two-tier system under which the supermarkets would pay new hires much less in wages and benefits than veteran employees. The impact, said *Los Angeles Times* columnist Michael Hiltzik, was that UFCW "membership will evolve from a group of decently paid workers into a group of poorly paid ones. Its resources to fight the employers will dwindle, and its prospects for growth will vanish. . . . The damage done by this dispute to the principle of providing a living wage and adequate health-care coverage for employees will be felt by workers—union and nonunion—around the state and across the country."

Some, including Hiltzik, maintained that Wal-Mart had been a convenient bugaboo for the supermarkets and that they were unlikely to pass along much savings from the new labor agreement to their customers; instead, they would reward their shareholders and senior executives. At the same time, others welcomed Wal-Mart, especially in the inner-city neighborhoods that the company had set its sights on. "I'd rather have a person on somebody's payroll—even if it isn't at the highest wage—than on the unemployment roll," said John Mack, president of the Los Angeles Urban League. Boosters predicted other positives as well. "Money that people save on groceries will be redirected to other items, including housing, savings, health, entertainment, and transportation," said a report from the Los Angeles County Economic Development Corporation. "This new spending will, in turn, create jobs outside the grocery industry."

But whatever pluses Wal-Mart was bringing, this much was beyond debate: another set of workers was now part of an industry that couldn't guarantee them a solid living. Under the old contract, a grocery clerk in Southern California could earn more than seventeen dollars an hour; under the new one, workers started at less than nine dollars and could make, at most, about fifteen. Overall, the average wage for a supermarket worker was poised to decrease between 18 and 28 percent. And anywhere from a quarter to nearly half of the unionized workforce would no longer be eligible for medical insurance. Employer pension contributions were also slashed 35 percent for current employees and 65 percent for new workers. "You're not going to be able to make a career out of it anymore," said Kerry Renaud, a produce worker at a Vons supermarket in Hollywood. Barbara Harrison, a bakery worker at Ralphs, put it this way: "With treatment like this from the company . . . the middle class is just becoming the lower class."

In 2007, the UFCW would win back some of what it had lost. Most important, the union was able to reverse the two-tier setup. With low employee morale plaguing the supermarkets, they apparently came to the realization that dividing the workforce wasn't so smart. The pact also included the first pay raises that workers had received in five years. But this wouldn't be a tale of sweet redemption. As the years went on, the social contract throughout the industry would continue to weaken. Wal-Mart and other nonunion grocers acquired more and more market share. And at the unionized chains, rule changes and scheduling tricks made workers wait an increasingly long time before they could move up the ladder and command the highest wages. By 2016, the average grocery worker in L.A. would be making less than $29,000 a year, down from more than $31,000 in 2005, when adjusted for inflation. "Grocery store jobs look much more like fast-food jobs than they used to," said Chris Tilly, director of the UCLA Institute for Research on Labor and Employment. "Lower pay, fewer benefits, more people part-time."

Meanwhile, Wal-Mart's sway extended to another batch of workers: those of its suppliers. "Your price is going to be whittled down like you never thought possible," said Carl Krauss, the owner of a Chicago company called Lakewood Engineering & Manufacturing. It produced the fan that Las Vegas ironworker Glenn Miraflor purchased at Wal-Mart for ten dollars. A decade earlier, it cost shoppers twice as much. But Wal-Mart, whose bigness gave it tremendous leverage over the companies whose wares filled its aisles, insisted that Krauss figure out how to make the appliance for less. "You give them your price," Krauss said. "If they don't like it, they give you theirs." To lower expenses, Krauss automated his factory: where it once required twenty-two people to assemble a product, it now took only seven. Krauss also leaned on his own suppliers to reduce prices for their components. Still, that wasn't enough. And so in 2000, Krauss opened a factory in Shenzhen, China, where workers earned twenty-five cents an hour, compared with thirteen dollars in Chicago. By 2003, about 40 percent of Lakewood's products were being made in China, including most heaters and desktop fans. For the box fan that Glenn Miraflor bought, the electronic innards were imported.

Many of Wal-Mart's suppliers found themselves in the same boat—or, more accurately, filling an endless string of container ships crossing the Pacific Ocean. In the mid-1980s, Wal-Mart had tried to score public-relations points by sourcing more products domestically. Under its "Buy American" initiative, patrons to its stores were greeted with red-white-and-blue banners and smaller signs that read, "This item, formerly imported, is now being purchased by Wal-Mart in the USA and is creating—or retaining—jobs for Americans!" By the mid-1990s, however, "Buy American" didn't pencil out for the company anymore. In 2002, Wal-Mart brought in $12 billion worth of Chinese-made goods, double the sum from five years earlier. By 2004, that was up to $18 billion, and by 2006 it had reached $27 billion, accounting for nearly a tenth of total US imports from China. "People say, 'How can it be bad for things to come into the United States cheaply? How can it be bad to have a bargain at Wal-Mart?'" said Steve Dobbins, president of Carolina Mills, a supplier of thread and yarn to the textile industry, which has watched as employment in American apparel factories has disappeared at a rate of more than 11 percent a year since the late nineties. "Sure, it's held inflation down, it's great to have bargains. But you can't buy anything if you're not employed. We are shopping ourselves out of jobs."

By one estimate, Chinese imports to Wal-Mart alone were responsible for wiping out more than 300,000 US manufacturing jobs between 2001 and 2013—a manifestation of what had suddenly become a very serious predicament across America. "Until about a decade ago, the effects of globalization on the distribution of wealth and jobs were largely benign," Michael Spence, a Nobel Prize–winning economist, wrote in 2011. "But employment in the United States has been affected . . . by the fact that many manufacturing activities, principally their lower-value-added components, have been moving to emerging economies." Through the 1990s, the United States ran a trade deficit, but it averaged only about 1 percent of the nation's economic output—a bearable volume. To be sure, the North American Free Trade Agreement caused some pockets of the nation to shed jobs, but the negative repercussions were quite small on the whole, and the losses may well have been eclipsed by new US employment that NAFTA helped to generate.

China was very different, however. After the country joined the World Trade Organization in 2001, giving it more access to markets across the globe, imports into the United States surged. The US trade deficit exploded, averaging about 5 percent of economic output in the 2000s. A consensus of economists and policymakers had long contended that free trade easily made for far more winners than losers. But, as the *Wall Street Journal* has pointed out, "China upended many of those assumptions. No other country came close to its combination of a vast working-age population, super-low wages, government support, cheap currency, and productivity gains." Within four years of the WTO admitting China, imports from there as a percentage of US economic output doubled. It took Mexico twelve years to do the same thing following the passage of NAFTA.

"China's low-cost imports swept the entire US," the *Journal* reported, "squeezing producers of electronics in San Jose, California; sporting goods in Orange County, California; jewelry in Providence, Rhode Island; shoes in West Plains, Missouri; toys in Murray, Kentucky; and lounge chairs in Tupelo, Mississippi, among many other industries and communities." Total manufacturing employment in the United States, which had held fairly steady through the 1990s, plunged after 2001. The harm inflicted would lead many Americans to regard globalization as more bad than good—an attitude that would help shape the contours of the 2016 US presidential race. "The Chinese export onslaught . . . left a scar on the American working class that has not healed," Eduardo Porter of the *New York Times* has written.

How much of this can or should be blamed on any single company—even a colossus like Wal-Mart—is certainly arguable. Not surprisingly, Wal-Mart itself has always made the case for total absolution. "Some well-meaning critics believe that Wal-Mart, because of our size, should play the role that General Motors played after World War II, and that is to establish the post-world-war middle class that the country is so proud of," said H. Lee Scott Jr., who took over as the company's CEO in 2000. "The facts are that retailing doesn't perform that role in the economy as GM does or did."

While Scott wasn't wrong, that was surely of little solace to millions of workers who'd seen the economy change, leaving them with fewer and fewer ways to get ahead. When GM and other manufacturers employed a quarter or more of the American workforce through the early 1980s, even those without much education could land a factory job and do quite well. But what were the two-thirds of Americans without a four-year college degree supposed to do now? Manufacturing, with its high wages and good benefits, employed just 10 percent of Americans by 2010. And even many of these industrial jobs and other blue-collar positions now demanded technical instruction beyond high school—something that far too few people had.

"The person who unloads the truck now has to have some training in logistics and inventory systems," said Anthony Carnevale, director of Georgetown University's Center on Education and the Workforce. "You don't become an auto mechanic any longer by getting a dirty rag and hanging out with your uncle." It wasn't that more of the nation hadn't grasped the value of being in a classroom. Between 1967 and 2012, the ranks of US adults with at least a four-year college degree rose from 13 percent to 32 percent, "a remarkable upgrading in the skills of America's workers," as a study by Carnevale has described it. Yet even when you added up all of those with four-year college diplomas, two-year associate degrees, and postsecondary vocational certificates, it still came out to less than half of the working-age population. Making things worse, many big companies—even while complaining about a "skills gap"—had stopped trying to develop their people. While both white- and blue-collar workers received on-the-job training as a matter of course in the 1950s and '60s, surveys now indicated that anywhere from about 50 percent to 80 percent of American employees got nothing of the sort.

For most of those without the right credentials, the only option was to try to make it amid a decidedly low-wage landscape, one now dominated by poorly paying service providers. In 1960, eleven of the fifteen biggest employers in the country made things, led by GM, with nearly 600,000 workers. By 2010, only four manufacturers were in the top fifteen; the rest were in services, including not only Wal-Mart but also McDonald's, Yum Brands (the parent of Taco Bell, KFC, and Pizza Hut), Target, and CVS. These occupations "are crucial to the support and growth of major industries across the country," officials at the San Francisco Federal Reserve said, "but many of these workers do not earn enough to adequately support their families, even at a subsistence level."

Yet for Lee Scott, paying more and offering larger benefits would have undercut Wal-Mart's reason for being. If "we raised prices substantially to fund above-market wages," he said, "we'd betray our commitment to tens of millions of customers, many of whom struggle to make ends meet."

Others, though, didn't buy it. "Being able to purchase groceries 20 percent cheaper at Wal-Mart," said Paul Samuelson, who is regarded as the father of modern economics, "does not necessarily make up for the wage losses." Besides, this wasn't the only way to do business. Some retailers had an alternate approach—most notably Costco, which paid an average of seventeen dollars an hour in 2005, more than 40 percent higher than the average wage at Wal-Mart's Sam's Club, its closest rival. What's more, a much bigger proportion of Costco workers had medical coverage and retirement plans than did their counterparts at Wal-Mart, and these benefits were far superior. After four and a half years, a full-time Costco worker would earn more than $46,000 a year; a full-time Sam's Club worker made $27,000. "We're not the Little Sisters of the Poor," said Jim Sinegal, Costco's longtime CEO. "This is good business."

By investing in his employees, Sinegal knew, they were bound to give excellent service to the company's customers, which helped to drive satisfaction and sales. "It starts with a living wage and affordable quality health benefits," said Richard Galanti, the chief financial officer at Costco, whose stock price would greatly outperform Wal-Mart's through most of the 2000s and beyond. "That's the initial basis for engagement."

Across most of the American economy, however, Costco has very much been the exception; Wal-Mart, the rule.

E conomically, the new century began with a whimper, as two recessions pummeled America within the first ten years.

The first slump, which began in March 2001, was a surprise to many. Even with all of the downsizing that had taken place during the 1990s, the Clinton expansion had gone on so long, it convinced some in Washington that they had—by virtue of their astute handling of fiscal and monetary policy—rendered the nation forever safe from any more broad-based economic declines. Theirs was a cocksureness akin to what President Kennedy's aides had exhibited in the early 1960s, though this latest exuberance was heightened by all of the dot-coms that had sprouted up during the mid-to-late nineties. The Internet seemed to be fundamentally remaking the way that one industry after another went about its work, spurring productivity that would result in widely shared prosperity. "The New Economy represented . . . a shift from the production of goods to the production of ideas, entailing the processing of information, not of people or inventories," Joseph Stiglitz, the chairman of President Clinton's Council of Economic Advisers, has written. "The New Economy also promised the end of the business cycle, the ups and downs that had, until now, always been part of capitalism, as new information technologies allowed businesses to better control their inventories."

But the bubble burst, as it inevitably does. A host of high-tech companies, many of which had been built largely on puffery, went under. Businesses, which had overinvested in IT, cut back. The stock market, which had become overinflated, tanked. As recessions go, this one was reasonably short (only eleven months long) and, according to some indicators, shallow. But it took the labor market an awfully long while to rebound completely—more than three years. Considering how slowly employment also had bounced back after the previous recession, a decade earlier, it was looking like "jobless recoveries" may have become the new normal.

The next economic upturn would last six years, but it wasn't the type of expansion that had nurtured and sustained the middle class in the decades after World War II. Corporate profits were strong, but total output was weak. Employment grew at less than a 1 percent annual rate, compared with the postwar average of 2.5 percent. Wages and salaries moved up at a rate just under 2 percent, half the postwar average. Few people, however, seemed to notice—or, if they did, to care—because one thing was going up and up and up: the value of their houses.

From 2000 through 2006, home prices increased across the country by more than 90 percent. In some places—Las Vegas, Phoenix, Miami—values more than doubled. It was the biggest housing boom in American history, and a cocktail of low interest rates and a growing populace had persuaded many in the industry that it might never end. For homebuyers, it was almost as easy to order up a mortgage as it was a Starbucks cappuccino, and many purchased properties far beyond what they could afford. It seems incontrovertible that lending money to people who don't have the means to pay it back is a stupid thing to do, but as Michael Lewis has detailed in his book *The Big Short*, those selling subprime mortgages operated by a different criterion: "You can keep on making these loans, just don't keep them on your books. Make the loans, then sell them off to the fixed income departments of big Wall Street investment banks, which will . . . package them into bonds and sell them to investors."

By the middle of 2007, the whole thing was toppling, sparking what would be the longest and most severe downturn since the Depression of the 1930s. The Great Recession began officially in December 2007; it ended in June 2009. But the worst was far from over. Nationwide, housing prices didn't bottom out until 2012, and by then they'd lost a third of their value from their pinnacle in 2006. In the interim, more than 4 million homes had been foreclosed upon.

The labor market was hit especially hard. The unemployment rate, which peaked at 10 percent in October 2009, was still sitting above 7 percent four years later. It would take six and a half years before all of the jobs that had been lost in the recession were regained. This was the most jobless of all the jobless recoveries yet. Of particular concern was the historically high number of Americans who were un-employed for six months or more, causing both their skills and feel-ings of self-worth to atrophy. Millions more "missing workers" left the labor force altogether. Growth in wages was modest, and five years into the recovery many workers—retail salespersons, waiters and wait-resses, food preparers, janitors, maids, and more—had actually seen their pay go down from where it had been when the economy had supposedly troughed. Many companies pulled back on their health care and retirement benefits, and it would take years to restore them to prerecession levels, if they ever got there.

The Great Recession was the proximate cause of much of this pain for workers, but in many ways the downturn had merely underlined deeper developments that had long been underway. "Arguably the most important economic trend in the United States over the past couple of generations has been the ever-more-distinct sorting of Americans into winners and losers, and the slow hollowing of the middle class," the journalist Don Peck has written. "For most of the aughts, that sorting was masked by the housing bubble, which allowed working-class and middle-class families to raise their standard of living despite income stagnation or downward job mobility. But the crash blew away that fig leaf. And the recession has pressed down hard on the vast class of Americans with moderate education and moderate skills."

It was difficult to find a company that the Great Recession hadn't touched. As most of the global economy tipped into crisis, Coca-Cola felt the effects of lower consumer spending; practically every region in the world was sick to some degree—be it the equivalent of "bad bron-chitis" or a "mild cold," said CEO Muhtar Kent. In response, Coke cut costs. But it also faced challenges beyond the ailing economy.

After Roberto Goizueta died in 1997, Coke's momentum faltered, and nobody seemed to have inherited his Midas touch; the company burned through two CEOs in just seven years—first Doug Ivester and then Douglas Daft. The latter had tried to right things in 2000 by im-plementing a restructuring, the likes of which Coke had never experi-enced before. Outside of its bottling network, the parent company had been able to preserve a familial spirit a lot longer than had most other American corporations. More concretely, Coke's employees had been spared from the mass layoffs that had punished their peers at General Electric, General Motors, Kodak, and so many other businesses during the 1980s and '90s. "At Coke," said Neville Isdell, a top executive who had joined the company in 1966, "a job had almost always meant a job for life." Not any more. Even at Coca-Cola, a social contract based on loyalty between employer and employee was now a thing of the past.

Daft's overhaul called for getting rid of more than 5,000 jobs out of a global workforce of 30,000. About half the pink slips were handed out at Coke's Atlanta headquarters. Entire departments, including payroll and building and grounds, were outsourced. Some employees, based abroad, were fired by voice-mail message. Many middle managers lost their stock options. "What that says to the remaining employees is, 'It doesn't matter what kind of job I do. We're all susceptible,'" remarked one executive who was let go. "It was cutting to the quick." People started calling the CEO "Daft the Knife."

The company, in the meantime, had its own harsh label to contend with: racist. In 1999, four current and former employees sued Coke, alleging disparities between whites and blacks in their promotions, performance evaluations, dismissals, and pay. The median annual salary for African Americans at the company was about $36,000 compared with $65,000 for whites. Some 2,000 employees soon became part of the class-action case. "In 114 years, you've only had one black senior vice president," Larry Jones, who had been a benefits manager at Coke, told Daft in April 2000 at the corporate annual meeting, where he led a delegation of protestors. "In 114 years, you only found one of us qualified? How long do we wait?"

In November, the company settled the suit for $192 million—about $40,000 per plaintiff—the most ever in a discrimination case. Even more extraordinary was that Coke agreed to have a panel of outside experts regularly review its pay and promotion practices, thereby ensuring that the company was making the necessary changes to truly become a place of equal opportunity. Managers' compensation was now tied to diversity goals. "The internal cultures of companies have been built on patterns of exclusion based on gender and race," said the Reverend Jesse Jackson, who had first condemned Coke's civil-rights record back in the early 1980s and had again voiced his disapproval of the soda giant after the latest lawsuit was filed. "This is a step in the right direction."

Most other corporations remained two steps behind. In 2014, minorities would make up 37 percent of workers at larger companies—but only 13 percent of executives and senior managers. African Americans accounted for about 15 percent of the workforce at these companies, but a mere 3 percent were executives and only 7 percent had reached middle management.

In the five decades since Walter Reuther had marched with Martin Luther King Jr. and riots had convulsed Rochester and other cities around America, you could make the argument that the nation had bent slowly toward racial justice. The black middle class had expanded fivefold since the early 1960s, and the share of African Americans with a college degree had more than tripled, to 22 percent. In 2008, an African American was elected president of the United States for the first time, and in 2012 Barack Obama would be reelected. But many other measures were troubling: blacks still earned about 25 percent less than whites on average and were twice as likely to be unemployed. In an economy now split between good-paying knowledge work and poor-paying service work, African Americans were clustered disproportionately at the low end. Blacks who grew up in middle-class families were apt to slide down the socioeconomic spectrum far more easily than were whites. Despite the educational strides that the community had made, black college graduates had a much harder time finding work than whites did, and when well-educated African Americans were employed, they were compensated badly. Hispanics, for their part, had to overcome comparable discrimination in the workplace.

Women were up against their own barriers. They had continued to pour into the labor force, so that by 2015 they would make up nearly half of it, a sharp increase from less than 30 percent in 1950. They were now earning about 80 percent of what men did, versus 60 percent fifty years earlier. But the pace of change had slowed. By 2000, the growth of women in the workforce had leveled off, and the pay gap stopped shrinking much. For many the glass ceiling never cracked, much less shattered. In 2014, less than 30 percent of the executives and senior managers at bigger companies were women. Of the 500 largest companies in the country, just twenty-one had a female CEO.

There were all kinds of theories for why women were still being held back, most of which could be condensed to a single word: sexism. One sociologist, for instance, found that women's pay got cut when they had children (because motherhood made them seem less committed to the job), while men were rewarded (because fatherhood made them seem more dependable and deserving). A woman's earnings, which were now often the same or even higher than those of her male colleagues when entering the workplace, tended to plateau by the time she was in her midthirties to midforties; men's salaries continued to climb. Another investigation showed that whenever a lot of women entered a field, the pay went down—for the very same work that men were doing in greater numbers before. Others pointed to surveys proving that men were just clueless; two-thirds thought that their female coworkers had equal opportunities on the job, making prejudice difficult to combat because it wasn't even recognized.

As for Coke, it would do much better than most employers, thanks to the goad of litigation. In 2000, just 8 percent of corporate officers had been racial and ethnic minorities, even though they constituted about a third of the company. By 2006, that was up to 22 percent. The share of women officers at Coke rose from 16 percent to 27 percent. The company's compensation system was also revamped to remove inequities.

The layoffs left their own mark. When Neville Isdell succeeded Daft as CEO, he found an "atmosphere of fear and disaffection" throughout Coca-Cola. He was able to revive employees' spirits before stepping down in 2008, however. And that cleared the way for Muhtar Kent, the next CEO, to map out a plan to double the size of Coke's business by 2020. To help meet his target—during a time when consumers were showing less and less appetite for sugary drinks, no less—Kent launched one of the most exhaustive leadership development programs in all of American industry. Still, even with that cultivation of talent, it wasn't as if Coke had resumed its old custom of giving a job for life. In 2015, as part of a multibillion-dollar cost-cutting bid, the company said it was severing about 1,700 white-collar positions, including 500 at headquarters. It was the largest reduction since the days of Daft.

The Great Recession also bruised Kodak. In late 2008, the company cited the "unprecedented amount of uncertainty surrounding the economic environment" before suspending its wage dividend for the first time since the Great Depression. But the truth was, Kodak had been trapped in a downward spiral for decades before the economy went sour. George Fisher, who bowed out as CEO in 2000, had done all he could to try to speed the company's transition to the world of digital photography. So had his two successors. But none of them got nearly far enough fast enough. In 2007, the company moved into the printer business, excited that its scientists had invented a pigment-based ink that didn't clog the nozzles of printing heads. It was an impressive innovation but didn't turn things around. Kodak lost money in 2008, 2009, 2010, and 2011. In 2012, it filed for bankruptcy. The judge who was in charge of Kodak's reorganization under Chapter 11 called the company's collapse "a tragedy of American economic life."

It was also a good reminder that the social contract between employer and employee can only function when a company is doing well. An unprofitable business isn't a stable place to work. By the time it emerged from bankruptcy in 2013, with a focus on commercial printing, Kodak employed fewer than 9,000 people worldwide, down from more than 50,000 in 2005 and 128,000 in 1980. In Rochester, just a couple of thousand folks were now left working for Kodak, barely a blip when compared with the 60,000-plus it employed there thirty years earlier. The company also ended health-care coverage for its 56,000 retirees and their dependents. Many lost their pensions as well.

Rochester's civic leaders expressed hope that the city, with its world-class universities and castoffs from Kodak, would become a breeding ground for a new crop of technology companies. And to some extent, their vision has been fulfilled, with young companies producing advanced manufacturing materials, chemicals, and more. But with Kodak in such a diminished state, others have bemoaned that the bountiful blue-collar work that so many locals once thrived upon—and which ranked Rochester near the top of American cities with the highest-wage jobs—was now gone and never coming back. "Good jobs," said Jennifer Leonard, president of the Rochester Area Community Foundation, have largely been overtaken by "service jobs that don't have benefits and don't pay well."

Of all the companies in America, General Motors was among those that the Great Recession rocked the most. The outcome was all the more heartbreaking because, for a time, it seemed like GM might finally have clawed past the calamities that the company had suffered during the 1980s and early '90s. In 1994, *Fortune* praised Jack Smith for having rescued GM and said that the company's "best days lie ahead."

And for a while, few could have taken issue with the magazine's assessment. The company remained profitable through the late 1990s, and even after the terrorist attacks of September 11, 2001.

Smith's successor, Rick Wagoner, displayed a willingness to tackle some of GM's long-unattended-to troubles, including closing its failing Oldsmobile division. At a company notorious for moving too slowly, Wagoner put in place a program called "Go Fast" to unclog snarls in the system. Under him, GM also showed another attribute that it was not known for in the past: humility. "Ten years ago we had a choice," the company said in a 2003 advertising blitz. "We could keep looking in the rearview mirror, or out at the road ahead. It was the easiest decision we ever made. The hard part meant breaking out of our own bureaucratic gridlock. Learning some humbling lessons from our competitors."

Before long, however, GM under Wagoner reverted to its old habits: proceeding tentatively, becoming too insular, not picking up swiftly enough on what car buyers wanted—more hybrids, fewer Hummers. The good years had fooled many into thinking that GM was in fine shape, but it never really had been. "If you're bleeding from the capillaries it's hard to notice," said Paul O'Neill, the former US treasury secretary, who served on the GM board during the mid-1990s. By 2005, GM was bleeding from everywhere. It lost more than $10 billion that year, as it fought a losing battle to contain costs while Toyota and other foreign automakers siphoned market share. The company reacted by announcing a new series of cuts, including the shutdown of all or parts of twelve factories in North America and the elimination of 30,000 more jobs.

By 2007, things were so bleak that the United Auto Workers agreed to historic compromises. In September, the union had undertaken its first nationwide strike against GM since 1970. But with no muscles to flex, it ended the walkout just two days later. The UAW then consented to the establishment of a two-tier wage structure under which many new hourly hires would earn half as much as current workers. These second-class employees would find themselves living in a way that autoworkers never had before—paycheck to paycheck. Their pension and health benefits also were curtailed. The Jobs Bank was trimmed back. And, in the most consequential part of the agreement, the union accepted that GM would no longer be responsible for blue-collar retirees' medical care. Instead, the company would put a capped amount into a union-controlled trust, and at that point GM was off the hook from any further obligations. If people's future health needs couldn't be met, that wasn't the company's worry anymore; it was the trust's, the UAW's, and the retirees'.

At first, the UAW was skeptical that GM's finances were as bad as the company claimed. But GM was happy to open its books—the very thing it had refused to do in the mid-1940s, when Walter Reuther was trying to draw attention to the company's amazing wealth—so as to make transparent how incredibly strapped it was now. "We showed these guys that the goose that laid the golden egg was about to die," remembered Kent Kresa, a GM board member. Yet even if the UAW had no alternative, it didn't lessen the magnitude of the moment. By acquiescing to the company's transfer of tens of billions of dollars in health-care liabilities, it revealed just how tattered the old employer-employee compact had become. The headline in the progressive publication *In These Times* said it all: "Treaty of Detroit Repealed."

As the recession deepened, things got worse for GM, which not only wasn't selling enough cars but also had exposure through its financing arm to the sinking home-mortgage market. In late 2008, as the Bush administration extended more than $13 billion in financing to GM as part of its bailout of the auto industry, Wagoner pledged to repair the company "once and for all." But he wouldn't get the chance. In March 2009, the Obama administration pushed him out as CEO. In June of that year, GM filed for bankruptcy.

The company would exit bankruptcy, lightning fast, a little more than a month later. It was now in a form that the Obama auto-industry task force liked to call "Shiny New GM." The company's debt had been sliced by more than 70 percent, and it had far fewer factories, brands, dealers, and employees to manage. In the United States, only 69,000 workers remained at GM—down about 90 percent from the late 1970s.

Even with a lower-wage tier, a GM job was still attractive in a service-heavy economy, and many felt lucky to get hired there. Debbie Werner earned about seventeen dollars an hour installing parts on Chevys and Buicks—a lot better than the nine she was making as a nursing-home worker. David Ramirez pulled down more than eighteen bucks an hour on a GM transmission line, more than double the eight that Wal-Mart had been paying him. Over the next few years, GM would only get stronger. A new CEO, Mary Barra, who had been with GM for more than three decades and was the daughter of a Pontiac die maker, won high marks for restraining costs, making the company's products more appealing, and holding employees more accountable. Her strategy was refreshingly simple: "No more crappy cars." By 2015, GM was doing well enough that it would end the two-tier wage and benefit system and give its more experienced workers their first raises since 2007. Profit-sharing bonuses were becoming routine.

Nevertheless, none of this suggested a return to the age of "Generous Motors," as GM had once been called. It would now take eight years for an hourly worker to reach top pay, instead of the three that it used to. The average wage for a factory worker at the company would be lower, in real terms, in 2019 than it had been in the 1990s or 2000s. And it was up to the union trust, not GM, to deal with the multibillion-dollar shortfall projected for blue-collar retirees' health care. The company also halted medical coverage for about 100,000 white-collar retirees—a big step beyond the cutbacks seen in the Sprague case—and it tried to buy out many of their pensions as well, in an attempt to save tens of billions of dollars more. "Everybody is trying to run leaner now," said David Cole, president emeritus of the Center for Automotive Research. "GM is not unique."

To many observers, such changes were long overdue, and if GM executives had only had the courage to make them sooner the company might never have gone bust. Others had a different take. "That argument," said Rick Wagoner, "ignores the fact that American automakers and other traditional manufacturing companies created a social contract with the government and labor that raised America's standard of living and provided much of the economic growth of the twentieth century. American manufacturers were once held up as good corporate citizens for providing these benefits. Today, we are maligned for our poor judgment in 'giving away' such benefits forty years ago."

In early 2011, President Obama named Jeff Immelt, the CEO of General Electric, as the chairman of his new Council on Jobs and Competitiveness. At first blush, it seemed perfectly reasonable for the White House to seek guidance on stimulating employment from a group of businesspeople headed by the leader of one of America's marquee companies. With the labor market still so anemic, what could be bad about getting advice from somebody with 285,000 workers of his own?

But to many on both sides of the ideological divide, Immelt was the wrong guy to be the nation's "jobs czar." Whether it was liberal Sen. Russ Feingold and Progressives United or conservative talk-show host Bill O'Reilly and the Tea Party, their reproof was the same: Immelt's company was mostly interested in doing business abroad.

In some ways, the criticism was uncalled for. While the majority of GE's employees were now based outside the United States—150,000 international workers compared with 133,000 domestic ones—that was hardly out of the ordinary. Through the 2000s, US multinational corporations added a total of nearly 3 million workers in foreign locations while chopping their payrolls at home by more than 860,000. And while many companies (including GE) continued to shift some production to other countries so as to lighten their cost of labor, globetrotters like Immelt were going overseas mostly to make money, not just to save money; GE's fastest-growing markets were no longer in the United States. "We go to Brazil, we go to China, we go to India," said Immelt, who'd replaced Jack Welch in 2001, "because that's where the customers are."

If anything, Immelt had done more than most to bring new manufacturing jobs to America, as he reoriented GE back toward its roots of industrial engineering and away from financial engineering. This born-again transformation would culminate in 2015 as the company set out to sell most of GE Capital, its finance unit—a divestiture that, in the view of many, signaled that Immelt was finally stepping out from Welch's long shadow. Along the way, GE reinvested in factories in Louisville, Schenectady, and other long-beleaguered towns. It was enough for some to submit that the United States was experiencing a full-blown manufacturing resurgence, especially with China's own labor costs increasing fast.

But this was a pipe dream, at least as far as creating lots of new jobs was concerned. Because of automation and the mix of goods being produced, US manufacturers had no use for anywhere near as many workers as they did from the 1950s through the 1970s—even though the nation's industrial output was actually much higher now. What once took 1,000 people to make could be cranked out these days by less than 200. "We need to get real about the so-called renaissance, which has in reality been a trickle of jobs," said Steven Rattner, who ran President Obama's auto-industry team.

To knock Immelt for any of this—for not having enough employees in the United States, for having too many across the sea—was to imply that the economy now behaved just as it had decades earlier. But this wasn't Ralph Cordiner's time or Reg Jones's, or even Jack Welch's. When Immelt came to the company in 1982, GE derived 80 percent of its revenue from within the United States. Now, 60 percent came from elsewhere. By 2016, 70 percent would. "I run an American company," Immelt said. "But in order for GE to be successful in the coming years, I've gotta sell my products in every corner of the world." If not, he added, "we'd have tens of thousands fewer employees in Pennsylvania, Ohio, Massachusetts, Texas. I'm never going to apologize for that, ever, ever."

And yet, as much as one might be willing to abide Immelt's embrace of becoming a "complete globalist," as he termed it, there were still plenty of other reasons to question his appointment as job czar. They might start with how GE was pushing workers at some of its factories to accept a two-tier wage structure, with new hires earning as little as $25,000 a year, while veterans took a pay freeze. Or how the company had closed its guaranteed pension plan to new white-collar employees—even though it was fully funded and could meet its obligations—giving them only the option of a 401(k). Or how it had changed its health coverage for salaried personnel to make them more responsible for the cost of their own care. Or how it no longer would provide supplemental medical insurance for its retirees older than sixty-five. Or how, while wearing down workers in all of these ways, it had done its best to take care of investors by buying back tens of billions of dollars worth of its own stock so as to attempt to raise the value of its shares.

On the other hand, all of the above was standard stuff for American business at this point: crimping workers' pay, reining in medical coverage, gutting retirement benefits. If President Obama had tried to find a jobs czar from a leading corporation that didn't do most of these things, he might have been hard-pressed to come up with a candidate. All of the trends that had started to sap workers' sense of security in the 1970s and '80s, and that had picked up in the '90s, were continuing apace through the 2000s. By now, the social contract for most employees was basically kaput—and it didn't matter what kind of company you were talking about, be it one with a history of troubles, like GM or Kodak, or one that had remained strong over a very long period of time, like Coca-Cola or GE. The story was pretty much the same everywhere.

For Immelt, the right way to think about people now seemed to lie out in Silicon Valley, where they practiced what he called "the essence of modern talent development." These were the words that Immelt used in endorsing a book called *The Alliance*, written by three California entrepreneurs, including Reid Hoffman, one of the founders of LinkedIn, the online social network for professionals.

"The old model of employment was a good fit for an era of stability," Hoffman and his coauthors, Ben Casnocha and Chris Yeh, declared. "In that era, careers were considered nearly as permanent as marriage." But such a construct, they said, was "too rigid" for today's highly dynamic world.

What the authors urged, instead, was that employees sign up for a "tour of duty," where it was spelled out what they were supposed to contribute over a prescribed period and what they'd gain in return, including skills and relationships. Toward the end of the tour, the employer and employee would discuss what should happen next— whether it was a new round at the company or a new job somewhere else. "Acknowledging that the employee might leave," they wrote, "is actually the best way to build trust."

This concept wasn't new. For high-tech companies, "taking time off between jobs, moving from one company to another and then back again, and job-hopping in general are a way of life," Paul Leinberger and Bruce Tucker noted in 1991 in *The New Individualists: The Generation After the Organization Man*. Still, it wasn't hard to see why tech was so intriguing, especially for an executive like Immelt, who was betting big on turning GE into a digital powerhouse in its own right. He wanted his employees to be more comfortable taking risks and making mistakes—as long as they learned from them.

Silicon Valley seemed to be the one place where workers could find "purpose, freedom, and creativity," as Google's Laszlo Bock summed up the goals for his company. Depending on the employer, there could be more or less stress involved. Either way, there were invariably great perquisites—a twenty-first-century version of welfare capitalism, with climbing walls, free life coaching, and complimentary sushi in the cafeteria.

Yet as cool as companies like Google, Apple, Amazon, and Facebook were as employers—and as much joy as they'd given us as knowledge seekers and music fans, shoppers, and social animals—they weren't job engines in the way that the big manufacturers once were. All combined, those four companies would employ about 300,000 people in the United States in 2015, less than half of what General Motors alone did in the late 1970s.

Software really was "eating the world," as venture capitalist Marc Andreessen said. But software developers weren't. The Labor Department counted a little more than 1 million Americans with such jobs in 2015—and they were terrific if you had the skills to get one, paying more than $100,000 a year on average. By comparison, there were more than 4.5 million people in retail sales, 3.5 million cashiers, 3 million food-service workers, 2.5 million waiters and waitresses, and 2 million secretaries and janitors. All of those jobs paid less than $27,000 a year.

"When George Eastman had a fantastic idea for photography, he got quite rich, and the city of Rochester became a flourishing city for generations, supporting thousands of middle-class workers," said Larry Summers, the former treasury secretary. "When Steve Jobs had remarkable ideas, he and his colleagues made a very large fortune, but there was much less left over—there was no flourishing middle class that followed in their wake."

Not everyone was ready to let the old social contract perish without a fight. Dennis Rocheleau, who was GE's labor relations chief under Jack Welch and then under Immelt before retiring in 2004, thought he might be able to prevail upon the company to reconsider its cutting of retiree medical benefits. Rocheleau wasn't concerned that he himself couldn't come up with the extra cash he'd now need to augment his Medicare coverage. As a top GE executive, he had made good money during his career—enough to fly back and forth between two residences: one in Connecticut and another in his home state of Wisconsin, a lakeside house filled with so many magnificent modern prints and crafts that it could have passed for a small museum. In addition, Rocheleau was still in good enough health in his early seventies that he would only be out about $1,000 a year because of the changes that GE was initiating.

But he worried that others among GE's 50,000-plus salaried retirees and their spouses, who were sicker and more reliant on this supplemental insurance, would be hurt much worse. In time, GE would institute the same cuts for its hourly retirees. "The people they're taking it from are the ones who can afford it the least," Rocheleau said. Beyond that, there was something else gnawing at him: GE had gone back on a promise. And that, he'd been taught, was never okay.

Rocheleau grew up in the Wisconsin town of Two Rivers, where his dad worked in a wood-products factory. He went on to Northwestern University on a full scholarship, and then Harvard Law. Long fascinated by industrial relations, he joined GE as a junior union negotiator a couple of years before the ultimate flashpoint: the 1969 strike. When it was finally over and Lem Boulware's formulation for beating down organized labor had been done away with, Rocheleau was pleased. GE's insistence that the unions "take it or leave it" had never sat well with Rocheleau's blue-collar pedigree. "I was schooled in Boulwarism," he said, "but graduated to a better place: the land of the negotiated settlement."

Over the next thirty-five years, as he moved up the organization, Rocheleau showed himself to be a hard bargainer. He was GE's top labor-relations executive when the unions walked out in 2003—the first national work stoppage at the company since '69. The key issue at the time: GE's attempt to have its hourly workers assume more of their health-care costs. "We are not advocates for mushy labor-management cooperation," Rocheleau once told an industry group. "We believe that there are conflicting interests within our industrial society and that the use of adversarial representation to accommodate those interests has been effective."

But once a contract was hammered out, Rocheleau did everything he could to ensure that the company made good on its word. As time went on, GE's unions weren't nearly the force that they once were. When Rocheleau started at the company, more than 140,000 employees were covered by collective bargaining agreements. When he retired, that was all the way down to 24,000, on its way to just 16,000 in 2015. But Rocheleau respected the union leaders that he jousted with, and he wanted them to respect him. "I always maintained that at GE, promises made were promises kept," he said. Rocheleau also took pride in another thing: speaking his mind. "I could have ass-kissed my way to success," he said. He chose not to and became well known among GE executives for his frankness.

Initially, Rocheleau had hoped that he would be able to remedy the retiree medical situation quietly. He wrote to Immelt in late 2012, telling him that "my faith in GE's expressed values has been seriously diminished," while also assuring him that he would contest the company "in a responsibly measured manner." "This isn't just another instance of 'Rocheleau going rogue,'" he said. He counseled restraint in others as well. When a retiree spokesman wanted to go to the company's annual meeting and publicly embarrass Immelt by asking him what the health-care cuts would mean for the CEO's father, who himself had worked at GE for forty years, Rocheleau got him to back off.

But Immelt never replied to Rocheleau's letter. In 2013 and again in 2014, Rocheleau spoke out at the annual meeting, saying that the company had "turned its back on its traditions" and that "morality and integrity must outweigh legality and ability if you are going to make a long-term, mutually beneficial relationship." Six months after the second meeting, Rocheleau sued GE—a case that, as of late 2016, was still pending.

As a senior manager at the company for so many years, Rocheleau knew full well why this was happening to its retirees: financial considerations were now preeminent, as GE made plain when it booked more than $4.5 billion in savings by dropping its post-sixty-five health-care obligations. But this was gravy. GE wasn't in terrible straits. The enterprise was profitable. It was nice to be able to tidy up the balance sheet like this. "But look," said Rocheleau, "a deal is a deal."

As he made that comment, he stood beside a beautiful metal grate that had come from an old GE administration office in Schenectady. Along with all of his art, Rocheleau had integrated into his house a bunch of this industrial flotsam, which he had bought from the company as it tore down different buildings. "They just destroy stuff," he said. "They have very little reverence for history."

C an the American corporate social contract ever be reconstructed? The short answer is no—at least not in the way it was before. The Golden Age was sui generis, and too much has changed since then.

Some unions and other labor groups are using online technology to organize employees and give them new tools to stand up for their rights, while helping to finance valuable campaigns for low-wage workers such as the Fight for $15. Still, we'll never again see private-sector unionization rates—and the potency that comes from widespread collective bargaining—like we had in the 1950s or '60s. Our economy isn't built for that anymore.

We must also accept that if artificial intelligence displaces masses of workers—and it well may, particularly those with few skills—we shouldn't try to stand in its way. If the economy is going to continue to grow, we must have technological progress. We shouldn't try to stop international commerce, either. It, too, is essential to our long-term economic growth, and trade restrictions won't be effective anyway. A third of the components used in products made in America are imported from overseas. Plus, the flow of goods is flattening while the flow of data, zipping invisibly across borders, is swelling.

What's required now is a new social contract that takes into account these realities.

The government has an enormous part to play. We need a higher federal minimum wage and, in our most expensive cities, a true living wage. Although organized labor won't recapture its former prominence, Washington needs to make it easier for workers to unionize. We need paid family leave. We need stricter enforcement of labor standards to help workers fend off wage theft—the denial of pay and benefits rightly owed them—and other violations, especially at a time when so much of the nation's employment is being generated among temps, freelancers, and others in contingent jobs. We need to expand the Earned Income Tax Credit.

We need portable benefits for Uber drivers and other "gig workers"—a still small but increasingly important segment of the labor market. We need the government to better support technological innovation and create an environment that fosters entrepreneurship, which, despite the radiance from Silicon Valley, has been at a low ebb in America for the past thirty years. We need the Federal Reserve to make full employment a priority.

And although it is easy to dismiss as a bromide, we really do need to revitalize public education from top to bottom.

We also need changes to our tax laws and accounting standards so that executives are induced to look beyond their company's quarterly earnings and daily share price. We need institutional investors to exhort corporations to keep sight of the long term, and not just pay attention to results in the short term.

But more than anything, we need to recognize that the social contract between employer and employee won't be strong unless our business leaders want it to be so.

"Companies once felt an obligation to support American workers, even when it wasn't the best financial choice," said Betsey Stevenson, who was chief economist at the Labor Department from 2010 to 2011. "That's disappeared. Profits and efficiency have trumped generosity."

We can't mandate that executives think the way they used to. We can't demand that they alter the norms by which they operate and—like the generation of executives who'd come through the crucible of the Great Depression and World War II—suddenly make it more about "we" and less about "I." We can't force them to invest in their workers through more training and higher compensation and stronger job security.

We—as employees and as consumers—can only encourage them to realize that corporate America's continuing fixation with putting shareholders above everyone else is ultimately bad for their companies. "A healthy business," wrote Peter Drucker, "cannot exist in a sick society." Restoring more balance between worker and investor would be a welcome balm.

A few may be starting to get it. Wal-Mart, of all companies, made *Fortune* magazine's Change the World list for 2016. It was so honored for raising its workers' pay to an average of $13.38 an hour and enrolling half a million employees in a curriculum "designed to teach job skills that could help them climb the income ladder."

And yet there is much, much more that Wal-Mart and many other corporations can do, and must do, if we are to come to grips with the most pressing issue of our time: distributing the nation's economic gains more broadly.

"The American people have continued up to now to tolerate abuses that have developed in our economic system because . . . they believe it can be made to work for the good of all," one business leader avowed. "They see in it a chance for a better life for themselves. Almost unanimously, they want it for their sons and daughters.

"Most Americans," he added, "would agree on the economic goals for America: a community permanently rich in opportunity and security."

More than seventy years after William Benton, vice chairman of the Committee for Economic Development, made that statement, it would be difficult to argue that our goals are any different today. What has corroded, sadly, is the underlying belief that the system can be made to work for the good of all.

ACKNOWLEDGMENTS

"Nobody can do it for you," Ralph Cordiner, the long-ago CEO of General Electric, remarked when discussing the need for business executives to develop their leadership skills. The same could certainly be said of authors, who must rely on a huge reservoir of self-motivation to take an idea for a narrative, flesh it out through many years of research and rumination, and then shape it onto the page.

Yet, as solitary as this pursuit is, no writer goes it alone.

This is my third book for PublicAffairs, and I can't imagine being at any other publisher. The house's commitment to telling the most important stories in the most engaging ways is all too rare. I will always be grateful to Peter Osnos and Susan Weinberg for bringing me in, and to Clive Priddle for keeping me around.

This book is undoubtedly better because of my editor, Ben Adams. He pushed on just the right spots, which is no small talent. I hope we'll get to collaborate again.

My longtime agent, Kris Dahl, is simply the best in the business. I am lucky to have her.

My mom, mother-in-law, two amazing kids, and friends—including Jeff Strauss and Mindy Schultheis, Erica and John Huggins, Mark Arax, Ellie Herman and David Levinson, Kathryn Kranhold and Lisa Banes, Kevin Conran, and Barry Greenberg—have never failed to ask me, with genuine curiosity and affection, "How's the book going?" And considering that I began this project back in 2009, that's a lot of asking. Their love and support have been sustaining.

No book like this can succeed without the ability to travel extensively to hunt through archives, transcribe endless hours of interviews, and purchase a library's worth of source material. You've got to have the stuff. Jeff and Madeleine Moskowitz helped to make that possible. I can't thank them enough for their generosity.

My colleagues at the Drucker Institute, now led by Zach First, have also been unfailingly supportive. Their passion for our mission—strengthening organizations to strengthen society—is an inspiration, and I hope that they will see some of that same spirit reflected in this work. Bridget Lawlor, the institute's archivist, deserves special thanks for the countless times she tracked down an article or congressional testimony for me, often at a moment's notice. "Can you just grab this one, too" are words that she will surely be delighted not to hear again. (At least not until my next book.)

Bryan Price, my researcher, provided excellent assistance along the way.

And then there were my readers. Paul Adler, my friend and a leading management scholar, furnished thoughts on some of the early chapters that helped to make the book stronger. The economist Jared Bernstein also shared valuable insights on pieces of the manuscript. And Anne Reifenberg, my dear friend and one of the most gifted editors I know, put her sharp eyes on every word.

No one, though, did more to nurture this book than my wife and best friend, Randye Hoder. One of the smartest and most widely read people I know, she pored over every chapter and offered the keenest criticism. At the same time, she has always been my most enthusiastic cheerleader. This book wouldn't be what it is without her. Neither would I.

A final note, in the interest of full disclosure: because of my position at the Drucker Institute, I've worked closely with a good many companies and executives, and some of them are part of this story. Former Coca-Cola executive Jack Bergstrand, who is a main character in chapter 9, is a personal friend, as well as a board member of and major donor to the Drucker Institute. Bill Casey, who is also quoted in chapter 9, has been a financial supporter of the institute. And the late Don Keough, Coca-Cola's former president, served on the Drucker Institute board before he died in 2015. Finally, the Drucker Institute at one point explored a business partnership with the Jack Welch Management Institute. But it didn't go anywhere.

A NOTE ON CITATIONS AND SOURCING

Because of the extensiveness of the endnotes, they are being published online. You can access them at www.hachettebookgroup.com/features /publicaffairs/endofloyalty.

BIBLIOGRAPHY

The books listed are those used by the author, not necessarily the original editions, so that the page numbers cited in the endnotes will correspond. An asterisk (*) indicates that this book was accessed through Google Play, which can affect the page numbers cited.

Abraham, Katharine G., James R. Spletzer, and Michael J. Harper. *Labor in the New Economy*. Chicago: University of Chicago Press, 2010.

*Ackerman, Carl W. *George Eastman: Founder of Kodak and the Photography Business*. Boston: Houghton Mifflin, 1930.

Alinsky, Saul D. *Rules for Radicals: A Pragmagtic Primer for Realistic Radicals*. New York: Vintage Books, 1989.

Allen, Frederick. *Secret Formula: How Brilliant Marketing and Relentless Salesmanship Made Coca-Cola the Best-Known Product in the World*. New York: Harper Business, 1994.

Allen, Frederick Lewis. *The Big Change: America Transforms Itself: 1900–1950*. New Brunswick, NJ: Transaction Publishers, 1993.

*Aronowitz, Stanley. *False Promises: The Shaping of American Working Class Consciousness*. Durham, NC: Duke University Press, 1992.

———. *From the Ashes of the Old: American Labor and America's Future*. New York: Basic Books, 1998.

Atleson, James B. *Labor and the Wartime State: Labor Relations and Law During World War II*. Urbana, IL: University of Illinois Press, 1998.

Aurand, Harold W. *Coalcracker Culture: Work and Values in Pennsylvania Anthracite, 1835–1935*. Selinsgrove, PA: Susquehanna University Press, 2003.

Bailey, Stephen Kemp. *Congress Makes a Law: The Story Behind the Employment Act of 1946*. New York: Vintage Books, 1950.

Baldwin, Richard. *The Great Convergence: Information Technology and the New Globalization*. Cambridge, MA: Belknap Press, 2016.

Bar-Haim, Aviad. *Participation Programs in Work Organizations: Past, Present, and Scenarios for the Future*. Westport, CT: Quorum Books, 2002.

Barabba, Vincent P. *Surviving Transformation: Lessons from GM's Surprising Turnaround*. New York: Oxford University Press, 2004.

Barker, Kathleen, and Kathleen Christensen, eds. *Contingent Work: American Employment Relations in Transition*. Ithaca, NY: Cornell University Press, 1998.

Barnard, John. *American Vanguard: The United Auto Workers During the Reuther Years, 1935–1970*. Detroit: Wayne State University Press, 2004.

*Baumol, William J., Alan S. Blinder, and Edward N. Wolff. *Downsizing in America: Reality, Causes, and Consequences*. New York: Russell Sage Foundation, 2003.

Bebchuk, Lucian, and Jesse Fried. *Pay Without Performance: The Unfulfilled Promise of Executive Compensation*. Cambridge, MA: Harvard University Press, 2004.

Bell, Daniel. *The Coming of Post-Industrial Society: A Venture in Social Forecasting*. New York: Basic Books, 1973.

*Bellah, Robert N., Richard Madsen, William M. Sullivan, Ann Swidler, and Steven M. Tipton. *Habits of the Heart: Individualism and Commitment in American Life*. Berkeley, CA: University of California Press, 1985.

Bennett, Amanda. *The Death of the Organization Man: What Happens When the New Economic Realities Change the Rules for Survival at Your Company*. New York: Touchstone, 1990.

*Berle, Adolf A., and Gardiner C. Means. *The Modern Corporation and Private Property*. New Brunswick, NJ: Transaction Publishers, 1991.

Bernstein, Irving. *The Turbulent Years: A History of the American Worker, 1933–1940*. Chicago: Haymarket Books, 2010.

Bernstein, Jared. *The Reconnection Agenda: Reuniting Growth and Prosperity*. Amazon Digital Services, 2015.

Bessen, James. *Learning by Doing: The Real Connection Between Innovation, Wages, and Wealth*. New Haven, CT: Yale University Press, 2015.

*Bhagwati, Jagdish. *In Defense of Globalization*. New York: Oxford University Press, 2004.

*Biven, W. Carl. *Jimmy Carter's Economy: Policy in an Age of Limits*. Chapel Hill, NC: University of North Carolina Press, 2002.

*Blackwelder, Julia Kirk. *Electric City: General Electric in Schenectady*. College Station, TX: Texas A&M University Press, 2014.

Blair, Margaret M., ed. *The Deal Decade: What Takeovers and Leveraged Buyouts Mean for Corporate Governance*. Washington, DC: Brookings Institution, 1993.

Blair, Margaret M., and Thomas A. Kochan, eds. *The New Relationship: Human Capital in the American Corporation.* Washington, DC: Brookings Institution, 2000.

*Blanding, Michael. *The Coke Machine: The Dirty Truth Behind the World's Favorite Soft Drink.* New York: Penguin Group, 2010.

*Blinder, Alan S. *Economic Policy and the Great Stagflation.* New York: Academic Press, 1979.

*———, ed. *Paying for Productivity: A Look at the Evidence.* Washington, DC: Brookings Institution, 1990.

Bluestone, Barry, and Irving Bluestone. *Negotiating the Future: A Labor Perspective on American Business.* New York: Basic Books, 1992.

*Bock, Laszlo. *Work Rules! Insights from Inside Google That Will Transform How You Live and Lead.* New York: Hachette Book Group, 2015.

Boulware, Lemuel R. *The Truth About Boulwarism: Trying to Do Right Voluntarily.* Washington, DC: Bureau of National Affairs, 1969.

Boyle, Kevin, ed. *Organized Labor and American Politics, 1894–1994.* Albany, NY: State University of New York Press, 1998.

———. *The UAW and the Heyday of American Liberalism, 1945–1968.* Ithaca, NY: Cornell University Press, 1995.

*Branch, Taylor. *Pillar of Fire: America in the King Years, 1963–65.* New York: Simon & Schuster, 1998.

Brandes, Stuart D. *American Welfare Capitalism, 1880–1940.* Chicago: University of Chicago Press, 1970.

Brayer, Elizabeth. *George Eastman: A Biography.* Rochester, NY: University of Rochester Press, 1996.

Brenner, Aaron, Benjamin Day, and Immanuel Ness, eds. *The Encyclopedia of Strikes in American History.* Armonk, NY: M.E. Sharpe, 2009.

Brenner, Robert. *The Economics of Global Turbulence: The Advanced Capitalist Economies from Long Boom to Long Downturn, 1945–2005.* London: Verso, 2006.

Brindle, Margret C., and Peter N. Stearns, *Facing Up to Management Faddism: A New Look at an Old Force.* Westport, CT: Greenwood Publishing, 2001.

Brinkley, Douglas. *Wheels for the World: Henry Ford, His Company, and a Century of Progress, 1903–2003.* New York: Viking, 2003.

Brown, Donaldson. *Some Reminiscences of an Industrialist.* Port Deposit, MD: Privately printed, 1957.

Bruner, Robert F. *Applied Mergers & Acquisitions.* Hoboken, NJ: John Wiley & Sons, 2004.

*Brynjolfsson, Erik, and Andrew McAfee. *Race Against the Machine: How the Digital Revolution Is Accelerating Innovation, Driving Productivity, and Irreversibly Transforming Employment and the Economy.* Lexington MA: Digital Frontier Press, 2011.

————. *The Second Machine Age: Work, Progress, and Prosperity in a Time of Brilliant Technologies*. New York: W.W. Norton, 2014.

*Buchholz, Todd G. *From Here to Economy: A Shortcut to Economic Literacy*. New York: Penguin Group, 1995.

*Buss, Terry F., and F. Stevens Redburn. *Shutdown at Youngstown: Public Policy for Mass Unemployment*. Albany, NY: State University of New York Press, 1983.

Cagan, Phillip, Marten Estey, William Fellner, Charles E. McLure Jr., and Thomas Gale Moore. *Economic Policy and Inflation in the Sixties*. Washington, DC: American Enterprise Institute, 1972.

*Cairncross, Alec, and Frances Cairncross. *The Legacy of the Golden Age: The 1960s and Their Economic Consequences*. London: Routledge, 1992.

*Capparell, Stephanie. *The Real Pepsi Challenge: The Inspirational Story of Breaking the Color Barrier in American Business*. New York: Wall Street Journal Books, 2007.

Cappelli, Peter. *The New Deal at Work: Managing the Market-Driven Workforce*. Boston: Harvard Business School Press, 1999.

Cappelli, Peter, Laurie Bassi, Harry Katz, David Knoke, Paul Osterman, and Michael Useem. *Change at Work*. New York: Oxford University Press, 1997.

Cecil, Andrew R. *Equality, Tolerance, and Loyalty: Virtues Serving the Common Purpose of Democracy*. Dallas: University of Texas at Dallas, 1990.

Chandler, Jr., Alfred D., Franco Amatori, and Takashi Hikino, eds. *Big Business and the Wealth of Nations*. New York: Cambridge University Press, 1997.

Cheatham, Mike. *"Your Friendly Neighbor": The Story of Georgia's Coca-Cola Bottling Families*. Macon, GA: Mercer University Press, 1999.

Cherney, Robert W., William Issel, and Kieran Walsh Taylor, eds. *American Labor and the Cold War: Grassroots Politics and Postwar Political Culture*. New Brunswick, NJ: Rutgers University Press, 2004.

Chinoy, Ely. *Automobile Workers and the American Dream*. Garden City, NY: Doubleday & Co., 1955.

Cobb, James C. *Industrialization and Southern Society, 1877–1984*. Lexington, KY: University Press of Kentucky, 2004.

*Cobble, Dorothy Sue. *The Other Women's Movement: Workplace Justice and Social Rights in Modern America*. Princeton, NJ: Princeton University Press, 2004.

Cole, Robert E. *Work, Mobility, and Participation: A Comparative Study of American and Japanese Industry*. Berkeley, CA: University of California Press, 1979.

Collins, Denis. *Gainsharing and Power: Lessons from Six Scanlon Plans*. Ithaca, NY: Cornell University Press, 1998.

Collins, Gail. *When Everything Changed: The Amazing Journey of American Women from 1960 to the Present*. New York: Little Brown, 2009.

*Collins, Robert M. *More: The Politics of Economic Growth in Postwar America.* New York: Oxford University Press, 2000.

———. *The Business Response to Keynes, 1929–1964.* New York: Columbia University Press, 1981.

Cordiner, Ralph J. *New Frontiers for Professional Managers.* New York: McGraw-Hill, 1956.

Cornelius, Peter K., and Bruce Kogut, eds. *Corporate Governance and Capital Flows in a Global Economy.* New York: Oxford University Press, 2003.

Cortada, James W. *The Digital Hand: How Computers Changed the Work of American Manufacturing, Transportation, and Retail Industries.* New York: Oxford University Press, 2004.

Cowie, Jefferson. *Stayin' Alive: The 1970s and the Last Days of the Working Class.* New York: New Press, 2010.

Crystal, Graef S. *In Search of Excess: The Overcompensation of American Executives.* New York: W.W. Norton, 1991.

Daft, Richard L., Martyn Kendrick, and Natalia Vershinina. *Management.* Boston: Cengage Learning, 2008.

Darden, Joe T., Richard Child Hill, June Thomas, and Richard Thomas. *Detroit: Race and Uneven Development.* Philadelphia: Temple University Press, 1987.

Davenport, Russell W. *U.S.A. The Permanent Revolution.* New York: Prentice-Hall, 1951.

Davin, Eric Leif. *Crucible of Freedom: Workers' Democracy in the Industrial Heartland, 1914–1960.* Lanham, MD: Lexington Books, 2010.

Davis, Bob, and David Wessel. *Prosperity: The Coming Twenty-Year Boom and What It Means to You.* New York: Random House, 1998.

Davis, Gerald F. *Managed by the Markets: How Finance Reshaped America.* New York: Oxford University Press, 2009.

———. *The Vanishing American Corporation: Navigating the Hazards of a New Economy.* Oakland, CA: Berrett-Koehler, 2016.

Davis, Mike. *Prisoners of the American Dream: Politics and Economy in the History of the US Working Class.* London: Verso, 1999.

Deal, Terrence E., and Allan A. Kennedy. *The New Corporate Cultures: Revitalizing the Workplace After Downsizing, Mergers, and Reengineering.* New York: Basic Books, 1999.

Delton, Jennifer. *Racial Integration in Corporate America, 1940–1990.* New York: Cambridge University Press, 2009.

Derickson, Alan. *Health Security for All: Dreams of Universal Health Care in America.* Baltimore: Johns Hopkins University Press, 2005.

Deslippe, Dennis A. *"Rights, Not Roses": Unions and the Rise of Working-Class Feminism, 1945–80.* Urbana, IL: University of Illinois Press, 2000.

Dhar, Rajib Lochan. *Strategic Human Resource Management.* New Delhi: Excel Books, 2008.

Dobbin, Frank. *Inventing Equal Opportunity*. Princeton, NJ: Princeton University Press, 2009.

Doeringer, Peter B. *Turbulence in the American Workplace*. New York: Oxford University Press, 1991.

*Domhoff, G. William, and Michael J. Webber, *Class and Power in the New Deal: Corporate Moderates, Southern Democrats, and the Liberal-Labor Coalition*. Stanford, CA: Stanford University Press, 2011.

Dorff, Michael B. *Indispensable and Other Myths: Why the CEO Pay Experiment Failed and How to Fix It*. Berkeley, CA: University of California Press, 2014.

Drucker, Peter F. *Adventures of a Bystander*. New Brunswick, NJ: Transaction Publishers, 1996.

———. *Concept of the Corporation*. New Brunswick, NJ: Transaction Publishers, 2008.

———. *Landmarks of Tomorrow*. New York: Harper & Row, 1957.

———. *Management: Tasks, Responsibilities, Practices*. New York: Harper & Row, 1973.

———. *The New Society: The Anatomy of Industrial Order*. New Brunswick, NJ: Transaction Publishers, 1993.

Eckholm, Erik, ed. *Solving America's Health-Care Crisis: A Guide to Understanding the Greatest Threat to Your Family's Economic Security*. New York: New York Times Co., 1993.

Ehrenreich, Barbara. *Nickel and Dimed: On (Not) Getting By in America*. New York: Metropolitan Books, 2001.

Eisenhower, Dwight D. *Waging Peace: The White House Years, 1956–1961*. Garden City, NY: Doubleday & Co., 1965.

El-Messidi, Kathy Groehn. *The Bargain: The Story Behind the 30-Year Honeymoon of GM and the UAW*. New York: Nellen Publishing, 1980.

Elliott, Charles. *Mr. Anonymous: Robert W. Woodruff of Coca-Cola*. Atlanta: Cherokee Publishing, 1982.

Ellis, Charles D., Alicia H. Munnell, and Andrew D. Eschtruth. *Falling Short: The Coming Retirement Crisis and What to Do About It*. New York: Oxford University Press, 2014.

Enrico, Roger, and Jesse Kornbluth. *The Other Guy Blinked: How Pepsi Won the Cola Wars*. New York: Bantam Books, 1986.

Evans, Chester E., and Laverne N. Laseau. *My Job Contest*. Washington, DC: Personnel Psychology Inc., 1950.

Evans, Thomas W. *The Education of Ronald Reagan: The General Electric Years and the Untold Story of His Conversion to Conservatism*. New York: Columbia University Press, 2006.

Farber, David. *Sloan Rules: Alfred P. Sloan and the Triumph of General Motors*. Chicago: University of Chicago Press, 2002.

Feldstein, Martin, ed. *American Economic Policy in the 1980s*. Chicago: University of Chicago Press, 1994.

———. *The American Economy in Transition*. Chicago: University of Chicago Press, 1980.

Felton, Mark. *Slaughter at Sea: The Story of Japan's Naval War Crimes*. South Yorkshire, England: Pen & Sword Books, 2007.

Ferguson, Karen, and Kate Blackwell. *Pensions in Crisis: Why the System Is Failing America and How You Can Protect Your Future*. New York: Arcade Publishing, 1995.

Fishman, Charles. *The Wal-Mart Effect: How the World's Most Powerful Company Really Works—And How It's Transforming the American Economy*. New York: Penguin Press, 2006.

*Fisse, Brent, and John Braithwaite. *The Impact of Publicity on Corporate Offenders*. Albany, NY: State University of New York Press, 1983.

Fitch, Lyle, and Horace Taylor, eds. *Planning for Jobs: Proposals Submitted in the Pabst Postwar Employment Awards*. Philadelphia: Blackiston Co., 1946.

Flamm, Kenneth. *Mismanaged Trade? Strategic Policy and the Semiconductor Industry*. Washington, DC: Brookings Institution Press, 1996.

Fleming, James S. *Window on Congress: A Congressional Biography of Barber B. Conable Jr.* Rochester, NY: University of Rochester Press, 2004.

Flynn, John T. *The Road Ahead: America's Creeping Revolution*. New York: Devin-Adair, 1949.

Fones-Wolf, Elizabeth A. *Selling Free Enterprise: The Business Assault on Labor and Liberalism, 1945–60*. Urbana, IL: University of Illinois Press, 1994.

*Ford, Martin. *The Lights in the Tunnel: Automation, Accelerating Technology, and the Economy of the Future*. Sunnyvale, CA: Acculant Publishing, 2009.

———. *Rise of the Robots: Technology and the Threat of a Jobless Future*. New York: Basic Books, 2015.

Foster, Richard, and Sarah Kaplan. *Creative Destruction: Why Companies That Are Built to Last Underperform the Market—And How to Successfully Transform Them*. New York: Currency, 2001.

Fountain, Clayton W. *Union Guy*. New York: Viking Press, 1949.

*Fox, Justin. *The Myth of the Rational Market: A History of Risk, Reward, and Delusion on Wall Street*. Petersfield, United Kingdom: Harriman House, 2010.

Frank, Dana. *Buy American: The Untold Story of Economic Nationalism*. Boston: Beacon Press, 1999.

Fraser, Jill Andresky. *White-Collar Sweatshop: The Deterioration of Work and Its Rewards in Corporate America*. New York: W.W. Norton, 2001.

Fraser, Steve. *The Age of Acquiescence: The Life and Death of American Resistance to Organized Wealth and Power*. New York: Little Brown, 2015.

Fraser, Steve, and Gary Gerstle, eds. *The Rise and Fall of the New Deal Order, 1930–1980*. Princeton, NJ: Princeton University Press, 1989.

Frederick, J. George, ed. *The Swope Plan: Details, Criticisms, Analysis.* New York: Business Bourse, 1931.

*Freeman, R. Edward, Jeffrey S. Harrison, Andrew C. Wicks, Bidhan Parmar, and Simone de Colle. *Stakeholder Theory: The State of the Art.* New York: Cambridge University Press, 2010.

Freeman, Richard B., and James L. Medoff. *What Do Unions Do?* New York: Basic Books, 1984.

French, Michael. *U.S. Economic History Since 1945.* New York: Manchester University Press, 1997.

*Friedan, Betty. *The Feminine Mystique.* 50th anniversary edition. New York: W.W. Norton, 2013.

Friedman, Benjamin M. *The Moral Consequences of Economic Growth.* New York: Alfred A. Knopf, 2005.

Friedman, Leon, and William F. Levantrosser. *Richard M. Nixon: Politician, President, Administrator.* Westport, CT: Greenwood Press, 1991.

Frost, Carl F., John H. Wakely, and Robert A. Ruh. *The Scanlon Plan for Organization Development: Identity, Participation, and Equity.* East Lansing, MI: Michigan State University Press, 1974.

*Galbraith, John Kenneth. *The Affluent Society.* 40th anniversary edition. New York: Houghton Mifflin, 1998.

Gandolfi, Franco. *Corporate Downsizing Demystified: A Scholarly Analysis of a Business Phenomenon.* Hyderabad, India: ICFAI University Press, 2006.

*Geis, Gilbert, ed. *White-Collar Criminal: The Offender in Business and the Professions.* New Brunswick, NJ: Transaction Publishers, 1968.

General Electric. *Professional Management in General Electric.* 4 books. 1953–1959.

General Motors. *The Worker Speaks: My Job and Why I Like It.* 1948.

*Geoghegan, Thomas. *Only One Thing Can Save Us: Why America Needs a New Kind of Labor Movement.* New York: New Press, 2014.

Gerling, Curt. *Smugtown U.S.A.* Rochester, NY: Plaza Publishers, 1993.

Gerstner, Jr., Louis V. *Who Says Elephants Can't Dance?* New York: HarperBusiness, 2002.

*Ghilarducci, Teresa. *When I'm Sixty-Four: The Plot Against Pensions and the Plan to Save Them.* Princeton, NJ: Princeton University Press, 2008.

Ginzberg, Eli, ed. *Business Leadership and the Negro Crisis.* New York: McGraw-Hill, 1968.

Glasner, David, ed. *Business Cycles and Depressions: An Encyclopedia.* New York: Garland Publishing, 1997.

Gleason, Sandra E., ed. *The Shadow Workforce: Perspectives on Contingent Work in the United States, Japan, and Europe.* Kalamazoo, MI: W.E. Upjohn Institute for Employment Research, 2006.

Glickman, Norman J., and Douglas P. Woodward. *The New Competitors: How Foreign Investors Are Changing the U.S. Economy.* New York: Basic Books, 1989.

Golden, Clinton S., and Virginia D. Parker, eds. *Causes of Industrial Peace Under Collective Bargaining.* New York: Harper & Brothers, 1949.

Goldin, Claudia, and Lawrence F. Katz. *The Race Between Education and Technology.* Cambridge, MA: Harvard University Press, 2008.

Gordon, Colin. *Dead on Arrival: The Politics of Health Care in Twentieth-Century America.* Princeton, NJ: Princeton University Press, 2003.

Gordon, Robert J. *The Rise and Fall of American Growth: The U.S. Standard of Living Since the Civil War.* Princeton, NJ: Princeton University Press, 2016.

Gosselin, Peter. *High Wire: The Precarious Financial Lives of American Families.* New York: Basic Books, 2008.

Gottschalk, Marie. *The Shadow Welfare State: Labor, Business, and the Politics of Health Care in the United States.* Ithaca, NY: Cornell University Press, 2000.

Green, James R. *The World of the Worker: Labor in Twentieth-Century America.* Urbana, IL: University of Illinois Press, 1998.

Greenhouse, Steven. *The Big Squeeze: Tough Times for the American Worker.* New York: Anchor Books, 2008.

Greenwald, Bruce, and Judd Kahn. *Competition Demystified: A Radically Simplified Approach to Business Strategy.* New York: Portfolio, 2005.

Greenwood, Ronald G. *Managerial Decentralization: A Study of the General Electric Philosophy.* Lexington, MA: Lexington Books, 1974.

Greider, William. *Secrets of the Temple: How the Federal Reserve Runs the Country.* New York: Simon & Schuster, 1987.

———. *Who Will Tell the People: The Betrayal of American Democracy.* New York: Simon & Schuster, 1992.

Greising, David. *I'd Like the World to Buy a Coke: The Life and Leadership of Roberto Goizueta.* New York: John Wiley & Sons, 1997.

Gross, James A. *Broken Promise: The Subversion of U.S. Labor Relations Policy, 1947–1994.* Philadelphia: Temple University Press, 1995.

———. *The Making of the National Labor Relations Board: A Study in Economics, Politics, and the Law, 1933–1937.* Albany, NY: State University of New York Press, 1974.

———. *The Reshaping of the National Labor Relations Board: National Labor Policy in Transition, 1937–1947.* Albany, NY: State University of New York Press, 1981.

Guttenplan, D. D. *American Radical: The Life and Times of I. F. Stone.* Evanston, IL: Northwestern University Press, 2012.

Hacker, Jacob S. *The Divided Welfare State: The Battle Over Public and Private Social Benefits in the United States.* New York: Cambridge University Press, 2002.

———. *The Great Risk Shift: The Assault on American Jobs, Families, Health Care, and Retirement and How You Can Fight Back.* New York: Oxford University Press, 2006.

Hacker, Jacob S., and Paul Pierson. *Winner-Take-All Politics: How Washington Made the Rich Richer—And Turned Its Back on the Middle Class.* New York: Simon & Schuster, 2010.

Halberstam, David. *The Fifties.* New York: Villard Books, 1993.

———. *The Reckoning.* New York: William Morrow, 1986.

*Hall, Bronwyn H., and Nathan Rosenberg. *Handbook of the Economics of Innovation,* Vol. 1. Amsterdam: Elsevier, 2010.

Halpern, Martin. *UAW Politics in the Cold War Era.* Albany, NY: State University of New York Press, 1998.

*Hamilton, Richard F., and James D. Wright. *State of the Masses: Sources of Discontent, Change, and Stability.* New Brunswick, NJ: AldineTransaction, 1986.

Hammer, Michael, and James Champy. *Reengineering the Corporation: A Manifesto for Business Revolution.* New York: Collins Business Essentials, 2001.

Hammond, John Winthrop. *Men and Volts: The Story of General Electric.* New York: J.B. Lippincott, 1941.

Harrigan, Kathryn Rudie. *Managing Maturing Businesses: Restructuring Declining Industries and Revitalizing Troubled Operations.* New York: Lexington Books, 1998.

Harrington, Alan. *Life in the Crystal Palace.* New York: Alfred Knopf, 1959.

*Harrington, Michael. *The Other America: Poverty in the United States.* New York: Simon & Schuster, 2012.

Harris, Howell John. *The Right to Manage: Industrial Relations Policies of American Business in the 1940s.* Madison, WI: University of Wisconsin Press, 1982.

Harrison, Bennett. *Lean and Mean: The Changing Landscape of Corporate Power in the Age of Flexibility.* New York: Guilford Press, 1994.

Harrison, Bennett, and Barry Bluestone. *The Great U-Turn: Corporate Restructuring and the Polarizing of America.* New York: Basic Books, 1988.

Hartley, Robert F. *Marketing Successes, Historical to Present Day: What We Can Learn.* New York: John Wiley & Sons, 1985.

*Hatton, Erin. *The Temp Economy: From Kelly Girls to Permatemps in Postwar America.* Philadelphia: Temple University Press, 2011.

Hays, Constance L. *The Real Thing: Truth and Power at the Coca-Cola Company.* New York: Random House, 2005.

Heald, Morrell. *The Social Responsibilities of Business: Company and Community, 1900–1960.* New Brunswick, NJ: Transaction Publishers, 2005.

Heckscher, Charles. *White-Collar Blues: Management Loyalties in an Age of Corporate Restructuring.* New York: Basic Books, 1995.

*Herzberg, Frederick, Bernard Mausner, and Barbara Bloch Snyderman. *The Motivation to Work.* New Brunswick, NJ: Transaction Publishers, 1993.

Hession, Charles H., and Hyman Sardy. *Ascent to Affluence: A History of American Economic Development.* Boston: Allyn and Bacon, 1969.

Hill, Herbert, and James E. Jones Jr. *Race in America: The Struggle for Equality.* Madison, WI: University of Wisconsin Press, 1993.

Hille, Waldemar, ed. *The People's Song Book.* New York: Oak Publications, 1948.

Hoffman, Reid, Ben Casnocha, and Chris Yeh. *The Alliance: Managing Talent in the Networked Age.* Boston: Harvard Business Review Press, 2014.

Hopper, Kenneth, and William Hopper. *The Puritan Gift: Triumph, Collapse, and Revival of an American Dream.* New York: I.B. Tauris, 2008.

Horwitt, Sanford D. *Let Them Call Me Rebel: Saul Alinsky—His Life and Legacy.* New York: Vintage Books, 1992.

Huberman, Leo. *The Labor Spy Racket.* New York: Modern Age Books, 1937.

Hufbauer, Gary Clyde, and Jeffrey J. Schott, *NAFTA Revisited: Achievements and Challenges.* Washington, DC: Institute for International Economics, 2005.

Ingrassia, Paul. *Crash Course: The American Automobile Industry's Road from Glory to Disaster.* New York: Random House, 2010.

Ingrassia, Paul, and Joseph B. White. *Comeback: The Fall and Rise of the American Automobile Industry.* New York: Simon & Schuster, 1994.

Isdell, Neville. *Inside Coca-Cola: A CEO's Life Story of Building the World's Most Popular Brand.* New York: St. Martin's Press, 2011.

Jacobs, Meg. *Pocketbook Politics: Economic Citizenship in Twentieth-Century America.* Princeton, NJ: Princeton University Press, 2005.

*Jacoby, Sanford M. *Employing Bureaucracy: Managers, Unions, and the Transformation of Work in the 20th Century.* Mahwah, NJ: Lawrence Erlbaum, 2004.

———. *Modern Manors: Welfare Capitalism Since the New Deal.* Princeton, NJ: Princeton University Press, 1997.

Johns, E. A. *The Sociology of Organizational Change.* Oxford, England: Pergamon Press, 1973.

Johnson, Christopher H. *Maurice Sugar: Law, Labor, and the Left in Detroit, 1912–1950.* Detroit: Wayne State University Press, 1988.

Johnson, Haynes, and David S. Broder. *The System: The American Way of Politics at the Breaking Point.* Boston: Back Bay Books, 1996.

*Johnston, David Cay. *Perfectly Legal: The Secret Campaign to Rig Our Tax System to Benefit the Super Rich—and Cheat Everybody Else.* New York: Penguin Group, 2003.

Judge, William Q. *The Leader's Shadow: Exploring and Developing Executive Character.* Thousand Oaks, CA: Sage Publications, 1999.

*Judis, John B. *The Paradox of American Democracy: Elites, Special Interests, and the Betrayal of Public Trust.* New York: Pantheon Books, 2000.

Jurgens, Ulrich, Thomas Malsch, and Knuth Dohse. *Breaking from Taylorism: Changing Forms of Work in the Automobile Industry.* Cambridge, England: Cambridge University Press, 1993.

Kale, Vivek. *Inverting the Paradox of Excellence: How Companies Use Variations for Business Excellence and How Enterprise Variations Are Enabled by SAP*. Boca Raton, FL: CRC Press, 2015.

*Kalleberg, Arne L. *Good Jobs, Bad Jobs: The Rise of Polarized and Precarious Employment Systems in the United States, 1970s to 2000s*. New York: Russell Sage Foundation, 2011.

Kanter, Rosabeth Moss. *The Change Masters: Innovation and Entrepreneurship in the American Corporation*. New York: Touchstone, 1983.

———. *Men and Women of the Corporation*. New York: Basic Books, 1977.

Katz, Harry C. *Shifting Gears: Changing Labor Relations in the U.S. Automobile Industry*. Cambridge, MA: MIT Press, 1985.

Kaufman, Alan, Lawrence Zacharias, and Marvin Karson. *Managers vs. Owners: The Struggle for Corporate Control in American Democracy*. New York: Oxford University Press, 1995.

Kaufman, Bruce E. *The Origins and Evolution of the Field of Industrial Relations in the United States*. Ithaca, NY: ILR Press, 1993.

*Kaufman, Bruce E., Richard A. Beaumont, and Roy B. Helfgott, eds. *Industrial Relations to Human Resources and Beyond: The Evolving Process of Employee Relations Management*. Armonk, NY: M.E. Sharpe, 2003.

Kaufman, Bruce E., and Daphne Glottlieb Taras. *Nonunion Employee Representation: History, Contemporary Practice, and Policy*. Armonk, NY: M.E. Sharpe, 2000.

Kawamura, Tetsuji, ed. *Hybrid Factories in the United States: The Japanese-Style Management and Production System Under the Global Economy*. New York: Oxford University Press, 2010.

Keen, Andrew. *The Internet Is Not the Answer*. New York: Atlantic Monthly Press, 2015.

Keller, Maryann. *Collision: GM, Toyota, Volkswagen and the Race to Own the 21st Century*. New York: Currency, 1993.

———. *Rude Awakening: The Rise, Fall, and Struggle for Recovery of General Motors*. New York: HarperPerennial, 1989.

Kelley, Robin D. G. *Into the Fire: African Americans Since 1970*. New York: Oxford University Press, 1996.

Kelly, Jeff, ed. *Best of Temp Slave!* Madison, WI: Garrett County Press, 1997.

Kelso, Louis O., and Mortimer J. Adler. *The Capitalist Manifesto*. New York: Random House, 1958.

Kennedy, David M. *Freedom from Fear: The American People in Depression and War, 1929–1945*. New York: Oxford University Press, 2005.

Keogh, James. *This Is Nixon: The Man and His Work*. New York: G.P. Putnam's Sons, 1956.

*Kessler-Harris, Alice. *In Pursuit of Equity: Women, Men, and Quest for Economic Citizenship in 20th-Century America*. New York: Oxford University Press, 2001.

————. *Out to Work: A History of Wage-Earning Women in the United States.* New York: Oxford University Press, 2003.

Khurana, Rakesh. *From Higher Aims to Hired Hands: The Social Transformation of American Business Schools and the Unfulfilled Promise of Management as a Profession.* Princeton, NJ: Princeton University Press, 2007.

*Kirk, Russell, and James McClellan. *The Political Principles of Robert A. Taft.* New Brunswick, NJ: Transaction Publishers, 2010.

*Kirsch, Max H. *In the Wake of the Giant: Multinational Restructuring and Uneven Development in a New England Community.* Albany, NY: State University of New York Press, 1998.

*Klein, Jennifer. *For All These Rights: Business, Labor, and the Shaping of America's Public-Private Welfare State.* Princeton, NJ: Princeton University Press, 2006.

Koistinen, Paul A. C. *Arsenal of World War II: The Political Economy of American Warfare, 1940–1945.* Lawrence, KS: University Press of Kansas, 2004.

*Krames, Jeffrey A. *Inside Drucker's Brain.* New York: Portfolio, 2008.

*Krysan, Maria, and Amanda E. Lewis, eds. *The Changing Terrain of Race and Ethnicity.* New York: Russell Sage Foundation, 2004.

Lambert, Josiah Bartlett. *"If the Workers Took a Notion": The Right to Strike and American Political Development.* Ithaca, NY: ILR Press, 2005.

Lane, Bill. *Jacked Up: The Inside Story of How Jack Welch Talked GE Into Becoming the World's Greatest Company.* New York: McGraw-Hill, 2008.

*Lash, Scott, and John Urry. *The End of Organized Capitalism.* Cambridge, England: Polity Press, 1987.

Lawler III, Edward E., Susan Albers Mohrman, and Gerald E. Ledford Jr. *Employee Involvement and Total Quality Management: Practices and Results in Fortune 1000 Companies.* San Francisco: Jossey-Bass, 1992.

Lawler III, Edward E., and James O'Toole. *America at Work: Choices and Challenges.* New York: Palgrave Macmillan, 2006.

Lee, R. Alton. *Truman and Taft-Hartley: A Question of Mandate.* Westport, CT: Greenwood Press, 1966.

Lee, Frederic S., and Warren J. Samuels, eds. *The Heterodox Economics of Gardner C. Means: A Collection.* Armonk, NY: M.E. Sharpe, 1992.

Leinberger, Paul, and Bruce Tucker. *The New Individualists: The Generation After the Organization Man.* New York: HarperCollins, 1991.

Lesieur, Frederick G., ed. *The Scanlon Plan: A Frontier in Labor-Management Cooperation.* Cambridge, MA: MIT Press, 1958.

Levinson, Harry, and Stuart Rosenthal. *CEO: Corporate Leadership in Action.* New York: Basic Books, 1986.

*Lewis, Michael. *The Big Short: Inside the Doomsday Machine.* New York: W.W. Norton, 2011.

Lichtenstein, Nelson, ed. *American Capitalism: Social Thought and Political Economy in the Twentieth Century.* Philadelphia: University of Pennsylvania Press, 2006.

*———. *Labor's War at Home: The CIO in World War II*. Philadelphia: Temple University Press, 2003.

*———. *The Retail Revolution: How Wal-Mart Created a Brave New World of Business*. New York: Metropolitan Books, 2009.

———, ed. *Wal-Mart: The Face of Twenty-First-Century Capitalism*. New York: New Press, 2006.

———. *Walter Reuther: The Most Dangerous Man in Detroit*. Urbana, IL: University of Illinois Press, 1995.

Liebschutz, Sarah F. *Communities and Health Care: The Rochester, New York, Experiment*. Rochester, NY: University of Rochester Press, 2011.

Linder, Marc. *Wars of Attrition: Vietnam, the Business Roundtable, and the Decline of Construction Unions*. Iowa City, IA: Fanpihua Press, 2000.

Lipsitz, George. *Rainbow at Midnight: Labor and Culture in the 1940s*. Urbana, IL: University of Illinois Press, 1994.

Locke, Robert R. *The Collapse of the American Management Mystique*. New York: Oxford University Press, 1996.

Loth, David. *Swope of G.E.: The Story of Gerard Swope and General Electric in American Business*. New York: Simon & Schuster, 1958.

Louis, J. C., and Harvey Z. Yazijian. *The Cola Wars: The Story of the Global Corporate Battle Between the Coca-Cola Company and PepsiCo Inc.* New York: Everest House, 1980.

Lounsbury, Michael, and Paul M. Hirsch. *Markets on Trial: The Economic Sociology of the U.S. Financial Crisis: Part B*. Bingley, United Kingdom: Emerald Group Publishing, 2010.

Lowenstein, Roger. *While America Aged: How Pension Debts Ruined General Motors, Stopped the NYC Subways, Bankrupted San Diego, and Loom as the Next Financial Crisis*. New York: Penguin Press, 2008.

Lubell, Samuel. *The Future of American Politics*. New York: Harper & Row, 1965.

Lutz, Bob. *Car Guys vs. Bean Counters: The Battle for the Soul of the American Business*. New York: Portfolio, 2011.

*Lynch, Timothy P. *Strike Songs of the Depression*. Jackson, MS: University Press of Mississippi, 2001.

Lynn, Barry C. *Cornered: The New Monopoly Capitalism and the Economics of Destruction*. Hoboken, NJ: John Wiley & Sons, 2010.

———. *End of the Line: The Rise and Coming Fall of the Global Corporation*. New York: Doubleday, 2005.

Madrick, Jeff. *Age of Greed: The Triumph of Finance and the Decline of America, 1970 to the Present*. New York: Alfred A. Knopf, 2011.

Magaziner, Ira C., and Robert B. Reich. *Minding America's Business: The Decline and Rise of the American Economy*. New York: Vintage Books, 1982.

Magill, Frank N., ed. *Chronology of Twentieth-Century History: Business and Commerce*. Vol 2. New York: Routledge, 2013.

Margolies, Daniel S., ed. *A Companion to Harry S. Truman*. Malden, MA: Wiley-Blackwell, 2012.

Markoff, John. *Machines of Loving Grace: The Quest for Common Ground Between Humans and Robots*. New York: Ecco, 2015.

*Marmor, Theodore R. *The Politics of Medicare*. New York: Aldine de Gruyter, 2000.

Marshall, F. Ray. *Labor in the South*. Cambridge, MA: Harvard University Press, 1967.

*Martin, Roger L. *Fixing the Game: Bubbles, Crashes, and What Capitalism Can Learn from the NFL*. Boston: Harvard Business Review Press, 2011.

Maslow, Abraham H. *Maslow on Management*. New York: John Wiley & Sons, 1998.

Matles, James J., and James Higgins. *Them and Us: Struggles of a Rank-and-File Union*. Englewood Cliffs, NJ: Prentice Hall, 1974.

Maynard, Micheline. *Collision Course: Inside the Battle for General Motors*. New York: Birch Lane Press, 1995.

Mayo, Elton. *The Human Problems of an Industrial Civilization*. New York: Viking, 1960.

McCartin, Joseph A. *Collision Course: Ronald Reagan, the Air Traffic Controllers, and the Strike That Changed America*. New York: Oxford University Press, 2011.

McColloch, Mark. *White-Collar Workers in Transition: The Boom Years, 1940–1970*. Westport, CT: Greenwood Press, 1983.

McCrohan, Donna. *Archie & Edith, Mike & Gloria: The Tumultuous History of All in the Family*. New York: Workman Publishing, 1987.

*McGregor, Douglas. *The Human Side of Enterprise*. Annotated edition. New York: McGraw-Hill, 2006.

*McQuaid, Kim. *A Response to Industrialism: Liberal Businessmen and the Evolving Spectrum of Capitalist Reform*. Washington, DC: Beard Books, 1986.

———. *Uneasy Partners: Big Business in American Politics, 1945–1990*. Baltimore: Johns Hopkins University Press, 1994.

*McWhorter, Diane. *Carry Me Home: Birmingham, Alabama, the Climactic Battle of the Civil Rights Revolution*. New York: Simon & Schuster, 2001.

Melman, Seymour. *Profits Without Production*. Philadelphia: University of Pennsylvania Press, 1983.

Metzgar, Jack. *Striking Steel: Solidarity Remembered*. Philadelphia: Temple University Press, 2000.

Meyer, G. J. *Executive Blues: Down and Out in Corporate America*. New York: Dell Trade, 1995.

Micklethwait, John, and Adrian Wooldridge. *The Company: A Short History of a Revolutionary Idea*. New York: Modern Library, 2003.

Milkman, Ruth. *Farewell to the Factory: Auto Workers in the Late Twentieth Century*. Berkeley, CA: University of California Press, 1997.

———. *Gender at Work: The Dynamics of Job Segregation by Sex During World War II.* Urbana, IL: University of Illinois Press, 1987.

———. *L.A. Story: Immigrant Workers and the Future of the U.S. Labor Movement.* New York: Russell Sage Foundation, 2006.

Miller, Casey, and Kate Swift. *Words and Women.* Lincoln, NE: iUniverse.com, 2000.

Miller, Douglas T., and Marion Nowak. *The Fifties: The Way We Really Were.* Garden City, NY: Doubleday, 1977.

Miller, Matt. *The Tyranny of Dead Ideas: Letting Go of the Old Ways of Thinking to Unleash a New Prosperity.* New York: Times Books, 2009.

Miller, Paul T. *The Postwar Struggle for Civil Rights: African Americans in San Francisco, 1945–1975.* New York: Routledge, 2010.

Millis, Harry A., and Emily Clark Brown. *From the Wagner Act to Taft-Hartley: A Study of National Labor Policy and Labor Relations.* Chicago: University of Chicago Press, 1950.

Mills, C. Wright. *The New Men of Power: America's Labor Leaders.* Urbana, IL: University of Illinois Press, 2001.

———. *White Collar: The American Middle Classes.* New York: Oxford University Press, 1951.

Mills, D. Quinn. *The IBM Lesson: The Profitable Art of Full Employment.* New York: Times Books, 1988.

Mishel, Lawrence, Josh Bivens, Elise Gould, and Heidi Shierholz. *The State of Working America.* 12th edition. Ithaca, NY: Cornell University Press, 2012.

Mizruchi, Mark S. *The Fracturing of the American Corporate Elite.* Cambridge, MA: Harvard University Press, 2013.

Monks, Robert A. G., and Nell Minnow. *Corporate Governance.* New York: John Wiley & Sons, 2008.

Moody, Kim. *Injury to All: The Decline of American Unionism.* London: Verso, 1988.

*Moore, Michael. *Here Comes Trouble: Stories from My Life.* New York: Grand Central Publishing, 2011.

Naisbitt, John. *Megatrends: Ten New Directions Transforming Our Lives.* London: Futura, 1984.

Nash, June C. *From Tank Town to High Tech: The Clash of Community and Industrial Cycles.* Albany, NY: State University of New York Press, 1989.

Nelson, Daniel, ed. *A Mental Revolution: Scientific Management Since Taylor.* Columbus, OH: Ohio State University Press, 1992.

Newman, Katherine S. *Falling from Grace: Downward Mobility in the Age of Affluence.* Berkeley, CA: University of California Press, 1988.

———, ed. *Laid Off, Laid Low: Political and Economic Consequences of Employment Insecurity.* New York: Columbia University Press, 2008.

Nicholson, Philip Yale. *Labor's Story in the United States.* Philadelphia: Temple University Press, 2004.

Nixon, Richard. *Public Papers of the Presidents of the United States.* Washington, DC: US Government Printing Office, 1971.

Noah, Timothy. *The Great Divergence: America's Growing Inequality Crisis and What We Can Do About It.* New York: Bloomsbury Press, 2012.

Northrup, Herbert R. *Boulwarism: The Labor Relations Policies of the General Electric Company.* Ann Arbor, MI: University of Michigan Press, 1964.

Northrup, Herbert R., and Richard L. Rowan, eds. *The Negro and Employment Opportunity: Problems and Practices.* Ann Arbor, MI: University of Michigan Press, 1965.

Nowak, Margaret Collingwood. *Two Who Were There: A Biography of Stanley Nowak.* Detroit: Wayne State University Press, 1989.

Nye, David E. *Image Worlds: Corporate Identities at General Electric.* Cambridge, MA: MIT Press, 1985.

O'Boyle, Thomas F. *At Any Cost: Jack Welch, General Electric, and the Pursuit of Profit.* New York: Vintage Books, 1998.

Oliver, Thomas. *The Real Coke, the Real Story.* New York: Penguin Books, 1986.

Osterman, Paul, ed. *Broken Ladders: Managerial Careers in the New Economy.* New York: Oxford University Press, 1996.

———. *Securing Prosperity: The American Labor Market: How It Has Changed and What to Do About It.* Princeton, NJ: Princeton University Press, 1999.

———. *The Truth About Middle Managers: Who They Are, How They Work, Why They Matter.* Boston: Harvard Business Press, 2008.

Parenti, Michael. *Democracy for the Few.* Boston: Wadsworth, 2011.

Parker, Mike, and Jane Slaughter. *Working Smart: A Union Guide to Participation Programs and Reengineering.* Detroit: Labor Notes, 1994.

Pasachoff, Naomi. *Frances Perkins: Champion of the New Deal.* New York: Oxford University Press, 1999.

Peck, Don. *Pinched: How the Great Recession Has Narrowed Our Futures and What We Can Do About It.* New York: Crown Publishers, 2011.

*Pelfrey, William. *Billy, Alfred, and General Motors: The Story of Two Unique Men, a Legendary Company, and a Remarkable Time in American History.* New York: Amacom, 2006.

Pendergrast, Mark. *For God, Country, and Coca-Cola: The Definitive History of the Great American Soft Drink and the Company That Makes It.* New York: Basic Books, 2000.

Perlstein, Rick. *Before the Storm: Barry Goldwater and the Unmaking of the American Consensus.* New York: Nation Books, 2001.

*Peters, Thomas J., and Robert H. Waterman Jr. *In Search of Excellence: Lessons from America's Best-Run Companies.* New York: Collins Business Essentials, 2006.

Phillips-Fein, Kim. *Invisible Hands: The Making of the Conservative Movement from the New Deal to Reagan.* New York: W.W. Norton, 2009.

Pierson, John H. G. *Essays on Full Employment, 1942–1972*. Matuchen, NJ: Scarecrow Press, 1972.

Piketty, Thomas. *Capital in the Twenty-First Century*. Cambridge, MA: Belknap Press, 2014.

Piore, Michael J., and Charles F. Sabel. *The Second Industrial Divide: Possibilities for Prosperity*. New York: Basic Books, 1984.

Piven, Frances Fox, and Richard A. Cloward. *Poor People's Movements: Why They Succeed, How They Fail*. New York: Vintage Books, 1977.

Porter, Michel E., ed. *Competition in Global Industries*. Boston: Harvard Business School Press, 1986.

*———. *The Competitive Advantage of Nations*. New York: Free Press, 1998.

Prestowitz, Jr., Clyde V. *Trading Places: How We Are Giving Our Future to Japan and How to Reclaim It*. New York: Basic Books, 1988.

Purcell, Theodore V. *Blue Collar Man: Patterns of Dual Allegiance in Industry*. Cambridge, MA: Harvard University Press, 1960.

Purcell, Theodore V., and Daniel P. Mulvey. *The Negro in the Electrical Manufacturing Industry*. Philadelphia: Wharton School of Finance and Commerce, 1971.

Quinn, Theodore Kinget. *Giant Business: Threat to Democracy*. New York: Exposition Press, 1953.

Rappaport, Alfred. *Creating Shareholder Value: A Guide for Managers and Investors*. New York: Free Press, 1998.

Rattner, Steven. *Overhaul: An Insider's Account of the Obama Administration's Emergy Rescue of the Auto Industry*. Boston: Houghton Mifflin Harcourt, 2010.

Reed, Susan E. *The Diversity Index: The Alarming Truth About Diversity in Corporate America and What Can Be Done About It*. New York: Amacom, 2011.

Reich, Robert B. *Locked in the Cabinet*. New York: Alfred A. Knopf, 1997.

———. *Saving Capitalism: For the Many, Not the Few*. New York: Alfred A. Knopf, 2015.

———. *Supercapitalism: The Transformation of Business, Democracy, and Everyday Life*. Alfred A. Knopf, 2007.

———. *The Work of Nations: Preparing Ourselves for 21st-Century Capitalism*. New York: Vintage Books, 1991.

Reichheld, Frederick F. *The Loyalty Effect: The Hidden Force Behind Growth, Profits, and Lasting Value*. Boston: Harvard Business School Press, 1996.

*Rickards, James. *Currency Wars: The Making of the Next Global Crisis*. New York: Portfolio, 2011.

Rielly, Edward J. *The 1960s: American Popular Culture Through History*. Westport, CT: Greenwood Press, 2003.

Rifkin, Jeremy. *The End of Work: The Decline of the Global Labor Force and the Dawn of the Post-Market Era*. New York: Tarcher/Penguin, 2004.

Rodgers, Daniel T. *Age of Fracture*. Cambridge, MA: Belknap Press, 2011.

Roethlisberger, F. J., and William J. Dickson. *Management and the Worker: An Account of a Research Program Conducted by the Western Electric Company, Hawthorne Works, Chicago.* Cambridge, MA: Harvard University Press, 1939.

Rosenbaum, David I., ed. *Market Dominance: How Firms Gain, Hold, or Lose It and the Impact on Economic Performance.* Westport, CT: Praeger, 1998.

Rosenfeld, Jake. *What Unions No Longer Do.* Cambridge, MA: Harvard University Press, 2014.

Rosengarten, Frank. *Urbane Revolutionary: C.L.R. James and the Struggle for a New Society.* Jackson, MS: University Press of Mississippi, 2008.

Ross, Robert J. S., and Kent C. Trachte. *Global Capitalism: The New Leviathan.* Albany, NY: State University of New York Press, 1990.

Rothschild, William E. *The Secret to GE's Success.* New York: McGraw-Hill, 2007.

Royce, Josiah. *The Philosophy of Loyalty.* New York: Macmillan, 1908.

Rubenstein, Saul A., and Thomas A. Kochan. *Learning from Saturn: Possibilities for Corporate Governance and Employee Relations.* Ithaca, NY: ILR Press, 2001.

Rucker, Walter, and James Nathaniel Upton. *Encyclopedia of American Race Riots.* Westport, CT: Greenwood Press, 2007.

*Rudacille, Deborah. *Roots of Steel: Boom and Bust in an American Mill Town.* New York: Anchor Books, 2011.

Sabato, Larry J. *The Kennedy Half Century: The Presidency, Assassination, and Lasting Legacy of John F. Kennedy.* New York: Bloomsbury, 2013.

Samuelson, Robert J. *The Good Life and Its Discontents: The American Dream in the Age of Entitlement, 1945–1995.* New York: Times Books, 1995.

———. *The Great Inflation and Its Aftermath: The Past and Future of American Affluence.* New York: Random House Trade, 2008.

Sass, Steven A. *The Promise of Private Pensions: The First Hundred Years.* Cambridge, MA: Harvard University Press, 1997.

Saval, Nikil. *Cubed: A Secret History of the Workplace.* New York: Doubleday, 2014.

Schatz, Ronald W. *The Electrical Workers: A History of Labor at General Electric and Westinghouse, 1923–60.* Urbana, IL: University of Illinois Press, 1983.

*Schieber, Sylvester J. *The Predictable Surprise: The Unraveling of the U.S. Retirement System.* New York: Oxford University Press, 2012.

*Schlesinger, Jr., Arthur M. *The Coming of the New Deal: 1933–1935.* Boston: Mariner Books, 2003.

———. *The Cycles of American History.* Boston: Mariner Books, 1999.

———. *A Thousand Days: John F. Kennedy in the White House.* Boston: Mariner Books, 2002.

Schriftgiesser, Karl. *Business Comes of Age: The Story of the Committee for Economic Development and Its Impact upon the Economic Policies of the United States, 1942–1960.* New York: Harper & Brothers, 1960.

Schultz, Ellen E. *Retirement Heist: How Companies Plunder and Profit from the Nest Eggs of American Workers*. New York: Portfolio, 2011.

Serrin, William. *The Company and the Union: The "Civilized Relationship" of the General Motors Corporation and the United Automobile Workers*. New York: Vintage Books, 1970.

Sethi, S. Prakash. *Business Corporations and the Black Man: An Analysis of Social Conflict: The Kodak-FIGHT Controversy*. Scranton, PA: Chandler Publishing, 1970.

*Shields, Charles J. *And So It Goes, Kurt Vonnegut: A Life*. New York: Henry Holt, 2011.

Shojai, Siamack, ed. *The New Global Oil Market: Understanding Energy Issues in the World Economy*. Westport, CT: Praeger, 1995.

Siracusa, Joseph M. *Encyclopedia of the Kennedys: The People and Events That Shaped America*. Santa Barbara, CA: ABC-CLIO, 2012.

Slater, Robert. *The Wal-Mart Decade: How a New Generation of Leaders Turned Sam Walton's Legacy into the World's #1 Company*. New York: Portfolio, 2003.

Sloan, Jr., Alfred P. *Adventures of a White-Collar Man*. New York: Doubleday, Doran & Co., 1941.

———. *My Years with General Motors*. New York: Currency, 1990.

Sobel, Richard. *The White-Collar Working Class: From Structure to Politics*. New York: Praeger, 1989.

Somers, Herman M., and Anne R. Somers. *Doctors, Patients, and Health Insurance: The Organization and Financing of Medical Care*. Washington, DC: Brookings Institution, 1961.

Stapleford, Thomas A. *The Cost of Living in America: A Political History of Economic Statistics, 1880–2000*. New York: Cambridge University Press, 2009.

Starr, Paul. *The Social Transformation of American Medicine: The Rise of a Sovereign Profession and the Making of a Vast Industry*. New York: Basic Books, 1982.

Staw, Barry M., and L. L. Cummings, eds. *Research in Organizational Behavior* Vol. 15. London: Elsevier, 1993.

*Stebenne, David L. *Arthur Goldberg: New Deal Liberal*. New York: Oxford University Press, 1996.

Stiglitz, Joseph E. *The Roaring Nineties: A New History of the World's Most Prosperous Decade*. New York: W.W. Norton, 2003.

Stout, Lynn. *The Shareholder Value Myth: How Putting Shareholders First Harms Investors, Corporations, and the Public*. San Francisco: Berrett-Koehler, 2012.

*Sugrue, Thomas J. *The Origins of the Urban Crisis: Race and Inequality in Postwar Detroit*. Princeton, NJ: Princeton University Press, 2005.

Sutch, Richard, and Susan B. Carter, ed. *Historical Statistics of the United States: Earliest Times to the Present*. New York: Cambridge University Press, 2006.

Swasy, Alecia. *Changing Focus: Kodak and the Battle to Save a Great American Company*. New York: Times Business, 1997.

Sweeney, John J., and Karen Nussbaum. *Solutions for the New Work Force: Policies for a New Social Contract*. Washington, DC: Seven Locks Press, 1989.

Tarbell, Ida M. *Owen D. Young: A New Type of Industrial Leader*. New York: Macmillan, 1932.

Taylor, Frederick Winslow. *The Principles of Scientific Management*. Norwood, MA: Plimpton Press, 1911.

Tedlow, Richard S. *Denial: Why Business Leaders Fail to Look Facts in the Face—And What to Do About It*. New York: Portfolio, 2010.

Tedlow, Richard S., and Geoffrey Jones, eds. *The Rise and Fall of Mass Marketing*. London: Routledge, 2014.

Teichmann, Howard, and George S. Kaufman. *The Solid Gold Cadillac*. New York: Dramatists Play Service, 1954.

Terkel, Studs. *Working: People Talk About What They Do All Day and How They Feel About What They Do*. New York: New Press, 1972.

Tichy, Noel M., and Stratford Sherman. *Control Your Destiny or Someone Else Will*. New York: Collins Business Essentials, 1993.

Tilly, Chris. *Half a Job: Bad and Good Part-Time Jobs in a Changing Labor Market*. Philadelphia: Temple University Press, 1996.

Tobin, James. *The New Economics One Decade Older*. Princeton, NJ: Princeton University Press, 1974.

Toffler, Alvin. *Future Shock*. New York: Bantam Books, 1970.

Tomasko, Robert M. *Downsizing: Reshaping the Corporation for the Future*. New York: Amacom, 1990.

Ton, Zeynep. *The Good Jobs Strategy: How the Smartest Companies Invest in Employees to Lower Costs and Boost Profits*. Boston: New Harvest, 2014.

Trahair, Richard C. S. *Elton Mayo: The Humanist Temper*. New Brunswick, NJ: Transaction Publishers, 1984.

Troy, Leo, and Neil Sheflin. *Union Sourcebook: Membership, Finances, Structure, Directory*. West Orange, NJ: Industrial Relations Data and Information Services, 1985.

Tucker, Spencer C. *World War II at Sea: An Encyclopedia*. Santa Barbara, CA: ABC-CLIO, 2012.

Uchitelle, Louis. *The Disposable American: Layoffs and Their Consequences*. New York: Vintage Books, 2006.

Ulrich, Dave, Steve Kerr, and Ron Ashkenas. *The GE Work-Out: How to Implement GE's Revolutionary Method for Busting Bureaucracy and Attacking Organizational Problems—Fast!* New York: McGraw-Hill, 2002.

Urofsky, Melvin I. *Louis D. Brandeis: A Life*. New York: Schocken Books, 2009.

Useem, Michael. *Executive Defense: Shareholder Power and Corporate Reorganization*. Cambridge, MA: Harvard University Press, 1993.

————. *Investor Capitalism: How Money Managers Are Changing the Face of Corporate America*. New York: Basic Books, 1996.

Vancil, Richard F. *Passing the Baton: Managing the Process of CEO Succession*. Boston: Harvard Business School Press, 1987.

Van Elteren, Mel. *Labor and the American Left: An Analytical History*. Jefferson, NC: McFarland & Co., 2011.

Van Horn, Carl E., and Herbert A. Schaffner. *Work in America: An Encyclopedia of History, Policy, and Society*. Santa Barbara, CA: ABC-CLIO, 2003.

Vogel, David. *Fluctuating Fortunes: The Political Power of Business in America*. Washington, DC: Beard Books, 2003.

Vonnegut, Kurt. *Player Piano*. New York: Dial Press, 1952.

Walton, Clarence C., ed. *Business and Social Progress: Views of Two Generations of Executives*. New York: Praeger, 1970.

Warner, W. Lloyd, Darab B. Unwalla, and John H. Trimm. *The Emergent American Society: Large-Scale Organizations*. New Haven, CT: Yale University Press, 1967.

Warren, Michael, and Peg Thoms. *Battleground Business*. Westport, CT: Greenwood Press, 2007.

Wasem, Ruth Ellen. *Tackling Unemployment: The Legislative Dynamics of the Employment Act of 1946*. Kalamazoo, MI: W.E. Upjohn Institute for Employment Research, 2013.

Waterhouse, Benjamin C. *Lobbying America: The Politics of Business from Nixon to NAFTA*. Princeton, NJ: Princeton University Press, 2014.

Watson, Jr., Thomas J. *A Business and Its Beliefs: The Ideas That Helped Build IBM*. New York: McGraw-Hill, 2003.

Watts, Steven. *The People's Tycoon: Henry Ford and the American Century*. New York: Vintage Books, 2006.

Webber, Michael J., and David L. Rigby. *The Golden Age Illusion: Rethinking Postwar Capitalism*. New York: Guilford Press, 1996.

Weekley, Thomas L., and Jay C. Wilber. *United We Stand: The Unprecedented Story of the GM-UAW Quality Partnership*. New York: McGraw-Hill, 1996.

Weil, David. *The Fissured Workplace: Why Work Became So Bad for So Many and What Can Be Done to Improve It*. Cambridge, MA: Harvard University Press, 2014.

Weir, Robert E. *Workers in America: An Encyclopedia*. Santa Barbara, CA: ABC-CLIO, 2013.

Weisbord, Marvin R. *Productive Workplaces: Dignity, Meaning, and Community in the 21st Century*. San Francisco: Jossey-Bass, 2012.

Weisman, Steven R., ed. *Daniel Patrick Moynihan: A Portrait in Letters of an American Visionary*. New York: PublicAffairs, 2010.

Weitzman, Martin L. *The Share Economy: Conquering Stagflation*. Cambridge, MA: Harvard University Press, 1984.

Welch, Jack. *Jack: Straight from the Gut.* New York: Business Plus, 2001.

Wells, Donald R. *The Federal Reserve System: A History.* Jefferson, NC: McFarland & Co., 2004.

Wells, Wyatt C. *Economist in an Uncertain World: Arthur F. Burns and the Federal Reserve, 1970–1978.* New York: Columbia University Press, 1994.

Whitten, David O., and Bessie E. Whitten. *Handbook of American Business History: Extractives, Manufacturing, and Services.* Westport, CT: Greenwood Press, 1997.

Whyte, William H. *The Organization Man.* Philadelphia: University of Pennsylvania Press, 2002.

Widick, B. J., ed. *Auto Work and Its Discontents.* Baltimore: Johns Hopkins University Press, 1976.

Wiener, Norbert. *The Human Use of Human Beings: Cybernetics and Society.* Boston: Houghton Mifflin, 1954.

Wilkerson, Isabel. *The Warmth of Other Suns: The Epic Story of America's Great Migration.* New York: Vintage Books, 2011.

Wilson, Sloan. *The Man in the Gray Flannel Suit.* Cambridge, MA: Da Capo Press, 2002.

Wilson, William Julius. *The Truly Disadvantaged: The Inner City, the Underclass, and Public Policy.* Chicago: University of Chicago Press, 1987.

*Woirol, Gregory Ray. *The Technological Unemployment and Structural Unemployment Debates.* Westport, CT: Greenwood Press, 1996.

Wolman, William, and Anne Colamosca. *The Great 401(k) Hoax: Why Your Family's Financial Security Is at Risk, and What You Can Do About It.* New York: Basic Books, 2002.

Wooten, James A. *The Employee Retirement Income Security Act of 1974: A Political History.* Berkeley, CA: University of California Press, 2004.

Wren, Daniel A., and Arthur G. Bedeian. *The Evolution of Management Thought.* New York: John Wiley & Sons, 2009.

Wright, J. Patrick. *On a Clear Day You Can See General Motors: John Z. DeLorean's Look Inside the Automotive Giant.* New York: Avon Books, 1980.

Wunnava, Phanindra V. *The Changing Role of Unions: New Forms of Representation.* London: Routledge, 2015.

Yankelovich, Daniel. *New Rules: Searching for Self-Fulfillment in a World Turned Upside Down.* New York: Bantam Books, 1982.

*Yergin, Daniel, and Joseph Stanislaw. *The Commanding Heights: The Battle Between Government and the Marketplace That Is Remaking the Modern World.* New York: Simon & Schuster, 1998.

Zelinsky, Edward A. *The Origins of the Ownership Society: How the Defined Contribution Paradigm Changed America.* New York: Oxford University Press, 2007.

*Zieger, Robert H. *For Jobs and Freedom: Race and Labor in America Since 1865.* Lexington, KY: University Press of Kentucky, 2007.

*Zieger, Robert H., Timothy J. Minchin, and Gilbert J. Gall. *American Workers, American Unions: The Twentieth and Early Twenty-First Centuries*. Baltimore: Johns Hopkins University Press, 2014.

Zimet, Melvin, and Ronald G. Greenwood, eds. *The Evolving Science of Management: The Collected Papers of Harold Smiddy and Papers by Others in His Honor*. New York: Amacom, 1979.

Zweigenhaft, Richard L., and G. William Domhoff. *Diversity in the Power Elite: How It Happened, Why It Matters*. Lanham, MD: Rowman & Littlefield, 2006.

CREDITS AND PERMISSIONS

PHOTO CREDITS

Chapter 2: From the collections of Kettering University. **Chapter 3:** Walter P. Reuther Library, Archives of Labor and Urban Affairs, Wayne State University. Press Picture Service photo. **Chapter 4:** Courtesy frontierfield.org. **Chapter 5:** Keystone Pictures USA/Alamy Stock Photo. **Chapter 6:** Courtesy City of Rochester, New York. **Chapter 7:** Richard Nixon Presidential Library and Museum. **Chapter 8:** miSci, Schenectady, New York. **Chapter 9:** The Coca-Cola Company. **Chapter 10:** Associated Press. **Chapter 11:** Courtesy OUR Walmart.

PERMISSIONS

INDEX

Rick Wartzman is the director of the KH Moon Center for a Functioning Society at the Drucker Institute, a part of Claremont Graduate University. He also writes about work for *Fortune* magazine online. His books include *Obscene in the Extreme: The Burning and Banning of John Steinbeck's The Grapes of Wrath*, which was a finalist for the Los Angeles Times Book Prize in History and a PEN USA Literary Award; *The King of California: J. G. Boswell and the Making of a Secret American Empire* (with Mark Arax), which won a California Book Award and the William Saroyan International Prize for Writing; and a collection of magazine columns called *What Would Drucker Do Now?* He previously served for twenty years as a reporter, editor, and columnist at the *Wall Street Journal* and *Los Angeles Times*.